The Nixon Presidency

Recent Titles in
Contributions in Political Science

American Conservative Thought Since World War II: The Core Ideas
Melvin J. Thorne

Mission in Mufti: Brazil's Military Regimes, 1964–1985
Wilfred A. Bacchus

Mr. Atomic Energy: Congressman Chet Holifield and Atomic Energy Affairs, 1945–1974
Richard Wayne Dyke

Vatican Policy on the Palestinian-Israeli Conflict: The Struggle for the Holy Land
Andrej Kreutz

Implementation and the Policy Process: Opening up the Black Box
Dennis J. Palumbo and Donald J. Calista, editors

Political and Social Change in China Since 1978
Charles Burton

Presidential Accountability: New and Recurring Problems
John Orman

The Modern Theory of Presidential Power: Alexander Hamilton and the Corwin Thesis
Richard Loss

Ethics for Policymaking: A Methodological Analysis
Eugene J. Meehan

Foreign Policy and Ethnic Groups: American and Canadian Jews Lobby for Israel
David Howard Goldberg

U.S. Senate Decision-Making: The Trade Agreements Act of 1979
Robert W. Jerome

Policy Theory and Policy Evaluation: Concepts, Knowledge, Causes, and Norms
Stuart S. Nagel, editor

The *NIXON PRESIDENCY*

Power and Politics in Turbulent Times

MICHAEL A. GENOVESE

Contributions to Political Science, Number 259

GREENWOOD PRESS
New York
Westport, Connecticut
London

Library of Congress Cataloging-in-Publication Data

Genovese, Michael A.
   The Nixon presidency : power and politics in turbulent times /
Michael A. Genovese.
      p.   cm.—(Contributions in political science, ISSN 0147-1066
; no. 259)
   Includes bibliographical references.
   ISBN 0-313-25506-7 (lib. bdg. : alk. paper)
   1. United States—Politics and government—1969–1974.   2. Nixon,
Richard M. (Richard Milhous), 1913–   I. Title.   II. Series.
E855.G46   1990
973.924'092—dc20   90-2713

British Library Cataloguing in Publication Data is available.

Library of Congress Catalog Card Number: 90-2713
ISBN: 0-313-25506-7
ISSN: 0147-1066

First published in 1990

Greenwood Press, 88 Post Road West, Westport, CT 06881
An imprint of Greenwood Publishing Group, Inc.

Printed in the United States of America

The paper used in this book complies with the
Permanent Paper Standard issued by the National
Information Standards Organization (Z39.48-1984).

10 9 8 7 6 5 4 3 2 1

To MLK and RFK

Contents

Tables

Preface

Writing this book was a much more formidable task than I had imagined, and as is the case with any author, I have acquired enormous debts. Scores of students, colleagues, friends, and scholars at other institutions deserve mention.

First of all, my thanks and gratitude extend to the many people at Loyola Marymount University who gave so generously of themselves to assist me in this work: to the students who constantly challenged and pushed me; to my colleagues upon whose expertise and friendship I called so often; to the staff of the Loyola Marymount University library, especially Tom Carter; and to Anthony B. Brzoska, S.J., and Albert P. Koppes, O.Carm., administrators who supported me throughout the course of my research and writing.

Research grants from Loyola Marymount University allowed me to spend considerable time examining the Nixon Presidential Papers. Jim Hastings, Fred Graboske, and the staff at the National Archives branch in Alexandria, Virginia (home of the Nixon presidential materials), were helpful beyond normal professional courtesy. The staff of the Nixon Book Collection at Whittier College's library were also very generous with their time. Friends in the Presidency Research Group gave generously of their time and expertise. And my thanks also to those who consented to be interviewed. I also owe a debt to the organizers of the 1987 Conference on the Nixon Presidency at Hofstra University, where I had the opportunity to meet with a number of officials from the Nixon administration.

My research assistants—Malia Adler, Ada Fermin, Sharon Morey, Kathleen Plaisted, Michelle Wright, and Alice Zayas—were patient and thorough, and put up with my many requests for "a little more material." Thanks also to my typists, Margaret Edwards, Ruth Goodrich, Debra McNamee, and Carole Keese.

A very special thanks to William Lammers of the University of Southern California, Seth Thompson of Loyola Marymount University, Michael Carey,

James Pfiffner of George Mason University, and Thomas E. Cronin of the Colorado College, who gave me valuable advice on all or parts of this book. I draw heavily upon their counsel, and while it is normally appropriate to absolve manuscript reviewers of all sins of omission and commission, I've decided to blame them for anything that goes wrong.

As this book goes into print, a great deal of material concerning the Nixon presidency remains unavailable to scholars. Former president Nixon's reluctance to release the bulk of his presidential papers makes writing any work on his presidency difficult and in many ways incomplete. But as former Nixon speechwriter Raymond Price wrote in his book *With Nixon*, he was not (and I am not) writing "*the* book about Richard Nixon and his presidency, but *a* book." I think it is fair to say that *the* book on Richard Nixon may never be written.

This book will try to piece together the many puzzles which make up Richard Nixon and his presidency. It is a study of Richard Nixon as a political leader, and focuses on Nixon's style of decision making and management. Organizationally, I begin with a brief biographical sketch of Nixon's early years and rise in politics; then look at the Nixon personality, how he approached and organized his administration, and how he handled domestic, economic, and foreign policy; and then examine the events which led to the fall of Richard Nixon known collectively as Watergate. I conclude with an analysis of the impact and legacy of Richard Nixon on the presidency and the United States, and try to place Nixon into a broader comparative perspective with other presidents. It is nearly impossible to think of Nixon without focusing upon his fall from grace: Watergate. But while the shadow of Watergate looms large over the Nixon legacy, it would be a mistake to see everything through the jaundiced eyes of that scandal. For the Nixon presidency was much more than the break-in of the Watergate complex and its aftermath. As important as Watergate is, both in U.S. political history and in understanding Richard Nixon, he and his career are too complex to be reduced to a single focal point. Watergate shows us Nixon writ large, but it does not show us all of Nixon. I hope that the multisidedness of the Nixon presidency is revealed in this work.

This is a study of the Nixon presidency, but it is also a study of "the presidency" broadly defined. In this sense, I share the concerns of traditional political biography along with the concerns of contemporary presidential scholarship. I hope this study is informed by the concerns of both schools.

By focusing on the Nixon administration from the perspective of presidential scholarship, we can get a clearer picture of why a book on the Nixon presidency is of importance. From this vantage point the Nixon presidency raises important issues and questions, such as:

- What is the impact of personality on performance and policies?
- What processes tend to produce what results?
- What is the relationship of policy outcomes to level of political skill, level of political opportunity, and political time?

- How were the key relationships of a presidency handled (e.g., management roles and relations with Congress and the media)?
- What are the implications of this presidency for our view of the institution, and what is the overall impact of the Nixon administration on the institution of the presidency?

As a note to the reader, at numerous points throughout this book references are made to the White House notes of Bob Haldeman, John Ehrlichman, and others. These notes are part of the archival material currently being stored at the National Archives branch in Alexandria, Virginia. All references to White House private notes are drawn from the National Archives material.

1

The Making of Richard Nixon

Biography should be written by an acute enemy.
> Arthur Balfour, former British prime minister, 1927

This political biography of Richard Milhous Nixon is not an effort to bury or resurrect Mr. Nixon. It is instead an effort to understand and explain one of the most mysterious, complex, and fascinating figures in modern history; an attempt to take a step back and reexamine and reevaluate Nixon, the man and his presidency. It does not fit into the literature on Nixon which puts the best possible construction on his behavior (e.g., Lord Longford's *Nixon* or Victor Lasky's *It Didn't Start with Watergate*), nor should it be considered in the company of those who place the worst possible construction on his behavior (e.g., Frank Mankiewicz's *Perfectly Clear* or Michael Myerson's *Watergate: Crimes in the Suites*).

The Nixon presidency is one of the most written-about, analyzed, discussed, and examined, yet least understood, administrations in American history. While we have a great many personality studies of Nixon (e.g., David Abrahamsen's *Nixon vs. Nixon*), policy studies (e.g., William Shawcross's *Sideshow*), memoirs (e.g., Nixon's own *RN*), and Watergate books (e.g., Leon Jaworski's *The Right and the Power*), a comprehensive overview of the Nixon presidency remains to be written. How, in short, do all the pieces fit together? How do the issues, people, and events interrelate? How do we explain Nixon's rise to power, his accomplishments, his landslide presidential victory in 1972, and ultimately, his downfall?

While much remains to be uncovered, and many mysteries are yet to be resolved, we need to look at the big picture as best we can piece it together to make sense of Richard Nixon and his era. This work aims at putting into perspective the events and personalities of an era of American history which was unusual and dramatic. But this book is only one piece of the puzzle.

Passing years, more books, and access to more information will be needed before we can get a more complete portrait of the presidency of Richard M. Nixon.

No one in the post–World War II period has been more central to America's political history than Richard Nixon. He is the one political figure about whom few people are neutral. He is loved and hated, glorified and vilified, honored and mocked. He is seen by some as a criminal and by others as a leader victimized and misunderstood.

Nixon was the quintessential post–World War II American figure. Indeed, it is not an exaggeration to call the quarter century from 1950 to 1975 the Age of Nixon. This period of his personal rise and fall coincides with the American rise to superpower status, the era of postwar U.S. dominance. His fall coincides with the decline of American hegemony. He was president in trying, turbulent, exciting times: the Age of Nixon.

Who was Richard Milhous Nixon, and how will history judge the thirty-seventh president of the United States, the only president to resign from office? So much is still unknown about Richard Nixon, this most private of public figures. Winston Churchill's description of the Soviet Union applies equally well to Nixon: "A riddle wrapped in a mystery inside an enigma."

Coming from rather humble beginnings, the young Nixon's rise in politics was nothing short of meteoric: election to the House of Representatives in 1946 at the age of thirty-three; reelection in 1948; election to the U.S. Senate in 1950. From Nixon's early campaigns, he developed the reputation as a hard-hitting, slashing campaigner. His attack style and "go for the jugular" approach became a Nixon trademark. So harsh was the Nixon campaign style that Walter Lippman described him as "a ruthless partisan [who] does not have within his conscience those scruples which the country has a right to expect,"[1] and Adlai Stevenson later said that "Nixonland was, a land of slander and scare, of sly innuendo, of a poison pen, the anonymous phone call, and hustling, pushing, shoving—the land of smash and grab and anything to win."[2] After a series of Nixon attacks alleging that Harry Truman was soft on communism, Truman, in an interview with Merle Miller, said "All the time I've been in politics there's only two people I hate, and [Nixon's] one. He not only doesn't give a damn about the people, he doesn't know how to tell the truth. I don't think that son of a bitch knows the difference between telling the truth and lying."[3] Because of the hard-hitting nature of the Nixon campaign style, and due to the use of misleading tactics, it was during his pre-presidential years that Nixon was first called Tricky Dick, an appellation which would plague him throughout his career.

Nixon emerged onto the national scene in the anticommunist hysteria of the 1950s. As a young congressman, Nixon was catapulted onto the national scene by the Alger Hiss case. The notoriety from this case put Nixon in the forefront of the Republican party and secured for him the nomination as Dwight D.

Eisenhower's vice presidential running mate at the age of thirty-nine. The future, it appeared, belonged to Richard Nixon.

During the 1952 presidential race Nixon the attacker found himself on the defensive. On September 18, 1952, the headline in the *New York Post* read, "SECRET NIXON FUND." The story revealed a "slush fund" of over $18,000, set up by sixty-six of Nixon's wealthy friends. At first, Nixon attacked the *Post*, calling the story a communist smear and saying that it was "completely false," but finally admitted that there was such a fund, but that the money went to pay his political, not personal, expenses.

In an effort to save his political life, Nixon went on television on September 23, 1952, to defend himself. The speech followed the popular "Milton Berle Show" and attracted approximately fifty-eight million viewers, the largest TV audience up to that time. In what became known as the Checkers speech, Nixon not only defended his use of the fund, but gave an accounting of his personal finances, questioned the ethics of his opponents Stevenson and Sparkman, spoke at length about his humble beginnings, his modest lifestyle, his wife Pat's lack of a mink coat ("but she does have a respectable Republican cloth coat"), and also brought the story of Checkers into the speech.

One other thing I probably should tell you, because if I don't they will probably be saying this about me, too. We did get something, a gift, after the nomination. A man down in Texas heard Pat on the radio mention the fact that our two youngsters would like to have a dog and, believe it or not, the day before we left on this campaign trip we got a message from Union Station in Baltimore, saying that they had a package for us. We went down to get it. You know what it was? It was a little cocker spaniel dog, in a crate that had been sent all the way from Texas—black and white, spotted, and our little girl Tricia, the six-year-old, named it Checkers. And you know, the kids, like all kids, loved the dog, and I just want to say this, right now, that regardless of what they say about it, we are going to keep it.[4]

While critics considered the Checkers speech "a crude exploitation of sentiment," for Nixon it was a phenomenal success. The Republican national headquarters was deluged with telegrams and mail supporting Nixon. More importantly, Eisenhower was impressed. After a few nervous days, Eisenhower and Nixon met in Wheeling, West Virginia, where Ike gave Nixon his blessing. "You're my boy," Eisenhower said to Nixon, at which the young vice presidential candidate wept openly. In the general election of 1952, Eisenhower and Nixon won 55 percent of the popular vote. In addition, the Republicans gained control of the House and Senate. And Richard Milhous Nixon, at the ripe young age of thirty-nine, had been elected vice president of the United States.

After two uneventful terms as vice president, Nixon was the obvious choice for the Republican presidential nomination in 1960. His opponent in the general election, Senator John F. Kennedy of Massachusetts, was a young, attractive Democrat, and the race seemed certain to be a close one. The election seemed a choice between the pragmatic conservative and the pragmatic liberal. Nixon had the experience and name recognition; Kennedy had great personal style and a reputation as a progressive. But Kennedy was a Roman Catholic, and no Catholic had ever been elected president. Nixon conducted the cleanest campaign of his political career. In the 1960 race, a "new Nixon" appeared.[5] Gone was the slashing, cutting aggressiveness of the fighting partisan. In its place a new, more statesmanlike Nixon emerged. Nixon knew that to win the election he had to appeal to independents and wavering Democrats, thus Nixon softened his rhetoric and sought to look presidential.

Nixon was ahead in the early polls, but was hurt by two factors in the election: Ike's lukewarm embrace of his former VP, and the debates between Nixon and Kennedy. In a press conference in 1960, Eisenhower was asked what decisions Nixon had helped him make in the past eight years. Ike's response, "If you give me a week, I might think of one. I don't remember," deflated the Nixon claim of "experience." While Ike once said that Nixon was the "most valuable member of my team," it was Eisenhower's offhand remark at the press conference that hounded Nixon.

The 1960 presidential debates also had a significant impact on the outcome of the election. Nixon was advised not to debate Kennedy. After all, Nixon was ahead in the polls and had little to gain. But Nixon, an accomplished debater, and experienced in the use of television, decided instead to take on his Democratic opponent in a series of four debates.

The results were disastrous for Nixon. In the first debate, viewed by eighty million people, Nixon did poorly. Not fully recovered from an injury, not as well prepared as he could have been, Nixon looked and sounded bad. Kennedy by contrast was rested, tanned, and relaxed. While on substance the debate was close, on appearance and style Kennedy was the clear winner. The experienced debater had lost the most important debate of his life. The three remaining debates were anticlimactic. An impression was stamped in the minds of the voters, and Nixon was not to recover.

The 1960 race was one of the closest in American history. Kennedy received 34,227,096 votes (49.7 percent) to Nixon's 34,107,646 (49.5 percent), a difference of only 113,000 votes. After the election, Nixon loyalists claimed that Kennedy—with the help of Chicago mayor Richard Daley and/or vote fraud in Texas—had "stolen" the election and that Nixon was the rightful winner. Nixon did not challenge the election because he said that such an effort would throw the nation into turmoil. While these charges are serious, there is no clear evidence to support the claim that Nixon was cheated out of victory in 1960.

After the 1960 race, the Nixons moved back to southern California. Nixon began to work at the law firm of Adams, Duque, and Hazeltine, and the former vice president began plotting his political comeback. During this period, Nixon wrote his autobiographical book *Six Crises*,[6] which was published in

1962. It dealt with the six significant crises of his public life: the Hiss case, the senatorial fund, Eisenhower's heart attack, his trip as vice president to Caracas, his meeting with Khrushchev, and the 1960 campaign.

Nixon set his sights on California's governorship. It would be an excellent stepping-stone back into the national political scene. But it was not to be. In the 1962 race Nixon faced his second consecutive defeat. Incumbent Pat Brown won 3,005,740 votes to Nixon's 2,721,933.

The aftermath of the '62 election was more noteworthy than the campaign itself. In what was dubbed "Nixon's Last Press Conference," an angry and disappointed Nixon went before the press, his usual self-control having deserted him, and proceeded to berate the press for its coverage of his campaign. Following his press secretary, Herb Klein, to the podium, Nixon said, "Now that Mr. Klein has made a statement, now that all the members of the press I know are so delighted that I lost, I would just like to make a statement of my own." It was a long, rambling statement in which he accused the press of giving him "the shaft," and concluded with the famous line, "I leave you gentlemen now, and you will now write it. You will interpret it. That's your right. But as I leave you I want you to know—just think how much you're going to be missing. You won't have Nixon to kick around any more, because, gentlemen, this is my last press conference."[7]

Indeed it did seem like Nixon's last press conference. Shortly after the meeting with the press, *Time* magazine featured a story which said that "barring a miracle, Nixon's public career has ended," and Howard K. Smith of ABC News broadcast the story of "The Political Obituary of Richard Nixon." Nixon began what Lord Longford called his "wilderness years."

Following his defeat in 1962 and his "permanent" retirement from politics, the Nixons moved to New York. There Nixon joined the Wall Street law firm of Mudge, Stern, Baldwin, and Todd in which John Mitchell later became a partner. Nixon himself became a partner in 1964. He bought an apartment at Sixty-second Street and Fifth Avenue (in the same building as Nelson Rockefeller, but the Nixons were never invited to the Rockefeller apartment) and began his new life. Nixon was becoming—or trying to become—a part of the Eastern establishment he so resented and so envied.

In spite of the advantages this new life offered Nixon and his family, a part of him was unsatisfied. The lure of public life still burned within him. He needed the political world to make him feel whole. But Nixon had lost two consecutive elections and had no power base. How would he, how could he, make his political comeback?

In many respects, the Goldwater debacle of 1964 that left the Republican party shattered was an excellent opportunity for a "new Nixon" to emerge as a unifying figure within the party. Shortly after the 1964 election (in which Nixon worked for Goldwater), Nixon crisscrossed the nation on behalf of the party, toiling in the Republican vineyards. It was a new, mellower Nixon who sought to heal the wounds of the divisive '64 race. He was reestablishing a presence in the party. In the 1966 midterm elections Nixon was a tireless campaigner for Republican candidates across the country. The results of the '66 election were very encouraging for the Republican party. They picked up forty-seven seats in the House, three in the Senate, and eight governorships. By early 1967, yet another "new Nixon" was once again running for the presidency.

As the 1968 presidential contest approached, events seemed to overshadow the individual candidates. The war in Vietnam was dragging on, and the war at home accelerated with massive antiwar marches, protests, and social upheaval. The universities were the scene of protests. Young people rejected convention, and the hippie movement flourished. Urban riots and racial unrest persisted. Political assassinations of President John Kennedy in 1963 and civil rights leader Martin Luther King, Jr., and presidential candidate Robert Kennedy in 1968 sent shock waves through the nation and the world. This "spectacle of violence" transformed the idealism of the Camelot era into a disenchantment and cynicism which threatened the bonds that held the nation together. Nixon was able to appear to be many things to many people in this unsettled and unsettling period. He was, in Garry Wills's words, "the right man for a period of resentment," who became "a virtuoso manipulator of discontents."

In this time of despair, disenchantment, conflict, and frustration, Richard Nixon—a "new" Richard Nixon—returned to the public arena. Gone was the aggressive, attacking Nixon. The new Nixon appeared calmer, more self-assured, thoughtful, compassionate, a healer of the nation's wounds. But was the new Nixon the real Nixon?[8]

In the general election Nixon benefited from the failure of the incumbent administration—of which his opponent Hubert H. Humphrey was vice president—to deal with the myriad problems of American society. Nixon also benefited from the collapse of the Democratic party. The assassination of Robert F. Kennedy during the primaries, the challenge to the Democratic establishment by Eugene McCarthy, the seemingly endless war in Vietnam, and the disastrous debacle during the Democratic Convention in Chicago, where protests and riots in the streets only added to the woes and conflicts going on within the convention hall, all conspired to put the Democrats on the defensive.

But by election eve the election was too close to call. When victory finally came, it was by an amazingly narrow margin. Nixon won by a 43.6 percent to 42.7 percent margin over Humphrey, with George Wallace getting 13.5 percent of the vote. Nixon's popular vote was 31,783,783 to Humphrey's 31,266,006, a plurality of only 517,777 votes. Nixon had lost the presidency by 113,000 votes in 1960, now, eight years later, he won by only a slightly greater margin. Nixon would be a minority president who was selected by the smallest vote percentage (43.6 percent) since 1912, when Woodrow Wilson won with only 41.9 percent of the vote. *And*, the House and Senate would be controlled by the opposition.

Table 1

Chronology of Richard Nixon's Pre-Presidential Years

Year	Event
1913	Born, Yorba Linda, California
1930	Graduated from Whittier High School
1930-34	Attended Whittier College
1934-37	Attended Duke University Law School
1937-41	Practiced Law, Whittier, California
1942	Worked for Office of Price Administration; Washington, D.C.
1942-45	Enlisted in Navy, Served in South Pacific
1946	Elected to U.S. House of Representatives
1948	Hiss Case
1948	Re-elected to House of Representatives
1950	Elected to U.S. Senate
1952	Republican presidential nominee Dwight D. Eisenhower nominated Nixon to be Vice-President. Secret Fund Case/Checkers Speech, Eisenhower-Nixon ticket elected.
1953-60	Nixon serves as Vice-President of the United States
1956	Re-elected as Vice-President
1958	South American trip
1959	Soviet Union trip/Kitchen debate with Krushchev
1960	Nixon runs for Presidency, loses to John Kennedy. Returns to California
1962	Runs for Governor of California, loses. Gives "last press Conference."
1963	Moves to New York to practice law.
1964	Campaigns for Republican candidates across the country.
1968	Elected President of the United States.

On election night, Nixon pledged to unify the country. "Bring Us Together" would be the theme of his administration. He continued, "That will be the great objective of this Administration at the outset: to bring American people together. This will be an open administration, open to new ideas . . . open to the critics as well as to those who support us. We want to bridge the generation gap. We want to bridge the gap between the races. We want to bring America together."

After the election, Nixon went about the important business of putting together his team and program for the challenge ahead. While his transition team was only loosely organized, Franklin Lincoln did put together a team of twenty task forces under the supervision of Paul W. McCracken.[9] On the surface, no man could have been better prepared for the presidency than Richard Nixon: the House, Senate, vice presidency; ups and downs; high points and low points. Nixon was a man who seemed trained for the office he was about to assume. (See Table 1.) But there was a fatal flaw. Former Nixon speechwriter William Safire called his ex-boss America's "first political paranoid with a majority," and Garry Wills called Nixon America's "first counterinsurgent president." For all his experience in politics, for all the "new" Nixons which had been developed and offered to the public, the essential core of Richard Nixon the person seemed to change very little. In spite of his vast experience, he never seemed to grow. As he approached the day when the prize would finally be his, questions remained: Who was Richard Nixon? What kind of a president would he make? What was the *real* Richard Nixon like?

NIXON'S POLITICAL PERSONALITY

Who is Richard Nixon? Perhaps this incident, related by Ellen K. Coughlin, best captures Nixon the man and the politician:

When his father died in 1956, Richard Nixon was campaigning for the Vice-Presidency of the United States. Soon after attending the funeral, the candidate was off again on a swing through upstate New York.

The first stop was Buffalo. He began a speech there with the words, "My father . . ." and then his voice faltered and he clung to the podium as if deeply moved.

He began again. "I remember my father telling me a long time ago, "Dick . . . Dick, Buffalo is a beautiful town."

"It may have been his favorite town."

Later, he moved on to Rochester, where he told the same story, substituting only the name of the city: "Dick, Rochester is a beautiful town." And then to Ithaca, where the performance was repeated once again.[10]

Richard Milhous Nixon is a complex, multidimensional figure. He is not, as some of his critics suggest, a shallow, one-dimensional person. He is a man of many contradictions. There were, as cartoonist Herblock oversimplified, two Nixons: the good Nixon and the bad Nixon, and they existed side by side within the man.[11]

Simple, easy descriptions do not apply to Richard Nixon. Is he, as Garry Wills suggests, "the least 'authentic' man alive," the "Market's servant," "plastic"? Is he, as Irving Brant wrote, "a synthetic figure"? Or is he, as Theodore White has written, "a quintessentially insecure man . . . uncomfortable with people"? Does Henry Kissinger's "the essence of this man is loneliness" apply? Or do Nixon's own "I'm an introvert in an extrovert's profession" and "I'm not a lovable man" apply? Arthur Miller wrote that he "marched instinctively down the crooked path," and George V. Higgins said that he was "a virtuoso of deception." Columnist Murray Kempton wrote that Nixon was "the President of every place in the country which does not have a bookstore." Bob Haldeman likens Nixon to a piece of quartz crystal, "He was very complex, with all kinds of light and dark facets, depending on where you're looking from."

Longtime Nixon friend and speechwriter Raymond Price sees his former boss as something of a paradox. Theodore White also noted the paradoxical quality of Nixon when he wrote of "the essential duality of his nature, the evil and the good, the flights of panic and the resolution of spirit, the good mind and the mean trickery." And former White House aide William Safire sees Nixon as a

complex man with mutiple layers, best seen as a layer cake, with the icing
(Nixon's public face) "conservative, stern, dignified, proper." But beneath the
icing one finds a variety of separate layers that reveal a complex, sometimes
contradictory, paradoxical human being. "One part of Nixon," Price writes, "is
exceptionally considerate, exceptionally caring, sentimental, generous of spirit,
kind. Another part is coldly calculating, devious, craftily manipulative. A third
part is angry, vindictive, ill-tempered, mean-spirited." Price notes that those
close to Nixon often referred to his "light side" and his "dark side," and suggests that over the years, the light side and the dark side "have been at constant
war with one another." Because of this, Price notes, "he has always needed
people around him who would help the lighter side prevail." Interestingly,
Price points out "the extent to which the dark side grew not out of his nature,
but out of his experiences in public life." The light side–dark side assessment
of Nixon is frequently referred to, especially by Nixon insiders. Some staffers
(e.g., Bob Finch) appealed to Nixon's better side, while others (e.g., Charles
Colson) appealed to the dark side. For the most part, the latter dominated in
the White House. This light side–dark side quality of Nixon made him a sort
of Jekyll and Hyde.

Bob Haldeman once described Nixon as "the weirdest man ever to live in
the White House," and John Ehrlichman described his former boss as "the
mad monk." Nixon has been a fascinating subject for analysis precisely because
he is so puzzling. As columnist Hugh Sidey has said, "He is an absolutely
sinister human being, but fascinating. I'd rather spend an evening with Richard
Nixon than with almost anybody else because he is so bizarre. He has splashes
of brilliance. He is obscene at times; his recall is almost total; his acquaintance-
ship with the world's figures is amazing. He is a fascinating human being."

The child being father to the man, we must, as David Abrahamsen notes,
"understand the hereditary and environmental elements, the developmental
factors, and the psychodynamics that determined his [Nixon's] personality
makeup."[12] If, as Garry Wills writes, "Nixon's background haunts him," what
can we say, what do we know of this background? How did this background
shape the man? Did he "overpersonalize" politics and policy? And when the
man became president, how did the office shape the man? As former Johnson
aide George Reedy points out, "The office neither elevates nor degrades a man.
What it does is to provide the stage upon which all of his personality traits are
magnified and accentuated."

One can see in Nixon's childhood certain recurring patterns or themes that
may have led to the development of psychological traits which affected his
adult behavior. The extent to which traits and characteristics developed early
in life impacted upon Nixon's behavior as president is shown in Nixon's relationship to his father and mother, the role illness and death played in his
childhood, and the view of the world Nixon developed out of his childhood
experiences. In many ways, Garry Wills's comment that "Nixon's background
haunts him" rings true.

From his relationship with his parents, young Richard's early development was, in David Abrahamsen's words, a tug of war between "two contrasting emotional antagonists, one parent unusually quiet and unyielding, the other often unruly and violent. Richard was caught in the middle." This forced Richard to walk a tightrope emotionally. Several psychobiographers characterize the home and family environment in which Richard grew as unhealthy and not conducive to the development of positive, secure personality traits. The relationship of Frank and Hannah Nixon was described by Nixon biographer Stephen Ambrose as "a union of opposites." Nixon's relationship to his parents rests at the center of many interpretations of the roots of Richard Nixon's problems.

Nixon's father, Frank, is variously described as "gloomy and argumentative" and "tyrannical" (Wills); as "a chronically angry man, ulcer-ridden from the early years of his marriage who invited hatred in his own family," who "punished his sons savagely," as "volatile, unpredictable and explosive" (Brodie); and as "a tyrant who intimidated his children. He spanked them on the slightest pretext." He was "unpredictable." "His children feared him" (Abrahamsen). In his autobiography, *RN*, Nixon writes of his father as a man with a "quick tongue and a ready pair of fists" who was a "natural fighter." When Frank was in one of his "black moods," young Richard knew to avoid him. Frank, his son Richard wrote, had a "brusque and bristly exterior."

The young Richard Nixon had difficulty warming up to and identifying with such a father. Frank was not very successful in business, not a warm, loving, or supportive father, and was prone to outbursts of temper, sometimes even violence. One neighbor remembers Frank Nixon as a man who "could be hard and he could be beastly . . . like an animal. He could be very hard on the children—spank them freely and give them cracks" (quoted in Abrahamsen).

By contrast, Nixon's mother, Hannah, was almost the direct opposite of Frank. Hannah Nixon is remembered as "saintly" (Wills), "shy and quiet" (Barber), "the epitome of self-control" (Di Clerico), and Nixon himself, on the eve of leaving the presidency, spoke of his mother as "a saint." A devout Quaker and pacifist, Hannah Nixon was the source of almost all of young Richard's security and affection in childhood. But this security was interrupted when Hannah was forced to leave Richard with his father for extended periods between 1927 and 1928, while Hannah took their tubercular sons to Arizona. Also, at the age of twelve, Richard was sent to live with an aunt for six months for reasons which are still unclear. These separations had a deep impact on young Richard Nixon.

These two parents of vastly different style, temperament, and outlook pulled in two different directions. All children need and reach out for parental love, but in Richard's case one can see a tug-of-war going on with the child as he attempted to please and draw affection from parents who were so different. This was complicated by the extended periods of separation from his mother that Nixon was forced to endure. David Abrahamsen believes this tug-of-war produced confusion, ambivalence, and identification problems for Nixon. As Abrahamsen writes, "Nixon had a double personality, a person who simultaneously seems to display entirely different thoughts, feelings, attitudes, and character." These behavior traits were imprinted on Nixon in childhood and extended into his adult life. It created, in Abrahamsen's terms, "an emotional conflict" wherein there was "an abyss between his higher, noble intentions and his aggressive, lower inclinations."

Illness played a significant role in Nixon's youth. At three, Richard was thrown from a horse-drawn carriage, falling on his head. He was rushed to the hospital, where Dr. A. L. Richards concluded that "had he reached the hospital emergency room just a few minutes later, Richard would have been dead on arrival." Nixon received a deep gash on his head that extended down to his neck and was severe enough to "separate his scalp from the bone." Ever since, Nixon has suffered from motion sickness believed to be caused by this accident.

A year later, Richard contracted a severe pneumonia from which he nearly died. Nixon also suffered throughout his childhood from hay fever. In his senior year in high school, Richard contracted a fever—believed to be undulant fever—causing him to run temperatures of 104 degrees and forcing him to miss much of his last year of high school.

Death also had a profound affect upon young Richard Nixon. Two of his brothers died of tubercular meningitis; the first, seven-year-old Arthur, with whom Richard was very close, died when Richard was twelve, the second, twenty-three-year-old Harold, died when Richard was twenty. Both had lengthy periods of illness which necessitated their mother's taking them to Arizona in an effort to find a healthful climate. During these times, Richard stayed at home with his father. The pain of separation from his mother was evident in this letter which the nearly eleven-year-old Richard wrote to his mother on November 23, 1923.

My dear Master:
   The two boys that you left with me are very bad to me. Their dog, Jim, is very old and he will never talk or play with me.
   One Saturday the boys went hunting. Jim and myself went with them. While going through the woods one of the boys tripped and fell on me. I lost my temper and bit him. He kicked me in the side and we started on. While we were walking I saw a black round thing in a tree. I hit it with my paw. A swarm of black things came out of it. I felt pain all over. I started to run and as both my eyes were swelled shut I fell into a pond. When I got home I was very sore. I wish you would come home right now.
                                                         Your good dog
                                                         RICHARD[13]

   The "good dog" letter reveals an anxiety for maternal nurturance and a self-image that is negative and submissive.
   Some psychohistorians note Nixon's reaction to the death of his two brothers as "survival guilt." This guilt may have led to an unconscious wish for injury or even a "death wish," a self-destructiveness which may have resulted in Nix-

on's behaving during the Watergate affair in a way that invited his own demise. He becomes, in David Abrahamsen's terms, "his own executioner. He punishes himself by arranging his own failures." His own doctor, at the height of the Watergate crisis, said that "the President has a death wish," and his head Secret Service guard said, "You can't protect a President who wants to kill himself."

The seeds of Nixon's low self-esteem and insecurity were sewn early in his life and would come back to haunt him as president. Essentially Richard Nixon had a warm, loving mother who abandoned him from time to time and a tough, harsh father whom he could never please. This seems to have taught Nixon that the soft and the nurturing are unreliable, that toughness and aggression are manly, and that the world is a harsh and cold place. Unable to attain a self-image that gave him satisfaction in what he was, he seemed constantly striving, compensating, and working hard to attain a sense of achievement based on what he did. He would face a hard world always ready to do battle, to attain a sense of self in outside achievements: winning. But at what cost?

From a psychohistorical or psychobiographical perspective, Richard Nixon is one of the most examined figures in history. A great many works have attempted to figure out "who" Nixon is. A brief review of some of the leading Nixon analysts may give us clues into what makes Nixon tick. Nixon himself was very sensitive about being psychoanalyzed from a distance, and in his memoirs attacked those who attempted such psychoanalysis.[14]

James David Barber (*The Presidential Character*, 1985) characterized Nixon as active-negative, a personality type that Barber describes as "exerting great effort but getting little emotional reward. The active-negative is compulsive, power-seeking, ambitious, striving. This personality type has low self-esteem, is rigid and insecure, and has difficulty managing aggressive feelings."

Barber believes that the seeds of Nixon's active-negative personality were sewn in a childhood in which he was "subject to strong deprivations of self-esteem" and that "out of his childhood Nixon brought a persistent bent toward life as painful, difficult, and—perhaps as significant—uncertain."[15]

Nixon is portrayed as a man driven by low self-esteem to compensate—sometimes overcompensate—for feelings of inadequacy. His lack of trust in people stemmed from a "view of human nature" which was "jaundiced" and is reflected in Nixon's comment that "most people are good not because of love but because of fear. You won't hear that in Sunday School, but it's true."

Bruce Mazlish's *In Search of Nixon*[16] offers a Freudian/Eriksonian version of Richard Nixon's psychological development. Mazlish focuses on Nixon's excessive fear of being unloved, his self-absorption, capacity for denial, avoidance, role absorption, ambivalence, opaqueness, loner tendencies, low self-esteem, compensatory behavior, feelings of inferiority, compulsiveness, need for control, projection, repressed hostility, lack of trust, and death wish. Mazlish asserts that Nixon had many "deep" needs, but fails to put them into context as Barber and others do. There is no diagnosis, no psychiatric conclusion or determination.

Eli Chasen's 1973 effort at understanding the Nixon personality *(President Nixon's Psychiatric Profile)* diagnoses the president as "a compulsive obsessive" person. Chasen points to Nixon's childhood years as stamping an identity on the president which would work against him. Chasen sees Nixon as identifying primarily with his mother, in part because he feared his father. This led to "significant feelings of uncertainty about himself as a male," and to doubts about his own sexuality and an "over concern with the important task of proving himself manly." He is unconsciously "helpless, dominated, and weak"[17] and must always prove himself. Nixon's ambivalence and internal conflicts led to a need for control, but since he could have only limited control over his environment, this led to anxiety.

David Abrahamsen, in *Nixon vs. Nixon: An Emotional Tragedy*, calls Nixon a "psychopathic personality" who is orally *and* anally fixated, who has "obsessive-compulsive longings," is egocentric, secretive, and manipulative, and who suffers from several "character disorders." The result is what Abrahamsen calls a "paranoid personality."[18]

Fawn Brodie, in *Richard Nixon: The Shaping of His Character*, sees Nixon as a "man of paradox". There was in Nixon, a "self-loathing," a "sense of being unloved". He developed a "paranoid style" and an "impulse toward self-destruction". Brodie writes of Nixon's "severely defective or almost nonexistent conscience," and of his "unconscious self-hatred."[19]

Throughout the psychobiographies of Richard Nixon several themes seem to dominate. (See Table 2.) A childhood marred by sickness and deaths in the family, as well as a self-image of insecurity and low self-esteem developing from his relationship to a stern, demanding father and a saintly mother, led to a personality development which most psychobiographers see as unhealthy. From Barber's active-negative categorization, to Mazlish's characterization of a boy unloved, to Chasen's "compulsive-obsesssive" personality diagnosis, to Abrahamsen's conclusion that Nixon has a "psychopathic personality" and "character disorder," to Brodie's view of Nixon as "self-loathing" and "paranoid," we see a psychiatric profile both disturbing and, perhaps, frightening.

If Nixon possessed these pathological characteristics, how did he rise to such heights, how did he achieve so many personal and political successes? In general, Nixon's psychobiographies argue that many of Nixon's psychological characteristics *aided* him in his political career! He was, by all accounts, a brilliant, hard-working man, and those "negative" psychological characteristics drove him to achieve, to succeed, to win. Thus, he sought in politics to compensate for his feelings of weakness by winning, by ambitious striving to succeed, by beating an opponent. In this way politics served as a temporary way of satisfying his feelings of insecurity and low self-esteem. Politics gave Nixon a way to attain through outward gratification some of the things he lacked internally. Politics satisfied a need.

Table 2
Richard Nixon's Psychological Characteristics

AUTHOR	CHARACTERISTICS	SOURCE
Abrahamsen	Psychopathic Personality Type Orally <u>and</u> anally fixated, obsessive-compulsive longings, passive-aggressive, secretive, egocentric, manipulative, paranoid personality, suffers from character disorders	Childhood
Barber	Active-Negative Type Vague self image, insecure, low self-esteem, lack of trust, need to manage aggressiveness, driven to compensatory behavior, feelings of inadequacy	Childhood
Brodie	Man of Paradox Self-loathing, paranoid style, sense of being unloved, impulse toward self-destruction, severely defective conscience, self-hatred	Childhood
Chasen	Compulsive-Obsessive Type Feeling of uncertainty, need to prove manliness need to control	Childhood
Mazlish	Fear of Being Unloved, Self Absorption Capacity for denial, low self-esteem, compensatory behavior, feelings of inferiority, compulsiveness, need for control, projection, repressed hostility, lack of trust, death wish	Childhood

Source: Adapted from David Abrahamsen, *Nixon vs. Nixon: An Emotional Tragedy* (New York: New American Library, 1978); James David Barber, *The Presidential Character* (Englewood Cliffs, N.J.: Prentice Hall, 1985); Fawn Brodie, *Richard Nixon: The Shaping of His Character* (New York: Norton, 1981); Eli Chasen, *President Nixon's Psychiatric Profile* (New York: Wyden, 1973); and Bruce Mazlish, *In Search of Nixon: A Psychohistorical Inquiry* (Baltimore: Penguin, 1972).

NIXON THE POLITICIAN

How can one see Nixon's personality impacting upon his behavior in politics? Clearly Nixon's operating style was deeply rooted in his personality, as he had a tendency to overpersonalize politics, and the operations of the White House began to function as an extension of President Nixon's character. He was unable to differentiate between disagreement and disloyalties; he had a tendency to see political opponents as enemies; and he looked upon the political world as an excessively hostile environment full of people out to get him. Aide Tom Charles Huston once remarked, "No one who has been in the White House could help but feel he was in a state of siege."

This led to a discernible, distinct, "operating style'" that guided Nixon's behavior as president. This style of operation can be seen in Nixon's relations with his staff and in the development and execution of policy, and in the end contributed to the downfall of the Nixon presidency. Richard Nixon developed a "paranoid style," which, while obscured at first, become more and more prevalent as his administration progressed. It was this paranoid style which eventually proved Nixon's undoing.

Nixon viewed politics as a battle, a struggle. He wrote: "I believe in the battle, whether it's the battle of the campaign or the battle of this office, which is a continuing battle. It's always there wherever you go. I perhaps, carry it more than others because that's my way."[20]

If politics is a battle, one must have enemies, and Nixon has a tendency to view political opponents as enemies. Internally, Nixon needed enemies to justify his own excessive actions. He also needed enemies on whom to project his own aggressive feelings. In March of 1973 Nixon told John Dean, "Nobody is a friend of ours. Let's face it." The view that the world around them was full of enemies pervaded the Nixon White House. And eventually a siege mentality took over, creating an isolated fortress around the president. He wasn't rich, or good-looking, or from the Eastern establishments and Ivy League, as was Kennedy. He wasn't as sophisticated, athletic, or graceful as Kennedy. This led to a sense of inferiority for which Nixon seemed always to be compensating. This chip on Nixon's shoulder, born of resentment, made Nixon more hostile and aggressive. He never really felt he had made it; even as president he was always the outsider fighting against a world out to get him. In John Ehrlichman's notes taken at a December 11, 1972, meeting with the president, Nixon is quoted as saying, "I'm one of the most hated MFs by Washington Estab, but I'm not captured by them. They know I'm not one of them."

Nixon speechwriter William Safire, discussing the "us versus them" attitude that pervaded the White House, suggested that while it may have been based on sound political reasoning, "it all got out of hand." This can be seen in the development of a White House "enemies list," a collection of names that ranged from Walter Mondale and Robert McNamara to Carol Channing, Steve McQueen, Barbara Streisand, Gregory Peck, Bill Cosby, and Joe Namath. Safire referred to Nixon as "the first political paranoid with a majority!" In some senses, Nixon did have enemies—as all politicians do. He also faced a hostile political environment—as all politicians do. But this is part of the governmental process. Nixon's real "enemies"—a Congress controlled by the Democrats, a bureaucracy staffed mostly by Democrats, an antiwar protest movement picking up steam, and the political legacy of the New Deal/Great Society—all worked against Nixon, but not in the way the president felt and saw. Nixon took real political adversaries and turned them into enemies; saw real political conflicts as battles to the death. He took hostile politicians and a hostile environment and blew both out of proportion.

In seeing his political opponents as enemies, Nixon had a tendency to overpersonalize every slight or insult. He harbored grudges and remembered every hurt. Abrahamsen calls him "an injustice collector." Evans and Novak, echoing this theme, wrote of Nixon's "invisible ledger of past wrongs" which was meticulously kept by Nixon himself. If you were in the ledger, Nixon would get you. John Dean told President Nixon that he was keeping notes "on a lot of people who are emerging as less than our friends," to which Nixon responded: "They are asking for it and they are going to get it. We have not used this power in this first four years as you know. We have never used it. We have not used the bureau and we have not used the Justice Department, but things are going to change now. And they are going to do it right or go." Dean then said to Nixon, "What an exciting prospect!"[21]

Nixon was the most "political" man imaginable. While he was a conservative by instinct and temperament, he had no deep-rooted ideological core, no guiding principles, beliefs, or ideals. This allowed him to shift policies so dramatically on such major issues as wage and price controls, China, the Soviet Union, and communism. This helped Nixon become a master of realpolitik, although one often didn't know where it was leading.

What were Nixon's values, what were his morals? In a very real sense, Nixon was amoral. He was not immoral, because he did not have a deep sense of morals. He was amoral in the Machiavellian sense. He had no real internal gyroscope to guide him morally. Power was the guide, winning his god. Thus, Nixon did not see himself acting immorally, he saw himself maximizing his power in a hostile and aggressive world.

Nixon's relationship to the general public was always ambiguous. He was not a warm, inspiring, or charismatic figure. He did not have the likability of a Ronald Reagan, the charm of a John Kennedy, or the ability to inspire confidence of a Franklin Roosevelt. Nixon was a somewhat awkward, uncomfortable man, who always seemed to be just slightly "off" in public. He did not inspire the trust of the public (critics mockingly asked, "Would you buy a used car from this man?").

Because of this, Nixon was the butt of some biting humor. Stephen J. Whitfield suggests that part of Nixon's public career cast him in the role of "comic figure," commenting that "it is doubtful whether any postwar American politician, or even any chief executive in our history, ever evoked so much mirth—much of it angry—as he."[22]

One of the most persistently hard-hitting of Nixon's comedic critics was Herbert Block, whose editorial cartoon "Herblock" graced the pages of the *Washington Post*. Herblock's most biting Nixon cartoon appeared during the 1954 campaign. The cartoon had Nixon emerging out of a sewer. For this, Vice President Nixon canceled his subscription to the *Post*, claiming that he wanted to protect his two daughters, who "were reaching an impressionable age." (In 1970, Herblock showed Nixon giving the vice president directions as Agnew descends into a sewer.)

Herblock's cartoons created powerful and lasting impressions. His Nixon—with his dark jowls and sinister looks, always in need of a shave—haunted Nixon throughout his career, bringing to mind Boss Tweed's lament about Thomas Nast's cartoons: "Them damn pictures."

Nixon became comedic cannon fodder for cartoonists, impersonators, and humorists such as David Frye, Art Buchwald, Mark Russell, Jules Feiffer, and others. He was parodied by noted author Philip Roth in the book *Our Gang (Starring Tricky and His Friends)* in which Trick E. Dixon, at the end of the book, gives a campaign speech in hell, where he is challenging Satan for the top job.

For all the humor directed at him, Nixon rarely used humor himself. Humor can deflate criticism or give a person a more human image, and as such can be a very valuable tool for politicians. Some presidents, such as Kennedy and Reagan, used humor with great success. But Nixon was almost humorless in public. He was rarely able to use humor to soften his public image. Nor did humor seem to be much of a part of Nixon's private side. He always seemed to take himself so seriously, and this is part of the reason why it was so easy to make him the butt of so many jokes.[23]

But the question remains: How, if he was so smart and experienced, could Watergate have happened? Since the answer defies outward logic, one must look within Nixon himself for the answer. Some tragic flaw within the man may have led to his downfall. Nixon was both prisoner and victim of his past.

Nixon Agonistes? In a way there is not one Nixon but many Nixons. Garry Wills has called him "the least 'authentic' man alive," and indeed he may have been. He seemed to create and re-create himself to fit the mood of the times. People constantly spoke of a "new Nixon," but it was really only a new image; in essence Nixon remained a political chameleon changing color to better fit into his environment.

H. R. Haldeman told interviewer Mike Wallace on television's *60 Minutes,* "Nixon is weird in the sense of being inexplicable, strange, hard to understand." That is because there are really several Nixons. He is a man pulled apart from within.

Nixon adviser Bryce Harlow summed up his former boss this way: "People didn't like him for the simple reason he didn't like people. . . . In the case of Richard Nixon, I suspect that my gifted friend somewhere in his youth, maybe when he was very young or in his teens, got badly hurt by someone he cared for very deeply or trusted totally—a parent, a relative, a dear friend, a lover, a confidante. Somewhere I figure someone hurt him badly, and from that experience and from then on he could not trust people."[24]

His inability to trust, his inability to make friends, his unwillingness to let people get close to him, all suggest that he is insecure, uncertain about his own identity, a man with low self-esteem. Life is a series of crises, many self-induced, which test his metal. He sees himself attacked by enemies, and this justifies his own dirty politics. He is a man who is haunted and hounded by his past. If child is father to the man, then the seeds of Richard Nixon's downfall can be traced back to a childhood of much pain, emotional deprivation, and ambivalence.

Richard Nixon was a brilliant man trapped in an insecure personality. He was a big thinker but a small man. He was brilliant, but this was a brilliance corrupted by smallness and hatreds. In the case of Richard Nixon, the tragedy was as much one of what might have been as one of what was. In the end, his paranoid style defeated him.

Richard Nixon was a complex man who governed in complex times. His fears, insecurities, repressed anger, and even paranoia produced a world image of Nixon alone, pitted against a hostile environment that was out to get him. He thus became excessive and self-righteous and played the game with one goal in sight: to win—by any means necessary.

NOTES

1. Quoted in Theodore H. White, *Breach of Faith: The Fall of Richard Nixon* (New York: Atheneum, 1975), p. 87.

2. Quoted in New York Times Staff, eds., *The End of a Presidency* (New York: Bantam, 1974), p. 17.

3. Merle Miller, *Plain Speaking* (New York: Putnam, 1974), p. 139.

4. Richard Nixon, *Six Crises* (New York: Warner, 1979), pp. 85–151.

5. Nixon, *Six Crises*, pp. 347–538.

6. Nixon, *Six Crises*, pp. 347–538.

7. Stephen E. Ambrose, *Nixon: The Education of a Politician, 1913–1962* (New York: Touchstone, 1987), pp. 650–674.

8. Theodore H. White, *The Making of the President, 1968* (New York: Atheneum, 1969), p. 148.

9. James Pfiffner, *The Strategic Presidency: Hitting the Ground Running* (Chicago: Dorsey, 1988), pp. 12–14.

10. Ellen K. Coughlin, "Putting Richard Nixon on the Couch," *The Chronicle of Higher Education*, February 13, 1979, p. 3.

11. In a 1988 discussion with Archibald Cox, I confessed that I was trying *not* to make this book into a psychobiography, but that so much of *what* Nixon did seemed to emanate from who he was, to which Cox replied, "Of course, with Nixon character is everything" (Loyola Marymount University, April 22, 1988).

12. David Abrahamsen, *Nixon vs. Nixon: An Emotional Tragedy* (New York: Farrar, Straus and Giroux, 1977), p. vi.

13. Quoted in James D. Barber, *The Presidential Character* (Englewood Cliffs, N.J.: Prentice-Hall, 1985), p. 401; and Bela Kornitzer, *The Real Nixon* (Chicago: Rand McNally, 1960), p. 57.

14. Richard Nixon, *RN* (New York: Grosset and Dunlop, 1978), p. 963.

15. Barber, *The Presidential Character*, pp. 9, 303, 350.

16. Bruce Mazlish, *In Search of Nixon: A Psychohistorical Inquiry* (Baltimore: Penguin, 1972).

17. Eli Chesen, *President Nixon's Psychiatric Profile* (New York: Wyden, 1973).

18. Abrahamsen, *Nixon vs. Nixon*, p. 116.

19. Fawn Brodie, *Richard Nixon: The Shaping of His Character* (New York: Norton, 1981), p. 505.

20. Quoted in Erwin C. Hargrove, *The Power of the Modern Presidency* (New York: Knopf, 1974), p. 177.

21. House Judiciary Committee, Recordings of Nixon White House, see Chapter 5 for more comprehensive review of contents of the Nixon tapes.

22. Stephen J. Whitfield, "Richard Nixon as a Comic Figure," *American Quarterly* 37, no. 1. (Spring 1985), p. 114.

23. Gerald Gardner, *All the Presidents' Wits: The Power of Presidential Humor* (New York: Beech Tree, 1986).

24. Bryce Harlow, "The Man and the Political Leader," in Kenneth W. Thompson, ed., *The Nixon Presidency* (Lanham, Md.: University Press of America, 1987) pp. 9–10.

2

Nixon in the White House

Richard Nixon's paranoid style permeated the administration. In almost every arena of behavior, that style took center stage and animated action: from the manner in which Nixon organized and dealt with Congress, to dealings with the courts and media, the paranoid style became standard operating procedure. The administration did not start with this style in full bloom. At the outset, the Nixon administration was a fairly balanced, dynamic group. But soon, the paranoid style began to take over and dominate. The movement toward this paranoid style planted the seeds of self-destruction at the very heart of the Nixon presidency.

RICHARD NIXON AS MANAGER

> Greater Love hath no man than this, that he lay down his friends for his political life.
>
> Jeremy Thorpe

The Nixon Team

The presidency is not simply one man, it is also an institution. With the growth of the positive role of the federal government since the 1930s, and with the rise of presidential power, an institution has grown around the president to serve his managerial, policy, and personal needs. This institution consists of the president's close personal staff, the peripheral staff, the cabinet, and the "permanent government," the bureaucracy. The president is the unmasterful master of this enormous and complex amalgamation, what Richard Rose calls a "chief, but not an executive."

The growth of the administrative side of the presidency has led some scholars to question what actually shapes a president's administration: the president or the presidency, the individual or the institution.[1] In this section we attempt to understand how Richard Nixon organized and managed the institution of the presidency, looking at how Nixon put his team together, the types of interactions between the president and his staff, the cabinet, and the bureaucracy, and the implications of his managerial arrangements for policy-making and advice.

How a president organizes his administration and *who* he chooses to serve him determines, to a great extent, *what* will be done.[2] In that sense, organizational and personnel decisions matter; they are not neutral. Organizing the machinery of government is one of the first tasks of a newly elected president. It is also one of his most important.

Presidents have tremendous latitude in determining how and for what purposes their administrations will be organized. In general, the president's choice of a managerial style will be based on a combination of the following: (1) *Personal Experience.* What style have the presidents employed in the past? Eisenhower, for example, was accustomed to a formal, hierarchical system from his military days and adopted that model in the White House; (2) *Personality.* What are the idiosyncratic characteristics of the President? Reagan, for example, had a very relaxed, laid-back, "don't bother me with the facts" style, well suited for a corporate or delegating management approach; and (3) *Policy Area Characteristics.* What different policy areas (foreign, economic, domestic) and types of policy decisions (routine, crisis) is a president required to make? Kennedy, for example, chose a special group of advisers, the EXCOM, to deal with the Cuban Missile Crisis. A president's choice of managerial style, which can be somewhat fluid but is surprisingly stable for each president, is based on the interaction of these three primary factors.

Overall, presidents have tended toward one of the following types of management styles: (1) *Formal.* This is a hierarchical style with clear lines of authority and formal structure. An example of this style would be Dwight Eisenhower; (2) *Competitive.* Here, the president sets his top advisers against one another in a friendly competition. Franklin D. Roosevelt is an example of this style; 3) *Collegial.* In this model, the president sits at the center of a cooperative unit of advisers. John Kennedy is an example of this management style;[3] and (4) *Corporate.* This is a delegating style in which the president remains fairly aloof from the day-to-day management of government. An example of this style is Ronald Reagan. Which style did Richard Nixon develop, and why? What were the implications of his choice of management style?

Nixon's Staff

Nixon's presidential team grew primarily out of his campaign organization.[4] It was a group with virtually no direct experience in electoral politics (with the exception of Robert Finch, secretary of the Department of Health, Education, and Welfare (HEW), but it was a team of Nixon loyalists. The original design, according to Bob Haldeman, was to have a "five equal assistants concept," with

Haldeman as the administrative head, John Ehrlichman to organize the domestic agenda, Henry Kissinger in charge of foreign policy, Bryce Harlow to head congressional relations, and Pat Moynihan in charge of urban affairs. But, as Haldeman notes, "the evolutionary process, once we were in place, moved us away from that fairly rapidly."

In point of fact, Haldeman quickly moved into the role he served during the campaign: chief of staff, protector of the president's time, and promoter of Nixon's interests. Because of Nixon's inclination, desires, and personality needs, a very *formal, structured,* and *hierarchical* system developed around the president, a palace guard. Nixon once said, "I must build a wall around me," and Haldeman would serve as the chief gatekeeper, protecting and isolating the president with his "zero-defect system," Haldeman's term for his tight management approach.

Deeply conservative, and sporting a crew cut in the long-haired days of the 1960s, H. R. ("Bob") Haldeman, the grim-faced former head of the J. Walter Thompson advertising agency in Los Angeles, boasted a fairly long history with President Nixon. Active in several of his previous campaigns, including managing the 1962 race for governor of California, Haldeman "organized" Nixon, in every aspect of that term. Haldeman had no independent duties or schedule; he served Nixon daily and closely. One Nixon aide estimated that the president spent more than seventy percent of his staff time alone with Bob Haldeman.[5]

Haldeman's skills and temperament were in many ways the ideal match for Nixon. He would and could do the president's dirty work, organize his time, protect him. But while Haldeman seemed just what the president needed (certainly what he wanted), James Shepley saw another dimension to the relationship: "When Nixon's need met Haldeman's abilities, you had an almost perfect formula for disaster."

Haldeman did what Nixon himself could not. Whereas Nixon disliked personal confrontations (he was unable to fire anyone; in fact Nixon once called FBI director J. Edgar Hoover into his office in order to fire Hoover, but by the end of the meeting the president ended up giving Hoover an increase in the number of agents the FBI could hire), Haldeman seemed to enjoy being tough and confrontational. Haldeman was Nixon's tough side in action. Haldeman used to say that "every president needs a son of a bitch, and I'm Nixon's. I'm his buffer and I'm his bastard. I get done what he wants done and I take the heat instead of him". At first Haldeman was able to exercise his considerable powers outside the glare of public attention. He believed that, as former FDR aide Louis Brownlow put it, White House assistants should have "a passion for anonymity." But it wasn't long before word got out that Haldeman was the Nixon gatekeeper, controlling access to the president by his tough, no-nonsense style and with the help of his young Haldeman clones known as "the Beaver Patrol."[6]

While most presidential observers warn of the danger of isolation, this was what Nixon sought.[7] John Ehrlichman once said, "We've [the White House staff] got the reputation . . . of building a wall around the President. The fact is that he was down under his desk saying 'I don't want to see those fellows,' and we were trying to pull him out."[8] Nixon demanded that Haldeman protect him from the outside world and control the flow of people and information. Haldeman once said of Nixon, "He doesn't want to organize, he wants to be organized." This gave Haldeman unprecedented power in the Nixon White House. But while Haldeman did the president's bidding, his one tragic flaw was that he had no real political experience and thus could not exercise any independent judgment so as to help the president avoid mistakes. Haldeman, in effect, did what the president wanted, right or wrong. His chief guiding principle was expediency. And while he did not isolate Nixon to the extent that some of his critics claim, he did reinforce Nixon's dark side.

With Haldeman installed as chief of staff, all others in the presidential orbit soon played a decidedly secondary role. John Mitchell, Nixon's 1968 campaign manager and attorney general, was at first an exception. While not mentioned by Haldeman as a part of the original inside team, Mitchell was indeed a close and influential adviser to the president in the early years of the administration. Nixon liked Mitchell's toughness and decisiveness. He was more than a member of the president's cabinet, he was a trusted adviser. In the first two years of the administration, Mitchell had a significant influence over policy, guiding the president on issues from desegregation, to Supreme Court nominations, to the 1970 decision to invade Cambodia. But as the decisions Mitchell was involved in soured, so too did his relationship with the president. After 1970, Mitchell concentrated on his duties as attorney general and later as campaign manager in 1972, and he was never as close to Nixon as he was in the early years of the administration.

John D. Ehrlichman, a Seattle zoning lawyer, was a college friend of Haldeman's at UCLA and another longtime Nixon campaign worker. With Haldeman's guidance and support, Ehrlichman moved smoothly and quickly from the relatively obscure post of counsel to the president to the center of power as coordinator of domestic policy.

With the exception of Henry Kissinger, who rose quickly to the core of the team and overshadowed Secretary of Defense Mel Laird *and* Secretary of State William Rogers, the other key advisers, Harlow, Moynihan, Charles Colson, Murray Chotiner, Arthur Burns, Robert Finch, et al., took a back seat to Haldeman and his close associate John Ehrlichman.

Through Haldeman, Nixon would control his administration via the staff. They were closer, more loyal, "his" men. The president would exercise his personal authority by creating a counter-cabinet and counter-bureaucracy located in the White House. Power would be personalized, and exercised through the staff. The normal counterweights of the cabinet and bureaucracy would be circumvented. Nixon, through Haldeman, would take control of government.

In a very real sense, the seeds of the Nixon administration's self-destruction were sewn early, as the organization of power built into the Nixon presidency a mechanism that fostered the negative aspects of the Nixon personality, the paranoid style. These negative aspects of the president—Nixon the loner, isolated, seeing adversaries as enemies, seeing political competition as war, distrusting, demanding loyalty—were nourished in the rarefied atmosphere of the White House organization he created. The structure built around the president fed into his dark side.

The organization centered in the White House was loyal and efficient but almost totally ignorant of national issues and the political process. With Haldeman, Ehrlichman, and Kissinger (especially the first two), critics saw a "Berlin Wall" in which the Huns, or the Germans, or the Teutonic Trio, as they were disparagingly called, ran the show for the president (Haldeman is actually Swiss). It was a closed system, a narrow passage through which ideas and information were filtered.

Relying so heavily on personal staff at the expense of cabinet and bureaucracy placed a great deal of power into the hands of Nixon's top staff members and necessitated an increase in the number of people who would serve the president. The budget for the White House staff increased from $8.5 million at the beginning of Nixon's term to $11.5 million in 1974.[9] The president, with the help of Haldeman, began to set a tone or a mood which was to seep down throughout the administration. All of Richard Nixon's fears and prejudices would be theirs. Of Nixon's two sides, the darker and lighter side, the administration began to move toward the darker. The president felt besieged, so the administration acted as if besieged. It was difficult to distinguish between real crises and imagined ones, between real enemies and imagined ones. In the end, all melted into one.

Bob Haldeman, in his memoirs *The Ends of Power*, claims that "Nixon was really the most *un*isolated [emphasis in original] President in history." He goes on to say he realized "that many problems in our administration arose not solely from the outside, but from inside the Oval Office—and even deeper, from inside the character of Richard Nixon. And to deal with these problems I realized I would have to turn myself into the man you know and don't love. And start to build a wall."[10]

Why the need to build a wall? Haldeman offers two reasons: (1) to conserve the president's time from unnecessary demands, and (2) because "*this* [emphasis in original] President had to be protected from himself." By this Haldeman meant that often, Nixon would issue "petty vindictive orders" such as an order to "put a 24-hour surveillance on that bastard," referring to a U.S. senator who had just given an anti–Vietnam War speech.

No one better exemplified the Nixon dark side than Charles ("Chuck") Colson. Jeb Magruder called him "an evil genuis." Colson shared Nixon's desire to go after the "enemies." Magruder gave Colson a great deal of blame for the White House mood that led to Watergate; he wrote, "I would have to say that—granting always Nixon's central responsibility for what happened in his administration—Colson was one of the men among his advisers most responsible for creating the climate that made Watergate possible, perhaps inevitable." Even Haldeman recognized the sinister impact Colson had on the president, writing that "Colson encouraged the dark impulses in Nixon's mind, and *acted* [emphasis in original] on these impulses instead of ignoring them and letting them die."

Garry Wills saw the early administration divided into three groups: the Law Firm (Mitchell et al.), the Nixon Regulars (Finch, Klein, et al.), and the Disneyland Mafia (Haldeman et al.).[11] It was also divided along policy and administrative lines, with Haldeman as the chief administrative officer, Kissinger as *the* foreign policy guru, Ehrlichman heading the domestic arena, and Arthur Burns and Daniel Moynihan in charge of economic and urban affairs.

How well was President Nixon served by his staff? In retrospect it is easy to say that his staff system served him poorly. It fed his darkest side and starved his best side. But it was a system that Nixon wanted, insisted upon; it fit his perceived political and personality needs.

But was Nixon ill served by the *structure* or the *people* around him? How different would things have been if good, experienced, honest people had staffed the top jobs in the administration? While one can only speculate, it appears that Nixon was ill served by *both* the structure and the people. The people fed his dark side and did not insist on a higher standard of behavior. The structure allowed Nixon to go on, isolated from those who might have stood up and cautioned him (the case of Secretary of the Interior Walter Hickel's being frozen out at a time when his warnings were most needed—during the Cambodian crisis—serves as a prime example). In short, the people closet to Nixon served him poorly, and the structure created a milieu in which isolation from essential information was possible.

Nixon's Cabinet

Cabinet government, the idea that the heads of the major administrative organs meet with the chief executive as a policy council and collectively govern, has never existed in the American political system. While most presidents pay lip service to the benefits of the cabinet, few make full use of them. In fact, cabinets have been of little importance in the areas of advice and policy making, as presidents prefer to use their staffs in making important political decisions.

Presidents soon come to doubt the loyalty and usefulness of their cabinets, as they feel that the cabinet has divided loyalties. While the staff is seen as loyal only to the president, the cabinet secretary is seen as dividing loyalty between the president who appointed him or her, the department or agency the official administers, the congressional committee most responsible for funding and issuing legislation for the department, and the client group that the department is to serve. However, the cabinet official is probably better situated than the White House staffer to give the president good political and policy advice. After all, who has his tentacles in more places than an astute cabinet member? But presidents, placing a higher value on personal loyalty than balanced political advice, opt for the staff over the cabinet.

President Nixon was no exception, and if anything, turned more toward his staff and further away from his cabinet than most. Nixon never really liked the personnel or organization of his cabinet and quickly distanced himself from the cabinet and relied very heavily on his top personal staff.

At first, Nixon did flirt with giving his cabinet real power, intending to reverse the highly personalized power then centered in the White House. The new president wanted to concentrate on foreign affairs and would leave the domestic side to the cabinet. At one of the early cabinet meetings in 1969, Nixon bolstered the independence of the cabinet when he told them that they were free to choose their own subordinates on the basis of ability, not loyalty to the president. Upon leaving the cabinet room, the president turned to an aide and said, "I just made a big mistake." From Nixon's perspective, he had. But he soon corrected this by centralizing more and more power in the White House. Nixon thus shifted from a view of his cabinet as a group of collegial advisers to one which relegated them to the role of mere managers. The Nixon cabinet never wielded significant influence with the president; power rapidly gravitated away from the departments and toward the White House. From the start, Nixon was unimpressed with his cabinet, particularly the three former governors: George Romney at the Department of Housing and Urban Development (HUD), Walter Hickel at Interior, and John Volpe at Transportation. Even longtime Nixon associate Robert Finch soon lost favor with the president. Only John Mitchell at Justice was to remain a part of the Nixon inner circle.[12]

Nixon's original cabinet was a diverse group of politically experienced men who soon faded in the eyes of the president. Things got so bad that after the first year, John Ehrlichman reports that the president "did not want to see most of the Cabinet." Attorney General John Mitchell and for a short time John Connally, treasury secretary (1971), were the exceptions. Nixon admired Mitchell's strength and intellect; he was drawn to Connally's strength and daring. But even these two shining stars were not enough to resurrect the dying cabinet, and the president refused to use the cabinet in any significant way. Cabinet meetings were rarely substantive and were generally, in John Ehrlichman's words, "show and tell. . . . There was very little deliberation." Upset that the cabinet "went native," Nixon came to view cabinet meetings as useless. John Ehrlichman quotes Nixon as saying, "We'll have no more unstructured Cabinet meetings. There'll be no hair-down political talk with those people. . . . We'll have a one-hour Cabinet meeting every two weeks, at which I intend to say less."[13]

Ehrlichman noted, "It got so bad that in about the third year we learned of a rump session of the Cabinet. They actually held a meeting over at Romney's conference room to discuss economic problems because they couldn't get any discussions at the Cabinet table when the Cabinet met." When the President got word of this he became very upset and tried—with limited success—to put a halt to these meetings.

Nixon's rapid transition from supporter of cabinet government in theory to an advocate of White House centralization also brought changes in the type of person appointed to the cabinet. From Nixon's original cabinet to those in office at the end of his administration, there is a pronounced decline in diversity, prior political experience, independent constituencies, and public reputation. It was a cabinet of anonymous managers.

The shift from stronger, independent, politically experienced people to more anonymous managers reflected the shift in Nixon's approach to cabinet government and his governing strategy. The last cabinet was weak on independence but strong on loyalty and execution. The last cabinet served no one but the president. It reflected the presidency-centered view of the president and helped centralize decision-making power in the White House. This shift gave the president more control and power, but meant that his advice would be less diverse and independent. In his less than six years as president, Nixon made over thirty appointments to the cabinet—more than any previous president.

Nixon and the Bureaucracy

Often called the fourth branch of government, the bureaucracy consists of the civil servants whose jobs are protected from changes in the political wind. They serve not at the pleasure of the president, but as the "permanent" government. These civil servants administer and execute the day-to-day business of government.

All modern presidents have expressed some distrust or hostility toward the bureaucracy, but none can ignore its role or importance in modern governance. The classic model of a bureaucracy exercising "neutral competence" has long ago been replaced by the recognition that the bureaucracy does indeed exercise a political and discretionary role in government. Bureaucrats do exercise administrative discretion, and presidents must be attentive to the politics of bureaucratic leadership, lest they risk having their policy initiatives thwarted. As more and more federal personnel became protected by civil service, problems of bureaucratic inertia, lack or responsiveness, and even disobedience to presidential orders became more prevalent.[14]

Richard Nixon had a hostility toward the bureaucracy that ran deep. His dislike for bureaucracy can be traced back to his brief but unpleasant experience in the federal government's Office of Price Administration (OPA) in the early days of World War II. Nixon said that from his OPA days, he learned how bureaucrats "at the top feathered their nests with all kinds of overlapping and empire building." In his memoirs Nixon wrote that "one of our most important tasks would be to place our stamp cn the federal bureaucracy as quickly and as firmly as we possibly could." The administration was going to,

in John Ehrlichman's words, engage in "guerrilla warfare" with the bureaucracy. As William Safire noted, "To Richard Nixon, government was half a
word—the whole word was 'damngovernment,' and the people who ran it contrary to his policies were the 'damnbureaucrats.'" In fact, the president tried to
establish a kind of counter-bureaucracy, centered—where else—in the White
House, under the control of John Ehrlichman and his Domestic Council. Nixon
would not limit himself to verbal bureaucracy-bashing, he would diminish their
importance by end runs around the bureaucracy.

Richard Cole and David Caputo write that "Nixon's struggle with the bureaucracy was more intense, more calculated, and far more political in design
than that of any previous president."[15] The ultimate goal of the Nixon strategy
was to use the techniques of management control to (a) eliminate or diminish
the independent power of the bureaucracy, (b) achieve via the executive branch
what the president could not get from a Congress controlled by the Democrats,
and (c) centralize power in the White House. Nixon felt, with some justification, that the bureaucracy was staffed by people who were against him. In
H. R. Haldeman's White House notes of June 29, 1971, he writes of Nixon as
saying, "Ninety percent of bureaucracy are against us/bastards who are here to
screw us." While it was certainly true that the bureaucratic tendency was to be
unresponsive to presidential initiatives, and while a good many of the career
civil servants were Democrats and/or liberals, the president took a grain of truth
and blew it out of proportion—much to his own detriment. The enemies mentality, so pervasive in the Nixon White House, soured relations between the
president and bureaucracy before the bureaucracy even had a chance to prove
itself. It was seen as an enemy.

Nixon was correct when he noted that most career civil servants were Democrats,[16] but the president overly personalized the partisanship of the bureaucracy and alternated between attacking, ignoring, bullying, or stripping power
from the bureaucracy. The president felt that the bureaucracy was partisan,
ideological, and hostile to the president's wishes and sought to replace top personnel where possible, or reorganize power where necessary. Nixon took a political environment that was not highly compatible to the president's desires (a
Democratic Congress, bureaucracy, and public and a media that was critical)
and saw mostly enemies. He thus assumed a "circle the wagons" mentality,
and this approach saw the bureaucracy as an enemy to be overcome, defeated.

This was a mistake, as John Ehrlichman later realized. Ehrlichman, who
early in the first term spoke of bureaucratic relations as guerrilla warfare, came
to feel that was a "big mistake." The bureaucracy, he found, had expertise and
experience which could have proven quite useful. Also, many in the bureaucracy exercised a level of professionalism which was impressive to those who
gave them a chance.[17]

But the die had been cast. Nixon, who so objected to what he felt was a
bureaucracy which was responsive to the liberal cause, wanted a bureaucracy
equally responsive to his needs. He sought to control the bureaucracy by a

highly centralized structure headed ultimately by H. R. Haldeman. With few top-level positions in the bureaucracy to fill, the president had to shift the centers of power from the bureaucracy to the White House.

To control the bureaucracy, a series of recommendations by Fred Malek, known as "The Malek Manual," presented a plan for bullying unresponsive bureaucrats into submission. Failing that, the president would centralize power and control into the White House.

As President Nixon's legislative proposals met with opposition in a Democrat-controlled Congress, he increasingly turned to attempts to achieve his policy proposals through administrative power, which had been centralized under the control of the White House, and took advantage of the wide latitude of administrative discretion to "interpret" laws in a manner favorable to his own views, and sometimes, as the impoundment of funds suggests, in direct opposition to the expressed will of Congress.

By the end of his first term, Nixon abandoned his legislative strategy in favor of an administrative approach to achieving his policy goals. The Nixon domestic agenda, frustrated by Congress, would be achieved through administrative techniques. This management approach to policy became the favored means of policy-making in the Nixon White House. Nixon would do administratively what he was unable to do legislatively. This required almost total control of the bureaucracy and caused a great deal of friction with the cabinet secretaries and the bureaucracy.[18] When it didn't initially work the way the president wanted, massive reorganization became the only answer. Nixon would take over the bureaucracy politically.[19]

Plans for Reorganization

Richard Nixon was never happy with the way his administration was managed. This was not due to any perceived failings on the part of his closest advisers, but flowed from that monolith known as "the government." It was large, unruly, and not part of the team. Failing in his attempts to tinker at the periphery of government, Richard Nixon was determined to reorganize the entire executive branch to better suit his needs.

Nixon was keen for reorganization. He eliminated the Department of the Post Office (and replaced it with a public corporation); merged the Peace Corps and Vista into a new agency called Action; created the Environmental Protection Agency, the National Oceanic and Atmospheric Administration, and the Federal Energy Administration; and proposed changes in the Atomic Energy Commission. He also eliminated several agencies and proposed the most ambitious reorganization of the executive branch in years. But the president had bigger ideas.

Nixon's approach to government reorganization focused on what Ronald Moe calls an "architectonic strategy," believing that the problem was principally "the machinery" of government. Thus, the president proposed comprehensive reforms.

Nixon had three major reorganization plans. The first, proposed in 1970, was the result of a report presented to the president by Roy Ash. This plan, submitted to the Congress, which had to approve executive branch reorganization, called for a reorganization of the Bureau of the Budget into the Office of Management and Budget, and the establishment of a Domestic Council. Congress did not nullify this proposal, and it went into effect in 1970.

The second, more ambitious reorganization plan was presented in 1971 in the State of the Union address, and called for a major cabinet reorganization. Nixon proposed that the twelve cabinet positions be reduced to eight; State, Treasury, Defense, and Justice would remain, but the others would be consolidated into four: Human Resources, Community Development, Natural Resources, and Economic Development. This was an effort to organize by function, not constituency. But the Congress refused to accept the president's reorganization proposal, and it was not implemented.

In 1973 President Nixon presented his third and most ambitious reorganization plan. But, frustrated by Congress's unwillingness to accept his 1971 reorganization plan, the president refused to submit this plan to the Congress and implemented it by executive fiat.

The day after his landslide reelection victory in 1972, the president met with top members of his administration. He thanked them for their efforts in the election, insisted that in his second term he would not be an "exhausted volcano," and then dropped a bombshell. Everyone, said the president, was required to submit letters of resignation. With that, the president left the room.[20]

Haldeman admitted that this was done "in a ruthless fashion" . . . but "ruthlessness was the only attitude that would work." Nixon, working from a plan orchestrated by John Ehrlichman, was to revive elements of the failed 1971 reorganization plan, but with several new twists.

The four super-cabinet officers—the heads of Economic Affairs, Human Resources, Natural Resources, and Community Development—would be elevated to the rank of assistants to the president and would serve as assistant or deputy presidents. Added to this would be Henry Kissinger as head of Foreign Affairs, and John Ehrlichman in charge of the Domestic Council. "These people," according to Ehrlichman, would be the "six-pointed Presidency." Named by designation and not statute, they would run the government and free the president's time for "big issues." In some ways it would be a collegial presidency—at least from an administrative standpoint. This new structure, according to Theodore White, "began to appear somewhat akin to Politburo control" of the government. Richard Nathan described this as an "administrative presidency."

The president, having called for the resignation of all his top officials, flew to Key Biscayne for a holiday. Nixon then went to Camp David for what the press came to call "the Mount Sinai shuttle." Helicopters flew in and out of

Camp David as senior administrative officials were shuffled in and out to get the news of their fate: in or out, up or down.

Some were treated to good news, others, like Transportation Secretary John Volpe, were treated, in Theodore White's term, "brutally." It was a house-cleaning with strong independent figures out and unknown Nixon loyalists and managers in. A new cabinet was created which would, in John Ehrlichman's words, "jump when the President says 'jump.'"

Nixon planned major surgery on the administrative apparatus of the government. Power was to be concentrated more and more within the White House, in the hands of the president's men. There was some logic to concentrating power in the White House, but the central problem is conveyed by an anonymous quote from a senior Nixon administration official who said, "The trouble is that Richard Nixon thought he could solve the problem by putting 'sons-of-bitches' in command."

This reorganization (and power-grabbing) plan died stillborn. As Watergate came to swallow the administration, and with the resignations of Haldeman and Ehrlichman, the super-cabinet faded away. The second Nixon term, rather than serving as a test case for the new administrative presidency, became a bunker-mentality presidency as the White House walls came tumbling in on Nixon and his top assistants.

Decision Making in the Nixon White House

How did Richard Nixon make decisions? By what process did the president decide? Nixon was a very disciplined person, and he had a very orderly, disciplined, structured decision process, mirroring his administrative vision and personal preferences.

Nixon the loner was uncomfortable with large groups and outward conflict. He preferred small groups and an orderly nonconflicted atmosphere. This necessitated a formal, hierarchical staff system, and required an advisory process which was narrow and tight knit. The president did not want aides and cabinet officials arguing in his presence. He wanted conflicts resolved outside the Oval Office. This meant that H. R. Haldeman played a central role in filtering issues and information for the president.

Unlike most of his predecessors, Richard Nixon did not like to announce his decisions directly to the affected parties. He preferred to have his decisions transmitted through Haldeman or other subordinates. This protected the president from the interpersonal clashes likely to develop if he were forced to get into a face-to-face battle with cabinet or other officials. Transmitting decisions in writing was tidier. Nixon used meetings not to decide but to sort out, not to reach a consensus but to air ideas.

Nixon's mind was truly astonishing, but his brilliance could not overcome the limitations he himself imposed on the decision-making process. Because he was a loner and sought physical isolation in order to think and decide, he was often a victim of his own process. Requiring that information go through written memoranda limited his own access to people and ideas. The best writers were often the most influential—this helps explain why Daniel Moynihan, a liberal, was so important in the early years of the Nixon presidency: Moynihan was a great writer.

The President preferred not to have advocates for and against positions engage in a tug-of-war in his presence but wanted recommendations and ideas in writing. This allowed him to sit alone, mull over ideas, and analyze them in his own mind. Of course, relying so heavily on written communication meant that those who were good writers—such as Daniel Moynihan—had a built-in advantage over those not as skilled at written communication. Likewise the filtering and written-communication process often made it difficult to discern the emotion, power, and intensity of an argument.

The president felt that he was able to overcome the potential pitfalls of this style of decision making because he was confident in his own ability, and because he was a man consumed with detail—even the most minute details.[21] H. R. Haldeman's notes of meetings with the president are full of Nixon giving orders about what to some might appear to be small "unpresidential" details: from "*never* serve California wine to a European" at a state dinner, to "change the [drinking] glass in Oval Office," to complaints that a picture hanging in the Defense Department was "much too severe." This attention to detail gave the president confidence that he could make decisions because he had all the information he needed.

Nixon's decision-making style was also affected by his personality needs. Nixon the loner, craving control and secrecy, demanding loyalty, trusting few, relying on a very few top advisers, closed himself off from people, ideas, and options. In short, Nixon decided *alone*, often without consulting his top aides. As Henry Kissinger noted, Nixon usually made "decisions in solitude on the basis of memoranda or with a few very intimate aides. He abhorred confronting colleagues with whom he disagreed . . . and he shunned persuading or inspiring his subordinates. He would decide from inside his self-imposed cocoon. . . . All this led to a vicious circle in which the President withdrew ever more into his isolation and pulled the central decisions increasingly into the White House."[22]

Thus, while Nixon was physically isolated, he did not feel that he was intellectually isolated—a mistake he would pay dearly for in the end. In the long run, President Nixon's decision-making style may have fit his personality, but it worked against his own best interests.

Conclusion

How effective was Richard Nixon as manager of the executive branch? In many ways, Richard Nixon cannot be considered a good manager. This is so in part because he didn't like the role of manager and delegated that role to

Bob Haldeman, in part because he resented the bureaucracy and his own cabinet, in part because certain personality quirks inhibited his ability to see and
judge clearly, in part because he doubted the loyalty of all but his closest advisers, and in part because he refused to spend the time necessary to be a good
manager.

The administrative side of the Nixon presidency went through three stages:
(1) *Cabinet Government*, an idea which lasted only a month or two; (2) *Staff
Government*, an idea that allowed Nixon to personalize power in the White
House; and (3) *Staff Kingship*, where management was further narrowed within
the White House, and an imperial presidency emerged. In this period, the
paranoid style was in full bloom.

Nixon's overreliance on his staff was understandable, given his personality
needs, but unfortunate for his presidency. The president tended to choose top
aides who mirrored his worst aspects—his dark side. Rather than recognizing
his weaknesses and developing counterweights, he chose people who fed into
his weaknesses. A "macho" style of staffing emerged, in which the tougher you
were, the more access to the center of power you had, and the weaker were
exiled to the periphery. Jeb Magruder identified the "losers" in this struggle as
Herb Klein, Bryce Harlow, and Robert Finch. The winners were Charles Colson, H. R. Haldeman, and John Mitchell.[23] Many years ago Harold Laswell
wrote that "the unconscious components of the personality result in poor personnel selection." This was dramatically clear in the case of Richard Nixon.

Instead of an open, healthy staff system, there developed under Richard Nixon
a closed, narrow system which was particularly prone to what Irving Janis called
"groupthink." The amazing thing is that Richard Nixon—on an abstract level—
recognized this problem. Notes taken by Haldeman at a meeting with the president quote Nixon as saying, "A man must not work with somebody who ac-
centuates his own prejudices." But Nixon was unwilling or unable to act on
this understanding. He did indeed choose aides who accentuated his own prejudices—and paid the price for this.

In dealing with the bureaucracy, Nixon, overly suspicious and distrustful,
tried to build a counter-bureaucracy within the White House. He refused to
seek cooperation with the bureaucracy and chose a frontal assault. This was
bound to fail, and in the long run impacted negatively on the president's performance.

The secrecy and isolation within which Nixon made decisions ran counter
to his own interests, but fit comfortably with his personality. He could not
overcome the fundamental weaknesses by exercise of brilliance. And Nixon's
inability to get what he wanted out of Congress and the bureaucracy led him
to pursue through administrative fiat what he could not achieve legislatively,
and to develop a counter-bureaucracy within the White House. The administrative presidency was bound to fail.

The collapse of the administrative presidency under Richard Nixon was for
the most part of his own doing. The fall of the house of Nixon resulted from

Table 3
Congressional Majorities during the Nixon Presidency

CONGRESS	HOUSE	SENATE
91st Congress (1969-71)	243 (D) - 192 (R)	57 (D) - 43 (R)
92nd Congress (1971-73)	254 (D) - 180 (R)	54 (D) - 44 (R)
93nd Congress (1973-75)	239 (D) - 192 (R)	56 (D) - 42 (R)

Source: Adapted from Gary King and Lyn Ragsdale, *The Elusive Executive: Discovering Statistical Patterns in the Presidency* (Washington, D.C.: Congressional Quarterly Press, 1988), pp. 426–29.

poor foundation, weak building materials, poor workmanship, and immense pressure from without. The house was weak, the pressure on it strong, the results predictable.

NIXON AND THE CONGRESS

I have been told I was on the road to hell, but I had no idea it was just a mile down the road with a Dome on it.

Abraham Lincoln

Since the 1930s, the voting public and the Congress have been essentially Democratic. The partisan realignment that resulted from the Great Depression of 1929 and came to life with Franklin Roosevelt's rise in 1932 changed the partisan distribution of power in the Democrats' favor and gave them control of the government for much of the postwar era. As the national majority party, the Democrats lost control of the Congress only twice: in 1946 and 1952, and then for only one term. When Richard Nixon became president in 1969, he was the first president in over one hundred years (since Zachary Taylor, in 1849, the last of the Whig presidents), to face opposition majorities in both houses of Congress at the start of his term (see Table 3).

As the minority party in the nation since the 1930s, the Republicans had played the role of loyal opposition to the Democratic majority. They were not compelled to provide coherent policy alternatives, nor were they accustomed to exerting leadership within the Congress. The Eisenhower presidency and the brief Republican control of the Senate by one seat, and by a 221–211 margin in the House in the 1953–55 term, passed without ceremony, and the Republicans seemed ill prepared to forge a national program through the Congress. Richard Nixon had experience in both the House of Representatives and the Senate. Also, as vice president he had presided over the Senate. But Nixon was never really a man of the Congress. He was never a congressional insider, didn't spend very many years in either chamber, and was never a legislative tactician.

Under the best circumstances, presidential influence with the Congress is only marginal. In the case of Richard Nixon, his level of opportunity to have an impact was low in that the opposition controlled both houses of Congress. But Nixon compounded his dilemma by not producing a legislative agenda early,[24] and thus, rather than hitting the ground running and attempting to take advantage of the opportunity afforded new presidents in the honeymoon period, Nixon hit the ground stumbling and was never able to recover.[25] The slim opportunity Nixon may have had was missed by his failure to go to Congress early with legislative proposals.

In his dealings with Congress, how did Nixon attempt to maneuver, work with, or work around the legislature? This section attempts to come to grips with the *process* of executive-legislative relations during the Nixon years. Policy dimensions are dealt with later in this book.

Moving quickly, at the height of opportunity, is a key to presidential success with Congress. Paul Light found that since 1960, of legislative items submitted by the president to Congress between January and March of the first year of a term, 72 percent were enacted. After that, the success rate drops dramatically to 39 percent in the next three months, and 25 percent in the following three months.[26] By the end of March, 1969, Nixon had submitted only 11 percent of his legislative programs to Congress.[27] It should not then be a surprise that President Nixon's proposals fared poorly in Congress.

Faced with opposition control of both houses, a weak Republican leadership structure in the House and Senate, and a lack of a clear legislative agenda, Richard Nixon decided that the Republican legislative void was perhaps as much an opportunity as a problem. It was an opportunity to remake the Republican leadership in Congress in his image. To do this, he would have to develop a congressional liaison apparatus that knew Nixon and knew the Congress. To head this unit he chose respected Washington insider Bryce Harlow.

Harlow was a longtime student of the Congress and, along with his assistant William Timmons (who later succeeded Harlow), put together the Nixon legislative strategy. But they did so without much assistance or input from the President, who displayed a profound lack of interest in the Congress. The early ambitions of creating a Congress in the president's image quickly gave way to an attitude of neglect, then contempt. This was exacerbated by the ill will and power struggle between Harlow and Haldeman. It was a power struggle over who would have the ear of the president and what strategy the administration would employ toward Congress. In this competition Harlow was bound to lose, and the loss spelt doom for Nixon's congressional relations.

The Republican minority leaders in Congress, Gerald Ford in the House and Hugh Scott in the Senate, never commanded the respect of Haldeman and the insiders in the White House and were never seriously used as advocates for the president's programs. Early efforts by Nixon to bring Democratic Senate leader Mike Mansfield into his confidence fell through.

Each year of his presidency, Nixon's contact with Congress declined. He felt uncomfortable with the back-slapping, hand-holding, persuading element of the relationship, and as time went on he sought other avenues to achieve his policy goals (administrative discretion, executive fiat, etc.)[28] and paid less and less attention to the Congress. His legislative scorecard suffered.[29]

Nixon's early superficial interest in building a strong relationship with Congress centered around Bryce Harlow's strategy to maximize the Nixon vote by building a solid Republican base, then attracting whatever Democratic votes they could get, mostly Southern conservative Democrats. While Nixon did not have a partisan majority in Congress, he did have something close to an ideological majority of Republicans and conservative Southern Democrats: the conservative coalition. In this way, Harlow saw Nixon attaining a number of legislative victories. But since the president minimized his role in this process, the Harlow strategy met with mixed results.[30]

When Timmons replaced Harlow in late 1969, a reevaluation of strategy took place. Timmons wished to follow the Harlow strategy, but Donald Rumsfeld (the only ex-Congressman on Nixon's top staff) promoted what could be called the "floating majority" strategy. This called for looking at each issue on a relatively nonpartisan or bipartisan basis. Depending on the issue at hand, it might be possible to build a liberal majority on one issue, a conservative majority on another, and a moderate majority on yet another.

After a while, discussions of strategy became less relevant as the essential disdain of Nixon toward the Congress emerged. Nixon was not willing to get his hands dirty in the congressional process, and soon legislative strategy was replaced by a veto strategy, and Nixon turned away from Congress in anger and frustration. But while the Democratic majority in Congress did cause Nixon problems, one cannot come away from an examination of executive-legislative relations during the early Nixon years without sensing the opportunities the president missed and the lack of interest he displayed toward the Congress. Rather than making a concerted effort at cooperation or even making serious attempts to work with the Congress, Nixon played the lone-wolf role. His inability to get his way with the Congress is not then surprising.[31]

As Nixon's problems with the Congress were compounded in the rejection of two Supreme Court nominees, problems ratifying the antiballistic missile treaty, and the inability to pass the Nixon legislative agenda, the president began to feel frustration and began to go on the attack. In the end Nixon saw the Congress as "cumbersome, undisciplined, isolationist, fiscally irresponsible, overly vulnerable to pressures from organized minorities, and too dominated by the media."[32]

Because of his early failures in the Congress—for which a great deal of blame rests on his shoulders—the president turned increasingly away from Congress

Table 4
Presidential Boxscore on Proposals Submitted to Congress

YEAR	PRESIDENT	NO. SUBMITTED	NO. APPROVED	% APPROVED
1954	Eisenhower	232	150	65
1955		207	96	46
1956		225	103	46
1957		206	76	37
1958		234	110	47
1959		228	93	41
1960		183	56	31
1961	Kennedy	355	172	48
1962		298	132	44
1963		401	109	27
1964	Johnson	217	125	58
1965		469	323	69
1966		371	207	56
1967		431	205	48
1968		414	231	56
1969	Nixon	171	55	32
1970		210	97	46
1971		202	40	20
1972		116	51	44
1973		183	57	31
1974		97	33	34
1974	Ford	64	23	36
1975		156	45	29

Source: Adapted from Gary King and Lyn Ragsdale, *The Elusive Executive: Discovering Statisti-cal Patterns in the Presidency* (Washington, D.C.: Congressional Quarterly Press, 1988), pp. 65–70.

and legislative solutions, began to see the Congress as yet another in the list of enemies, and began to search for ways to "get around" Congress. An independent strategy—one which sought ways to act *without*, or over the heads of, the Congress emerged. It was a strategy that included vetoes, impoundment of funds, use of administrative discretion and executive orders, *and* secrecy.

Nixon's legislative agenda was meager compared to that of his predecessors. He did not—in part because of partisan opposition majorities in both houses—pursue a comprehensive set of legislative proposals. And his success rate, even on his rather limited agenda, was not especially impressive (see Table 4).

With a thin legislative agenda, one might have thought Nixon could focus his energies on getting his bills through Congress, but that was not the case. Nixon disdained the legislative process, and his lack of success in Congress reflects this. The president simply did not put time, thought, or effort into the Congress. Moynihan wrote that Nixon's "initial thrusts were rarely followed up with a sustained . . . second and third order of advocacy. . . . The impression was allowed to arise . . . [that] the President wasn't really behind them."[33] The president quickly lost interest in his own legislative proposals but continued to use the Congress as his whipping boy in public. Nixon's emotional outburst after the Senate rejected G. Harold Carswell for a seat on the Supreme Court is but one of many examples of Nixon lashing out at Congress.[34] This Congress-bashing extended to Nixon's top aides as well. John Ehrlichman was said to have "arrogant disdain" for Congress, suggesting its members were a "bunch of clowns."[35] And Bob Haldeman was quoted as saying, "I don't think Congress is supposed to work with the White House."[36] Nixon's adversarial relationship with the Congress led the president to attempt to act above the Congress, by executive orders or administrative discretion. It only exacerbated his problems with the Congress.

Nixon's relations with a Democratic Congress were generally hostile and contentious (it went both ways). After several half-hearted efforts at working with Congress, Nixon moved to a more confrontational or a bypass approach. Not a coalition builder, Nixon, as was often the case, ended up as a polarizer and divider.[37]

To varying degrees, Nixon made efforts to ignore, circumvent, *and* take away the powers of Congress. It was, once again, elements of the paranoid style that came to dominate Nixon's relations with the Congress. Nixon's grab at congressional power can be seen in his efforts to expand the president's war powers (e.g., Cambodia), take the power of the purse from Congress (e.g., impoundment), limit access to information (e.g., executive privilege), and ignore the legislative process (e.g., the administrative presidency). While other presidents used these devices on occasion, Nixon made them part of a *broad policy* to circumvent the legislative process and move toward an imperial presidency.

RICHARD NIXON AND THE COURTS

> A man who aspires to any high office should have three qualifications: first, he should be prepared to support the constitution of his country; second, he should have a special aptitude for the office he desires; and third, he should have virtue and justice as they are understood by his fellow-citizens.
>
> Aristotle

Traditionally, the courts have not been a very effective check on presidential power.[38] More often than not, the courts have legitimized or added to the powers of the president rather than attempted to halt presidential extensions of power. Judicial scholar Glendon Schubert has written that "the most significant aspect of judicial review of presidential orders is its ineffectiveness. If the courts are the most important bulwark of freedom and liberty in the United States, then we have every right to view with alarm the future security of the republic."[39]

The judiciary was designed to serve as one of a number of checks on governmental power. One branch was to check and balance the other, power was meant to counteract power. But the role played by the courts when facing the presidency is far less significant than one might expect. As far as presidential power is concerned, the judiciary could more often be likened to the lamb, bowing to the superior power of the presidential wolf.

The normal pattern of court-president relations was for the president to act, and for the courts to either ignore such acts or give them judicial sanction.[40] This was especially true in the area of foreign policy, which the courts have traditionally viewed as the sacred province of the president, immune from judicial intervention.[41] But in recent years, a different picture has emerged. This picture paints a far more complimentary portrait of the courts when facing the presidency. In the past two decades, the frequency of court decisions against the presidency has increased to unprecedented levels. Presidency-curbing efforts by the courts came to a head during the presidency of Richard Nixon. Let us begin with a brief exploration of some of the major issues of the Nixon years and examine the courts' responses.

Court-president relations during the Nixon years were strained, and so were issues surrounding judicial politics. Nixon's two Supreme Court nominees who were rejected by the Senate in bitter political battles, the politicization of the crime issue, the attack on the courts during the 1968 campaign, all contributed to a confrontational mood and adversarial relationship where judicial issues were involved.

Nixon and the Supreme Court

As a politician of great skill and insight, Richard Nixon saw the Supreme Court in 1968 as a hot campaign issue. The liberal/activist Warren Court was under siege from the right, and a significant segment of the public, fearing the rise of crime, looked to the Supreme Court as one of the problems. Nixon campaigned hard on this issue, promising to name "strict constructionists" to the Court. Nixon wanted judges who would strictly and objectively interpret the Constitution, and not "make laws." The Warren Court had, according to Nixon, gone soft on crime.[42] Attacking the Court became good politics.[43] As America grew more and more fearful of street crime, as urban unrest and riots made the headlines, as the campuses exploded with protest, Nixon seized the issue and put much of the blame on the courts.

Nixon appears to have been attracted to the "attack the Warren Court" strategy for two reasons: (1) ideology (Nixon was, by inclination and design, a "law and order" advocate), and (2) politics (it would help him get elected and fit into his broader scheme of a Southern strategy). And since the court was powerless to fight back, it became an even more attractive target.

In his six years in office, Richard Nixon had the opportunity to appoint four justices (including the chief justice) to the Supreme Court. Being one vote short of a majority gave Nixon the opportunity to remake the Court in his own political and philosophical image. Nixon, like most presidents, tried to use his power to appoint justices as a way of promoting his political and philosophical goals. While Nixon's appointment of federal judges was no more partisan than most, he did pay particularly close attention to the political nature of his Supreme Court appointments.

Nixon's first opportunity to recast the composition of the Court came with the appointment of Warren E. Burger as chief justice. Burger was a Nixon discovery who had a long record of activism in the Republican party and who fit the Nixon model: strict law-and-order judge, conservative, a critic of the Warren Court. Burger was easily confirmed by the Senate, and the search then went on to fill the seat being vacated by Abe Fortas.

The Fortas seat opened up after some behind-the-scenes maneuvering by John Mitchell and Nixon, who presented to Chief Justice Warren information about some questionable financial dealings by Fortas. Rather than face the charges against him, Fortas resigned his seat on the Court. Nixon used this opening to send a signal to the South. This appointee would be a Southern conservative who would be seen as an early installment in the Southern strategy. But whom to chose?

Attorney General Mitchell suggested, and President Nixon accepted, Clement F. Haynsworth as the nominee for associate justice. Haynsworth, a fifty-seven-year-old lawyer from Greenville, South Carolina, was then serving as chief judge of the Fourth Circuit Court of Appeals. Initially, he seemed an ideal choice. But upon further investigation, serious problems emerged.

It should be noted that some Democrats in the Senate were predisposed to find fault with Haynsworth due to displeasure over the way the Nixon team pressured Abe Fortas into resigning from the Court, and also due to the unnecessary and futile threats of impeachment against Justice William O. Douglas.

This, coupled with several serious charges against Haynsworth, promised a battle over Nixon's first Southern nominee to the Supreme Court. Haynsworth was somewhat vulnerable on the issue of race, and Joseph L. Rauh, Jr., counsel for the Leadership Conference in Civil Rights, called him a "hard-core segregationist." Labor also had problems with the nominee, with AFL-CIO president George Meany calling him "antilabor." But it was questions of Haynsworth's judicial ethics, based on several questionable decisions that may have benefited him financially, that placed the nomination in deep trouble. The charge of conflict of interest in several cases was leveled against Haynsworth. The charges were serious, and needed to be answered. But the Nixon administration so botched their effort to defend Haynsworth that even the charges of questionable validity appeared to be true. Clark R. Mollenhoff, who was charged eventually with orchestrating the Haynsworth defense for Nixon, wrote that "the Administration's handling of the Haynsworth case . . . demonstrated to me that Nixon's White House team captains were rank amateurs in the operation of government. Through arrogance, superficiality, ignorance, and ethical insensitivity they could destroy the very people they hoped to use to their political advantage."[44]

The Judiciary Committee of the Senate approved the nomination by a 10–

7 vote. But when the nomination reached the floor of the Senate, it was clear that things had gone from bad to worse. The Nixon forces could not hold the line. On November 21, the Senate rejected the Haynsworth nomination by a 55–45 vote, with seventeen Republicans voting against the president's choice.

Nixon was, to put it mildly, outraged. But he would stay the course and appoint another Southerner to the Court. His commitment to the Southern strategy was unshakable, and three months later, Nixon nominated G. Harold Carswell to the Supreme Court.

Carswell, an activist in the Republican party in Florida, was a U.S. attorney, a district judge for the Northern District of Florida, and at the time of his nomination to the Supreme Court, a U.S. court of appeals judge for the Fifth Circuit. Even his supporters had difficulty defending Carswell as a man deserving of a seat on the Supreme Court. He was, in the words of Evans and Novak, "not a first-class judge or, as the Senate became convinced after full study of the record, even a first-class man."[45] Some of Nixon's critics thought that the Carswell nomination was a deliberate insult, offered after the Haynsworth defeat, in the belief that the Senate would never reject two nominations in a row.

At first it appeared as if the Senate would unenthusiastically but overwhelmingly consent to the nomination. But problems arose which began to threaten the status of the Carswell nomination: a 1948 speech in which Carswell proclaimed, "I am a Southerner by ancestry, birth, training, inclination, belief, and practice. I believe that segregation of the races is proper and the only practical and correct way of life in our states. I have always so believed and I shall always so act. . . . I yield to no man as a fellow-candidate, as a fellow-citizen, in the firm, vigorous belief in the principles of white supremacy, and I shall always be so governed"; his involvement in the transfer of a golf course from municipal to private control in an effort to evade a Supreme Court integration ruling; his misrepresentation of his own involvement in that matter; an unusually high rate of reversal of his judicial decisions by higher courts; and the failure of many of his colleagues on the Fifth Judicial Circuit to endorse him. These among other charges spelled trouble for the nomination. Perhaps the final humiliation, though, came in an effort to defend Carswell. Senator Roman Hruska, Republican from Nebraska, arguing against Carswell's critics, defended the judge's competence by arguing that "even if he were mediocre, there are a lot of mediocre judges and people and lawyers. They are entitled to a little representation, aren't they, and a little chance? We can't have all Brandeises and Frankfurters and Cardozos and stuff like that there."[46] These problems, coupled with repeated Nixon administration blunders,[47] led to the full Senate rejecting the Carswell nomination by a 51–45 vote.

Amazingly, Nixon had been turned down twice in a row on Supreme Court nominations. This had never happened in U.S. history, and the president took it personally. Nixon's response—which he himself characterized as "cold and reasoned anger"—was harsh.

I have reluctantly concluded, with the Senate presently constituted, I cannot success-fully nominate to the Supreme Court any federal appellate judge from the South who believes as I do in the strict construction of the Constitution. . . . I understand the bitter feeling of millions of Americans who live in the South about the act of regional discrimination that took place in the Senate yesterday. They have my assurance that the day will come when men like Judges Carswell and Haynsworth can and will sit on the high Court.[48]

But even in losing, Nixon may have gained something. By fighting so hard "for the South," Nixon displayed his loyalty to them and furthered the cause of the Southern strategy. Nixon *and* the South were victims; together they would march ahead.

Nixon still had a Supreme Court seat to fill, and he turned to an old friend of the chief justice, Harry A. Blackmun. Blackmun was on the U.S. Court of Appeals at the time of his nomination. He was a conservative, but not an extremist, and was confirmed by the Senate, 94–0.

President Nixon soon had two more chances to fill Supreme Court vacan-cies, and he chose Lewis Powell, Jr., and William Rehnquist. In the first seat, the president originally favored appointing a woman, California Court of Ap-peals judge Mildred L. Lillie (a conservative Democrat and a Catholic), but Chief Justice Warren Burger hinted that a woman on the Court was unaccept-able to him, and Nixon backed away. Tennessee senator Howard Baker was offered a seat on the Court, but turned down an appointment. Powell, of Vir-ginia, was a Southerner with a distinguished career in the law, serving as, among other things, president of the American Bar Association; Rehnquist was an assistant attorney general in the Nixon administration and was extremely conservative. Both were easily confirmed. Now it truly was the Nixon Court.

Having nominated four of the nine Supreme Court justices, Richard Nixon had, in effect, a Court majority, needing only one of the remaining five jus-tice's votes to attain a majority. Did the Court perform as Nixon had hoped and anticipated?

While the Nixon Court did not quickly overturn all the Warren Court de-cisions, it did begin a slow, measured retreat away from some of the policies of the Warren Court. A type of "gradual withdrawal" characterized the Nixon/Burger Court approach: the Court demonstrated a more lax attitude on charges of discrimination, manifested a belief that capital punishment is not "cruel and unusual," and was less sympathetic to labor, less sympathetic to the rights of the accused person, less sympathetic to demands of the poor, less sympathetic to civil liberties and the rights of the press, more concerned with the sanctity of property rights, and—perhaps surprisingly—somewhat supportive of wom-en's rights. In short, while the Nixon/Burger Court retreated from the policies of the Warren Court, it did so slowly and cautiously.

The courts entered political conflict with President Nixon very slowly. Being used to passive acceptance of presidential domination, the courts were at first reluctant to challenge the power and prestige of the presidency. The Vietnam War serves as an excellent example of judicial timidity.[49] Facing a "presidential war," the courts refused to face the heated question of the legitimacy of American involvement in the war in Southeast Asia. Time after time the courts backed away from conflict with the president over the war in Vietnam.[50]

The Pentagon Papers case[51] was one of the early president-curbing cases (see Chapter 4) in which the Supreme Court rejected a Nixon bid for expanded power. This was followed by a series of court decisions relating to the presidential impoundment of congressionally appropriated funds in which the courts restrained presidential power.[52]

The impoundment cases serve as an example of the courts standing up to the president. After successfully standing up to the Nixon administration in the Pentagon Papers case, the courts seemed more willing to take on questions of presidential power. In case after case, courts throughout the country ruled against executive impoundments and ordered the Nixon administration to release congressionally appropriated funds. Law professor Arthur Miller once noted that the power of the president to impound funds could be exercised "to the extent that the political milieu in which he operates permits him to do so."[53] In the case of the Nixon administration, it was an example of presidential overload. The political system could take a lot, but it could not take these numerous intrusions into the realms of congressional policy-making.

The courts were joined by the Congress, which wanted the funds released, along with different interest groups and state and federal agencies, and this coalition was able to halt a president who seemed determined to breach the boundaries of the political milieu in which he was operating.[54]

Overall, more cases were decided against the president than in any other period in American history—more than during the Civil War and New Deal era combined. The courts, contrary to historical tradition, played a significant role during the Watergate period.[55] Early decisions by federal judge John Sirica helped force an otherwise slow proceeding and investigation further along, and without Judge Sirica, there is a good chance that the political sins of Richard Nixon might have gone undetected. It was in Judge Sirica's court that the early Watergate defendants were tried and convicted, that the Senate and House committees went to battle over the acquisition of presidential tape recordings, and that the highest Nixon administration officials were tried and convicted: all except the president himself, who retreated to the safety of San Clemente with a presidential pardon as an "unindicted co-conspirator."

Richard Nixon in Court

Early in the first term of Richard Nixon, the courts adhered to the traditional role played by courts in American history: they stayed away from the president. But slowly, as the activities of the Nixon administration began to stray further from both the law and reason, the courts began to enter the legal/political scene. With Watergate, court involvement peaked in the court of federal judge John Sirica, and ultimately, the Supreme Court. Buttressed by the support of the Congress and the public, the Supreme Court stood up to the president, and the fate of Richard Nixon was all but sealed.

In what can only be described as an atypical historical occurrence, the courts took an active and clear stand in putting a halt to excessive claims of presidential power during the Nixon years. At no period in American history have the courts stood up so often to a president as they did to Nixon.[56]

NIXON, THE MEDIA, AND THE PUBLIC

> I don't mind a microscope, but when they use a proctoscope. . . .
>> Richard Nixon, on the tendency of the press
>> to place the president under a microscope

All presidents dislike the press at times. As an avenue to the public, the press reveals more than most presidents wish and usually exposes warts that presidents would prefer to keep concealed. (As one wag commented, "Presidents hate the press because they quote them.")

From the beginning of the republic, presidents have bemoaned what they saw as the irresponsibility or downright scandalousness of the press. George Washington once wrote that he was tired of being "buffeted in the public prints by a set of infamous scribblers," and John Adams complained of being "disgraced and degraded" in the press, and was president while the Alien and Sedition acts were used to arrest and prosecute opposition news editors. Thomas Jefferson, America's most eloquent advocate of press freedom ("Our liberty depends on the freedom of the press, and that cannot be limited without being lost," or "Where the press is free, and every man able to read, all is safe"), once wrote that "even the least informed of the people have learnt that nothing in a newspaper is to be believed."

In spite of the press's role as presidential irritant, presidents need and use the press. While it is a source of irritation, it is also a source of power. All presidents use, and most presidents dominate, the press. It is their vital link to the public and the best route to persuading the people and the Congress.

Thus the press can serve as an occasional check on presidential power as well as—and more often as—a tool for presidential power. Which of these it tends to be (and for all presidents it is at times both) depends on the *issues* (are they working for or against the president?); the personal *skills* of the president (is he persuasive?); and the *management* of the media (how well orchestrated is the president's public relations team?).

Whether the president is more or less skillful at manipulating and using the press to his advantage, one thing remains clear: the president is in a position to command the attention of the media and the nation as no other public figure can. His every move, every action, every word is news which must be covered and reported. Presidents thus have the capacity to set the national agenda and focus the country's attention on issues as no one else can.

In general, presidents get fairly soft treatment in the press. Other than the final year of the Johnson, Nixon, and Carter presidencies, one would be hard pressed to find a year in which—overall—any president received a "bad" press. On balance, presidents receive fairly positive coverage at the hands of the national media.

In relations, adversarial or otherwise, between the president and the press, the president has a distinct advantage. While both sides have tools at their disposal, presidents hold the most powerful ones. Presidents have the capacity to reward friends through access, interviews, leaks, and so on, and to punish adversaries. A skillful president can use the media to exploit his office as a "bully pulpit," and the "communicator-in-chief" role gives presidents considerable power. The press is the president's conduit to the people, the primary link between president and public. The press is a two-edged sword. It brings power or pain to presidents.

Richard Nixon has always had a love-hate relationship with the press, although, in his early years in the House and Senate, Nixon had greater contact with reporters and often fed and received information from them. But later, each seemed to love hating the other. "Criticism from the press has been my lot throughout my political life," said Richard Nixon, and to an extent this was true. Former aide Bryce Harlow once went so far as to say that "the press was hooked on an anti-Nixon drug and could never break the addiction. It was a terrible drag throughout Nixon's political career."

Washington Post reporter Lou Cannon said of the relationship, "Nixon hated us. It was reciprocated in some ways, but not as much as he thought." Nixon speechwriter William Safire has written that "when Nixon said, 'The press is the enemy,' . . . He was saying exactly what he meant: 'The press is the *enemy*, to be hated and beaten' " (emphasis in original). To Safire, this attitude was Nixon's "greatest personal and political weakness and the cause of his downfall." Columnist Hugh Sidey went so far as to say that "Nixon's paranoia about the press was world class."

Nixon's problems with the press began in earnest during the 1960 presidential race. In his first campaign for president, Nixon blamed his loss—in part—on the media. Kennedy "looked" better than Nixon, the debates became, in Nixon's view, more a beauty contest than a genuine exchange of ideas, and Nixon felt victimized by the media. If style triumphed over substance, Nixon would blame the messenger. He vowed *never* to let the media—especially television—do him in again. After losing the race for governor of California in 1962, Nixon finally blew up in public at the press. Apparently blaming the press for his defeat, Nixon held his infamous "last press conference," where an angry Nixon blasted the press for giving him "the shaft" and told the press that "you won't have Nixon to kick around any more."

But of course, that was not the end of Richard Nixon, and six years later, when he again ran for president, Nixon was determined *not* to let the press do him in again. This time Nixon would control, as much as possible, how the press saw, reported, and dealt with him. He would tightly control access to himself and information about the campaign. Leaving almost nothing to chance, Nixon's 1968 campaign was the most tightly controlled presidential campaign to date.

The '68 campaign was chronicled by Joe McGinniss in *The Selling of the President 1968* as an exercise in media control and manipulation. It was an effort to "sell" Nixon as one would a product. A "new" Nixon was created and presented to the American voter. As McGinniss writes of the media control on behalf of Nixon's effort to reshape his public image: "Television was the only answer, despite its sins against him in the past, but not just any kind of television. An uncommitted camera could do irreparable harm. His television would have to be controlled. . . . This would be Richard Nixon, the leader, returning from exile. Perhaps not beloved, but respected. Firm but not harsh; just but compassionate. With flashes of warmth spaced evenly throughout."[57]

Nixon ran a controlled, closed media campaign. Determined not to expose himself to a hostile press, he carefully orchestrated his public exposure so as to present the image he chose to have the public see. While Nixon said a few days after his nomination that "I am not going to barricade myself into a television studio and make this an antiseptic campaign," that is precisely what was done. And it worked.

Roger Ailes, who orchestrated Nixon's 1968 media image, knew why he had to produce shows that re-created Nixon. As Ailes said: "Now you put him on television, you've got a problem right away. He's a funny-looking guy. He looks like somebody hung him in a closet overnight and he jumps out in the morning with his suit all bunched up and starts running around saying, 'I want to be President.' I mean this is how he strikes some people. That's why these shows are important. To make them forget all that."[58]

There did seem to be a "new" Nixon: more relaxed, more controlled, mature and strong. He would be a man of peace who would end the war in Vietnam. The new Nixon was ready to lead. Having been victimized by the press in the past, Nixon used the press and media in 1968. It would be Nixon's preferred image that the voter saw, not the image the press wanted to promote; a "new" Nixon, not the real man. Television gave Nixon the means to re-create himself in the eyes of the American public. He would be television's master, not its victim.

In his bid for reelection in 1972 Nixon would control his image to an even greater degree than in the 1968 campaign.[59] Nixon could do this because he had (a) more than twice as much money as his opponent; (b) the advantage of incumbency; (c) a weak opponent; (d) a fairly submissive press; and (e) a fairly strong claim to success in his first term. Even the Watergate break-in received little adverse media attention, and Nixon was able to slide into his second term confident that he had indeed won the upper hand in dealing with the media.

How did Nixon deal with and attempt to control and manipulate the media during his presidency? How did he create, by 1972, an atmosphere in which he could dominate a sheepish press? Why did the press, in 1974, gang up on the president?

Nixon and the Press

All presidents complain about the press they get. This is part of the adversarial nature of presidential-press relations. But Nixon's bad relationship with the press—certainly on Nixon's part, and on the part of some in the press—went deeper, hit more primitive chords, called for action. Nixon once said that "I have had the most unfriendly press in history." But in fact, until the Watergate story gained momentum *after* the 1972 presidential election, Nixon had received fairly mixed treatment from the press.

If one compares the treatment Nixon received from the press to that of other presidents, one finds that by a variety of measures, Nixon received fairly favorable treatment. One measure is the percentage of newspaper endorsements a candidate receives in the presidential election. By this standard Nixon did quite well, receiving 54 percent of the newspaper endorsements over John Kennedy's 15 percent in 1960, a 60.8 to 14 percent margin over Hubert Humphrey in 1968, and an astronomical 71.4 to 5.3 percent margin over George McGovern in 1972.

While the everyday news reporter is slightly more liberal than the average voter, it is still difficult to find many reporters who were consistently critical of Nixon. And a study by John Orman of the balanced reporting in the periodical press found Nixon received a demonstrably good press compared to other presidents (even though he took a beating in 1973 and 1974 from the press).[60] In short, other than during the Watergate period, Richard Nixon received fairly favorable press coverage.[61]

But Nixon *believed* the press was out to get him, and he classified them as an enemy. If an enemy was going to attack, it called for a counterattack. In fact, the Nixon administration developed the most complex and elaborate attack on the national press in our nation's history. It was an attack on the tone, content, and personnel of the news industry.[62]

What emanated from the Nixon White House was an attack aimed not at a single reporter deemed to be biased or unfair, but at the entire news industry, from news reporters to editors to publishers.

Richard Nixon's paranoia about the press teamed up with his excessive desire for secrecy and found an outlet for his anger when leaks began to spring in the ship of state.[63] Troubled by what he saw as excessive leaking—especially relating to the duplicitous stance the United States was taking in the India-Pakistan war—and egged on by Henry Kissinger, the president ordered that the leaks be plugged up. This led to the creation of the "Plumbers" who committed a variety of crimes that in the long run contributed to the president's downfall.

Part of the strategy of plugging leaks and punishing critical news reporters and columnists was the imposition of a wiretapping program—again at the insistence of Henry Kissinger—which targeted a number of media stars. Among those victimized by the wiretapping program were Hedrick Smith and William Beecher of the *New York Times*, Henry Brandon of the *London Sunday Times*, and Marvin Kalb of CBS News. Such invasions of privacy—which the courts judged to be illegal—were justified on national security grounds, but probably had more to do with Nixon's own feelings toward the press.

The goals in dealing with the press were: (a) discredit the media; (b) get the best coverage possible for the administration; and (c) go over the heads of the press—directly to the American public. Nixon wanted to turn public opinion *against* the news media, thus discrediting the source of criticism against the administration. If this could be done, if the press could be painted as part of the "radiclib" cabal out to get the president, then criticism of the administration could be discounted.

President Nixon decided in 1968 not to have a press secretary in the conventional sense. He assigned Ron Ziegler to run the press office, and Herb Klein was appointed director of communications. At first, Klein was to serve as the communications powerhouse, but his star quickly descended and press spokesman Ron Ziegler rose to become the administration's public voice.[64]

"Make the press look bad, make the President look good" was the overarching goal of the Nixon press machinery. To do this, an elaborate public relations effort was put into effect. John Ehrlichman notes that "Richard Nixon at times seemed to believe there was no national issue that was not susceptible to public relations treatment." Nixon organized the administration so as to maximize the opportunities afforded the president. As Ehrlichman notes, "Nixon came into the White House determined to exercise the fullest possible influence over what the press said about him and his administration." He and Bob Haldeman shared the view that no previous president had properly organized and staffed the White House to manage the news. They set about constructing an apparatus that would appear to serve the White House press corps, while, at the same time, sending volumes of information over their heads to small newspapers and television stations out in the hinterlands. The White House would try to systematically propagandize the general public.[65] The "five o'clock group" met almost daily to discuss how to "play" stories in the media.

The president himself was rarely openly engaged in antipress rhetoric or action. He would remain above the fray. But it is clear that the overall leitmotif of the antipress campaign came from Nixon himself. Throughout H. R. Haldeman's notes are references from the president such as "freeze out" this or that reporter; "no one to see press at all"; "All NY Times reporters—*all* off list [emphasis in original] including K. punish the whole institution." This "freeze out" policy reflected Nixon's long-running battle with the press, a battle fought through Haldeman and his aides. In his memoirs, *The Ends of Power*, Haldeman writes that "I can't remember all of the reporters and newspeople he [Nixon] asked me to 'go after' in one way or the other."

Nixon was especially sensitive to press criticism, took it personally, and sought revenge. H. R. Haldeman's notes taken in meetings with the president are full of critical references made by Nixon to news reporters. Nixon reserved a special contempt for the *New York Times*, the *Washington Post*, and *Newsweek* magazine. For example, on July 20, 1969, Nixon is quoted as saying, "Absolute order—complete cut off of *Times*"; or on July 18, 1969, "get *Time* in on Friday and *US News* give them the whole story . . . don't tell *Newsweek* anything."

The Nixon team's effort to manipulate the image presented of their president and manipulate the news media itself was not unique in kind, only in volume. All presidents try to influence or manage the news. But no previous president (and only Reagan since) went to the lengths that Nixon went to manipulate the media.[66]

John Ehrlichman called Nixon "a talented media manipulator." But the most aggressive aspect of the Nixon press strategy was the "attack strategy" employed by the administration. Presidents have tended to use both the carrot *and* the stick when dealing with the press: Nixon emphasized the stick. He believed the media represented "the greatest concentration of power in the United States,"[67] and were part of the elite Eastern establishment that was out to get him. Walter Cronkite once accused the Nixon administration of "a grand conspiracy to destroy the credibility of the press," of a "clear effort at intimidation" of the press. This effort to discredit the press was carefully planned and elaborately orchestrated.

If the press was the enemy, Nixon would go over their heads, directly to the American people, "his" people. Nixon had a fear that if he gave his message to the press, they would distort the message he was trying to get across. "My object," Nixon once said, "was to go over the heads of the columnists." The president often sought—and was granted—prime-time television access to make major policy and political speeches. This allowed the president to go directly to the voters *without* the filtering effect of TV and news reporters. Nixon, for example, gave more television addresses (32) than Kennedy (9), Johnson (15), and Ford (6) combined.

To Nixon, public speaking was "performance not communication."[68] His communication theory was to: "(1) speak for the institution, not for oneself; (2) speak in controlled settings, not those permitting interlocutors; (3) speak for the ages, not for the tempestuous moment."[69]

In this sense, Nixon furthered his goal of appearing presidential. By using this method and speaking directly to the people, Nixon had almost total control of the medium and the message. He could surround himself with the symbols and paraphernalia that would help create the image *he* wanted. Nixon could speak to the people in words he chose. The press was effectively excluded from this process.

Nixon chose to communicate with the public through televised speeches and not through press conferences, which could not be controlled, had too many loose ends, and too many things that could go wrong. In fact, the only modern president to hold fewer press conferences than Nixon was Ronald Reagan.

The overall control of the antipress strategy went through Haldeman's office, but day-to-day control was assumed by Jeb Magruder and Charles Colson. The initial strategy was laid out in a remarkable October 17, 1969, memorandum from Magruder to Haldeman entitled "The Shot-Gun Versus the Rifle." The memorandum advised dealing with press criticism not in a case-by-case way (Magruder cited twenty-one instances of the president, in a thirty-day period, requesting action against news stories), but in a broader, more general manner.

The real problem, Magruder wrote, was "to get to this unfair coverage" in a way that "the networks, newspapers and Congress will react to and begin to look at things somewhat differently." To do this Magruder suggested that the administration "begin an official monitoring system"; he also proposed utilizing "the anti-trust division to investigate various media relating to anti-trust violations. Even the possible threat of anti-trust action I think would be effective in changing their views"; and "utilizing the Internal Revenue Service as a method to look into the various organizations that we are most concerned about. Just a threat of an I.R.S. investigation will probably turn their approach."

Magruder also proposed that the administration "begin to show favorites in the media," and "utilize Republican National Committee for major letter writing efforts." Out of this memorandum sprang a series of actions designed to discredit the media, put it on the defensive, and hopefully, get more favorable coverage. This started an avalanche of activity directed against the press.

The goal, as Haldeman aide Lawrence Higby noted in a memorandum to Magruder, was not to go after individual newsmen: "What we are trying to do here is to tear down the institution."

The president himself was very interested in a broad monitoring of television. In a March 11, 1969, memorandum to John Ehrlichman, the president notes that he wants to "monitor television programs—not only the political programs but the entertainment programs in which there are often deliberately negative comments which deserve some reaction on the part of our friends. One of the programs . . . was the 'Smothers Brothers.' In looking at it Sunday night . . . one said to the other that he found it difficult to find anything to laugh about—Vietnam, the cities, etc., but 'Richard Nixon solving these problems' and 'that's really funny.' " Nixon then added, "The line didn't get a particularly good reaction," but it was "the kind of line that should . . . receive some calls and letters strenuously objecting to that kind of attack."

The most visible arm of the attack on the news media was seen in a series of speeches given by Vice President Agnew. The idea of using Agnew in this manner came, according to Haldeman, "right from the Oval Office." The first salvo was fired by Agnew in a November 13, 1969, speech written by Pat Buchanan and delivered in Des Moines, Iowa. In the speech, Agnew launched an all-out assault on the integrity of the three television networks. Noting that he was not proposing government censorship, Agnew asked "whether a form of censorship already exists" with the networks, "a small and unelected elite" determining what the people will see and hear. Later in the speech, the vice president reminded the networks that they enjoyed "a monopoly sanctioned and licensed" by the government (a warning of things to come) and called on the networks to be "made more responsive to the views of the nation." Agnew continued:

A small group of men, numbering perhaps no more than a dozen anchormen, commentators and executive producers, settle upon the twenty minutes or so of film and commentary that's to reach the public. . . . They decide what forty to fifty million Americans will learn of the day's events in the nation and in the world. . . . We do know that to a man these commentators and producers live and work in the geographical and intellectual confines of Washington, D.C., or New York City, the latter of which James Reston termed the most unrepresentative community in the entire United States. Both communities bask in their own provincialism, their own parochialism. We can deduce that these men read the same newspapers. They draw their political and social views from the same sources. Worse, they talk constantly to one another, thereby providing artificial reinforcement to their shared viewpoints.[70]

A week later, in a speech in Montgomery, Alabama, Agnew again went on the attack, this time broadening his accusations to include the *New York Times* and the *Washington Post*.

Agnew's public attack on the honesty and integrity of the press was followed by a series of moves designed to put pressure on the media from a variety of fronts. Dean Burch, chairman of the Federal Communications Commission (FCC), called the heads of all three networks the day after President Nixon gave a major speech on Vietnam and requested transcripts of the news analyses the networks carried. He was doing so, he claimed, "at the request of the White House." Such thinly veiled efforts at intimidation were reinforced with other, more hard-hitting, actions.

By the summer of 1971 the White House pushed ahead even more forcefully: the enemies list was forwarded to John Dean for action; the Pentagon Papers case went ahead, the Plumbers broke into one of Daniel Ellsberg's psychiatrist's offices, and the FBI began investigating CBS correspondent Daniel Schorr. It was a full-court press.

Attorney General John Mitchell contributed substantially to the antimedia effort with a legal assault on press freedom and the First Amendment by challenging the privacy of a reporter's sources. Mitchell also executed the first attempt by the U.S. government at prior restraint of the press in the Pentagon Papers case (see Chapter 4).

Clay Whitehead, head of the White House Office of Telecommunications Policy, criticized news coverage of the president in forceful language and in 1972 announced that the administration would soon propose legislation that would hold local stations responsible at license-renewal time for the content of the network news and all the network-provided programming they broadcast. He also suggested that the FCC impose licensing-renewal requirements with "teeth." Whitehead wanted the local stations to pressure the networks to refrain from what he called "ideological plugola" and "elitist gossip in the guise of news analysis." By threatening to use the licensing-renewal procedure, Whitehead hoped the local affiliates would pressure the networks into altering their news program. He concluded his speech by saying, "Station managers and network officials who fail to act to correct imbalance or consistent bias from the networks—or who acquiesce by silence—can only be considered willing participants to be held fully accountable by the broadcaster's community at license-renewal time."

In connection with this, the administration orchestrated a letter-writing campaign that generated thousands of letters to the networks supporting the administration. This letter-writing campaign—in which it was made to appear that thousands of ordinary citizens were spontaneously making their views known— was used throughout the Nixon presidency.[71]

The two-pronged goal of discrediting the news media in the eyes of the public and frightening the press into submission continued as the administration pressed the networks on the fairness issue. Chuck Colson set up a series of off-the-record meetings with the network heads in which Colson introduced the possibility of government intervention in television news. In a memorandum to Haldeman describing the meetings, Colson wrote that "the networks are terribly nervous over the uncertain state of the law. . . . They are also apprehensive about us. Although they tried to hide this, it was obvious. The harder I pressed them (CBS and NBC) the more accommodating, cordial, and almost apologetic they became." He further wrote, "They were startled by how thoroughly we were doing our homework . . . the way in which we had so thoroughly monitored their coverage and our analysis of it. . . . They are terribly concerned with being able to work out their own policies with respect to balanced coverage and not to have policies imposed on them." Colson continued, "They are very much afraid of us and are trying hard to prove they are 'good guys.' " He concluded, "This all adds up to the fact that they are damned nervous and scared and we should continue to take a very tough line, face to face, and in other ways."[72]

The threat of license challenges became a reality when the administration discussed the future of two CBS affiliates, WJXT in Jacksonville and WPLG in Miami, both owned by the *Washington Post*, whose investigative reporting helped undo the Watergate cover-up. Part of a White House conversation between the president and Bob Haldeman deals with this matter.

The President: The main thing is the *Post* is going to have damnable, damnable problems out of this one. They have a television station and they're going to have to get it renewed.

Haldeman: They've got a radio station, too.

The President: Does that come up, too? . . . It's going to be goddam active here. . . .
   Well, the game has to be played awfully rough.

Soon thereafter, the federal licenses under which these two stations operated came up for renewal. But their licenses were challenged by people with known associations to the president, and this sent a chill throughout the industry. The *Post* was being made to pay for its reporting.

The administration was also displeased with the fledgling Corporation for Public Broadcasting (CPB).[73] Annoyed at what they considered anti-administration reporting, the president vetoed the 1972 Public Broadcasting Bill and killed its funding for a two-year period.

The administration further turned up the heat in the spring of 1972 when Patrick Buchanan, in an interview, complained about the bias on network news programs and cautioned that "a monopoly like this of a group of people with a single point of view and a single political ideology" was creating a situation in which they were "going to find something done in the area of anti-trust-type action." As a prelude to the 1972 presidential campaign, such a warning spoke volumes.

As the '72 campaign approached, and as the Democrats self-destructed and the McGovern candidacy declined, the Nixon administration eased up on the media. But the easing of pressure was short-lived. On October 29, 1972, Chuck Colson telephoned CBS president Frank Stanton to complain about the station's coverage of the Watergate break-in. Asked if the reporting was unfair, Colson responded, "Whether the report was fair or not, it should not have been broadcast at all." For the next few weeks CBS seemed to back off on its Watergate coverage.

Just after the '72 campaign, Colson again called Stanton. According to an affidavit of Stanton's, Colson "said in substance that unless CBS substantially changed its news treatment of the Nixon Administration 'things will get much worse for CBS.' " Colson added that CBS " 'didn't play ball during the campaign . . .' and that 'We'll bring you to your knees in Wall Street and on Madison Avenue.' "

As the administration's attempts at media manipulation increased, the president's contacts with the press decreased. The president's handlers jealously guarded Nixon, and he remained aloof and isolated from the press. In fact, Nixon held fewer press conferences than any modern president until Ronald Reagan (see Table 5).

After the 1972 election, the administration continued to heat up the media attack as FCC chair Dean Burch leaked word that he had proposed a rule-making proceeding to determine whether the ownership of the major networks was in the public interest. As Watergate became a bigger story, the president felt compelled to go public himself with the antipress line. In an October 26, 1973, press conference Nixon said: "I have never heard or seen such outra-

Table 5
Presidential News Conferences, 1949–1984

PRESIDENT	TOTAL CONFERENCES	YEARLY AVERAGE	MONTHLY AVERAGE
Truman	160	40	3.3
Eisenhower, I	99	25	2.1
Eisenhower, II	94	24	2.0
Kennedy	65	22	1.9
Johnson	132	26	2.1
Nixon, I	30	8	0.6
Nixon, II	9	5	0.5
Ford	41	19	1.4
Carter	59	15	1.2
Reagan	23	6	0.5

Source: Gary King and Lyn Ragsdale, *The Elusive Executive: Discovering Statistical Patterns in the Presidency* (Washington, D.C.: Congressional Quarterly Press, 1988), p. 268.

geous, vicious, distorted reporting in twenty-seven years of public life. I'm not blaming anybody for that. Perhaps what happened is that what we did brought it about, and therefore the media decided that they would have to take that particular line. But when people are pounded night after night with that kind of frantic, hysterical reporting, it naturally shakes their confidence."

In 1973, in an effort to determine the extent of the administration's repeated accusations of media bias, the National News Council was formed. The council made numerous attempts to get the administration to document its charges against the media, but the administration could not or would not cooperate. Finally this effort was abandoned.

As the Watergate story grew, the Nixon effort at media attack accelerated, but there was little the administration could do. The cumulative weight of revelation after revelation finally turned the public against the president, and all the attacks upon the press could not change the damaging impact of the facts of Watergate.[74]

Since the administration was brought down due, in part, to the media's investigating and reporting about Watergate, one must ask, how successful was the Nixon attack on the media?

By the end of the 1972 campaign it appeared as if the Nixon campaign against the press had indeed worked. The criticism against the president in the '72 campaign was very mild, and indeed, it was the McGovern campaign that received the harshest treatment. The networks, the major newspapers, seemed to be on the defensive. For a time, the Nixon strategy did work. But as the Watergate story picked up steam, the full weight of the charges against the president eventually overwhelmed the administration.

In the long run, Nixon's obsessive hatred of the press contributed mightily to his own undoing. Many of the crimes and accusations of Watergate related to abuses of power concerning efforts to control or punish the press. Illegal wiretaps against newsmen, efforts to cover up crimes, the Ellsberg psychiatrist's break-in, excessive secrecy, the creation of the Plumbers to control news leaks, and a variety of other activities relating to the media contributed substantially to the decline and fall of Richard Nixon. His paranoia about the press proved to be part of his own undoing.

Had Nixon a healthier, more balanced attitude about the press, he might not have been inclined to engage in the excesses that brought his presidency down. As Nixon speechwriter William Safire has written: "A hatred of the press . . . . caused Nixon to go over the brink, to lose all sense of balance, to defend his privacy at the expense of everyone else's right to privacy, and to create the climate that led to Watergate."[75]

Nixon and the Public

Nixon's suspicions of the media forced him to "go public" in manners slightly different than his predecessors. All presidents seek to control, to whatever degree possible, the kind of coverage they get and the terms of that coverage. But Nixon, convinced that the press was an enemy, sought to go around the press, directly to the people. Rather than let the news commentators filter his message, Nixon would go straight to the people via major presidential addresses. Nixon's tendency was to make a decision, then announce it via a major address. He did not use speeches to generate support as Reagan would, but as a means of announcing an act already taken or a decision already made. Thus, Nixon went public selectively, in a controlled manner, at a time and place of his choosing.[76] The media would not set his agenda, he would set theirs. How did he approach the media? Why did he use this method? How well did it work?

Nixon's controlled approach to going public involved these components: (1) use major speeches to go directly to the people (he did so frequently); (2) use press conferences infrequently (he had the lowest average per year until Reagan); and (3) be careful of meetings with outside groups (Nixon left this to Colson and his staff).

Why choose this method? Primarily because Nixon viewed the press as the enemy, and any chance to circumvent them was seen as a plus. Going directly to the people allowed Nixon to gain access on his own terms in the manner with which he felt most comfortable. It suited Nixon's personality needs and his style. He could cut back on contact with the press (a group he feared) and cut back on contact with interest groups (small talk made him uncomfortable). Plus, using the vehicle of the major speech satisfied Nixon's flair for the dramatic.

How well did this insulated presidency work? Nixon's popularity was moderately high by modern standards. Nixon was never highly popular (his high point was only 68 percent) but throughout the first four years of his presidency he maintained a fairly moderate and stable level of popularity. His high point, 68 percent in 1973, after the election and Vietnam settlement, were very low highs (Truman peaked at 87 percent, Ike at 78 percent, Kennedy at 84 percent, Johnson at 80 percent, Ford at 71 percent, Carter at 72 percent, and Reagan at 68 percent). But in general he hovered in the 50 percent range. Until Watergate! From his 68 percent rating after the Vietnam settlement, Nixon's popularity plummeted, until by late 1973 he was below 30 percent. Nixon's popularity stayed in the 20 percent range for all of 1974.[77]

The combination of Nixon's hostility toward the media, his personality needs, and his style in reaching out to the public meant that his level of opportunity to persuade the nation was (self-) limited. Since Nixon was not a charismatic leader, since he saw the bureaucracy as staffed with enemies, and the Congress controlled by Democrats, how would he govern? It was his effort to govern "on his own terms" within a politically pluralistic arena that started Nixon down the road to his own downfall.

NOTES

1. Bruce Buchanan, *The Presidential Experience: What the Office Does to the Man* (Englewood Cliffs, N.J.: Prentice-Hall, 1978).

2. James P. Pfiffner, *The Strategic Presidency: Hitting the Ground Running* (Chicago: Dorsey, 1988).

3. For elaboration on the first three styles, see: Richard T. Johnson, *Managing the White House* (New York: Harper & Row, 1974). See also, Colin Campbell, S.J., *Managing the Presidency* (Pittsburgh: University of Pittsburgh Press, 1986).

4. Rowland Evans, Jr., and Robert D. Novak, *Nixon in the White House: The Frustration of Power* (New York: Random House, 1971), Chaps. 1, 2, and 3.

5. Alexander Butterfield, *Testimony before the Committee on the Judiciary, House of Representatives*, 93rd Cong. 2d sess., July 2, 1974.

6. Alexander Butterfield's testimony regarding the operation of the Nixon White House; *Testimony of Witnesses, Hearings before the Committee on the Judiciary, House of Representatives*, Book 1, July 2, 3, and 8, 1974, pp. 6–122.

7. See: Dan Rather and Gary Paul Gates, *The Palace Guard* (New York: Harper and Row, 1974). See also, Michael Medved, *The Shadow Presidents* (New York: Times Books, 1979).

8. Thompson, *The Nixon Presidency*, p. 132.

9. *National Journal*, April 6, 1974, p. 495.

10. H. R. Haldeman, *The Ends of Power* (New York: Times Books, 1978), pp. 57–58.

11. Garry Wills, *Nixon Agonistes* (Boston: Houghton Mifflin, 1971), pp. 410–411.

12. For comments by several Nixon cabinet members, see: Thompson, *The Nixon Presidency*. See also, Stephen Hess, *Organizing the Presidency* (Washington: Brookings Institution, 1988).

13. John Erlichman, *Witness to Power* (New York: Simon & Schuster, 1982), p. 108.

14. Joel D. Aberbach and Bert A. Rockman, "Clashing Beliefs within the Executive Branch: The Nixon Administration Bureaucracy," *American Political Science Review* (June 1976), pp. 456–468.

15. Richard L. Cole and David A. Caputo, "Presidential Control of the Senior Civil Service: Assessing the Strategies of the Nixon Years," *American Political Science Review*, (June 1979), pp. 389–400.

16. Aberbach and Rockman, "Clashing Beliefs."

17. Pfiffner, *The Strategic Presidency*, p. 99.

18. Richard P. Nathan, *The Plot That Failed: Nixon and the Administrative Presidency* (New York: Wiley, 1975).

19. Fred Malek, "Federal Political Personnel Manual: The 'Malek Manual,' " *The Bureaucrat* (January 1976), pp. 13–21.

20. Haldeman, *The Ends of Power*. For a comprehensive treatment of presidential reorganization plans, see: Peri E. Arnold, *Making the Managerial Presidency* (Princeton, N.J.: Princeton University Press, 1986).

21. For a review of the president's work habits and decision-making style, see testimony of Alexander Butterfield, *Testimony before the House Committee on the Judiciary*, pp. 31–35.

22. Henry Kissinger, *White House Years* (Boston: Little, Brown, 1979), pp. 45, 482, 483.

23. Jeb Magruder, *An American Life* (New York: Atheneum, 1974), pp. 55–60, 112.

24. Paul C. Light, *The President's Agenda: Domestic Policy Choice from Kennedy to Carter* (Baltimore: Johns Hopkins University Press, 1982).

25. Pfiffner, *The Strategic Presidency*.

26. Light, *The President's Agenda*, p. 45.

27. Light, *The President's Agenda*, p. 44.

28. Nathan, *The Plot That Failed*.

29. George C. Edwards, *Presidential Influence in Congress* (San Francisco: Freeman, 1980), pp. 16–29, 138–145, and 161–172.

30. Stephen J. Wayne, *The Legislative Presidency* (New York: Harper and Row, 1978), pp. 45–51.

31. Nelson W. Polsby, *Congress and the President* (Englewood Cliffs, N.J.: Prentice-Hall, 1986), pp. 43–52.

32. Nixon, *RN*, p. 770.

33. Theodore C. Sorensen, *Watchmen in the Night* (Cambridge: MIT Press, 1975), pp. 57–58.

34. Richard Harris, *Decision* (New York: Dutton, 1971), pp. 155–156, 158, 209; Evans and Novak, *Nixon in the White House*, pp. 106–108, 166, 170–172.

35. Rather and Gates, *The Palace Guard*, p. 271.

36. Rather and Gates, *The Palace Guard*, p. 279.

37. Nathan, *The Plot That Failed*.

38. Michael A. Genovese, "The Supreme Court as a Check on Presidential Power," *Presidential Studies Quarterly* 6, nos. 1 and 2 (Winter-Spring 1976), pp. 40–44.

39. Glendon A. Schubert, *The Presidency in the Courts* (Minneapolis: University of Minnesota Press, 1957), p. 347.

40. Genovese, "The Supreme Court as a Check."

41. *United States v. Curtiss-Wright Export Corp.*, 299 U.S. 304, 319 (1936); *Chicago and Southern Air Lines v. Waterman S.S. Corp.*, 33 U.S. 103, 110 (1948); *The*

Prize Cases, 2 Black 635 (1863); *U.S. v. Belmont*, 301 U.S. 324 (1937); and *U.S. v. Pink*, 315 U.S. 203 (1942).

42. Paul N. McClosky, Jr., *Truth and Untruth* (New York: Simon and Schuster, 1972), p. 189.

43. James F. Simon, *In His Own Image: The Supreme Court in Richard Nixon's America* (New York: McKay, 1973), p. 18.

44. Clark R. Mollenhoff, *Game Plan for Disaster* (New York: Norton, 1976), p. 56.

45. Evans and Novak, *Nixon in the White House*, p. 164.

46. Quoted in Harris, *Decision*, p. 110.

47. Harris, *Decision*, p. 192.

48. Quoted in Evans and Novak, *Nixon in the White House*, pp. 170–171.

49. *Mora v. McNamara*, 389 U.S. 934 (1967); *Orlando v. Laird*, 443 F. 2d. 1039 (1971); *Massachusetts v. Laird*, 400 U.S. 886 (1970); and *Da Costa v. Laird*, 448 F. 2d. 1368 (1971).

50. Anthony A. D'Amato and Robert M. O'Neil, *The Judiciary and Vietnam* (New York: St. Martin's, 1972).

51. *New York Times Company v. United States*, 403 U.S. 713 (1971).

52. *Kendall v. United States ex rel Stokes*, 37 U.S. (12 Pet.) 524 (1838).

53. Arthur Miller, "Presidential Power to Impound Appropriated Funds," *North Carolina Law Review* 43 (1965), pp. 502–547.

54. For additional information on impoundment, see: Warren J. Archer, "Presidential Impoundment of Funds: The Judicial Response," *The University of Chicago Law Review* 40, no. 2 (Winter 1973), pp. 328–356; Mark Cohn, "Impoundment of Funds Appropriated by Congress," *Ohio State Law Journal* 34, no. 2 (1973), pp. 416–427; Louis Fisher, "Funds Impounded by the President: The Constitutional Issue," *George Washington Law Review* 38 (October 1969), pp. 124–137; Louis Fisher: "Impoundment of Funds: Uses and Abuses," *Buffalo Law Review* 23, no. 1 (Fall 1973), pp. 141–200; Nile Stanton, "The Presidency and the Purse: Impoundment 1803–1973," *University of Colorado Law Review* 45 (Fall 1973), pp. 25–50; and Sally Weinraub, "The Impoundment Question—An Overview," *Brooklyn Law Review* 40 (Fall 1973), pp. 342–389.

55. *United States v. Nixon*, 418 U.S. 683; 94 S.Ct. 3090; 41 L.Ed. 2d 1039 (1974).

56. Michael A. Genovese, *The Supreme Court, the Constitution, and Presidential Power* (Lanham, Md.: University Press of America, 1980).

57. Joe McGinniss, *The Selling of the President, 1968* (New York: Trident, 1969), p. 34.

58. McGinniss, *The Selling*, p. 103.

59. Kathleen Hall Jamieson, *Packaging the Presidency: A History and Criticism of Presidential Campaign Advertising* (Oxford: Oxford University Press, 1984), Chaps. 6 and 7.

60. John Orman, "Covering the American Presidency," *Presidential Studies Quarterly* (Summer 1984), pp. 381–390.

61. Several studies attempted to document media bias in the 1968 and 1972 presidential campaigns. For a study purporting *bias against Nixon*, see: Edith Efron, *The News Twisters* (Los Angeles: Nash, 1971). For a study which found *no anti-Nixon bias*, see Richard Hofstetter, *Bias in the News* (Columbus: Ohio State University Press, 1976).

62. Ehrlichman, *Witness to Power*, Chap. 15.

63. There are two types of leaks, *controlled leaks* (those which the president and his

top advisors choose to give to the press to serve their own purposes); and *uncontrolled leaks* (when a disgruntled individual gives information to the press which the president wishes to keep secret).

64. Herbert Klein, *Making It Perfectly Clear* (Garden City, N.Y.: Doubleday, 1980).

65. Ehrlichman, *Witness to Power*, Chap. 15.

66. Joseph C. Spear, *Presidents and the Press: The Nixon Legacy* (Cambridge: MIT Press), 1984.

67. Nixon, fifth syndicated television interview with David Frost.

68. Robert P. Hart, *The Sound of Leadership: Presidential Communication in the Modern Age* (Chicago: The University of Chicago Press, 1987), p. 99. Also see: Michael Grossman and Martha Kumar, *Portraying the President: The White House and the News Media* (Baltimore: Johns Hopkins University Press, 1981).

69. Hart, *The Sound of Leadership*, p. 100. Also see James Keogh, *President Nixon and the Press* (New York: Funk and Wagnalls, 1972).

70. Wills, *Nixon Agonistes*, pp. 357–359.

71. Thomas Whiteside, "Annals of Television: Shaking the Tree," *The New Yorker*, March 17, 1975, pp. 82–97.

72. William E. Porter, *Assault on the Media: The Nixon Years* (Ann Arbor: University of Michigan Press, 1976).

73. David M. Stone, *Nixon and the Politics of Public Television* (New York: Garland, 1985).

74. John Herbers, *No Thank You, Mr. President* (New York: Norton, 1976).

75. For a thorough review of Safire's analyses of Nixon and the press, see: William Safire, *Before the Fall: An Inside View of the Pre-Watergate White House* (Garden City, N.Y.: Doubleday, 1975), pp. 341–365.

76. Samuel Kernell, *Going Public: New Strategies for Presidential Leadership* (Washington, D.C.: Congressional Quarterly, 1986).

77. For popularity data across presidencies, see: Gary King and Lyn Ragsdale, *The Elusive Executive: Discovering Statistical Patterns in the Presidency* (Washington, D.C.: Congressional Quarterly, 1988), pp. 292–304.

3

Economic, Domestic, and Social Policy

In the major policy arenas, three very distinct patterns emerge. In economic policy, we find Nixon attempting to manipulate the economy for short-term political gain; in domestic/social policy, early efforts at conservative reform give way to policy degeneration and dismantling; and in foreign affairs—where Nixon took special pride—the president developed an ambitious plan for creating a new "structure of peace." While the administration's behavior in each policy arena is distinct, one can nonetheless see the impact of Nixon's paranoid style influencing each policy arena.

ECONOMIC POLICY

> Being a President is like riding a tiger. A man has to keep on riding or be swallowed.
>
> Harry S Truman

Richard Nixon became president when the world economy—and the United States' place in it—was going through profound changes. These changes would alter the political and economic landscape and leave the United States in a weaker, less independent position than at any time in the previous twenty-five years.

World War II left the United States in a position of economic ascendancy. The Allied and Axis powers were crushed economically, their physical plants lay in rubble, and the cost of rebuilding their infrastructure was enormous. With American help, the participants in the Second World War began to rebuild, and the United States found itself as *the* hegemonic power of the West. Talk of an "American Century" abounded, as the United States made plans to use its power and affluence. The international financial capital shifted from

London to New York, and American economic might was the envy of the world.

But the American Century lasted only twenty years, and as Nixon ascended to the presidency, U.S. economic and political decline was already evident—changes in both the international and domestic economies meant trouble for American hegemony.[1]

On the international front, Japan and Western Europe went through miraculous economic recoveries, and their new, rebuilt industrial bases began to compete with the United States. This greater competition put stress on the Atlantic Alliance as the European Economic Community and Japan began to capture a larger and larger share of world trade. The oil producing nations (OPEC) banded together to raise prices and put an economic squeeze on the industrial nations. U.S. goods also began to decline on the international markets. "Made in America," once a proud stamp of quality, declined relative to perceptions of Japanese and West European products. As the sunset of American economic hegemony was upon us, managing the mixed economy became a necessity.

On the domestic front, productivity in a variety of basic industries began to decline. In steel, autos, and other industries, the United States was not producing up to world standards and prices. Inflation and slow growth began to further erode the U.S. economy. Also, the financial drain of a war in Southeast Asia and a domestic war on poverty without a tax hike began to put great budgetary pressure on the United States.

All these factors added up to a relative decline in the U.S. position in the international and domestic economic spheres. New strains, new demands, new pressures were being applied. How did the Nixon administration deal with these emerging new economic realities?

As with domestic policy, Richard Nixon did not have the driving interest in economic policy that he did for foreign affairs. But unlike the domestic side, Nixon recognized how vital economic success was to his efforts on other policy and political fronts. So, while no expert in the field, and with no great interest in economics, Nixon felt compelled to spend time—and political capital—on the economic front.

There was another, deeper reason why Richard Nixon felt compelled to aggressively tackle economic problems. Immediately before the 1960 presidential election, the nation went into a mild recession. Then–vice president Nixon was hoping that Eisenhower would provide a slight fiscal boost to the economy so as to improve Nixon's chances in the upcoming election, but Ike did no such thing. Nixon still felt the scars of 1960 and would intervene in the economy if it were politically necessary. It would be impolitic to do otherwise.

Since Nixon himself was not an economic expert, he knew he had to surround himself with the best and the brightest in the field. But not being a trusting man, and harboring resentment toward the "Eastern elite," Nixon did not draw his economic team close to himself and eschewed the Ivy League economists who had so much Washington experience.

The Nixon economic team was nevertheless a distinguished group. Such highly respected men as Paul McCracken, Arthur Burns, Robert Mayo, and David Kennedy were brought into government in 1969, and later such luminaries as Herbert Stein and George Schultz were added to the select lot. In general, these men were moderate-to-conservative Republicans who were highly regarded in the financial and academic communities. Kennedy, the CEO of the Continental Illinois Bank, would be Nixon's treasury secretary. Robert Mayo, a vice president at the Continental Illinois Bank, was the budget director. Paul McCracken, of the University of Michigan, was chair of the Council of Economic Advisers. Maurice Stans headed Commerce, and George Schultz was the labor secretary. And Arthur Burns, a prominent adviser on domestic affairs, also served as an informal Nixon adviser on economic issues, as did Daniel P. Moynihan. It was a highly qualified, distinguished team.

As economic issues have become more important and time-consuming, and as success or failure in dealing with the economy has had a spill-over effect into other presidential endeavors, presidents have developed more self-conscious, formal, and elaborate organizational structures to deal with economic management. In this sense, an "economic subpresidency" has developed within the executive branch.[2] This economic subpresidency consists mainly of four units usually referred to as the quadriad: the Treasury Department, the Council of Economic Advisers (CEA), the Office of Management and Budget (OMB), and the Federal Reserve Board (Fed), along with other actors such as members of the White House staff, other Cabinet departments, and outside advisers who will sometimes enter into this orbit. Each component of this subpresidency is different, maintains different norms, and serves different constituencies. Yet, the president's task is to develop some coordination out of these fragmented parts of the economic subpresidency. It is just such a problem that led Richard Rose to comment that the "President's title of chief executive is a misnomer; he can more accurately be described as a nonexecutive chief".[3]

In general, Nixon's economic policies could be described as a zigzag of competing, sometimes contradictory steps, designed both to boost Nixon's reelection bid of 1972 and to readjust U.S. economic power in a more competitive world. The policies emerged out of a fluctuating process that saw the center of economic policy-making shift from a Cabinet committee to an economic czar (John Connally), and finally to a troika of policy advisers. The policies shifted with four different "game plans," culminating in the dramatic New Economic Policy of 1971 (NEP), which, on the international front, took the United States off the gold standard and negated the Bretton Woods agreement, and on the domestic front, imposed wage and price controls and overheated the economy prior to the '72 election.

Nixon was able to make these bold moves because his level of opportunity on economic policy was fairly substantial. The Congress gave Nixon tremendous latitude on economic policy, and while many limitations remained,[4] he was still able to move aggressively on the economic front. This chapter explores the *process* and *policy* of the Nixon administration on economic matters. It attempts to illustrate how policy was made, what was attempted, and why these moves were made.

How did Richard Nixon deal with and manage his economic subpresidency? Richard Nixon, a highly formalistic, even rigid manager, began his term by using a Cabinet Committee on Economic Policy (CCEP), a group consisting of the vice president and the treasury, commerce, labor, agriculture, and housing and urban development secretaries, along with the director of the Bureau of the Budget, chairman of the CEA, and a variety of other officials, often chaired by Nixon himself. But Nixon was uncomfortable with this collegial, interdepartmental approach and shifted in the opposite direction. Nixon found the CCEP too unwieldy, but rather than abolish it, he made the vice president chairman, stopped attending meetings himself, and soon afterwards, the cabinet members took to sending their under secretaries, and the CCEP withered away to insignificance.

In early 1971, Nixon designated treasury secretary John Connally as his "economic czar." Nixon was more comfortable with an approach in which Connally worked through the troika, then met with Nixon in one-on-one sessions. Nearly all decisions were made in this one-on-one setting, with Connally bringing the options and a recommendation to Nixon, and the president normally approving Connally's suggestion. When Connally was succeeded by George Schultz (and later Kenneth Rush), the process became slightly more collegial.[5]

The one-on-one meetings with Connally fit Nixon's personality needs and satisfied his flair for the dramatic. In fact, Nixon imposed wage and price controls and "closed the gold window" (that is, ceased to allow dollars to be converted to gold), against the advice and without the knowledge of most of his economic advisers, but with the strong support of Connally, who became head of the Cost of Living Council, which was to oversee wage and price guidelines. This was the centerpiece of economic policy-making during the period. But the one-on-one approach did not satisfy the broader institutional needs for a wide range of economic advice. When Phase I of the wage and price guidelines was lifted, and George Schultz took over as treasury secretary in 1972, the process was opened, and while there was no formal transfer of power to a troika/quadriad, Schultz did restore some of the advisory power to these other significant actors. Nixon delegated a great deal of control to Schultz, and when the 1972 election, and then Watergate, dominated Nixon's attention, economic policy became less and less salient for the president.[6]

Nixon's relationship with John Connally is a fascinating one. The president would occasionally, in William Safire's words, "fall in love" with an adviser.[7] It happened early in the president's first term, with Moynihan and Mitchell, and for a time, Nixon fell in love with John Connally. Nixon was intrigued by

Connally, the flamboyant, urbane conservative Democrat. As former Nixon aide Harry Dent said, "Connally turned Nixon on."[8] The president felt that every Cabinet should have someone of "presidential" quality, and to Nixon, Connally was the one. In fact there was very serious consideration given to dumping Vice President Agnew from the 1972 ticket and having Connally switch parties and become the vice presidential candidate (and Nixon's successor in 1976). In a July 20, 1971, meeting discussing the move, Nixon said that the "only one who has the stuff is Connally."

Nixon treated Connally with a respect that sometimes bordered on subservience. In meetings between the president and Connally, it was Connally who called the shots, controlled the meeting. And almost every recommendation Connally made was accepted by the president. Connally even lorded over the fearsome Bob Haldeman.

How did process affect policy? In the case of CCEP, Nixon received fairly standard, conventional advice. When Connally rose to prominence, Nixon moved to bold, even radical policy initiatives. When Nixon moved to the troika, he returned to more conventional steps.[9] Clearly, the change in process had an impact in policy. How did the policy moves change during the Nixon years?

Nixon, a longtime proponent of free trade, sought negotiated reductions in trade barriers between the United States and its trading partners, especially Japan. But there were stirrings in Congress toward protectionism, and the president opposed these efforts. Congressional pressures limited the president's freedom to negotiate on several trade fronts, and the United States ceased to be a leader in the international free trade movement.

In 1969 the president sought to take a strong stand internationally on free trade, but protectionist forces in Congress threatened to undermine his efforts. Trade protectionist bills continued to pop up in Congress, and by 1970, it appeared that a protectionist bill which would have imposed quotas (forbidden by the General Agreement on Tariffs and Trade) on textiles and footwear might get through the Congress. While the bill never came to a vote, it reflected a growing protectionist mood in the Congress.

In 1972, the Foreign Trade and Investment Act of 1972 (known as the Burke-Hartke bill), a piece of protectionist legislation, began to move through Congress. Due to efforts by the administration, the bill never came to a vote, but once again the threat of protectionism loomed over the president. In the face of congressional pressure, Nixon eventually forced our trading partners to accept "voluntary" export restraints (VERs), but the forces of protectionism continued to hound the president (things got so bad that in 1971 when the Japanese refused to come to terms on a proposal to limit textile exports, the president felt compelled to request mandated quotas from Congress).

Nixon greatly expanded East-West trade (though originally the administration opposed such trade) as part of the fruits of détente. After Nixon's 1972 visit to the Soviet Union, a variety of agreements intended to normalize U.S.-Soviet commercial relations were signed. The key to this trade relationship was a major grain sale to the Soviet Union. Over nineteen million tons of wheat, corn, and soybeans were bought by the Soviet Union. But the Congress put restrictions on the granting of most-favored-nation status for the Soviet Union and placed other restrictions on U.S.-Soviet trade in an attempt to extract concessions from the Soviet Union on internal Soviet policies.

Led by the Democrats in Congress, an effort was made to grant most-favored-nation status and access to Eximbank Agreements only if the Soviet Union would allow for an opening of emigration. This restriction (the Jackson-Vanik amendment to the Trade Reform Bill of 1973), aimed primarily at allowing Jews to leave the Soviet Union, caused great concern for Nixon, not because he didn't care about the emigration issue, but because he hoped to achieve that result via other means. The president resisted the congressional effort, and eventually the trade negotiations broke down and Watergate took center stage. It was not until after President Nixon resigned that negotiations got back on track.

If Nixon had trouble with an "unruly" Congress on trade, his New Economic Policy [10] was designed—in part at least—to silence his critics. By August of 1971, the president was proposing a 10 percent surcharge on imports and a realigned currency standard to help the U.S. trade imbalance. The United States began to demand concessions from its trading partners in the West to produce a "permanent" trade surplus, [11] which the European and Japanese eventually rejected. But perhaps because of the new aggressiveness of the Nixon administration, the trading partners did not take retaliatory steps, and eventually the United States softened its position. Renewed multilateral negotiations eventually led to the Tokyo Economic Summit in September 1973.

Richard Nixon was a longtime critic of government regulations, feeling they were too intrusive and complex. Yet, during Nixon's presidency, according to Herbert Stein, "Probably more new regulation was imposed on the economy . . . than in any other presidency since the New Deal, even if one excludes the temporary Nixon foray into price and wage controls." [12] The main areas in which Nixon extended federal regulations were in energy and environmental concerns. The energy regulations dealt primarily with domestic oil production and were a reaction to OPEC's growing power. The environmental regulations dealt with cleanups of the environment and other "externalities" such as occupational health and safety and consumer protection. While some deregulation did take place (e.g., air, truck, and rail deregulation), the trend clearly was toward more federal regulations.

On assuming the presidency, Nixon faced several problems. The budget deficit, predicted by LBJ to be approximately $15 billion, swelled to over $25 billion, the highest by post–World War II measures. Inflation was near five percent, and real purchasing power was threatened. Although by contemporary standards these figures are desirable, in 1969 they were seen as serious problems.

The standard Republican bromide—a tight monetary policy, lower social welfare spending, reduction of the size and cost of government—were initially attractive to Richard Nixon, but they were soon seen as ineffective. While Nixon accepted the idea that inflation was the number-one problem, he was not comfortable with the traditional Republican solution of higher unemployment.[13] The initial Nixon "game plan," as they referred to it, called for a tight money policy and higher interest rates to slow down inflation and cause a slight recession. But Nixon, who firmly believed in the free enterprise system, but whose overall interest in economic policy was not high, felt that the usual Republican solutions were insufficient, and thus, as Herbert Stein notes, "His aim to be a conservative man with liberal policies" (again the Disraeli analogy comes to mind) became the order of the day.

But Nixon's advisers were split on what to do next, and the president was only peripherally involved. In fact, Nixon was so disenchanted with economic and budgetary problems that he refused to even see Budget Direct Robert Mayo, and used John Ehrlichman as his go-between with Mayo.[14] As the first year of the Nixon presidency came to a close, the economy had worsened (inflation *and* recession were a reality), the economic policy team was divided, and the president was unsure. A new economic game plan was in order.

In economic policy, the Nixon administration went through four distinct phases, what they called "game plans" in honor of the president's love of football. Game Plan I, from 1969 to 1970, represents the "old Nixon." It was classic conservative economics, a laissez-faire approach to the economy. In this phase, inflation was seen as the chief enemy and the cure was to cool off the economy, slow down the growth of federal expenditures, tighten the money supply (several of the president's key advisers were disciples of Milton Friedman), cut taxes, and hope for a slight recession. Putting the economy through these "slowing pains" was exactly what one expected of a Republican administration. Pressured by business to get a grip on inflation and ease wage pressures (at a February 22, 1970, meeting between the president, Bob Haldeman, and others, Haldeman notes that "Bus Council *want* a little recession to drive labor down"), Nixon sought a slowing down of the economy but not a recession.

But the results of Game Plan I were not as expected. The economy did slow down, and unemployment rose, but inflation continued to climb! It didn't seem possible, but simultaneously there was a mild recession *and* inflation. A judgment of sorts was leveled against Game Plan I in the midterm congressional elections of 1970. The Republicans did not do as well as they had hoped or expected (although by historical standards they did fairly well), and part of the blame was placed on poor economic conditions. The failure of Game Plan I to produce electoral victories led to a reshuffling of economic policy.

Game Plan II (1970 to late 1971) involved a seemingly sudden and abrupt conversion on the part of the president. Nixon declared, "I am now a Keynesian," indicating a change of economic stripes from a tight-money/budget balancing manager to a full-employment expansionist. The old Nixon gave way to a "new Nixon," a Disraeli-like conservative reformer. The change came swiftly. Only days after the November 1970 elections, Nixon's Council of Economic Advisers chairman Paul McCracken indicated that a change was on the horizon when he said that "economic policy like other [policies] have to be responsive to the national will." The CEA was proposing an expansionary, full-employment economic policy. The decision amounted to an admission of defeat on the inflation front and a frontal assault on recession. Nixon was to prime the economic pump, expand the money supply, move toward some type of income policy, and pursue an expansionary/deficit economic policy in hopes of stimulating the economy. It was Richard Nixon gingerly embracing the Democratic economic agenda.

Much of the new economic policy was geared to the upcoming presidential election of 1972. Nixon was determined not to have the liability of a weak economy as he had had in 1960. Many scholars have noted an electoral cycle in American economic policy wherein incumbents give an extra boost to the economy prior to an election. Edward Tufte cites Nixon as an example of an incumbent who, determined to increase the amount of disposable income in the hands of the voters just prior to his 1972 reelection bid, artificially overheated the economy, thereby improving his electoral chances but hurting the long-run interests of the nation's economy.[15] But soon, Nixon felt compelled to take dramatic steps to improve the domestic economy, because Game Plan II wasn't working.

On August 6, 1971, treasury secretary John Connally gave the president a report on how to get the economy back on track. In his memoirs, Nixon described how Connally loved the "big play" but noted that he was surprised at how big a play Connally was proposing: wage and price controls.[16]

In August of 1971, the president convened an economic summit of all his top advisers at Camp David to discuss the problem.[17] The Camp David Summit resulted in a major policy shift for the administration. Called the New Economic Policy (NEP), it marked the complete shift from laissez-faire Friedmanism to aggressive Keynesianism. This was a "Really New" Nixon who favored a managed, controlled economy. No one could have guessed that the Richard Nixon who took office in 1969 would, by August of 1971, make such a startling and complete philosophical reversal. But then, Richard Nixon was known for surprises.

On the afternoon of August 13, 1971, the president met with his top economic advisers, Stein, Peterson, Volker, and a few others. Drastic action was needed. Game Plans I and II were not working. The 1972 election was fifteen months away. The president spoke of the gravity of the situation, then turned the meeting over to Connally. John Connally insisted that the gold window had to be closed, but this would necessitate an import tax of 10 to 15 percent.[18] He went on to describe the other actions needed, then he dropped the bombshell: a wage and price freeze was needed!

While some in the Nixon inner circle saw this coming, others could not believe what they had heard. The president interrupted Connally to assure the group that wage and price controls could only work if imposed for a limited time. A free-flowing discussion followed, with each member of the group arguing over parts of the policy. The most heated conflict erupted over closing the gold window, with Arthur Burns arguing that closing it was too drastic and unnecessary, given the other steps the president proposed taking. Burns spoke of the economic and political risks of such a move (he could, he said, see the headlines in *Pravda*, "Sign of Collapse of Capitalism"). What would the stock market do? How would this affect trade? Would other countries retaliate? Burns suggested that the president take the other actions, send Volker abroad to explain things to our allies, then have Volker negotiate on exchange rates.

It was the president who answered Burns, suggesting that speculations would start a run on the dollar. But Burns said that if that happened, the gold window could be closed the next day, and asked if they could at least try to get by without closing the gold window. The president countered, arguing that the action on gold was needed for domestic reasons, and then went over the range of reasons for closing the gold window.

Unconvinced, Burns asked, if it all works, how do we know it won't collapse two months before the election? Connally jumped in to remind Burns that the main problem was "international gold," so the administration must act on that immediately. Arguing that "we're broke, anyone can topple us" (which was only technically correct—our gold reserves were not sufficient to cover demand should all the holders of dollars insist on a payment in gold, but such an event was not realistic), Connally insisted on the need to act on gold, "We don't have alternatives." Burns continued to argue, but the president had made up his mind.

Then the president turned to the wage and price freeze. Herbert Stein explained the details of the president's proposal, with the president reiterating that the freeze would only be temporary. Burns, perhaps surprisingly, went along with the plan. The only questions involved the duration of the controls and technical questions of implementation. Otherwise there was surprising unanimity about wage and price controls.

Discussion next turned to the budget. Nixon wanted to cut taxes but not have a budget deficit. The discussion drifted to the post-Vietnam budget situation, and the president spoke of the challenges of peace and prosperity. The meeting ended with a new economic game plan for the future.

Game Plan III, which the president announced on August 15, 1971, was, by Republican standards, a radical departure from tradition. But Richard Nixon thought it a necessary one. After two years of economic gradualism, the economy needed a drastic shot in the arm. The New Economic Policy was, Mr. Nixon said, the most comprehensive economic program since Roosevelt's New Deal.

In essence, the NEP sought to move in two opposite directions simultaneously: stimulate the economy, but drive inflation down. To do that, the president's policy consisted of closing the gold window, allowing the dollar to float, imposing a 10 percent import tax, reinstating the investment tax credit, providing income tax relief, repealing the excise tax on automobiles, and instituting spending cuts *and* a ninety-day freeze on wages and prices. To implement these policies, the president created a Pay Board, Price Board, and Cost of Living Council.

How was Nixon able to impose such sweeping economic restrictions? The authority for these drastic steps was conferred upon the president by Congress in the form of the Economic Stabilization Act of 1970. Just prior to the 1970 midterm election, the Democrats passed legislation giving the president the power to "stabilize prices, rents, wages, and salaries" by issuing "such orders and regulations as he may deem appropriate." This was principally a political move on the part of the Democrats. Secure in the belief that a conservative Republican would never resort to such liberal measures, the Democrats hoped to use the legislation as a way to taunt Nixon, who was not using the powers available to solve the economic crunch. When the president acted on August 15, the Democrats were forced to go along. Nixon had successfully surprised, coopted, and silenced his critics. As he had done a month before in announcing his trip to China, the surprising Mr. Nixon had once again turned the tables on his opponents.

The NEP went through three different phases before all restrictions were lifted in 1974. It succeeded in controlling inflation, and some of the other economic indicators improved as well. In the eyes of the president, while wage and price controls made him uncomfortable, the NEP was a success. (In his memoirs, Nixon says that the economic controls were politically necessary and popular, but wrong.)[19] But with the 1972 election imminent, short-run concerns were paramount. The dramatic Nixon turnaround was primarily electorally inspired. As John Ehrlichman said, "The overriding issue of 1972 would be the economy,"[20] and Richard Nixon knew that tinkering wouldn't do the job. A strong fiscal stimulus and a strong image on the economy were necessary. The NEP was the dramatic step that let the American electorate know that Richard M. Nixon was in command.

As the 1972 election approached, a more aggressive fiscal boost was needed to get the economy well oiled for election time. As defense secretary Melvin Laird said, "Every effort was made to create an economic boom for the 1972 election. The Defense Department, for example, bought a two-year supply of toilet paper. We ordered enough trucks to meet our expected needs for the next several years."[21] Other actions designed to boost the economy were implemented. The Fed, under the leadership of Arthur Burns, dramatically increased the money supply. For 1972, the money supply was increased by 7.9 percent, and by 8.7 percent during the final quarter of 1972.[22] Federal spending increased by 11 percent in 1972. And Congress passed a 20 percent increase in Social Security, for which the president claimed credit. The economic stimulation had its predicted effect. By the final quarter of 1972, the economy was booming forward at an 11.5 percent growth rate. The artificial boosting of the economy is something nearly all presidents do in election years, but Richard Nixon took the art form to new extremes.[23] It was a cynical effort to overheat the economy prior to the election, and a stiff price would later be paid.

With a sound economy at home, and peace at hand in Vietnam, Richard Nixon won a landslide victory in the 1972 election. But the economic piper had to be paid for the pre-election splurge. By 1973, when economic controls were lifted, inflation returned with a vengeance. This led to Game Plan IV, a return to tight fiscal and monetary policies—back to the old Nixon. Growth in the Gross National Product slowed, inflation rose, and the Fed tightened the money supply (but inflation became so serious that the president briefly returned to a wage and price freeze).

In an effort to cut the federal budget *and* control the policy agenda, Nixon began to step up his impoundment of funds. Of questionable legal authority, past presidents have impounded (refused to spend money appropriated by Congress) funds on occasion. But Nixon began to impound funds on policy issues he had lost in the legislative process. At levels unprecedented in U.S. history, Richard Nixon refused to obey the stated will of Congress (and the law) and withheld funds appropriated by the Congress. The president used impoundment as a way of substituting his will for the law as passed by Congress. But eventually the courts (and later the Congressional Budget and Impoundment Control Act of 1974) ordered the president to release impounded funds.

By this time Watergate began to progressively consume the administration, and attention turned away from the economy and toward impeachment. Game Plan IV, the partial return to conservative economics, never really got off the ground.

In the end, the Nixon economic policy was a zigzag of policies that ran the political gamut from classical conservative, to mainstream Democratic, to leftist controls, and back to conservative economics. There is no real philosophical consistency, so how does one explain the apparent economic multiple personalities of the Nixon administration? Clearly, Nixon's economic changes were driven by a desire to improve the economic situation but were primarily animated by the need to improve the president's political status.

In economic terms, the president simply did not know what to do. His reliance on traditional conservative bromides failed, and then, after the voters had spoken in the 1970 midterm elections—but before they had a chance to speak in the 1972 reelection—Nixon took drastic, un-Republican-like steps to boost his electoral appeal. While the president was very concerned with the overall health of the economy, the main driving force of economic policy during the Nixon years was the 1972 presidential election.

DOMESTIC AND SOCIAL POLICY

> I sit here all day trying to persuade people to do the things they ought to
> have sense enough to do without my persuading them. That's all the pow-
> ers of the President amount to.
>
> Harry S Truman

It is commonly believed that Richard Nixon was not very interested in domestic policy. He cultivated the image of a president concerned with the big issues of war and peace, the dramatic policies such as opening the door to
China, détente, and Middle East shuttle diplomacy. Nixon reveled in the
glow of his role as international statesman. Domestic policy? Small pota-
toes.[24]

Nixon even went so far as to tell Theodore White in 1967 that "I've always
thought this country could run itself domestically without a President, all you
need is a competent Cabinet to run the country at home. You need a President
for foreign policy." Several members of the Nixon administration lend cre-
dence to this notion. Joseph J. Sisco, under secretary for political affairs in the
State Department, said that Nixon "had a monumental disinterest in domestic
policy" and that he "found domestic policies a bore." Leonard Garment, who
held several posts in the Nixon White House, said that "a great deal of ground
was freely given on the domestic side because it was a matter of secondary
importance to the President."[25]

But is the image—sometimes cultivated by Nixon himself—an accurate one?
John Ehrlichman, head of Nixon's Domestic Council, disagrees. "It has become accepted 'fact,' " he writes, "that Richard Nixon was preoccupied with
foreign affairs, to the exclusion of domestic issues. . . . Writers have built on
the misinformation of other writers, layer after layer, until this nonsense has
become doctrine."

Nixon *did*, according to Ehrlichman, spend a considerable amount of time
(and some political capital) on the domestic side, and he "insisted on personally
making all the decisions on abortion, race, aid to parochial schools, labor legislation, drugs, crime, welfare and taxes, for example." In other areas, Ehrlichman continues, "notably the environment, health (except cancer research),
campus unrest and antiwar demonstrations, hunger, transportation, consumer
protection, youth, housing and revenue sharing—he delegated to others to look
after." In fact, Ehrlichman continues, "Nixon insisted I not bother him about
many things" (on the domestic agenda).[26]

Nixon's attention to domestic policy varied from issue to issue, and from
time to time, as circumstances and interest warranted. It is true that the president was more concerned with foreign affairs, but not to the total exclusion of
domestic issues.

Nixon's level of opportunity in domestic affairs was fairly low. He was a
Republican president facing Democratic majorities in both houses of Congress;

he did not have a burning interest in domestic affairs; presidential power is more limited in the domestic area than in foreign policy; and upon entering office, Nixon hit the ground stumbling.

On most domestic policy issues, a policy transformation took place. The pattern was a familiar one. Since Nixon had very few clear ideas as to what he wanted to do in the domestic arena, the pre-presidential transition task force (Stage I, 1969) served as an idea-generating group. Once in office (Stage II, 1969–70) these ideas were bounced around by a very open, competitive, lively staff structure. In this period, a dynamic, idea-oriented one, some of the best intellectual work of the administration took place. Bold ideas, innovative approaches were entertained. In many ways the first chaotic six months were the best of Nixon's presidency.

But such an open, competitive style did not suit Nixon. He needed order, craved privacy, hated being in the center of arguments. Nixon was a loner and wanted to be protected by the hierarchical structure H. R. Haldeman provided. Thus, from dynamic to static went the Nixon system, and the new order— more rigid, closed, hierarchical—sought order out of chaos (Stage III, 1970–73).

While the new system did bring order, it was at the expense of ideas and creativity. The trade-off suited Nixon's personality. With Haldeman as his chief of staff, Ehrlichman in charge of the domestic side, Kissinger heading foreign affairs, and John Connally in charge of economic policy, Nixon had the order he craved.

As the policy ideas settled in, so too did the wall around Nixon. The president began to personalize the White House to an extent many thought dangerous (Stage IV, 1971–74).[27] Now, only a small circle of people would meet with and influence the president. Those who appealed to the light side of Nixon (Finch, Price) were excluded, while those appealing to Nixon's darker side (Haldeman, Mitchell, Colson) were drawn closer to the presidential orbit. In this period, the administration turned away from most of the progressive reforms of the first year, and a revolution took place. Nixon as Disraeli was replaced by Nixon as Uriah Heep.

As the wall around Nixon became more fortified, and as Nixon felt the outside environment becoming more hostile, a *dismantling strategy* emerged in the domestic arena (e.g., illegally dismantling the Office of Economic Opportunity). Here (Stage V, 1972–74), the president sought to prevent Congress and the bureaucracy from getting their way by using what Richard Nathan calls the "administrative presidency"[28] to dominate the policy process. Rather than promoting new legislation, Nixon sought to exercise a negative or dismantling approach by the use of vetoes, administrative roadblocks, reorganization, executive orders, and impoundment of funds.

By early 1972, Nixon began to oppose the Great Society more actively, to use domestic issues for partisan gain, and to use the power of the federal government against political enemies/adversaries. Nixon never had a great interest in domestic policy, but by 1972 he became even more aloof from the domestic policy arena. More of his attention was directed at foreign affairs, the war in Vietnam, détente, and the upcoming reelection campaign. Instead of developing new ways to deal with old problems, Nixon abandoned the Disraeli model and began to show a disinterest in domestic affairs.

Since Nixon did not have much of a domestic agenda, he began to become reactive, nay-saying. He developed a policy of opposition. Perhaps responding to what he saw as a hostile political environment, Nixon began to look at domestic politics as an extension of the political battlefield.

In the aftermath of the 1972 landslide, Nixon sought to extend the administrative presidency, but Watergate quickly dominated the political landscape, and a bunker mentality emerged. In this period, domestic policy was on automatic pilot, as Kenneth Cole replaced Ehrlichman and the president's attention was focused on Watergate (Stage VI, 1973–74). The last year of the Nixon presidency was not a time of domestic policy activity. As the president struggled to save his political skin, domestic policy took a decidedly back seat.

Nixon's Domestic Agenda

When Nixon became president in 1969 after years in public life, he did not have a domestic agenda. He had many ideas about what he wanted to do in foreign policy, but surprisingly for a career politician, his domestic cupboard was nearly bare.

In the period immediately following his election in 1968, Richard Nixon appointed Arthur Burns to head his domestic policy task force for the transition to the presidency. Nixon did not give Burns clear and explicit policy guidelines, and the domestic agenda was unclear from Nixon's campaign statements. Nixon did criticize the Great Society, but in rather vague terms. Postelection planning was thus uncoordinated and haphazard, and the president-elect did not provide the direction Burns needed.

When Richard Nixon ascended to the presidency, the expectation—drawn from his previous political statements and campaign speeches—was that Nixon would begin to retreat from the federal commitment to solve social problems. The New Deal of Franklin Roosevelt and the Great Society of Lyndon Johnson appeared to be in jeopardy. After all, as Nixon speechwriter Raymond Price wrote, "It was the Roosevelt pattern in domestic policy that Nixon sought to reverse, the Roosevelt coalition he sought to replace, the Roosevelt legacy he sought to supplant."[29] The real questions were, how fast would Nixon march backwards, and what kind of a fight would the Congress put up?

To compound matters, in the early stages of the administration, an institutional conflict was built into the domestic arena as Nixon set Arthur Burns up against Daniel P. Moynihan as his top advisers. The conflict and competition between Burns and Moynihan could have produced an open, dynamic advisory system if someone were there to manage the conflict, control the competition.

Nixon's intent was to balance the conservative Burns against the liberal Moynihan. No one, including the president, managed the balancing act, and soon the competition adversely affected the domestic team. "Before long," John Ehrlichman wrote, "each was seeing the President behind the back of the other, hoping to gain the final favorable decision on some disputed issues."

The confusion, conflict, and competition could not last. "Why," Ehrlichman recalls Nixon asking, "do I have to put up with this on the domestic side? There's got to be a more orderly way of going about the development of domestic policy than this. Henry [Kissinger] never bothers me like this. Henry always brings me nice, neat papers on national security problems and I can check the box. Nobody badgers me and picks on me. But these two wild men on the domestic side are beating me up all the time."

The solution was to create a Domestic Council modeled loosely after the National Security Council, and to reorganize the Bureau of the Budget as the Office of Management and Budget. Together, these two agencies were to coordinate and control the domestic policy agenda in the Nixon administration.[30]

Very quickly, the Domestic Council, headed by John Ehrlichman, became the primary coordinating agency in domestic affairs. It moved to the forefront because (a) Ehrlichman was one of Haldeman's protégés and was pushed by his mentor to the center; (b) the Domestic Council was located in the White House—it belonged to the president and no one else; and (c) John Ehrlichman was a brilliant, capable administrator.

Executive Order 11541 created the Domestic Council in 1970. Formally the council consisted of the president, the vice president, and several cabinet officers and agency heads. But the real work was done by the staff, headed by John Ehrlichman. As John Kessel notes, the Domestic Council soon became the "principal locus of domestic decision-making," and it quickly became John Ehrlichman's domain.

The council itself met infrequently, and even those meetings were, in John Ehrlichman's words, "largely show and tell." The real work was done by Ehrlichman's support staff, whose day-to-day operations were controlled by one of his assistants (usually Kenneth Cole) working with council committees. These committees would submit reports to Ehrlichman, who made whatever changes he felt appropriate, then passed them on to the president. Nixon would normally read the reports and make marginal notes to Ehrlichman.

In the early days of the Nixon presidency, the Burns-Moynihan conflict did produce a dynamic, idea-oriented policy atmosphere (resembling Franklin Roosevelt's competitive staff system), but the tug and pull made Nixon uncomfortable, and since the president did not often intervene to give direction, the system went from being dynamic to being deadlocked. Nixon preferred a more orderly, hierarchical, formal system, and John Ehrlichman and the Domestic Council provided the president with such a conflict-free atmosphere. But Nixon paid a price for the shift to a more hierarchical, closed system. He was less involved in and aware of the domestic issues and provided less direction and leadership. Thus, by 1970, the domestic agenda became more the property of John Ehrlichman than of the president, and while Ehrlichman provided competent leadership, the character, tone, and direction of the domestic agenda began to shift.[31] Since the transition team did not supply the president with a domestic legislative program Nixon wished to pursue, and since the president seemed ambivalent about what role government should take on the domestic front, the new administration hit the ground stumbling. So, the early days of the administration were spent arguing, proposing, suggesting new and old ideas. This—perhaps surprisingly—produced some fascinating results.

Nixon's early legislative proposals (e.g., postal system reform) were meager by contemporary standards. This did not allow the president to take advantage of the "honeymoon period." But by the summer, the Burns-Moynihan system began to produce. The ambitious and innovative Family Assistance Plan (FAP), revenue sharing, environmental legislation, and an increase in food stamps all indicated that Nixon—to the surprise of many—was not out to dismantle the Great Society or the federal government's role in social welfare, but was in many ways expanding it.

In his first months in office, Nixon had no domestic agenda to speak of. Out of the Burns-Moynihan clash of the next few months emerged a Disraeli-like liberal agenda. But by 1971, as John Ehrlichman took control of domestic policy, Nixon began to move back to the political right. But in early 1971, Nixon still had a split personality on the domestic front.[32]

In his 1971 State of the Union message, Nixon called for a "New American Revolution." His domestic agenda, designed to achieve this revolution, consisted of what the White House called the Big Six, a combination of liberal proposals (FAP, a "full-employment" budget, environmental programs, medical programs) and conservative proposals (revenue-sharing, executive branch reorganization). This agenda, while still generally liberal, was the beginning of Nixon's return to more familiar ground on the political right.

But while a policy tug-of-war took place on the domestic front, a tug-of-war was also going on over the political soul of Richard Nixon. The battle here was over the light side and the dark side of Richard Nixon. Upon entering the White House, Nixon had all the hopes and high intentions of any new president. His early domestic efforts, as confusing and sometimes contradictory as they were, nonetheless represented a genuine effort by the president to face up to and solve the domestic ills that plagued the nation. But as time went by, things began to change. Adversaries became enemies, frustrations set in, roadblocks persisted, the weight of the war in Vietnam infected everything, marches and demonstrations persisted, and the dark side of Richard Nixon began to come to the forefront.

The New Federalism

The cornerstone of Nixon's domestic policy agenda was introduced in an August 8, 1969, television address and was called the New Federalism. It was a legislative program without a theory of government, a collection of policy proposals without a conception of how and why things fit together.[33] The two primary components of the New Federalism were General Revenue Sharing and welfare reform.

In broad terms, Nixon wanted to return power to the states. Ever since the New Deal, power had been shifting from state and local governments to the federal government. The Great Society of LBJ increased the federal role in social welfare policies, and Nixon was determined to reverse this trend. But Nixon was no knee-jerk conservative who blindly disparaged the federal role in solving problems. He was conservative, but a pragmatist. He wanted to shift some power back to the states, but still understood that the federal government had a significant role to play.

Nixon the conservative reformer simultaneously embraced contradictory goals and values. Since his domestic agenda was not as well thought-out or as integrated as it could have been, Nixon was able to pursue both centralizing (FAP) and decentralizing (revenue sharing) policies at the same time. The umbrella under which the Nixon domestic agenda was subsumed was called New Federalism, and it suggested that there would be a redistribution of power within the federal system. But as FAP promised to centralize welfare, revenue sharing sought to decentralize the federal-state-local relationship.[34]

Revenue Sharing

General Revenue Sharing (GRS) marked a bold shift in intergovernmental relations. It was a plan to share revenue *and* powers with state and local governments. This decentralizing move fit with Nixon's conservative taste and gave the president a domestic issue to pursue.

GRS was an idea that had been floating around Washington for almost a decade. The idea behind it was that while the responsibilities of state and local governments had grown in the past few decades, the tax base of these governments had not expanded at a rate comparable to the growth of demand and cost. A fiscal crisis in the cities put enormous strain on their capacity to serve the needs of their residents. If the federal government could share its revenues with the cities, this crises could be relieved. As Moynihan wrote:

Behind the idea of revenue sharing was the belief that the ills of urban government arose at least in part from the imbalance that had gradually developed between the revenue generating capacity of the property tax, on which municipal government heavily depended, and the graduated income tax which provided revenue for the Federal government. The remedy for this imbalance was to begin sharing the proceeds of the latter tax with state and local government, leaving them to do with the funds exactly what they would, and requiring compliance only with general policies of the national government.[35]

But revenue sharing was designed to do more than share revenues, it was also designed to move power downward, closer to the people: a classically conservative goal. It was a conservative readjustment in power. GRS consisted of a mixture of formula funding and discretionary state and local spending with few strings attached, and was *very* popular with state and local officials.

The idea for revenue sharing first came to Nixon in November of 1968 in a report from the transition team's Intergovernmental Fiscal Relations Task Force. For both fiscal and philosophical reasons, the task force strongly endorsed the concept of revenue sharing. In April 1969, the president ordered an inter-agency committee to give him a report on revenue sharing, and at this point Arthur Burns began to actively promote revenue sharing within the administration.[36] The president liked the idea and gave his approval, but Nixon never displayed the kind of commitment to revenue sharing one might expect. John Ehrlichman recounts that Nixon kept wanting to cut GRS for budgetary reasons and that he, Ehrlichman, had to keep saving revenue sharing. This view is confirmed by a number of other sources.[37] Despite Nixon's lukewarm embrace of GRS, legislation was drafted and sent to the Congress, which began to drag its feet on this issue.

The White House lobbying effort got cranked up, state and local officials were activated (New York's governor, Nelson Rockefeller, was especially important in promoting GRS in Congress), and the president began to contact congressional officials. In the end, the House passed GRS by a 223–185 vote, and the Senate passed a bill by a 64–20 margin. The State and Local Fiscal Assistance Act of 1972 (GRS) was the law.

General Revenue Sharing was an effort to reduce the power of the federal government and its bureaucracy. While it did this to a degree, it never met the expectations of its proponents. It did not, as Nixon once said, mark the beginning of the second American Revolution. In its early stages, the New Federalism contained elements that genuinely sought to transfer power downward within the federal system. It was not, as some critics suggested, a dismantling strategy. Only later, in 1972 and beyond, did Richard Nixon begin to move in that direction.

The Family Assistance Plan

The genesis of the innovative welfare reform proposal that eventually became known as the Family Assistance Plan (FAP) stems from initial confusion over what to do about the growing problem of poverty and welfare dependence. Nixon had no firm ideas about solving this problem, but a transition-team task forced headed by Richard Nathan made an ambitious proposal to establish a minimum floor for welfare to be funded by the federal government and administered by the states.

Early in the first term, HEW secretary Robert Finch and newly appointed head of the Council for Urban Affairs Daniel P. Moynihan began to push the Nathan proposal. The proposal itself had roots in an idea promoted by Sargent Shriver, LBJ's director of the Office of Economic Opportunity. Johnson rejected the proposal as too costly, especially given the cost of the war in Vietnam. As the Nathan plan worked its way through the Urban Affairs Council, it met with opposition from several cabinet officials. A new plan had to be drawn up. A subcabinet task force was given the job of redrafting a welfare reform package.[38]

The Burns-Moynihan conflict began to impact upon the deliberations, Burns opposing the establishment of national standards (a guaranteed income) and Moynihan favoring such standards. The Nathan proposal gave way to political and personal pressures from every direction, and a new, bolder plan began to take shape.

The Family Security System (FSS), an ambitious, innovative step in welfare reform, was a liberal program, presented by the Urban Affairs Council and proposed by a conservative president. Arthur Burns was shocked. "It ran counter to everything I knew about Dick Nixon. . . . It seemed that he might do the unthinkable." Indeed, Nixon began to warm up to the FSS concept, but insisted on revisions. At this stage, the debate between the house conservative (Burns) and house liberal (Moynihan) became more harsh and counterproductive. The president asked labor secretary George Shultz to serve as mediator. Shultz put a work incentive into FSS (to satisfy conservatives) and orchestrated other changes. But again things bogged down. The president then turned to John Ehrlichman to steer the proposal through the maze. But opposition within the administration did not wane. Vice President Agnew said of FSS, "It will not be a political winner," and other in-house conservatives fought the proposal as too costly and too liberal.[39]

Finally, on August 6, 1969, after the name of FSS was changed to the more palatable Family Assistance Plan, the president met with his cabinet at Camp David, where, as Moynihan recalls, "his decision to propose a guaranteed income was set forth to the discomfort, even the dismay, of most of those present." Two days later, in a television address, the president proposed his legislative agenda. It contained a four-part package: FAP, a job-training program, a revamping of the Office of Economic Opportunity, and revenue sharing.

It was a radical solution to the welfare problem. But the president made it sound almost conservative. It was, the president assured his audience, workfare, not welfare. In his memoirs, *RN*, Nixon called FAP "simple, but revolutionary." It was anything but simple. It called for what amounted to a guaranteed income for all Americans, a revolutionary proposal. Nixon wanted to abolish the existing welfare system and replace it with a more costly program establishing, in the president's words, "a foundation under the income of every American family." Couching his proposal in conservative rhetoric (e.g., "not a guaranteed income"), the president nonetheless proposed a radical reshaping of the nation's welfare system.

The initial responses to the president's program were supportive. Politicians and press alike applauded the president. The liberal journal the *New Republic* called it "the most substantial welfare reform proposal in the nation's history." But once the legislative proposal itself was submitted to the Congress, both the left and right began to pick it apart. To the left, it was not generous enough; to the right, it was too generous and was philosophically repugnant. After introducing FAP, the president seemed almost uninterested in his proposal. He let it drift in Congress and did not seem anxious to spend his political capital on pushing FAP through the legislative process. It was not until late winter that Nixon became actively involved in lobbying for FAP.

The push helped get a slightly modified FAP through the House by a vote of 243 to 155. But things did not go as well in the Senate. It was in the Senate that the left and right began to gang up on FAP. And at the early stages, when FAP was having its troubles in the Senate Finance Committee, the president stayed on the sideline. The president didn't get involved until well after the Finance Committee refused to deal with FAP until changes in the proposal were made.

A revised FAP was submitted, and the Finance Committee resumed hearings on welfare reform. By August the president lobbied more forcefully for his bill. But Nixon's efforts lasted less than a month, and several prominent Democrats on the Finance Committee said they were never lobbied by the White House on FAP. Finally, on October 8, the Committee voted FAP down by a 14–1 vote, with all six Republicans voting against the president's bill.

The administration made one last effort to revise and resubmit FAP, but all was for naught. A compromise effort linked the Senate liberals with the president in a case of strange bedfellows that ultimately failed to revive FAP, and in spite of Nixon resubmitting FAP in 1971, it was never to pass. Nixon's highest domestic priority, welfare reform, died. Nixon's sporadic support for his own proposal and the odd coalition of opposition from the left and right doomed FAP. Richard Nixon's radical proposal on welfare reform was not to be.

Why? Why did Nixon, the longtime conservative and critic of big government, emerge out of the Burns-Moynihan conflict as something of a liberal? The answer, it seems, is that Nixon was captivated (Safire called it "falling in love") by Moynihan the thinker and writer. Moynihan was impressive, persuasive, *and* he gave Nixon the rationale for pursuing a liberal-expansionary agenda: the Disraeli analogy. "Tory men and liberal policies are what have changed the world," Nixon concluded after reading a biography of Benjamin Disraeli. Disraeli had broadened his political base, coopted his opponents, expanded his power, *and* begun a tradition of "Tory reform." Nixon, William Safire writes, was "delighted with the Disraeli comparison." His would be a "reform administration",[40] leading the nation into a future of progressive conservatism. But Nixon's flirtation with progressive reform would be short-lived. Moynihan's star descended, hard-liners took over in several domestic areas, and when John Ehrlichman took over as head of the Domestic Council, more traditionally Republican policies dominated the Nixon Agenda.

Nixon and Civil Rights

> Don't look at what we say, but what we do.
>
> Attorney General John N. Mitchell

Richard Nixon entered the presidency in a time of social and political unrest. One element of that unrest was reflected in the civil rights movement that gained momentum in the late 1950s and emerged as a powerful force in American politics in the 1960s. The movement reflected the demands of black Americans for equal rights and opportunities and challenged the white power structure in America.[41]

Nixon owed his election in part to the forces opposing the civil rights advances, and as Representative Paul N. McClosky, Jr. (R. Calif.), wrote, "In 1968 the workings of our political system had produced a President who owed his nomination and election to a coalition of forces dependent upon the same elements in the Deep South which had for so many years blocked the evolution of civil rights for black people."[42]

At the Republican Convention in 1968, Nixon was challenged for the party's presidential nomination by Ronald Reagan on the right and Nelson Rockefeller on the left. In order to get the 667 delegates necessary to win, Nixon knew he had to get the Southern delegates. As it turned out, of the 292 delegates available from the Southern states, Nixon got 228 votes. This allowed Nixon to win the Republican nomination on the first ballot with 692 delegate votes, a bare 25 votes more than necessary. The Deep South helped Nixon, and he would try to repay them.

In the general election, Nixon won the presidency by an even narrower margin, in part with the help of third-party candidate Governor George Wallace of Alabama, who attracted normally Democratic votes away from Hubert Humphrey and won five Southern states. With Nixon carrying five other Southern states, he was able to squeak by Humphrey with 43.6 percent of the popular vote to Humphrey's 43.2 percent. Nixon received less than 10 percent of the black vote in the 1968 election. The white South had indeed helped Richard Nixon carry the prize of the presidency. How would Nixon repay his debt?

In fact, Nixon had never received the support or votes of blacks in the United States. In his loss to Kennedy in the 1960 presidential election, the 1962 loss to Pat Brown for the California governorship, and even in his 1972 presidential landslide victory, blacks voted overwhelmingly for Nixon's Democratic opponents. Since Nixon neither had nor needed the support of blacks to win the presidency, and since there was little likelihood that he would be able to win over black voters, it is not surprising that his administration was at best lukewarm to the promotion of civil rights.

While he claimed not to owe political debts to any side, in fact, Nixon owed a great deal to the whites of the Deep South.[43] His debt was paid in what became known as the Southern strategy.

One of the chief operating officials of Nixon's Southern strategy, Harry Dent, says that the president's critics are wrong when they accuse him of retreating on civil rights. Dent saw not retreat but a shift from the use of fund cutoff procedures (Civil Rights Act of 1984, Title VI), to litigation procedures (Title IV of the same act) on the grounds that fund cutoffs were not an effective tool to generate compliance and were, in the president's view, "heavy-handed." According to Dent, Nixon's litigation method was one of "firmness tempered with conciliation." Thus to Dent, the president favored desegregation, but by a more "accommodating method."[44]

Scholar Hugh Davis Graham sees a different picture. "From the documents in the Nixon archives one reconstructs a different picture of evolving civil rights policy. It is characterized chiefly by neglect and inattention, by ill-prepared reactions (with some few striking exceptions) to poorly anticipated legislative confrontations, by divided leadership with no one clearly in command. Perhaps most important, although not surprising, one detects no generally coherent theory of civil rights to govern the new Republican Administration's policy choices."[45]

Civil Rights lawyer Eleanor Holmes Norton sees "two civil rights Nixons": "There have been two civil rights Nixons, neither of them ever particularly principled. The more benevolent has moved but only with calculation, taking initiatives where opposition seemed least likely but stopping short when challenged. The other seems to have enjoyed leading a popular retreat as the majority indicated those civil rights gains it could not stomach. Both these Nixons were beholden to the idea of the supremacy of majoritarian preference."[46]

While Nixon had always seemed a moderate on civil rights throughout his public career, in terms of the private Nixon, we get very few glimpses of how he felt about blacks and racial equality. One of the few insiders to reveal how Nixon may have felt is John Ehrlichman, who wrote that "twice in explaining all this [racial equality] to me, Nixon said he believed America's blacks could only marginally benefit from Federal programs because blacks were *genetically inferior* to whites"[47] (emphasis in original). In handwritten notes taken by Chief of Staff H. R. Haldeman in a March 5, 1970, meeting with the president, Haldeman notes that "P-has concluded blacks really want tokenism *instead* of results—(based on meeting today with black admin officials."

Just prior to Nixon's inauguration, six black leaders met with the president-elect to discuss racial problems. Nixon was quoted as telling the group that he would "do more for the underprivileged and more for the Negro than any President has ever done."[48] But the two civil rights Nixons were not evenly divided, and the president would not keep this promise. For, while Nixon could point to several positive steps taken to promote civil rights (moving forward—slowly—on affirmative action early in his presidency, developing plans to increase minority participation within the construction trade, the Philadelphia Plan, attempts to eliminate discrimination against women and minorities in college and university hiring, voluntary councils to promote Southern desegregation), overall, the Nixon approach to civil rights was "withdraw and retreat."

If there were two individual Nixons on civil rights, there were two bureaucratic Nixons as well, and this is the key to understanding the evolution of civil rights policy in the Nixon administration. The split within the administration occurred between the Department of Health, Education, and Welfare, headed by Robert Finch, which was seeking to promote several civil rights reforms and continue—at slightly slower pace—the work done by the Kennedy-Johnson administrations, and the Justice Department, headed by John Mitchell, which was seeking retreat on the civil rights issue while promoting the Southern strategy. In the long run, the HEW crowd was no match for Mitchell at Justice, and the Nixon administration marched a quick retreat away from the early efforts of HEW at civil rights reform. As early as October of 1969, H. R. Haldeman's notes reflect great displeasure with the job being done by Robert Finch at HEW and a growing concern over pressure from Southern conservatives over school desegregation and the Voting Rights Act. From this point on, the goal within the administration was to get everyone "tracking together" on civil rights. This meant "all moving steadily at one in the same direction, with the same destination in mind, and, hopefully, with an identical map in each tracker's hand."[49] If there were two Nixons on civil rights early in 1969, by late 1970, it was the anti–civil rights side of the Nixon personality that would come to dominate the policy and political agenda.

The bureaucratic battle within the Nixon administration over control of the civil rights agenda reflected a reversal of sorts from the approach taken during the Kennedy-Johnson years. When Robert F. Kennedy and then Ramsey Clark served as attorney general, it was the Justice Department that spearheaded the civil rights push within the government; HEW took a back (though supporting) seat. In the Nixon years, HEW's early attempts to promote civil rights were blocked by Justice. The Justice Department was no longer to be the driving force to promote civil rights in the United States.

By 1970, when Justice had won control of the civil rights issue, there emerged a marriage of John Mitchell's Southern strategy to Nixon adviser Daniel P. Moynihan's benign neglect on civil rights. The full weight of this marriage crushed HEW's efforts to stay the course on civil rights.

The Southern strategy was an effort to play up to white Southern voters in an effort to woo them away from the Democratic party. This meant retreating on black civil rights and giving special favors to Southern segregationists. As Reg Murphy and Hal Gulliver saw it, the Southern strategy represented "a deal" between Nixon and the Southern segregationists. As they put it,

The essential Nixon bargain was simply this: I'm president of the United States, I'll find a way to ease up on the federal pressures forcing school desegregation . . . this was a long-range strategy. Nixon clearly hoped to woo Southern support so ardently that there might once again develop a solid political South—but this time committed as firmly to the Republican party as it once had been to the Democratic party. It was a cynical strategy, this catering in subtle ways to the segregationist leanings of white Southern voters—yet pretending with high rhetoric that the real aim was simply to treat the South fairly, to let it become part of the nation again.[50]

Benign neglect represented a belief, presented to the president by Daniel Moynihan in a memo written in early 1970, that "the time may have come when the issue of race could benefit from a period of 'benign neglect.' The subject has been too much talked about. The forum has been too much taken over by hysterics, paranoids, and boodlers on all sides. We may need a period in which Negro progress continues and racial rhetoric fades."[51]

While Nixon and Moynihan insisted that this was merely an effort to deflate the hot rhetoric of the race issue, critics saw it as yet another piece of a policy of civil rights retreat. But as Robert Finch's political star descended, benign neglect *and* the Southern strategy fit together as parts of the civil rights policy that did indeed mark a backing away from the federal government's affirmative role of promoting civil rights.

The core of the Nixon civil rights policy can be seen in the Southern strategy and the demands it made on the administration of justice. Nixon knew that, as notes taken by Bob Haldeman in meetings with the president reveal, "there's no political gain in integrating!" On top of that, the president was doubtful that integration was a good idea at that time. As notes taken by Haldeman in an August 4, 1970, meeting with the president reveal, Nixon said, "Law does not require integration not sure integration will work serious reservations re interracial playgrounds not right for this year—maybe in 10 years."

The Southern strategy was developed in part by Kevin Phillips, who worked for John Mitchell in the Justice Department and later published *The Emerging Republican Majority* (1969). This book laid out a blueprint for a realignment of the American voting public toward the Republican party. Nixon was well aware of Phillips's thesis and attempted to develop policies designed to implement Phillips's vision of a new American majority consisting of a combination of the Nixon and Wallace vote of 1968 along with the social policy conservatives and white ethnics.

But as the administration began to pull the federal government back from an advocacy position, a broader "policy" on civil rights began to emerge. This policy reversal was fully expected by the white South, but while the administration sought to accommodate the demands of Southern segregationists, it found that there were roadblocks in the way of the retreat. They could not change the law, they could not force the courts to reverse themselves, and they could not move the nation away from its legal and moral commitment to civil rights. However, even within these limitations, there were actions that the administration could take which were designed to fulfill its Southern strategy. One thing that could be done was to limit or control the level of civil rights enforcement. As Haldeman notes in a July 22, 1970, meeting with the president, Nixon orders "nothing more done in South beyond law requires." Again, on August 4, 1970, in Haldeman's notes of a meeting with the president, we find, "Only do what law requires—*nothing more*" (emphasis in original). The administration could also delay implementation of the law, as it did in school desegregation cases.[52]

While administration officials denied that there was a Southern strategy, an examination of the Nixon presidential papers reveals that indeed this is precisely what motivated the president. In notes taken by John Ehrlichman at a November 28, 1972, meeting with the president, Ehrlichman writes "[President]—continue The Southern Strategy." And Southerners were aware of the strategy, as a Republican state chairman from Georgia, Wiley A. Wasden, Jr., wrote to Nixon's liaison to the South, Harry Dent, in 1969 that "maybe the southern strategy is beginning to work."

The Nixon policy on civil rights emerged piecemeal, but nowhere was it more evident than in the attempt to limit the Voting Rights Act of 1965. This act was one of the most effective civil rights laws ever passed, as it promoted voter registration among blacks in the South and began to give the black community some hope for gaining political power. On June 26, 1969, Attorney General John Mitchell testified in Congress against renewal of the Voting Rights Act and suggested a much weakened bill in its place. Evans and Novak said that this was "by far the most ominous break with civil rights that the administration had yet attempted."[53] In addition, six weeks after taking office, Nixon pulled federal voting registrars out of Mississippi, and the administration began to deliberately underenforce the Voting Rights Act.[54]

On school desegregation, Nixon sought to satisfy the demands of Republican senator Strom Thurmond of South Carolina and withdraw the federal government from its efforts at desegregation. Leon Panetta, former director of HEW's Office for Civil Rights during the early days of the Nixon administration, recognized the difficulty Nixon had in attempting to reconcile his campaign promises to Thurmond and the South with the need to obey the court decisions on school desegregation, and saw Nixon giving in to the political pressures from Thurmond.[55]

Nixon's liaison to the South, Harry Dent, wrote a January 23, 1969, memo to the president in which he stated that "so far as Southern politics is concerned, the Nixon Administration will be judged from the beginning on the manner in which the school desegregation guidelines problem is handled. Other issues are important in the South but are dwarfed somewhat by comparison."

Of course, the demands of the law and the needs of politics could not, at least in this case, be reconciled. And Nixon gave a clear signal of intent when he fired Leon Panetta in early 1970 and issued a lengthy position paper on school desegregation in which Nixon pledged that "we are not backing away" but which, the *Wall Street Journal* said, signalled "a go-slow approach geared to maximum political mileage."[56]

In point of fact, the Nixon administration was severely restrained in what it could do to back away from school desegregation by court decisions tracing back to *Brown v. Board of Education* in 1954, followed by two recent court rulings—*Green v. (New Kent) County School Board* (1968), which dealt a blow to Nixon's "freedom-of-choice" option, and *Swann v. Charlotte-Mecklemburg Board of Education* (1971), which set tough requirements on districts with one-race schools. The administration sought to overturn these orders, but in the end, the decisions stood. This forced Nixon to back down slightly from his position, and in the end he urged only "minimal compliance with the law."[57]

On the busing issue, Nixon attempted to make a quick retreat from the court-ordered busing that was the law, and instead proposed in 1972 a moratorium on all busing, which, in his own words, "would put an immediate stop to further new busing orders by the federal courts."[58] While the *Brown, Green, Holmes,* and *Swann* decisions stood in his way, Nixon repeatedly sought to enact policies based on his belief, stated in a January 28, 1972, memorandum to John Ehrlichman, that "this country is not ready at this time for either forcibly integrated housing or forcibly integrated education." Nixon hoped for what he called "a middle course" on school desegregation, but on October 29, 1969, the Supreme Court announced that "the obligation . . . is to terminate dual school systems at once." Nixon delayed, and when the Court forced him to comply, he did so reluctantly and slowly.

Beginning in 1970 and running through 1972, there was a great deal of discussion within the administration about sponsoring a constitutional amendment to prevent forced busing. At first the issue was promoted by Harry Dent and opposed by HEW and Robert Finch's assistant Len Garment. Later John Ehrlichman pushed for an antibusing amendment, in part, as a May 19, 1972, memo reveals, to smoke out the Democratic presidential candidates. Notes by H. R. Haldeman of a February 27, 1970, meeting with the President, Haldeman, and Ehrlichman contain the following: "move fast on Constit. amendment re schools should bite bullet now & bite it hard if it's racism—so be it."

Murphy and Gulliver describe Nixon as a "reluctant integrationist." Forced by the courts to move ahead on desegregation, Nixon nonetheless used the issue to pursue his Southern strategy and ingratiate himself to the white segregationists of the South. As Murphy and Gulliver note:

The terrible cruelty of the Nixon administration's indecision on school desegregation was that it gave direct encouragement to those white Southerners *least* reconciled to the ending of an era. . . . Richard Nixon . . . gave them reason to hope that the clock could be turned back, that at the very least the *direction* of change could be somewhat altered, the movement of it slowed down, that quite possibly, for instance, some form of token integration might satisfy the laws and the courts. . . . The law had not changed, nor had the court decisions or the HEW guidelines. But Nixon managed to let many white Southerners suddenly *believe* that things had changed.[59]

An area in which Nixon tried to take a constructive role was "black capitalism," or as it later became known, "minority business enterprise." Nixon felt that this was an area in which he could satisfy some of the demands of the black community, while not alienating whites, especially in the South.

In the 1968 campaign, candidate Nixon endorsed efforts by the government to promote black capitalism, and the reaction was generally favorable. Nixon had found a policy that served many needs: it fit into his philosophy of government, helped blacks, and did not seem to anger whites. On March 5, 1969, President Nixon announced the signing of Executive Order 11456, which created a new agency, the Office of Minority Business Enterprise (OMBE), within the Department of Commerce. With the signing of this order, Nixon announced, "I have often made the point that to foster the economic status and the pride of members of our minority groups, we must seek to involve them more fully in our private enterprise system."[60]

OMBE would have the power to coordinate all existing federal efforts at promoting minority enterprise (116 programs within 21 departments and agencies) and would, in Nixon's words, "be the focal point of the Administration's efforts to assist the establishment of new minority enterprises and expansion of existing ones." Unfortunately, OMBE was not to have any funds to give financial assistance to minority business but was only to serve as a coordinating agency. In this way, it generated a great deal of good publicity at a very low cost.

Once again however, the early efforts of the administration gave way to the demands of the Southern strategy, and by 1971 the president had all but forgotten minority business enterprise as an issue. By late 1971 Nixon had virtually no constructive plan for promoting civil rights or minority economic development.[61]

Overall, the Nixon policy on civil rights unfolded piecemeal through bureaucratic in-fighting, the law, campaign rhetoric, political needs, and public relations imperatives. It was not a well thought-out, carefully crafted package of programs and initiatives that fit together tightly, but a randomly organized forcing together of ideas and programs to which only periodic attention was focused.

What little was attempted in support of civil rights was only lukewarmly proposed, and even that support was often withdrawn in midstream. In the end, the Nixon civil rights policy was best summed up in November of 1971 in a report of Father Theodore Hesburgh, chairman of the U.S. Civil Rights Commission, when he wrote, "The President's posture . . . has not been such as to provide the clear affirmative policy direction necessary to assure that the full weight of the federal government will be behind the fight to secure equal rights for all minorities."[62] Or, as Hugh Graham concluded, "The direction of civil rights policy seemed to be determined by its political play."[63] And conservative A. James Reichley noted, "It would be hard not to conclude that his [Nixon's] judgment [on civil rights and busing] was heavily influenced by his immediate political interests."[64]

Eleanor Holmes Norton sums up the Nixon Civil rights policy in comparison to other presidents, writing,

Examined in the traditional areas of civil rights concern—employment, education, and housing—the Nixon record fails the test of the times, the test by which previous presidents have been judged. . . . Nixon took virtually no risks at a time when aggressive action to enforce equal rights was easily possible for the first time in our history. He chose the opposite course—totally to politicize an issue which, because it affects a disfavored minority, cannot survive a uniformly political approach.[65]

Nixon and Crime

Before 1968, crime and "law and order" were not significant issues in presidential campaigns. Normally considered within the domain of state and local governments, crime became one of the chief campaign themes for Richard Nixon in the 1968 race.

The law and order issue did not rise in a vacuum. The urban riots of the mid 1960s, rising crime rates, campus unrest, and other symptoms lifted crime to a national concern. Richard Nixon ran on a tough anticrime plank in the 1968 campaign. Nixon had to seize the law and order issue because George Wallace was using it to promote his independent bid for the presidency, and Nixon feared that his own natural constituency would be drawn away by the Wallace appeal. After Nixon was elected, he had to convert campaign rhetoric into policy.

Nixon's law and order policy emerged—as was true of so many domestic concerns to which Nixon gave only secondary consideration—piecemeal, and gradually. In 1969, the president spent a great deal of time on the crime issue but became frustrated by the limited options available to him. In early 1970, Nixon ordered Haldeman to "do something on crime *now*" (emphasis in original). But the president didn't know *what* to do. In a June 9, 1971, meeting with his chief of staff, Haldeman's notes reveal the president saying:

look in terms of how create issues
   need an enemy, controversy
drugs and law enforcement. May be one
   esp. since so weak in polls.

In 1970, the Domestic Council, headed by John Ehrlichman, was given responsibility for giving coherence to the disparate parts of the Nixon law and order policy. Ehrlichman, with the help of his assistant Egil ("Bud") Krogh, and always with the input of Attorney General John Mitchell, put together an anticrime package. Beginning in April of 1969, the administration sent four major pieces of anticrime legislation to the Congress. The most controversial was the District of Columbia Crime Control Bill.

The federal government could do little on the crime issue nationally, so they focused on the District of Columbia. The Nixon District of Columbia anticrime policy consisted of a variety of "get tough" proposals designed to give police greater freedom and power, including provisions that empowered judges to jail criminal suspects ("preventive detention") for sixty days before trial and allowed police to break into houses without showing a search warrant ("no-knock").

Senator Sam Ervin (D. N.C.) denounced the plan as a "blueprint for a police state" and called it a "repressive, nearsighted, intolerant, unfair, and vindictive legislative proposal."[66] Beyond the D.C. plan, the Nixon administration waged a high-visibility campaign against organized crime. While this program got headlines, it did not produce very significant results.

The public relations offensive on crime became a central concern in 1970, as revealed in March 10 notes taken by Haldeman of a meeting with the president, Attorney General John Mitchell, Ehrlichman, and Haldeman himself, held in the Executive Office Building. From the meeting Haldeman's notes read:

problem is not what we do—but the appearance
  not getting the points we should on crime
Agnew can lead on this should take strong
  position as crime fighter but can't do as
his views—must be Admin.
  should have Mitchell do like J. Edgar used
to no one else in Admin. can put this on play
  tough SOB role—as crime fighter
time to go on real crusade—not just do good
  put all PR effort we can into this area
need to make asset of Mitchell's toughness
  should do more on TV, speeches, etc.
VP & others should build up Mitchell *and* our
  appts—Attys, Judges, etc.

Nixon also stepped up the war on drugs. The Nixon administration felt that if the flow of narcotics into the United States could be decreased, street crime would also drop. Led by Bud Krogh, efforts increased in this area (e.g., Special Action Office for Drug Abuse Prevention, and the Office of Drug Abuse Law Enforcement), but in spite of the effort, the results were disappointing. While an internal memo written by Egil Krogh admitted that "nothing really was accomplished,"[67] it did generate a great deal of favorable publicity for the administration. The pattern of devising policies for their favorable press as a way to boost the image of Nixon as tough on crime replaced substantive policy as a means of reducing crime.

The politics of Nixon's crime policy, like the policy itself, became an attempt to make it appear as if Nixon was trying to act, trying to move, but was frustrated by the Democrats who controlled Congress. An internal memo by Egil Krogh written in July of 1970, entitled "Crime Control and Law Enforcement, Current Status: Political Position for the 1970 Elections," stated that "the Administration position in the crime field depends on our ability to shift blame for crime bills inaction to Congress."[68] This policy failed when the Congress, afraid of appearing soft on crime, passed Nixon's bill.

There was only limited success on the policy front, so the administration pursued extensive efforts on the political front, which reflected the recognition by the administration that there wasn't a great deal it could do about crime. It was a local issue, and the federal government, short of giving money and aid, was severely limited in what it could accomplish. This led Nixon to rely on dramatic gestures and symbolic leadership in the crime area. Nixon would talk tough, make dramatic speeches, propose strict legislation, primarily for the impact or symbolic power it could achieve. As Edward Jay Epstein notes: "In retrospect the 'law and order' campaign seemed to have had a much more marked effect on public opinion than on crime in America. It etched on the public consciousness the image of an unmerciful 'law and order' administration."[69]

Despite the campaign rhetoric, Nixon never developed a thought-out, coherent anticrime program. In part because there was little the federal government could do in the area, in part because Nixon quickly became distracted by other issues, symbol replaced substance in the crime area. The politics of crime took precedence over the policy, as evidenced in notes taken by Bob Haldeman on July 13, 1970, of a meeting in which the president orders: "Mitchell—no prosecutions whatever re Mafia for any Italians until Nov." Law and order was a theme used to give the appearance of toughness, but there was no sustained attempt to put meat onto the bones of a legitimate anticrime program.

Nixon and the Environment

Environmental protection was not a major issue in the 1968 campaign. But soon after taking office, Nixon found himself pressured from all sides on the environment. Significant movement had developed around environmental issues, and on April 22, 1970, the nation celebrated Earth Day, a massive outpouring of support for environmental protection. The public very quickly recognized the hazards to the environment and overwhelmingly supported increased protections and greater federal regulations and spending.

But industry, always a backer of Nixon and the Republican party, urged restraint. Industry spokesmen began to portray environmentalists as hysterical radicals who wanted to bring the nation to its knees. In general, American business downplayed the environmental risks and suggested that business be allowed to clean up the environment on its own, without more government regulations.

Richard Nixon was caught in the middle. The problem, he knew, was real. But the solutions were costly, both financially and politically. After early efforts to deal with environmental issues, the Nixon administration began to back into a pattern of bold rhetoric and mild actions. As the public, Congress, and environmental groups became activated, Nixon attempted to talk tough but water down congressional efforts to impose stricter, costlier restrictions on industry.

On signing the National Environmental Policy Act (NEPA), Richard Nixon said that "the 1970s absolutely must be the years when America pays its debt to the past by reclaiming the purity of its air, its waters, and our living environment. It is literally now or never." But such bold rhetoric was not to be translated into policy, and when speaking to the Detroit Economic Club on September 23, 1971, Nixon assured the auto industry that he would not allow environmental concern "to be used sometimes falsely and sometimes in a demagogic way basically to destroy the system."

In his 1970 State of the Union address, Nixon created the impression that his administration would lead the way in an environmental movement that would redress the imbalances and clean up the pollution that had been threatening the nation. But when it came time to translate words into action, the administration practice was to downgrade the environmental threat and attempt to weaken environmental legislation while talking tough and taking credit for legislation that the administration often fought against.

The Democrats in Congress were proposing a series of strict and costly bills on the environment, and industry was fighting hard to reduce environmental regulations. Nixon was caught in the middle and attempted to chart a moderate course. In the end Nixon's efforts on the environment were moderate but positive.

On May 29, 1969, Richard Nixon formed a cabinet committee, the Environmental Quality Council, headed by Dr. Lee DuBridge. This group was to advise Nixon on environmental policy. But Nixon soon became dissatisfied and put John Ehrlichman in charge. Ehrlichman, a former land-use lawyer in Seattle, had some knowledge of environmental issues and, along with Egil Krogh, got the ball rolling within the administration. They in turn gave John C. Whitaker the task of shepherding environmental policy for the president.

Whitaker, heading an environmental task force (which was replaced by Nixon's Council on Environmental Quality), gave the president a sixty-five-page outline of recommendations that Nixon read over Thanksgiving of 1969 at Key Biscayne. This report was to serve as the basis of Nixon's February 1970 environmental message to Congress. There was intense internal squabbling over the report as several cabinet officials wanted their pet projects put in or taken out. Whitaker called the report's recommendations "modest" but felt that they were a step in the right direction.[70]

Within the White House there was a confusing tug-of-war going on over who should and would control environmental policy. Walter Hickel, secretary of the interior, who was out of favor with Nixon, did a great deal to make the environment a prominent issue, but the president did not respect the counsel Hickel gave and kept him out of the inner circle. Russell Train, head of the Council of Environmental Quality, was a forceful spokesman for the environment, but he too failed to get close to the president. William Ruckelshaus, head of the Environmental Protection Agency, was a moderate on the issue and did not exert forceful leadership on behalf of the environment. Commerce secretary Maurice Stans turned out to be the in-house advocate for industry, repeatedly counseling the president to be careful of the environmental "extremists." (In fact, it was Stans who led the fight to weaken clean air and water regulations promoted by William Ruckelshaus.) Stans was joined by Peter Flanagan in defense of industry, and the battle for the mind of Richard Nixon was on.

By 1971, after much confusion, industry had won the day. Hickel was fired and replaced by Rogers Morton, who was more friendly to industry. Russell Train was neutralized, and by summer of 1971, the president attached a message to the Council of Environmental Quality's Second Annual Report that stated that "it is simplistic to seek ecological perfection at the cost of bankrupting the very tax-paying enterprises which must pay for the social advances the nation seeks." Industry had won! From the early days, when it appeared Nixon wanted to strike a balance between the demands of the environmental movement and the demands of business, to 1971, Nixon's policy shifted. He moved farther and farther away from the environmental side, and closer and closer to industry.[71]

During the Nixon years several things happened to the environmental field that are of importance. The environmental movement, assisted by Congress, and sometimes with the help of, other times in spite of, the president, created the Council of Environmental Quality and the Environmental Protection Agency, passed clear air and water legislation, and pushed the nation ahead in the environmental area.

Nixon's record on the environment is mixed. Nixon himself appointed the Council of Environmental Quality, created the National Oceanic and Atmospheric Administration, and early in his presidency advocated stronger environmental protection laws. But as time went by he was won over by industry, and the administration sought to water down the environmental bills before the Congress. Toward the end of his presidency Nixon actively worked against the environmental laws by impounding money earmarked for environmental protection.

The journey of Richard Nixon from being a mild advocate of environmental protection, to being mildly pro-industry, to being actively pro-industry reflects a process that was matched in a variety of other domestic areas. As time went on, several factors coalesced to lead a retreat on environmental issues: Nixon's darker side began to dominate the policy agenda, the interplay of other actors and institutions pulled the administration back, and in the end, Nixon retreated.

On other major domestic issues, Nixon's policies fluctuated dramatically. On women's rights, the president has a very mixed record. He supported but did not work for the Equal Rights Amendment. He appointed women to some fairly high posts, but no woman was in his inner circle. He appointed a task force on women's rights and all but ignored its recommendations. His promotion of affirmative action for women in civil service (April 1971) was a major step forward for women's rights, but the president succeeded in diluting the Equal Opportunity Act of 1972 in Congress. He fought against liberalization of abortion laws. On education, Nixon cut higher education funds, then impounded further funds. In housing, Nixon orchestrated a policy of retrenchment by ordering a moratorium on the federal housing subsidy program, and did a retreat on federal low-cost housing. His farm policy marked a retreat from price supports, and he attempted to kill the school milk program.

As the Democrats in Congress refused to pass most of Nixon's domestic legislative proposals, Nixon went more and more to an administrative strategy for achieving his goals.[72] Using administrative discretion and impoundment of funds to achieve policy goals, Nixon attempted to bypass the Congress and act on his own independent authority.

While previous presidents defended impoundments on the basis of their power as commander in chief or by citing the Anti-Deficiency Act, Nixon went much further and boldly declared, "The constitutional right for a President of the United States to impound funds and that is not to spend money, when the spending of money would mean either increasing prices or increasing taxes for all the people, that right is absolutely clear."[73]

This gave Nixon almost unlimited power to control spending and turned upside down the roles of Congress and the president. As Larry Berman noted, "In this interpretation, the president faithfully executes the laws of Congress by not spending money that Congress appropriates."[74]

Nixon impounded nearly $20 billion in congressionally authorized funds. Sometimes, as was the case in Nixon's impoundment of money for a waste treatment program, the money was impounded in spite of the Congress overriding Nixon's veto of the authorizing legislation. The Supreme Court and several lower courts found Nixon's use of impoundment illegal (see: *Train v. City of New York*)[75] and ordered the release of the impounded funds. Nixon's efforts led to the Congress passing the Budget and Impoundment Control Act in 1974, an effort to codify and control the impoundment of funds by presidents. Nixon often used impoundment for purely political purposes, as notes of a White House meeting taken on May 13, 1971, by Bob Haldeman suggest. Haldeman's notes have the president saying:

re impounded funds

> release any that will get <u>us</u> a vote
>
> <u>don't</u> <u>worry</u> <u>about</u> <u>ultimate</u> <u>deficit</u>
>
> (underlining in original).

Did Nixon keep his campaign promises in the domestic field? Did he follow through on the promises he made when he asked the citizens for their votes? Political scientist Jeff Fishel did an extensive comparative study, entitled *Presidents and Promises*,[76] which attempted to measure the frequency with which presidents kept their campaign promises. Fishel's findings indicate that of all presidents from Kennedy to Reagan, Nixon did not fare well. In efforts to develop legislation or advance executive orders that were fully or partially consistent with campaign promises, Kennedy led all modern presidents (67 percent), followed by Carter (65 percent), Johnson (63 percent), Nixon (60 percent), and Reagan (53 percent). Of the campaign promises dependent upon congressional approval, Johnson led (89 percent), followed by Kennedy (81 percent), Carter (71 percent), Reagan (68 percent), and Nixon (61 percent).[77] (Nixon, however, faced a Congress with Democratic majorities in both houses.)

What then can be said of Richard Nixon's domestic policies? In spite of a good deal of backtracking, in spite of Nixon's efforts late in his administration to retreat from the Great Society, President Nixon did preside over an expansion of the welfare state, and for the first time in the postwar era, domestic spending exceeded military spending. He proposed a guaranteed income for all Americans, and achieved revenue sharing. During his presidency the Environmental Protection Agency and the Occupational Safety and Health Administration were formed, more money went to supporting the arts and humanities, food-stamp money was increased, funds for the needy and handicapped were increased, indexing of Social Security took place, the Legal Services Corporation was established, and efforts to create the Federal Energy Administration got under way.

Nixon first used a competitive process for dealing with domestic affairs. While this was highly dynamic and idea-oriented, it was also time-consuming and didn't fit comfortably with Nixon's preferred operating style. He moved to a more formalistic, hierarchical Domestic Council, which the president preferred. This system was not as dynamic but was more organized. The result of this process shift was a policy shift. Nixon almost immediately moved toward more conventional, more traditional approaches in domestic policy.

Given Nixon's sporadic interest in domestic affairs, his poor timing, his squandering of political resources, and given his slow start and the limited level of opportunity he had in the domestic area, it is not surprising that his accomplishments were so limited. But a persistent question remains: was Nixon a liberal or conservative in domestic policy? He was a conservative in a liberal era, facing a liberal Congress and a public still loyal (though not as loyal) to the Great Society. But beyond liberal or conservative, Nixon was a pragmatist. His policy about-faces on welfare, U.S.-Soviet and U.S.-Chinese relations, and wage and price controls reflect not so much a staunch conservative as someone who surveys the political landscape and acts accordingly. David Abrahamsen writes that "Nixon had no ideological core; in both his personal and political life he had no guiding principles, no genuine ideals."

While Nixon did sponsor (early in the first term) legislation that could be called liberal (e.g., FAP), and while the welfare state did expand on his watch, Nixon's instincts, constituency, and most of his domestic policies were conservative. Notes taken by Bob Haldeman of a June 2, 1971, meeting with the president reflect this. Haldeman's notes read:

We're screwing up (unintelligible) many things
    have to be tougher on domestic
    P is *not* lib—is conserv—
    all our programs are wrong—
    gain nothing plus wrong for country—

Though Nixon was not a classic or extreme conservative, the main thrust of his domestic policies was indeed to the political right. The White House notes of John Ehrlichman are replete with orders from the president to cut or eliminate Great Society programs. Nixon wanted to eliminate the Job Corps (Ehrlichman's notes: "[President] wants Schultz to get *rid* of Job Corps"); cut Head Start (Ehrlichman's notes: "May be too late to abolish" . . . "no increases"); eliminate Vista (Ehrlichman's notes: "Vista—no good"); eliminate the Office of Economic Opportunity (Ehrlichman's notes: "See what we said in campaign re OEO—*no increases*"); and he wanted to cut back the Peace Corps. Further, Nixon vetoed legislation that would have increased federal funding of day care, declared a moratorium on new federal commitments to subsidized housing, impounded billions of dollars in social welfare spending (e.g., education and health), and by the second term, opposed expansion of welfare spending. While Nixon was no doctrinaire conservative, his policies did lean to the political right.

NOTES

1. Michael A. Genovese, "The Presidency in an Age of Decline" (Paper presented at the Western Political Science Association annual meeting, Salt Lake City, Utah, March 1989).

2. James E. Andersen, "Managing the Economy" (Paper delivered at the American Political Science Association annual meeting, August 1980).

3. Richard Rose, "Governments against Sub-government," in Richard Rose and Ezra Suleiman (eds.), *Presidents and Prime Ministers* (Washington, D.C.: American Enterprise Institute, 1980).

4. Michael A. Genovese, "The Presidency and Styles of Economic Management," *Congress and the Presidency* (Autumn 1987), pp. 151–167.

5. Herbert Stein, *Presidential Economics* (New York: Touchstone, 1984).

6. Genovese, "The Presidency and Styles."

7. Safire, *Before the Fall*, Chap. 4; and Klein, *Making It Perfectly Clear*, p. 353.

8. Dent, *The Prodigal South Returns to Power*, p. 272.

9. Genovese, "The Presidency and Styles."

10. Roger L. Miller and Raburn M. Williams, *The New Economics of Richard Nixon* (New York: Harper's Magazine Press, 1972).

11. Joan Spero, *The Politics of International Economic Relations* (New York: St. Martin's, 1985), pp. 109–112.

12. Stein, *Presidential Economics*, p. 190.

13. Stein, *Presidential Economics*, pp. 135–138.

14. Ehrlichman, *Witness to Power*, p. 90.

15. Edward R. Tufte, *Political Control of the Economy* (Princeton, N.J.: Princeton University Press, 1978).

16. Nixon, *RN*, p. 518.

17. Nixon, *RN*, pp. 518–520.

18. Events described are taken from H. R. Haldeman's notes from the meetings.

19. Nixon, *RN*, p. 521.

20. Leonard Silk, *Nixonomics* (New York: Praeger, 1973).

21. Kim McQuaid, *Big Business and Presidential Power* (New York: Morrow, 1982), Chap. 8.

22. Harold Barger, *The Impossible Presidency* (Glenview, Ill.: Scott Foresman, 1984), p. 348.

23. Tufte, *Political Control of the Economy*.

24. In his memoirs, Nixon devotes less than 5 percent of the book to social or domestic policy issues.

25. Thompson, *The Nixon Presidency*, p. 104.

26. Ehrlichman, *Witness to Power*.

27. George Reedy, *Twilight of the Presidency* (New York: World, 1970).

28. Nathan, *The Plot That Failed*.

29. Raymond Price, *With Nixon* (New York: Viking, 1977), p. 64.

30. John H. Kessel, *The Domestic Presidency* (North Scituate, Mass.: Duxbury Press, 1975).

31. Ehrlichman, *Witness to Power*.

32. Light, *The President's Agenda*.

33. A. James Reichley, *Conservatives in an Age of Change* (Washington, D.C.: Brookings Institute, 1981). Also see: Timothy Conlan, *New Federalism: Intergovernmental Reform from Nixon to Reagan* (Washington, D.C.: Brookings Institute, 1988).

34. Nathan, *The Plot That Failed*.

35. Daniel P. Moynihan, *The Politics of a Guaranteed Income: The Nixon Administration and the Family Assistance Plan* (New York: Random House, 1973), p. 164.

36. Kessel, *The Domestic Presidency*, pp. 103–108.

37. David Caputo, "Richard M. Nixon, General Revenue Sharing and American Federalism," *Annals of the American Academy of Political and Social Science*, no. 372 (1975), pp. 5–9.

38. Vincent J. Burke and Vee Burke, *Nixon's Good Deed: Welfare Reform* (New York: Columbia University Press, 1974).

39. Barbara Kellerman, "Richard Nixon and the Family Assistance Plan," in Kellerman, *The Political Presidency* (New York: Oxford University Press, 1984).

40. Moynihan, *The Politics of a Guaranteed Income*.

41. Nixon, *RN*, p. 435.

42. McClosky, *Truth and Untruth*, pp. 152–153.

43. Nixon, *RN*, p. 435.

44. Harry S. Dent, *The Prodigal South Returns to Power* (New York: Wiley, 1978), pp. 136–139.

45. Hugh Davis Graham, "The Incoherence of Civil Rights Policy in the Nixon Administration" (Paper presented at Hofstra University conference on the Nixon presidency, November 1987), pp. 5–6.

46. Eleanor Holmes Norton, "Civil Rights: Working Backward," in Alan Gartner et al., *What Nixon Is Doing to Us* (New York: Harper & Row, 1973), p. 204.

47. Ehrlichman, *Witness to Power*, p. 223.

48. Quoted in Evans and Novak, *Nixon in the White House*, p. 134.

49. Leon Panetta and Peter Gall, *Bring Us Together* (Philadelphia: Lippincott, 1971), p. 165.

50. Reg Murphy and Hal Gulliver, *The Southern Strategy* (New York: Scribner's, 1971), pp. 2–3.

51. Memo quoted in Nixon, *RN*, p. 437. See also, Wills, *Nixon Agonistes*, pp. 471–494.

52. Barbara Luck Graham and Augustus Jones, "A Comparative Analysis of Executive Branch Influence on Civil Rights Policy" (Paper presented at the 1988 annual meeting of American Political Science Association, Washington, D.C., 1988). See especially references to *Alexander v. Holmes County Board of Education*, 396 U.S. 19 (1969).

53. Evans and Novak, *Nixon in the White House*, p. 150.

54. McClosky, *Truth and Untruth*, pp. 152–172.

55. Panetta and Gall, *Bring Us Together*.

56. Quoted in McClosky, *Truth and Untruth*, p. 158.

57. McClosky, *Truth and Untruth*, p. 160.

58. Presidential Message sent to Congress, March 17, 1972.

59. Murphy and Gulliver, *The Southern Strategy*, pp. 66–67.

60. Arthur I. Blaustein and Geoffrey Faux, *The Star-Spangled Hustle: The Story of a Nixon Promise* (Garden City, N.Y.: Anchor, 1972), p. 130.

61. Blaustein and Faux, *The Star-Spangled Hustle*, pp. 212–213.

62. Quoted in McClosky, *Truth and Untruth*, p. 151.

63. Graham, "The Incoherence of Civil Rights Policy," p. 18.

64. Reichley, *Conservatives in an Age of Change*, p. 204.

65. Norton, "Civil Rights: Working Backward," p. 215.

66. Sam Ervin, *Preserving the Constitution* (Charlottesville, Va.: The Michie Co., 1984), p. 277. See also: Thomas E. Cronin, Tania Z. Cronin, and Michael F. Mila-

kovich, *U.S. v. Crime in the Streets* (Bloomington: Indiana University Press, 1981), ch. 6–7.

67. Edward Jay Epstein, "The Krogh File—the Politics of 'Law and Order,' " *Public Interest* (Spring 1975), pp. 99–124.

68. Epstein, "The Krogh File—the Politics of 'Law and Order,' " p. 101.

69. Epstein, "The Krogh File—the Politics of 'Law and Order,' " p. 121.

70. John C. Whitaker, *Striking a Balance: Environment and Natural Resources Policy in the Nixon-Ford Years* (Washington, D.C.: American Enterprise Institute, 1976).

71. James Rathlesberger, ed., *Nixon and the Environment: The Politics of Devastation* (New York: Village Voice Books, 1972).

72. Richard Nathan, *The Plot That Failed.*

73. Allen Schick, *Congress and Money,* (Washington, D.C.: Brookings Institution, 1980), pp. 44–47.

74. Larry Berman, *The New American Presidency,* (Boston: Little, Brown, 1987), p. 85.

75. Michael A. Genovese, *The Supreme Court, the Constitution, and Presidential Power* (Lanham, MD: University Press of America, 1980), pp. 166–67, 222–35.

76. Jeff Fishel, *Presidents and Promises* (Washington, D.C.: CQ Press, 1985).

77. Fishel, *Presidents and Promises,* pp. 39, 90, 42.

4

Foreign and Defense Policy

America is a large, friendly dog in a very small room. Every time it wags its tail, it knocks over a chair.

Arnold Toynbee

INTRODUCTION

The Nixon years were a time of dramatic, bold, innovative approaches and overtures in the field of foreign affairs. They were years when the conventional wisdom was challenged and when conventional solutions were eschewed for a new strategic approach to foreign policy.

It was a new era that brought about an opening of relations with China, détente with the Soviet Union, a strategic arms limitation agreement with the Soviets, a period when America's military involvement in Vietnam and Southeast Asia was expanded, then ended, and when a relatively new approach and strategic orientation was introduced into American foreign policy thinking.

Under Richard Nixon and Henry Kissinger, a reexamination and reorientation of the United States' role in the world produced a different vision. There was a recognition of the changing role and capacity of the United States, a recognition of the limits of power and an attempt to match America's strategic vision with its capabilities. Had it not been for Watergate and the self-destruction of the Nixon presidency, there is no telling how the early stages of the Nixon foreign policy revolution might have eventually changed the United States and the world.

In collaboration with Henry Kissinger, Nixon promoted a far-reaching, forward-thinking approach to foreign policy that had a momentous impact on the world. As Crabb and Malcahy note: "Nixon's impact was felt in several ways—in the theoretical framework which his foreign policy initiatives were cast (the so-called 'Nixon Doctrine'), in the specific content of the policies themselves (for example, in détente and the normalization of Sino-American relations), and in the process by which these policies were formulated, especially regarding the role of Kissinger and his White House staff." [1]

As was the case in so many other aspects of his presidency, the foreign policy Nixon promoted was full of irony and contradiction. How could one of America's premier anticommunists open the door to China and promote détente and arms control with the Soviet Union? How could the politician who kept promoting an "America first" attitude negotiate a deal with the Soviets that effectively granted them equality with the United States? How could a president who promoted American hegemony relinquish economic power and prestige? What accounts for these metamorphoses?

Even Nixon's most skeptical critics recognized that his truly was a different and more sophisticated approach to American foreign policy. Nixon had a vision—a new strategic orientation—and attempted to take the steps necessary to bring this vision to fruition. One could argue that Nixon's vision was inappropriate or incorrect, but that Nixon had an integrated, complex, and sophisticated worldview seems clear. What that vision was, on what ideas it was based, and how it fit into the realities of world politics is the subject of this chapter.

To understand the Nixon foreign policy, we will examine the roots of Nixon's views on international politics, the issues and world he faced as president, the level of opportunity to maneuver in foreign affairs, and Nixon's grand design for reshaping the world. We will also look at process issues in foreign policy management and selected case studies—Vietnam, U.S.-Soviet relations, and so forth—and finally, evaluate Nixon as a foreign policy president.

Nixon, from his earliest days in politics, was an internationalist. Building his early career on a staunch anticommunism, Nixon was also a consistent supporter of a broad international role for the United States and was an early supporter of the Marshall Plan. He always displayed a deep interest in foreign affairs, but Nixon's foreign policy education did not take place at the feet of the Eastern establishment but was for the most part self-taught.

By the time he rose to the presidency, Nixon had a clearer idea of where he wanted to lead the nation in foreign affairs than in any other area of policy. Nixon felt that the domestic arena could be run by a cabinet, but only the president could lead in foreign policy. Foreign policy was Richard Nixon's domain, the area in which he felt most comfortable, most in command. And Nixon had some definite ideas as to where he wanted to lead the nation, the Western alliance, and the world.

Nixon came to office at a time when U.S. foreign policy was ripe for reexamination and redesign. The post–World War II consensus that had guided the nation for twenty-five years was collapsing, and America's role in the world was going through some convulsive changes. By the late 1960s, an era of U.S. foreign policy was coming to an end.

For the two decades immediately following World War II, the United States served as the dominant, hegemonic power of the West. It was the beginning, many thought, of the "American Century," a period in which the United States would provide a benevolent leadership and direction. After the decline of Great Britain in the postwar era, the United States inherited hegemonic control, which placed it in the lead of the Western alliance. This role was challenged by the Soviet Union in the years following World War II, but by virtue of vast military and economic superiority, the United States was able to spread its protective umbrella over Western Europe and eventually over much of the rest of the world.

Empire was costly, but in the 1940s and 1950s, the United States had the resources to spend. We could afford a costly web of military ventures and economic aid to contain the expansion of communism. But, by the 1960s, America's role was proving to be a burden—a burden costly in lives and resources. By the time Richard Nixon took office, the American empire was in the early stages of decline. The American Century lasted barely thirty years.

The combination of the war in Vietnam and the multiple changes taking place in the world left the United States without an acceptable road map for the future. Strategically the United States was adrift and floundering. The war in Vietnam deeply divided the American people. Relations with the Soviet Union were in flux. As the Soviets approached strategic parity with the United States, questions of how best to deal with the Russians proved confounding. Should the United States continue containment? Search for coexistence? Move to confrontation? These questions confused us at a time when a further Cold War belief was being dispelled. The assumption regarding monolithic communism was being reexamined because of deep rifts between the Soviet Union and China, and trouble with the communist satellite states. Tight bipolarity seemed to be giving way to a kind of global pluralism, and the United States was without a plan for dealing with these changes.

Other changes in the world proved equally perplexing to American policy makers. Members of the Western alliance, which the United States had dominated for twenty years, were showing signs of independence as the European economies rebounded from the war with vigor and the American economic dominance was being threatened. The third world and less-developed nations were becoming more independent and nationalistic, the oil-producing nations were forming a cartel, and the post–World War II world seemed to be going through changes that the United States could neither control nor comprehend.

The United States' leadership was being challenged. Twenty years after World War II, the world was a vastly different place. Europe and Japan were thriving, even challenging the United States for economic dominance. The Soviet Union had approached military parity with the United States, and the limits on power became more and more pronounced, brought home by the inability to win the war in Vietnam. America's vulnerability, as evidenced by our dependence on foreign oil, rose as America's power declined relative to the rest of the world. The postwar world America had done so much to create was beginning to close in on the U.S.

The world was becoming more complex, more interdependent, and less amenable to U.S. dominance. This, at a time when America's resources—military and economic—were declining relative to the demands placed upon the United States. Nothing seemed to be working as it should. The center did not hold. Amidst this policy incoherence and confusion, the time was right for a fundamental change in American foreign policy. But how could the United States respond to this changing world?

Vietnam was the most glaring symptom of America's relative decline. Henry Kissinger recognized this "new" relationship when he wrote in his memoirs:

We were in a period of painful adjustment to a profound transformation of global politics; we were being forced to come to grips with the tension between our history and our new necessities. For two centuries America's participation in the world seemed to oscillate between over-involvement and withdrawal, between expecting too much of our power and being ashamed of it, between optimistic exuberance and frustration with the ambiguities of an imperfect world. I was convinced that the deepest cause of our national unease was the realization—as yet dimly perceived—that we were becoming like other nations in the need to recognize that our power, while vast, had limits. Our resources were no longer infinite in relation to our problems; instead we had to set priorities, both intellectual and material.[2]

Gone were the days when American power was so preponderate that the United States seemed capable of solving problems by simply overwhelming them with America's superior economic or military power. The world had changed; the United States had changed. Not having overwhelming resource superiority, the United States had to be more careful, more selective. But how does one adjust responsibilities to match declining power while still exerting hegemonic control? Could the United States make this transition, or was decline inevitable?

In effect, Nixon and Kissinger attempted to deal with relative decline by developing slightly more modest international commitments (the Nixon Doctrine), developing a new international system (Nixon's ambitious "Grand Design" or "structure of peace"), exerting dramatic international leadership (shuttle diplomacy), and refashioning our relations with the two most powerful communist nations (détente with the Soviet Union, opening the door to China). Osgood called the new strategy "military retrenchment without political disengagement,"[3] and Nixon attempted to deal with the overextension of American power, not by retreating from American globalism, but in an orderly, controlled readjustment, a measured devolution. In light of the new limits on America's capabilities and resources, the United States could not bear the international burdens it had accumulated for the last twenty-five years.[4] Now, the United States would have to settle for less, set clearer priorities, redefine the national interest. But could this be done while still playing the role of hegemon? Could the United States continue to lead but at a reduced cost?

Could Nixon orchestrate this dramatic transformation of policy? Could the U.S. maintain its preeminent position at reduced costs by instituting a new structure of relationships in the international system?

THE GRAND DESIGN: NIXON'S STRUCTURE OF WORLD PEACE

Facing a changing world, with limited power, Richard Nixon nonetheless attempted to refashion and redesign America's foreign policy and the international context in which the United States operated. It was a new, global vision that surprised many, and one which promised a "new structure of world peace." When he entered office, Richard Nixon was cognizant of the increasing demands placed on American world leadership, but was also sensitive to the limited—even declining—resources available for his use. More of the same would not be sufficient; things had to be different.

Nixon had a vision of a "structure of world peace" that was bold, innovative, at times confusing, and always controversial. In attempting to build this new structure of peace, Nixon and Kissinger overly relied on secrecy and personal diplomacy, failing to institutionalize their vision, but their daring approach brought some extraordinary breakthroughs and stunning policy reversals. Some commentators argue that the Nixon/Kissinger design was a well thought-out, integrated vision of the future. Others claim that it was merely a dramatic set of improvised acts glossed over by the patina of overall planning. Whatever the truth, no one could dispute the frenetic, action-oriented pace at which Nixon and Kissinger sought to refashion America's foreign policy.[5] The cumulative impact of Nixon's foreign policy innovations was, in Tad Szulc's words, to set the United States "on a wholly new course in its foreign relations. These policies, irreversible in many areas, marked a most momentous shift in America's posture toward allies and adversaries alike. Basic relationships were realigned, and progressively, new truths were recognized." He adds that "during the Nixon years the United States went a long distance to adjust its position to the global realities of the 1970s."[6]

Nixon, with his global vision, helped reshape the world and America's place in it. After years of study, continuous world travel, and a fascination with how the world worked, and could work, Richard Nixon entered the presidency with a clear view of the problem faced by America and some definite views as to what needed to be done. Nixon saw a deterioration of America's world power and was faced with the dilemma of what to do: rebuild power to the point of renewed American hegemony, or readjust America's goals to match its declining resources while simultaneously restructuring the international arena to build a more stable structure of power. Nixon chose the latter.

Nixon wanted to redesign the international arena, not merely respond to it. His strategic sense sought to exploit opportunities that existed in the changes taking place in the world. He took the world as it existed and attempted to redefine the bonds that linked nations together. In global terms, Nixon attempted to adapt American power to the end of an era of U.S. dominance. As America's military and economic resources were found insufficient to maintain hegemony, U.S. interests and goals had to be readjusted. Nixon was farsighted enough to recognize these momentous global changes and attempt to deal with them *before* they reached crisis proportions. It was an effort to protect America's role in the world by redefining it.

Nixon saw a changing world, and he had an astute grasp of how the changing geopolitical situation impacted upon America's opportunities to further its interests. He understood how the many parts of the foreign policy puzzle fit together to form an interconnected whole, and how the United States could pursue a cohesive foreign policy, and not simply react to the world. It was an ambitious vision.

A stable structure based on order had to be built. But how, in an international system based on force, where anarchy and power determined behavior, does a nation seek to curb aggression, create a stable set of restraints to deter potential aggressors, and still protect its interests?[7]

The "structure of peace," Nixon noted in 1972, "has to be built in such a way that all those who might be tempted to destroy it will instead have a stake in preserving it." Nixon's structure of peace tried to draw the different nations of the world into the status quo, sought to give them a definite stake in preserving that status quo, and to build disincentives into the process.

But how does one achieve this in the midst of a system of international anarchy? The first step was to restore America's power. But Nixon knew that efforts to revive hegemony were doomed to fail. American power should find a new role that would restore, albeit in different form, some of the status America was losing.

Only a radical reorientation of American foreign policy would do. Thus, Nixon and Kissinger departed dramatically from the approach of previous administrations in dealing with foreign affairs. They de-emphasized the role of ideology in foreign affairs, employed "creative diplomacy" as opposed to routine diplomacy, ambitiously sought to create a new international system, centralized policy-making authority in their hands (thus overpersonalizing and deinstitutionalizing policy), placed a great emphasis on secrecy and drama, and attempted to restore American power and prestige.

To Nixon, restoring America's power involved several interconnected steps. First, military strength had to be maintained. This did not mean military superiority, but as Eisenhower sought, military *sufficiency*. Second, the war in Vietnam had to be ended, and ended with honor. The United States could not appear to be abandoning an ally to communism. Third, the Western alliance had to be rejuvenated. This was especially true regarding Western Europe. Fourth, American self-confidence had to be restored. The Vietnam War had shattered America's optimism, and psychologically, the United States needed a renewed self-confidence. Fifth, American leadership had to resume a world leadership role. Preoccupation with Vietnam had diverted America's attention from the rest of the world, and the American president had to resume the role of leader of the Western world. Sixth, a new approach to diplomacy and international relations toward the communist world was needed. This would eventually lead to détente with the Soviet Union and improved relations with China. Seventh, America had to reorder its foreign policy priorities. No longer could the United States afford to squander its limited resources in both manpower and materials on peripheral concerns. This would lead to what became known as the Nixon Doctrine. Finally, a new international order had to be constructed that would promote stability. This was the basis of Nixon's ambitious goal of building a new structure of world peace.

Of course, sufficiency was ambiguous enough to mean different things to different people, and Nixon's description of the purpose of the U.S. nuclear strategy as "the maintenance of forces adequate to prevent us and our allies from being coerced" did not clear up the confusion. Nixon sought a defense strategy that did not limit U.S. options to doing nothing *or* fighting a nuclear war.

In line with the new grand design, tactics and strategies had to be developed to bring America's resources in line with its new commitments. This called for a new defense strategy. As the Soviet Union approached parity in strategic arms with the United States, Nixon moved from a defense strategy based on nuclear superiority, to an acceptance of "mutually assured destruction" (MAD) and an arms position of "sufficiency." MAD implied that no degree of superiority could protect a nation in a nuclear exchange, so, to accept MAD meant that superiority had no tangible meaning. What nuclear arsenal was appropriate? Taking a page from Ike, Nixon's approach was that sufficiency was all that is necessary. As Nixon pointed out, "this is an absolute point below which our security forces must never be allowed to go. That is the level of sufficiency."[8]

Sufficiency was to be the justification for the reduced worldwide role that the Nixon Doctrine envisioned. Nixon would give greater responsibility to allies, boost certain regional powers, and not play as aggressive a role as the world's policeman. It was not meant to be a retreat from commitments, only a reordering or balancing of resources to commitments. Thus, the defense budget was stabilized, the draft was eliminated, an all-volunteer army was instituted, and arms control proceeded. Ultimately, Nixon was able to announce that the McNamara goal of preparing to fight "two and a half wars" (which was never practical) would be scaled down to a "one-and-a-half-war" strategy.

An integral part of the restoration and reordering of American power was the Nixon Doctrine. First discussed by the president on July 23, 1969, in Guam, the Nixon Doctrine rested on the belief that a type of retrenchment was necessary to allow for the more efficient and effective use of American power. It was also a tacit recognition that the United States could no longer, and would no longer, serve as policeman of the Western alliance. In this sense it recognized the limits of American power.

Animated by both the lessons of Vietnam and a recognition that the United States had to alter its international commitments to match its resources and capabilities, the Nixon Doctrine stressed three points: (1) the United States would keep all its treaty commitments; (2) the United States would continue to provide a nuclear umbrella to the Allies; and (3) in conventional or guerrilla conflicts, the United States would provide military assistance and economic aid to countries wishing to defend themselves, but American manpower would not be furnished. This was not, Nixon insisted, an early step in America's withdrawal from the world, but was one which, according to Nixon, was the only practical way for the United States to stay involved in the world.[9]

This more-limited American role was described by Nixon in the First Annual Report to the Congress on United States Foreign Policy for the 1970s, submitted on February 18, 1970. In this document the president wrote of the Nixon Doctrine: "Its central thesis is that the United States will participate in the defense and development of allies and friends, but that America cannot—and will not—conceive *all* the plans, design *all* the programs, execute *all* the decisions and undertake *all* the defense of the free nations of the world. We will help where it makes a real difference and is considered in our interest."

Nixon called for "a more responsible participation by our foreign friends in their own defense." In light of the lessons of Vietnam, Richard Nixon was calling for "a more balanced and realistic American role in the world," if "American commitments are to be sustained over the long pull."[10]

The Nixon Doctrine was part of the reordering of American power to fit the demands of a changing world. It sought to marshal America's resources so the structure of peace could be implemented. The Nixon Doctrine attempted this readjustment within the continued framework of containment. With power restored, Nixon could go about building his complex structure of peace. But could a nation, historically withdrawn from the complexity of world power politics and disillusioned by the divisive war in Vietnam, adapt its outlook and policies to the complexities of a changing international environment?

Eschewing what they saw as the misguided utopianism of *idealpolitik* (which in actuality was a straw man, never practiced by postwar presidents), Nixon and Kissinger embraced a concept of *realpolitik* in which the world was not seen as divided between good guys and bad guys, but was seen as consisting of a variety of powers, all claiming a stake in the world. Downplaying the internal politics of the various nations, Nixon assumed that all states had certain legitimate interests that they had a right to pursue—within limits. Gone were the excesses of ideological anticommunism that obscured rather than enlightened international debate. Nixon was not blind to the role of ideology in international affairs, but he downplayed its significance. Relations between nations were seen not so much in terms of ideology as in terms of power. Nixon sought a realpolitik which redefined American interests in a more limited, or realistic way. Nixon sought a negotiated balance of power, not the role of policeman of the world; he sought stability, not reform of the world. Gone were Kennedy's calls to pay "any price" or bear "any burden" to promote liberty. Nixon and Kissinger became the masters of realpolitik in, as Stephen Ambrose notes, "both its subtle and brutal forms."

Interests, not morality, and *power*, not ideology, were to guide American action. This was not an immoral view of world politics, but an amoral view. Nations used their power to achieve what they felt was in their interests. A stable international order had to be built in which the major powers saw it within their interests to protect the status quo, to act with restraint and within limits. This did not mean that the United States would completely abandon its idealistic values, but it did mean that values and morals would play a distinctly secondary role in foreign policy formulation. While America was used to thinking internationally in moral terms, Nixon sought to direct policy based on power. Using power as a conceptual base, Nixon and Kissinger began to implement their idea for a structure of peace.

Nixon and Kissinger sought that elusive system of international stability. But they were aware that stability could be achieved only if a framework of rules and guidelines could be established which the major powers found it in their interests to maintain. But what of the "revolutionary states," those states that did not accept, in rough form, the status quo? How could they be brought into the system, or isolated by the other powers?

To bring revolutionary states into the framework, it had to be made clear that they had a significant stake in preserving the status quo. Thus, the development of an international framework and the establishment of mutually binding links to that framework was the goal of the Nixon-Kissinger foreign policy.

What was the Nixon-Kissinger design for a new structure of world peace? Since Nixon and Kissinger never clearly defined or articulated the vision but only revealed it piecemeal, more in action than in words, commentators are split, interpreting the Nixon framework as one of two classical models from international relations: *balance-of-power* politics, or the *concert of Europe* model. The Nixon-Kissinger approach seemed to contain elements of both approaches, applied to the twentieth-century world.

The Nixon-Kissinger structure of world peace is of mixed intellectual pedigree. The union of balance-of-power politics (Nixon) to the nineteenth-century concert of Europe (Kissinger) model, served as the basis of the new effort at world peace. Since the Nixon-Kissinger structure was never fully articulated or codified, this not completely compatible heritage never became a significant problem for Nixon.[11]

The president was a believer in classical balance-of-power politics. In January of 1972 he stated that "the only time in the history of the world that we have had any extended period of peace is when there has been a balance of power. . . . I think it will be a safer world and a better world if we can have a strong, healthy United States, Europe, Soviet Union, China, Japan, each balancing the other, not playing one against the other, an even balance."

In general, balance of power signifies the maintenance of a power equilibrium. This approximate power equilibrium further requires a domestic environment in which the leader is relatively free from the pressures of internal constraints of public opinion, clearly understood "rules" among the participating countries, and a common understanding that the balance ought to be maintained and protected. Since the international environment did not seem especially amenable to classical balance-of-power politics, critics of the president faulted him for strategic shortsightedness.[12]

Henry Kissinger's contribution to the structure of peace came from the lessons of history that he studied and wrote about throughout his academic career. In essence, Kissinger's blueprint for the future came from lessons of the past applied to the present. Most important among the lessons of the past was the concert of Europe of the early nineteenth century.[13] Kissinger, a student of Metternich, envisioned a modern concert of the world's powers. The concert system of Europe existed roughly from 1815 and the Congress of Vienna, to 1848, the beginnings of Europe's revolutionary upheavals. During this period there were a series of congresses that established a pattern of interaction, a mode of diplomatic relations and a more or less agreed-upon set of rules and norms to guide behavior. All parties felt a stake in the status quo and had certain rights and duties to maintain. Threats to the system were met in concert by the other participating states, and changes in the system required a consensus among the various states. It was a modern variation of this system that Henry Kissinger envisioned for the United States and the world.

The stability of such a system is based on the shared belief that the system is legitimate and worth maintaining. It is not a static system, but is a dynamic one that accepts change within certain limits. Kissinger attempted to incorporate the principles of this concert in American foreign policy. Kissinger recognized that the concert consisted of rules, and that states would still pursue self-interest. But it would be a self-interest sought within defined boundaries. Kissinger, like Metternich, believed that order was a necessary precondition of peace, that stability was predicated on legitimacy, and that self-interest had to be accommodated within a dynamic equilibrium based on an approximate balance of power.

The Nixon-Kissinger goal of "linkage" fit into the concert approach to international relations.[14] Linkage saw an interconnectedness (link) in world events. Behavior of the great powers on any one issue could not be seen in isolation from other issues. The interlocking webs of behavior were an attempt to promote adherence to the rules necessary for establishing and maintaining concert. It was a system of carrots and sticks, rewards and punishments. Proper behavior resulted in carrots, improper behavior in sticks. This was to be the enforcement mechanism of the new concert. International behavior was part of an organic whole; violations in any area were a threat to the concert, so linkages were a necessary means of enforcing proper behavior.

Nixon's goal of linkage can be seen in early efforts to get the Soviet Union to pressure North Vietnam to accept the American peace proposal. If the Soviets would help the United States in Vietnam, the United States might be willing to put pressure on Israel to grant more concessions to Moscow's Arab friends. While this has the sound of big powers using little powers as pawns, it was a means to complement the concert Nixon and Kissinger sought.

But were the Soviets, not to mention the other great powers, really interested in reviving such a concert? There is no indication that Moscow was interested in playing the game by the rules Nixon sought to establish. While they did negotiate several agreements that Nixon chose to interpret as a victory for concert, the Soviets saw these agreements in another light entirely.

This not completely compatible marriage between Nixon's interest in a balance of power and Kissinger's interest in a revived concert of Europe was not wholly integrated or mutually reinforcing. It was a complex, multidimensional view of international politics that required American leaders to look at foreign policy-making more as a game of chess than checkers. Each move was designed to affect the next several moves. Each step was connected to others.

While the structure of peace led to détente with the Soviet Union and improved relations with China, the overall approach was never sufficiently conceptualized or articulated. In this sense, the nations that were to be a part of the new concert were not fully aware of the Nixon-Kissinger design and could thus never fully buy into the process, assuming they wanted to. Nixon and Kissinger attempted to establish the process by which the structure could exist and then let the concert develop around those agreements. But the overall plan remained vague. The overall rationale was never clearly articulated, either at home or abroad.

The structure of peace promoted by the Nixon administration had three fundamental problems. The first related to *purpose*. The second concerned *process*. The third hinged on *design*. Since the new structure of peace did not appeal to a higher moral goal, its purpose left critics wondering if Nixon was abandoning the higher goals traditionally associated with American foreign policy— human rights, freedom, and so forth. Nixon was not unconcerned about purpose, but his overarching goal was stability. He sought to create a world where a form of international pluralism could exist; one where the threat of nuclear war was reduced; one where our differences did not lead to hostility. The internal policies of nations, though important, were not primary to the Nixon structure.

Process problems loomed larger, as it is not clear that the prospective participants in the process were even interested in reviving a concert system. And even if they were, could a worldwide concert led by the major powers really be fit into the twentieth century?[15]

The design problems further complicated matters. The concert assumed some continuity of leadership, something which the United States and other countries could not guarantee. Also, the concert assumed that leaders understood, accepted, and were willing to act upon the needs of the concert system, regardless of public opinion or other competing demands. Certainly in the West, and somewhat so in the Soviet Union, public opinion had become a powerful force to empower and inhibit leaders. Thus, Western leaders did not have a free hand in concert.

The lynchpin of the process was, of course, the Soviet Union. Nixon and Kissinger believed that by setting up new rules of the game and by establishing a system of inducements, the United States could get the Soviets to play our game by our rules. But there is no indication that the Soviet Union was interested in a new game or new rules. American efforts to draw the Soviets into the new system were mixed.

In point of fact, Nixon may have had an exaggerated impression of just how much power and influence the Soviet Union had over world events. Repeatedly Nixon tried to get the Soviets to exert pressure on North Vietnam to get its ally to accept a negotiated settlement of the war. But the Soviets most likely did not have the power to do so. Nixon continued to look at the concert in superpower, East-West terms, at the exclusion of other powers. This conceptual and operational flaw further inhibited the chances for the concert's success.

The way Nixon and Kissinger operationalized the concert design further inhibited chances for success. They overly personalized their system. Not trusting others to implement the design, Nixon and Kissinger jealously guarded and personalized their roles in the process. Kissinger's dramatic personal style of diplomacy, "shuttle diplomacy," produced some striking successes, but this style was dependent upon Kissinger playing the Lone Ranger role—a role in which he relished.

There was nothing to keep the concert alive after Nixon and Kissinger passed from the scene. The process was never institutionalized. Nixon and Kissinger so distrusted the bureaucracy that the process was never institutionalized. With the concert dependent on the personalities of the chief participants, it is no surprise that as Watergate brought on the collapse of Richard Nixon, it also spelled doom for the structure of peace. There was simply no one left behind with a stake in picking up the mantle of the Nixon-Kissinger design. Since the public, the Congress, and the bureaucracy were never brought into the process, they had no vested interest in fighting to keep the structure alive.

Finally, just how realistic was the Nixon-Kissinger effort at practicing realpolitik? While the practice of downplaying the importance of ideology allowed the administration to pursue a more positive—and realistic—policy toward the Soviet Union and China, the overall approach to world politics—the Grand Design—may not have been a realistic goal. It was an ambitious plan, perhaps too ambitious. In any event, even if the goal of reviving a concert-type system was not unrealistic, the problems in execution caused many to doubt the overall schematic design of the new structure of world peace.

There is understandably some disagreement as to just how deliberate and self-conscious the implementation of the Grand Design may have been. Was the Grand Design an intellectual construct Nixon had envisioned prior to, or early in, his term as president? Did he take that framework and then seek to take the steps necessary for its full implementation? Or, did the Grand Design emerge piecemeal, as the result of accumulated small steps (e.g., Nixon Doctrine, linkage, détente)? Did the pieces come first and the framework later as an afterthought? Were the pieces developed to fit the mold, or vice versa?

THE MANAGEMENT OF FOREIGN POLICY

Richard Nixon was determined to run foreign policy personally, from the White House. Deeply suspicious of the State Department and bureaucracy in general, Nixon excluded his own secretary of state, William Rogers, from several major decisions and even excluded Rogers from the first meeting with Anatoly Dobrynin, the Soviet ambassador. Richard Nixon, along with national security advisor Henry Kissinger, would be in control of foreign policy. It would be a highly personalized process, with powers jealously guarded by Nixon and Kissinger. This overpersonalization and deinstitutionalization of foreign policy decision making was a distinctive characteristic of the Nixon style in foreign affairs.

That Nixon and Kissinger got together in the first place is something of a surprise. Kissinger worked for Nixon's rival, New York governor Nelson Rockefeller, and Nixon, who so valued loyalty, was not expected to choose someone from the enemy camp. Nixon himself described the choice of Kissinger, a man he hardly knew, as "uncharacteristically impulsive." But Nixon was so secure in his knowledge of foreign affairs, unlike other areas, that he did not feel threatened by having an outsider fill so vital a role. Nixon and Kissinger seemed to be on the same wavelength from the beginning. Kissinger set out to construct a power base at the National Security Council (NSC) which was unequalled by any other national security adviser, and which eclipsed the power of the secretaries of state and defense. Kissinger became Nixon's "foreign minister."

Richard V. Allen was the foreign policy coordinator during the campaign. A firm anticommunist, Allen at thirty-two was too young to serve in a top foreign policy position such as national security adviser, but he promoted Henry A. Kissinger for the job. Kissinger, a Harvard professor of government, had written extensively about international politics. Nixon admired his work and during the transition invited Kissinger to the Pierre Hotel to discuss the new administration's foreign policy. Several days after their meeting, Richard Nixon offered Kissinger the job of national security adviser. On December 2, 1968, Kissinger's appointment was announced to the press, at which time Nixon remarked that Kissinger was "keenly aware" of the necessity not to set himself up as a wall between the president and the secretary of state or the secretary of defense. But this was not to be.

Immediately after his appointment Kissinger began a thorough reevaluation of American foreign policy. This study was coordinated by Kissinger and his staff, and all contents of the reports had to be approved by Kissinger himself. The reports that the Kissinger team prepared gave area and subject reviews of U.S. foreign relations and problems along with policy options for the president's review. Known as National Security Policy Memoranda (NSPM), these reports were the basis of many of the early Nixon administration policies.

Also in the transition period, the seeds of discontent and disagreement began to sprout between Kissinger and Nixon's appointees as secretary of state, William Rogers, and secretary of defense, Melvin Laird. It would be the flamboyant Kissinger against the bureaucratic Rogers and Laird. Given the president's style and tastes, Kissinger was bound to win.[16]

Nixon and Kissinger had a complex, symbiotic relationship. Before the meeting at the Pierre Hotel, Nixon had only met Kissinger once, but he admired Kissinger's book *Nuclear Weapons and Foreign Policy*. As Nixon noted in his memoirs, "I had a strong intuition about Henry Kissinger," and he added, "I decided on the spot that he should be my National Security Adviser." It was a strange match, this small-town, Quaker politician and the German Jewish academic and refugee from Nazi Germany, but it was a match that worked to the advantage of both parties.[17] As Nixon had done with Mitchell, and was yet to do with Moynihan, then Connally, the president "fell in love" with Henry Kissinger. In a variety of ways (intellectually, conceptually, emotionally, and psychologically), Kissinger quickly rose to the apex of foreign policy power, the prime currency of his power being his rock-solid relationship with the president.

Kissinger's style and intellect were an excellent complement for the new president. Kissinger would be the front man for Nixon, his voice in shuttle diplomacy, his alter ego in world politics. Kissinger, like Nixon, had a flair for the dramatic and liked acting alone. As he told Italian journalist Oriana Fallaci:

I've always acted alone. Americans admire that enormously. Americans admire cowboys leading the caravan alone astride his horse, the cowboy entering a village or city alone on his horse. Without even a pistol, maybe, because he doesn't go in for shooting. He acts, that's all: aiming at the right spot at the right time. A Wild West tale, if you like. . . . This romantic, surprising character suits me, because being alone has always been part of my style, or of my technique if you prefer. Independence too. Yes, that's very important to me and in me.[18]

Kissinger was flamboyant where Nixon was staid, the darling of the press where Nixon was their adversary, a master at bureaucratic manipulation where Nixon was aloof. They were perfectly matched. Kissinger set out to redefine the role and power of the National Security Council. Although not officially a member of the NSC, the assistant to the president for national security affairs began to use his position to remold the NSC and make it the preeminent place for foreign policy making in the Nixon presidency. Kissinger recruited an outstanding staff and quickly began to centralize power in his hands at the expense of State and Defense. When Nixon signed National Security Decision Memorandum 2 (NSDM2) on January 19, 1969, Henry Kissinger was in the foreign policy driver's seat. The NSC would run foreign policy, or more accurately, Nixon and Kissinger would centralize and control foreign policy. The bureaucracies of State and Defense would take a decidedly back seat.

Since Nixon held an antipathy toward the U.S. career foreign service professionals, it is not surprising that the State and Defense departments played a secondary role in foreign policy making during the Nixon years. Kissinger noted this when he wrote that Nixon "had very little confidence in the State Department. Its personnel had no loyalty to him; the Foreign Service had disdained him as vice-president and ignored him the moment he was out of office. He was determined to run foreign policy from the White House."[19]

Kissinger was Nixon's chief coordinator of foreign policy, and he set up a highly structured, White House–centered system. Information and planning went through Kissinger, who chaired the newly formed National Security Council Review Group. Nixon was dependent on Kissinger, but it was so by choice. As the first term progressed, Kissinger assumed greater power, even assuming operational responsibilities. He became Nixon's alter ego and personal envoy, soaring above the bureaucracy and becoming the superstar of the Nixon foreign policy apparatus.

Nixon had appointed foreign policy novice William P. Rogers as secretary of state. While Rogers and Nixon had a good personal relationship based on their professional contacts when Rogers was attorney general during the Eisenhower administration, this relationship proved insufficient to salvage Rogers and State during the Nixon presidency. Melvin Laird, the secretary of defense, fared no better. While Laird contributed greatly in the early months of the administration (he is generally credited with developing the broad contours of the Nixon Doctrine and Vietnamization), Laird's role declined as Kissinger's rose.

The most obvious and heated internal foreign policy dispute revolved around the Kissinger-Rogers feud. Not only did Nixon permit this feud to take place, he often sought to play Kissinger off against Rogers. Nixon once told William Safire, "Henry thinks Bill [Rogers] isn't very deep and Bill thinks Henry is power crazy. In a sense they are both right."[20]

Rogers was often kept in the dark about the most important decisions and actions taken by the president. In effect, Henry Kissinger had arranged to go around Rogers, and he set up a "rival State Department" in the White House.[21] The National Security Council preempted many of the powers and functions of the State Department during the Nixon years. It was the primary vehicle for foreign policy advice, articulation, and implementation. The NSC grew from a staff of ten during the early Truman years, to one hundred fifty during the Nixon presidency. It was considered a first-rate staff of highly competent foreign policy analysts. Nixon and Kissinger developed a NSC system similar to that used by Eisenhower, but less formal and modified in three ways. First, they made greater use of policy option papers for presidential use; second, the NSC staff was given broader powers and responsibilities; and third, a series of interdepartmental committees, chaired by Kissinger, provided some coordination of policy.

Overall, the system was designed to centralize power in the White House and give Nixon the opportunity to "create" his new structure of world peace, rather than simply react to events. But Nixon and Kissinger kept tight control at all times, creating a highly personalized institutional system. The "Lone Ranger" image was one that Kissinger relished, and Nixon loved the dramatic big-play style of personal diplomacy. Overall, the Nixon-Kissinger NSC system and style (it is impossible to divorce one from the other) can be characterized as highly personalized, closed, antibureaucratic, highly centralized, and disdainful of the foreign policy establishment.[22]

NSC meetings were generally not open policy discussions. The meetings, attended by the president, vice president, secretaries of state and defense, director of the Office of Emergency Preparedness, Kissinger, other invited officials, and—at Nixon's insistence—the attorney general, were not debating sessions. The president would normally open the meetings and lead the discussion. Kissinger's role was to summarize reports and participate in discussions. But this process was a formality. Rarely were decisions made at NSC meetings. The real policy debate/discussion took place at the daily meetings between Kissinger and Nixon in the Oval Office or in Nixon's Executive Building office. Decisions were made by Nixon, alone, often at night, and reflected the president's preferred style of decision making: he would be alone, reflect upon the information and options before him, and decide, then the decision would be relayed to Kissinger. This self-imposed isolation was Nixon's preferred decision-making style in foreign policy as well as all other policy areas.

As Watergate began to consume the Nixon presidency, the president believed he needed a stronger, even more centralized voice in foreign affairs. Since Nixon was distracted by Watergate, his solution was to make Kissinger both national security adviser and secretary of state. In August, 1973, Kissinger became secretary of state, and because of Nixon's preoccupation with Watergate, became the central foreign policy figure for the United States.

With so much power consolidated in the hands of so few, it is sometimes difficult to determine who was the *real* architect of foreign policy in the Nixon years, the president or Henry Kissinger. While the two benefited from each other's intellect and abilities, it is clear that Richard Nixon was the central figure in developing foreign policy during his presidency. Elliot Richardson, who served Nixon as both secretary of state *and* defense, has said, "I can attest, without any equivocation at all, that Nixon was the architect of the Nixon foreign policy." Many of Nixon's eventual foreign policy moves were hinted at in his pre-presidential writings and conversations with friends and officials. While

Kissinger helped fine-tune the Nixon strategic approach, it was Nixon who constructed and formulated his own foreign policy.[23]

How well did this system serve Nixon, and the nation? Nixon wanted a closed system that he—with Kissinger—could dominate. This gave him a tremendous amount of control over the foreign policy process, but in overpersonalizing foreign affairs, Nixon cut out the bureaucracy and by not bringing the State Department into his orbit, doomed any hope of long-term success. When Watergate forced Nixon to resign, there was no institutional need to continue with Nixon's policies. The Nixon-Kissinger policy was dependent upon their presence.

The overpersonalization of foreign policy not only excluded the bureaucracy but also excluded the public. Thus, while the public could applaud Nixon's dramatic achievements, no ongoing consensus was ever developed in support of the policies. Nixon treated foreign affairs as an elite domain, and he didn't bother to persuade the public of the appropriateness of his policies. So, when Nixon was gone, support for his policies evaporated. In short, Nixon didn't leave very much behind. He took much of his foreign policy with him when he left office. While U.S.-Chinese relations progressed, in many areas, Nixon's foreign policy moves proved transitory. This gives pause to those who claim that Nixon was a foreign policy "genius." After all, few of his policies outlasted his tenure in office, and while he was conceptually brilliant in foreign affairs, his execution was often shortsighted and flawed.

VIETNAM AS ROOT OF ALL EVIL

Nixon's Grand Design for peace was a complex, ambitious formula that required short-term and long-term plans. Premier among the short-term plans was ending the long, internally divisive war in Vietnam. If a structure of peace was to be built, the first step had to be extricating the United States from Vietnam—with honor! But for Nixon and Kissinger, Vietnam became a personal test of will as well as a test of America's credibility. As such, getting out of Vietnam proved to be a more difficult problem than either Nixon or Kissinger had anticipated. "Peace with honor" proved elusive. For Nixon's Grand Design to work, American power had to remain a credible force in world politics. Thus, Vietnam became an important—and annoying—piece in the larger puzzle Nixon and Kissinger were trying to put together.

In the pre-inaugural days at the Pierre Hotel, Nixon reviewed a variety of options on Vietnam. A military victory could be attained with massive, perhaps even nuclear, bombing, but the domestic and international reaction to such a move was unacceptable. A conventional escalation, it was felt, could take at least six months—too long a time, Nixon felt. A negotiated settlement was the only viable option. What about simply pulling out? This option defeated Nixon's larger plans, as it would have abandoned the South to communism, put into doubt America's word and power, and undermined Nixon's own credibility. "Ending the war honorably is essential for the peace of the world. Any other solution may unloose forces that would complicate the prospects of international order," said Henry Kissinger.

Vietnam was the war Nixon inherited. At the time Nixon came to the presidency, the war was stalemated, with no victory in sight. It caused a tremendous amount of domestic strife—protest marches, civil disobedience, the emergence of a counterculture among the young. The war was tearing the nation apart. It was a long, slow, almost unnoticed process that got the United States into Vietnam. Decisions by Eisenhower, Kennedy, and Johnson brought the United States further and further into a Southeast Asian land war that, in 1969, many saw as unwinnable.

The United States had approximately 520,000 troops in Vietnam when Nixon took office. In fact, a great deal of Nixon's success in the 1968 election was attributed to the failure of Lyndon Johnson and the Democrats to win or effectively prosecute the war in Vietnam. This left the Democrats deeply divided and allowed candidate Nixon to talk of a plan to end the war. Nixon was, in 1968, the peace candidate.

In point of fact, Nixon's "plan" to end the war wasn't much of a plan at all. His early efforts at a negotiated compromise didn't work, as North Vietnam wanted victory, not compromise. On July 15 of his first year in office, Nixon secretly sent what he thought to be a rather conciliatory letter to President Ho Chi Minh of North Vietnam in which Nixon called for serious negotiations and an early end to the war.

At the same time Henry Kissinger, without the knowledge of Secretary of State Rogers, was setting up secret negotiations with North Vietnamese officials (Xuan Thay). But Ho Chi Minh's reply to Nixon's letter, signed on August 25, a week before Ho's death, was disappointing to the president. Ho, in effect, blamed the United States for the war, reiterated his determination to settle for nothing less than full independence of his country, and called for a complete U.S. withdrawal from Vietnam.

Nixon and Kissinger did not take Ho's letter very seriously. They viewed it as Ho's effort to take a tough initial bargaining position from which he would eventually back away. Nixon and Kissinger were convinced that, faced with the superiority of America's military might, the North could not long withstand an American military barrage. The assumptions of Nixon and Kissinger about Vietnam, almost always wrong, reflect both the historically developed "arrogance of American power" and a profound ignorance of Vietnam and its history. Incorrect or faulty assumptions got us into Vietnam, they would also keep us there.

The Kissinger-Xuan Thay meeting, held in Paris on August 4, led nowhere. With Ho's death later that month, the president hoped for a more-encouraging response to his overtures. Again he was to be disappointed. If the North would not cooperate, if talking wouldn't work, perhaps increased military pressure would. Nixon would not pull out, he would plunge forward.

In an effort to get the Paris negotiations going, Nixon decided to play a carrot-and-stick game with the North Vietnamese. He would offer them incentives to negotiate and disincentives to stalling. The incentive was a phased withdrawal of American combat troops from Vietnam. The stick was simultaneous bombing of the North, the invasion of Cambodia, invasion of Laos, and an intensified pressure on North Vietnam's allies, China and the Soviet Union, to pressure the North to end the war.

Nixon's letter to Ho didn't work. Secret negotiations by Kissinger didn't work. Would military pressure? Nixon was convinced it would. We could, Nixon felt, bomb the North Vietnamese to the bargaining table.

Nixon was determined. In notes Bob Haldeman took at a September 27, 1969, meeting with the president, Nixon says:

VN—enemy
   Misjudges 2 things
     -the time—has 3 yrs + 9 mo
     -the man—won't be 1st P to lose war[24]

Nixon's confidence was displayed in notes taken by John Ehrlichman at an October 7, 1969, meeting with the president in which Ehrlichman wrote that the president says, "War will be behind us by the end of next year . . . or at least see the end of the Tunnel."[25] Nixon fell into the same trap Lyndon Johnson had fallen into. He simply couldn't believe that the North Vietnamese would or could hold out much longer. After all, the United States was the mightiest military power in the world. How could a tiny, backward (in Nixon's view) country stand up to U.S. power?

So the United States would continue to prosecute the war in Vietnam. Nixon would not be the first president to lose a war! To Nixon, it was a matter of both individual and national pride. He would not be defeated, and the United States could not be defeated. Both personal and national credibility were at stake here.

But how long would it be before Vietnam became *his* war? And if it did, would Nixon be dragged down as Johnson was? As the "plan" to end the war evaporated, the protest movement accelerated. The marches became bigger, the crowds, more middle-class, and Nixon began to take it personally.

The chief goals of Nixon in Vietnam were to get out of Vietnam, preserve American honor, get the American prisoners of war home, and hopefully, give South Vietnam a chance for independence from the North. It was the last goal that proved to be America's undoing, because the North Vietnamese would not accept a divided nation. They wanted victory and were determined to achieve it regardless of cost.

But Nixon knew the war had to be ended and ended soon, lest he be dragged down by it. "I'm not going to end up like LBJ, holed up in the White House afraid to show my face on the street. I'm going to stop that war fast," he said.[26] Vietnam became *the* overriding issue of the first term. In effect, everything else—internationally and at home—was predicated on ending the war in Vietnam. But how?

In late January of 1969, Nixon decided that he could not simply pull out of Vietnam, but he couldn't continue to prosecute the war as Johnson had. He would execute a gradual withdrawal of American fighting forces—thereby diffusing the antiwar movement at home; he would seek a negotiated agreement with the North—something which allowed the United States to preserve its honor; and he would dramatically increase the bombing in Southeast Asia—thereby bombing the North into an agreement.

VIETNAMIZATION

The American troop pullout was part of what was called Vietnamization, a plan promoted by Secretary of Defense Melvin Laird that called for turning the war over to the South Vietnamese. Vietnamization fit into the Nixon Doctrine, and it was seen as a sign of good faith being sent to the North. But the North read this signal as a sign of weakness, and Nixon's announced troop withdrawal only strengthened the resolve of the North. Like his predecessors, Nixon had misunderstood and misread his opponents. The three-pronged strategy of Vietnamization (U.S. troop withdrawal), bombing increase, and negotiation was not to work.

It was hoped that Vietnamization would ease the pressure on the administration from congressional doves and the antiwar protesters, thus giving Nixon more time to pursue a negotiated settlement giving the United States "peace with honor." Nixon called on the "great silent majority" to support him in his efforts and called for national unity, saying in a November 3, 1969, speech: "Let us also be united against defeat. Because let us understand: North Vietnam cannot defeat or humiliate the United States. Only Americans can do that."

Vietnamization was doomed. There was no way that the South could assume fighting responsibility for the war. But Vietnamization had a strong domestic component, and Nixon hoped that announcements of troop pullouts would soften the antiwar criticism and allow the other parts of the Vietnam strategy to take effect. It allowed Nixon to simultaneously be the dove, with a troop pullout, and the hawk, with increased bombing. Vietnamization was only one element of the Nixon strategy, and it was in the other areas where Nixon hoped to make gains.

The negotiating strategy the United States pursued with the North was based entirely on the mistaken belief that the North Vietnamese were interested in— or were at least willing to consider—a negotiated compromise on the future of their nation. But the North wanted victory, not compromise, and when President Nixon announced the first troop withdrawals, the North was confident that it could outlast Nixon and win the ultimate victory.

They knew they could defeat a reconstructed South Vietnamese army and were confident that they could withstand increased levels of American bombing. In fact Nixon's massive bombing seemed only to strengthen the resolve of the North. Nixon, like Johnson before him, had misjudged his adversaries.

The administration had weakened its own bargaining position with the North by announcing unilateral troop withdrawals. Had it used the withdrawals as a bargaining chip, the North might have reacted differently, but now, everything was dependent upon the ability of the South to take up all the fighting. The North was confident it had little to fear.

The negotiations, held in Paris, produced a clear and unalterable position from the North: no end to the war until and unless the United States withdraws its troops and its support for the Thieu government of the South. While the North knew the United States had massive military superiority, Hanoi also knew that the United States had backed itself into a corner and felt that it, not the United States, was negotiating from a position of strength. In the first three years of the war, the North's terms were unacceptable to Nixon.

To force the North to the bargaining table and to a negotiated settlement, Nixon was prepared to expand the war into Cambodia and Laos and increase bombing of North Vietnam. One of the early options that was ruled out was to use tactical nuclear weapons against the North. But Nixon decided instead to order a massive bombing of the North and ultimately the mining of North Vietnam's ports as well as a naval blockade of the ports.

So, while American combat troops were being withdrawn, B-52s began massive bombings of the North. "I refuse to believe," Kissinger is reported to have said, "that a little fourth-rate power like North Vietnam doesn't have a breaking point."[27] The bombing targets included Hanoi and Haiphong, as well as other cities, main roads and passageways to the South around the Ho Chi Minh Trail, and the railroads linking the North to China. Between 1969 and early 1973, the United States dropped on Vietnam an average of a ton of bombs each minute. It would be what Nixon and Kissinger called "a savage blow." But in the end, it would not be enough.

Nixon hoped to strike fear in the hearts of the North Vietnamese. This was to be done by massive bombing and the "Madman Theory." Nixon told Bob Haldeman that he wanted the North Vietnamese to believe he might do *any-thing* to win the war, including possibly using nuclear weapons.[28]

THE WAR SPREADS: CAMBODIA AND BEYOND

In 1969, despite Nixon's repeated promises to wind down the war, the president ventured into an expansion of the war into Cambodia. Nixon widened the war by secretly bombing North Vietnamese based inside the neutral nation of Cambodia. In 1970, Nixon sent troops into Cambodia. It was, for Nixon, a tacit claim of war-making powers that suggested an expansive, even imperial, interpretation of presidential power. The secret war in Cambodia was truly a presidential war, conducted by the executive branch on its own, with no congressional approval or oversight, no public scrutiny, and no democratic controls. This was Nixon's war.

Nixon's goal in Cambodia was to disrupt enemy supply lines and attack the North Vietnamese in their "safe" havens inside of Cambodia. But to keep this mission secret, the military had to set up improvised command chains outside of normal military channels, file false reports, and create a duel reporting system.

After reviewing the military options in Southeast Asia, the president met on Sunday, March 16, 1970, with Secretary of State Rogers, Defense Secretary Laird, Henry Kissinger, and chairman of the Joint Chiefs, General Earle Wheeler. In his memoirs, the president recalls saying that the choice was either "to bomb or not to bomb," and that the only way to get the stalled negotiations untracked was to do something "they will understand": bomb.[29] But for the operation to be a success, the president felt that the bombing had to be kept secret.[30]

On March 18, 1969, the first B-52 raid against Cambodia took place.[31] Operation Menu, as it was called, the first phase of the bombing, lasted over fourteen months. In that period, B-52s flew 3,875 sorties into Cambodia and dropped 108,823 tons of bombs. After that, the operation became public knowledge as U.S. troops invaded Cambodia on April 30, 1970. Bombing missions continued into Cambodia until August 1973, when Congress forbade all such bombings. The total tonnage of bombs dropped on Cambodia in approximately four years was 540,000.[32]

The decision to expand the war in Cambodia from bombing raids to a land invasion was reached after extensive discussion within the administration. The policy alternatives—do nothing or invade Cambodia with American troops—were both fraught with problems. William Rogers and Melvin Laird spoke against the invasion, arguing that an invasion meant widening the war, incurring the wrath of Congress and the protest movement while promising only limited military gains. Rogers argued for having the South Vietnamese, not Americans, invade Cambodia. But the military argued that a full American troop commitment was necessary if the invasion hoped to be a success.

After over three hours of debate, the president went to his office in the Executive Office Building and on a yellow legal-size pad, wrote down the arguments for and against an American troop invasion. Nixon could not decide. Finally, he contacted Vietnam field commander General Creighton Abrams and asked for "the unvarnished truth." American troops were essential, Abrams replied. Nixon ordered the attack.[33]

On April 30, 1970, the president went on national television and shocked the nation with his announcement that he had ordered American troops into

Cambodia. "The time has come for action," the president said. This decision went to "the heart of the trouble." The president said he was outraged that the enemy had violated the neutrality of Cambodia by setting up sanctuaries there, and said that "American policy has been to scrupulously respect the neutrality of the Cambodian people." He continued by saying that "neither the United States nor South Vietnam has moved against these enemy sanctuaries, because we did not wish to violate the territory of a neutral nation."[34]

President Nixon went on to say that "we live in an age of anarchy both abroad and at home. We see mindless attacks on all the great institutions which have been created by free civilizations in the last five hundred years. Even here in the United States, great universities are being systematically destroyed." With so much in the balance, the president issued a warning. "If, when the chips are down the world's most powerful nation, the United States of America, acts like a pitiful, helpless giant, the forces of totalitarianism and anarchy will threaten free nations and free institutions throughout the world."

In that speech, the president said, "We will not be humiliated. We will not be defeated," and "it is not our power but our will and character that is being tested tonight . . . if we fail to meet the challenge, all other nations will be on notice that despite its overwhelming power, the United States, when real crisis comes, will be found wanting."

The overall military impact of the invasion of Cambodia was such that it damaged the communists, but not fatally. It did buy time for Nixon as he pursued Vietnamization, but since Vietnamization did not stand the test of time, such an expenditure of arms, men, and, at home, political capital, proved extremely damaging to the president.

Because of the Cambodian invasion, the war at home heated up beyond anything the president expected. The campuses immediately erupted. Nixon's comment about "bums blowing up campuses" was published and further fired up the already outraged protesters. Four hundred forty-eight colleges declared themselves "on strike." Many rioted. Police had to protect the White House from the over one hundred thousand protesters who converged on Washington.

The mood in the White House was tense. A siege mentality captured the president and his top aides. Then on May 4, tragedy struck. At an antiwar demonstration at Kent State University, in Ohio, National Guardsmen opened fire on a group of protesters and bystanders. Fifteen people were wounded; four were killed.

The biggest student strike in U.S. history followed. On May 9, over two hundred fifty thousand demonstrators descended on Washington, and across the country campuses shut down. Dr. Clark Kerr, who chaired a Carnegie Commission study on higher education, reported that 89 percent of all independent universities and 76 percent of all public universities held demonstrations.[35]

The president's response was brief and insensitive. In a statement read to the press by Ron Ziegler, the president said that "this should remind us all once again that when dissent turns to violence, it invites tragedy. It is my hope that this tragic and unfortunate incident will strengthen the determination of all the nation's campuses—administrators, faculty, and students alike—to stand firmly for the right which exists in this country of peaceful dissent and just as strongly against the resort to violence as a means of such expression."[36]

Less than two weeks later, two more students were killed at Jackson State College in Mississippi.

The public pressure on Nixon was enormous. The expanded war with only a marginal hope for an honorable settlement, domestic turmoil, dissension within his own administration, all ate at the president. Nixon seemed near the breaking point on May 8 when a series of bizarre incidents occurred. He spent nearly the entire evening and early morning on the telephone, calling officials, friends, relatives; some of them he called several times. (According to White House logs, the president called Bob Haldeman seven times, and Henry Kissinger eight times, the last call taking place at 3:38 A.M.) He wanted to know what they thought of him, how they viewed events of the past weeks. In all, Nixon made fifty-one calls the evening and morning of May 8–9.

The president had trouble sleeping that night, so just before 5:00 A.M. he ordered his limousine, and he and valet Manolo Sanchez drove to the Lincoln Memorial, where a group of antiwar protesters were camping out.

Upon arriving at the Lincoln Memorial, the president got out and began talking to them. Nixon defended the invasion of Cambodia, saying that he hoped it would bring a quicker end to the war. Then he began to reminisce about his youth, urged the young people to travel, and then he was gone. From there, Nixon ordered his driver to go to the Senate Building, where, upon finding the building locked, Nixon went to the House, where a custodian let the president in. Nixon went to the seat he had occupied as a congressman and told Manolo Sanchez to sit in the Speaker's chair and make a speech. Then, Nixon went to the Mayflower Hotel for breakfast, after which he returned to the White House at 7:30 A.M.[37] In the long run, the bombing and the invasion of Cambodia backfired on the president. A limited military success, the event sparked a storm of domestic protest, led to a major political setback as the Congress passed a resolution prohibiting funds from being used in Cambodia, and with the invasion, Vietnam became "Nixon's war."

The secret bombing of Cambodia set in motion a series of events that would lead the administration down a path of illegality and impropriety that culminated in Watergate and the resignation of a president.

THE WAR AT HOME

The domestic upheaval created by the war in Vietnam had a profound impact on the Nixon administration. As the war dragged on, the general public became increasingly dissatisfied with the way first Lyndon Johnson, then Richard Nixon were handling the war. Johnson was driven from office, declining to run for reelection in 1968 because of opposition to his Vietnam policies among the public. When Richard Nixon won the presidency as the "peace candidate" promising to end the war, hopes that his plan could quickly be implemented soon gave way to frustration and anger among the public, and as the war dragged on and on, the antiwar movement picked up numbers with each passing day.

Richard Nixon seemed to take the antiwar marches personally. Politically he knew that the growing antiwar movement was narrowing both his time and his options in Southeast Asia. But on a personal level Nixon felt a special uneasiness about the demonstrators. The opponents of the war seemed to tap something deep within Nixon, something dark and menacing. Nixon felt threatened by the protesters and would not, could not, sit idly by while the protesters dragged him down as they had done to his predecessor. Nixon was determined not to be their victim. He would act. But these acts were to plant seeds of illegal and immoral activities that would eventually lead to the president's downfall. The roots of Watergate can be traced to the war in Vietnam and Nixon's reaction to the war at home.

The antiwar movement started slowly, as did the war in Vietnam itself. But by 1966, marches, moratoriums, demonstrations, and isolated incidences of violence mounted. The United States had seemingly backed into a commitment in Vietnam that it found difficult to resolve, and by the mid 1960s, protest against that war escalated.

When Nixon became president, the demonstrations against the war were already large and frequent and growing increasingly menacing. Isolated incidences of violence sprang up, and levels of nonviolent civil disobedience increased. As Nixon expanded the war, he added fuel to the already heated fires of protest and with the extension of the war in Cambodia, stirred the embers of student protest to its hottest point.[38] Nixon saw the demonstrating not simply as a protest against the war, but as a fundamental threat to the ideas and values of America. He was convinced that the protest movement was financed from abroad, and Vice President Agnew said, referring to demonstrators, "I think a lot of them are connected with foreign powers" and have "received instructions from active Communist leaders of the world." Nixon asserted that in drastic times, drastic measures were called for. If the republic was in danger from the lawless demonstrators, then it was not only all right to go beyond the law to protect the republic, but it was Nixon's duty to do so. After all, reasoned Nixon, that is what Lincoln had done during the Civil War.

Vice President Agnew became the administration point man in its "war" against antiwar protesters. In May of 1969, Agnew said, "In my judgment, the war in Vietnam would be over today if we could simply stop the demonstrations in the streets of the United States." Later Agnew said that "a society which comes to fear its children is effete. A sniveling, hand-wringing power structure deserves the violent rebellion it encourages. If my generation doesn't stop cringing, yours will inherit a lawless society where emotion and muscle displace reason." Agnew promised that the Nixon administration would "separate them from our society with no more regret than we should feel over discarding rotten apples from a barrel." Since most of the vice president's speeches were approved by the White House, and since the president took a great deal of interest in Agnew's speeches, it is clear that the vice president was not speaking on his own, but with the blessing, and speechwriters, of the White House. Agnew was to Nixon what Nixon was to Eisenhower a decade earlier.

In August of 1967, the CIA set up the "Special Operations Group" (later called Operation CHAOS) to see if antiwar groups in the United States were financed by any foreign governments. The reports to President Johnson were all negative. When Nixon became president, he was shown the reports but did not believe them. On June 20, 1969, he ordered the CIA to do another study into the subject, and a report entitled "Foreign Communist Support to Revolutionary Protest Movements in the United States" again found no evidence of outside funding.

Nixon wanted more. On May 14, 1969, Attorney General Mitchell and CIA director Richard Helms met to discuss domestic intelligence gathering. Operation CHAOS expanded and was coordinated with Justice Department groups monitoring domestic disturbances. In July of that year, military intelligence groups were added. Also in July, White House aide Tom Huston instructed the IRS to harass "Ideological Organizations." In early 1969, a web of domestic intelligence operations, ordered by the White House, began to operate and grow.

A complex and elaborate series of domestic intelligence operations, directed against the peace movement, were organized by the Nixon White House. Nixon was determined not to be the victim of these protesters. He would be tough.

To successfully prosecute the war, Nixon needed a stable base of domestic support, which the antiwar movement was clearly undermining. Nixon could not accept this. So began a series of domestic activities aimed at stifling dissent and protest. It was the beginning of the end of the Nixon presidency. H. R. Haldeman wrote that "I firmly believe that without the Vietnam War there would have been no Watergate."[39]

PLUGGING LEAKS

The failure of the president's Vietnam policy to achieve its desired peace, the mounting pressure of domestic protest, the seeming disloyalty of some administration officials, Nixon's predisposition to see adversaries as enemies, and the leaks of information to the press all came together and helped create a siege mentality in the White House. A form of paranoia began to creep in and distort the judgment of administration officials.

One of the most serious irritants to Nixon and Kissinger was the profusion of information being leaked to the press. Both Nixon and Kissinger believed that some of the leaks endangered national security and undermined the administration's position. Consequently, the president and his national security adviser set out to plug the leaks.[40]

From the first months in office, top Nixon people were complaining of leaks, and the president himself was furious about them, repeatedly complaining to Bob Haldeman at their daily meetings. Nixon wrote in his memoirs that leaks started at the very beginning of his administration.[41] In an effort to stop the leaks, Nixon ordered investigations, interviews, lie detector tests, sworn affidavits, depositions, and finally, the administration engaged in wiretaps and break-ins. As the president wrote, "It was decided that when leaks occurred Kissinger would supply [FBI director] Hoover with the names of individuals who had had access to the leaked materials and whom he had any cause to suspect. I authorized Hoover to take the necessary steps—including wiretapping—to investigate leaks and find the leakers." And the president wanted "maximum secrecy on this wiretap project."[42]

THE WIRETAPS

The president's legitimate need to protect the privacy of executive branch information and Nixon's near paranoia about loyalty and secrecy led to acts of illegality. Real needs and false fears led to a series of warrantless wiretaps in 1969, which marked the beginning of the descent of the Nixon administration into the morass of Watergate.

Leaking information was an art deftly used by Nixon and especially Kissinger. At his first staff meeting in January of 1969, Kissinger declared, "If anybody leaks anything, I will do the leaking."[43]

In early May of 1969, in an article in the *New York Times*, William Beecher revealed the secret of the bombing of Cambodia. The revelation, according to William Safire, "drove Henry up his basement office wall."[44] Nixon and Kissinger were furious. Kissinger spoke to J. Edgar Hoover several times that day, insisting that the FBI find the source of the leak. According to a Hoover memorandum, the White House would "destroy whoever did this if we can find him, no matter where he is."[45]

Nixon and Kissinger were so outraged at the leak of information that after only three months in office, they took matters into their own hands and instituted a series of wiretaps aimed at discovering the source of the Beecher leak. The fact that so early in his first term the president had decided to bypass the FBI and act independent of the other agencies of government speaks volumes on Nixon's distrust of others—even the FBI.

The Beecher story was the immediate cause of Nixon and Kissinger's decision to begin a series of wiretaps that they believed were necessary for national security reasons. Newspaper reporters (e.g., Beecher), Nixon administration officials (e.g., NSC staffer Morton Halperin), and others (e.g., Defense Department aides) were tapped with the approval of the president. Kissinger and NSC aide Alexander Haig supplied the names of suspected leakers to the FBI and at least one of the taps (Halperin's) was installed before Attorney General Mitchell signed the authorization for the wiretap (the Halperin wiretap remained active for twenty-one months). The way the wiretaps were organized is explained by William Safire:

As it was explained to me later by an embarrassed and worried Kissinger and Haig, the tapping procedure was this: the President, FBI Director J. Edgar Hoover, and Kissinger discussed the need for wiretaps in April 1969. The arrangement was made for Kissinger to supply the names to the Director, the conduit being Al Haig to William Sullivan of the FBI. Hoover required that each authorization be signed by John Mitchell, which he thought would make the taps lawful (although the Supreme Court later decided that such taps were unlawful).[46]

Kissinger danced deftly around his own role in the ordering of wiretaps, but there can be no doubt of the central role he and the president played in this affair. All the participants were aware of the need to keep the wiretaps a secret, and each knew of the danger if the existence of the taps were revealed. In notes taken by Bob Haldeman of a 1969 meeting with the president, Ehrlichman, and Kissinger, Ehrlichman gives the following cautionary advice:

re taps—impt. for K. to get the files out of his office
    thru E & Mitchel find someone to read taps
        maybe use Huston etc. for this
work out a scheme—minimize what done thru Hoover
        esp. newsmen—shld be done outsider
K. shldn't be reading these.

Soon, other reporters were added to the list to be wiretapped (e.g., Hedrick Smith, Marvin Kalb, Joseph Kraft). All the taps were installed *without warrants.*[47] But afterwards, when the wiretaps were revealed, the president, Kissinger, and Haig had conflicting stories about who ordered what, and all had partial memory lapses concerning the events.

ALL FALL DOWN: THE HUSTON PLAN

The process of the Nixon administration's moral and legal deterioration from within took a foothold early in the first term. In his speech on the Cambodian invasions, the president spoke of being in the "age of anarchy," and Nixon was determined not to let the age get the best of him. Nixon wrote in his memoirs of 1970 at a time when the nation was faced with an "epidemic of unprecedented domestic terrorism," and of the "evolutionary cycle of violent dissent," of "highly organized and highly skilled revolutionaries dedicated to the violent destruction of our democratic system."[48] Thus, in June of 1970, the president ordered a reassessment of the government's domestic intelligence gathering capacity. Bob Haldeman assigned aide Tom Huston, a former defense intelligence officer, to oversee the project.

On June 5, 1970, CIA director Helms, FBI director Hoover, National Security Agency head Vice Admiral Noel Gayler, Defense Intelligence Agency head Lieutenant General Donald Bennett, Haldeman, Ehrlichman, and the president met to coordinate their activities against the domestic disturbances. After several subsequent meetings, the group (called the Intelligence Evaluation Committee) arrived at a plan, called the Huston plan.

This plan, which Sam Ervin later described as evidence of a "Gestapo mentality," called for opening of mail and tapping of telephones without warrants, breaking into homes and offices, and spying on student groups. Huston admitted to Nixon and the others that "covert [mail] coverage is illegal and there are serious risks involved," and that surreptitious entry "is clearly illegal; it amounts to burglary. It is also highly risky and could result in great embarrassment if exposed."[49]

On July 14, 1970, Bob Haldeman sent Huston a memo that read: "The recommendations you have proposed as a result of the review, have been approved by the President. He does not, however, want to follow the procedure you outlined on page four of your memorandum regarding implementation. He would prefer that the thing simply be put into motion on the basis of this approval."[50] The president approved the plan.

But it was not long before J. Edgar Hoover raised objections. "The risks are too great," Hoover told Nixon through Huston, "these folks are going to get the President into trouble." Nixon reluctantly withdrew his approval.

Nixon would defend his approval of the Huston Plan with an "everybody does it" defense.[51] In a response to a Senate interrogatory in 1976, Nixon said his approval was based on what previous administrations had done, and claimed inherent powers that were legal when the president acted for national security reasons.

While the Huston Plan died, the idea of developing an expanded domestic intelligence operation run out of the White House did not. Through the Justice Department and John Mitchell, a new Intelligence Evaluation Committee was formed, and through the CIA, domestic intelligence gathering, which is illegal under the CIA charter, expanded, in the form of Operation Chaos. The web of illegal activities was spreading. It would soon snare the very life of the administration. The Huston Plan was one of the early steps down a road leading to Watergate.

Monday Melee and Teamsters Thugs

As the antiwar demonstrations grew, a fortress was erected around the White House, and the administration felt besieged. In May of 1971, a demonstration was scheduled for Washington, D.C., with the ambitious goal of "stopping the government." The demonstration did succeed in stopping D.C. traffic and interfering with daily commuters as they tried to get to work, but by no means was the government shut down.

Initially the D.C. police acted with restraint and flexibility. But on instructions from the president, who was at the Western White House in San Clemente, Attorney General Mitchell was put in charge of dealing with the protesters. With the help of the National Guard, the army, and marines, the D.C. police conducted a massive and indiscriminate arrest operation. On Monday, May 3, 7,200 people—protesters as well as innocent bystanders, reporters, and people trying to get to work—were incarcerated, the most ever incarcerated in the United States in a single day. Thirteen thousand, four hundred people were arrested over a four-day period.

The jails could not accommodate so many people, and 1,700 were taken to a practice field around RFK Stadium, where they were locked up, few were read their rights or charged with any crime, normal arresting procedures were ignored, and some were kept locked up over twelve hours with no toilet facilities, unable to make any phone calls, and unable to contact lawyers. The inevitable consequence of these wholesale arrests and violations of civil liberties was that of the over thirteen thousand people who were incarcerated, all but about two dozen had their cases thrown out of court.

Nixon returned to the White House from San Clemente in the midst of the May Day demonstrations. Infuriated at the protesters, Nixon wanted a firmer, more-forceful response on the part of the government. On May 5, the demonstrators marched on the Capitol. Twelve hundred people were taken into custody. In the White House, Nixon and Haldeman discussed ways to deal with the protesters.

A tape recording of the May 5, 1971, conversation between Nixon and Haldeman reveals a bizarre and frightening discussion between the president and his chief of staff. Perhaps nowhere is the dark side of Nixon more clearly seen than in this tape. The president, angered by the activities of the antiwar protesters, endorsed a suggestion that "thugs" from the Teamsters' Union be used to attack demonstrators. According to the president, the Teamsters were to "go in and knock their heads off." "Sure," Haldeman replied, "murderers. Guys that really, you know, that's what they really do . . . it's the regular strikebusters-types and all that . . . and then they're gonna beat the [obscenity] out of some of these people. And, uh, and hope they really hurt 'em. You know . . . smash some noses."[52] The thought of the president of the United States demeaning his office by advocating that Teamsters thugs go after American citizens and "knock their heads off" is shocking. But this is not the first time the president discussed roughing up American citizens. On Air Force One, on a trip to California, Bob Haldeman's notes of a July 24, 1970, inflight meeting with the president contain the following note:

Get a goon squad to start roughing up demo's
VFW or Legion—no insults to P.
use hard hats

On May 26, Nixon met with a group of construction workers and longshore-men who had attacked some antiwar marchers in New York. The president told the group he found their actions "very meaningful." There is no evidence to suggest that the president or Haldeman directly ordered or encouraged these men to attack the marchers.

THE PENTAGON PAPERS

Slightly more than one month after the Mayday melee, another shock hit the administration: the publication of the Pentagon Papers. It led to an unprec-edented effort by the administration to exercise prior restraint and censorship against the press.

On June 13, 1971, the *New York Times* began to publish excerpts of a top-secret study of the origins and conduct of the war in Vietnam. The study was begun in 1967 by Secretary of Defense Robert McNamara and was given to the *Times* by Daniel Ellsberg, a former employee of McNamara who had be-come disillusioned with the war. Ellsberg made copies of the study while an employee of the Rand Corporation in California.

The study, a forty-seven-volume report entitled "History of U.S. Decision-Making Process on Vietnam Policy," became known as the Pentagon Papers. It included a detailed account of how President Johnson had misled the Con-gress and public about Vietnam. The Nixon administration, through the Jus-tice Department, got the Federal District Court for the Southern District of New York to issue a temporary injunction, ordering the *Times* to cease publi-cation of stories based on the Pentagon Papers on national security grounds.

But other papers also received copies of the Papers, and began to publish them. These newspapers were also ordered to cease publication. The case very quickly got to the Supreme Court, and on June 30, 1971, the Court ruled against the government, allowing publication of the Pentagon Papers.[53] The Court's vote was 6 to 3, and it rejected the administration's claim of an inher-ent power to prevent publication of material on national security grounds.[54] In the arguments of the Nixon administration, there developed an expansive no-tion of a powerful "national security state," with rights and powers which went far beyond the Constitution and laws. The sweeping claim of inherent powers and the covert "national security" apparatus set up by the Nixon administration distorted the impact of the Constitution and created the framework for an in-crease of presidential power, as well as the abuse of presidential power.

While the Pentagon Papers did not deal directly with the Nixon administra-tion, there were several concerns the president had about the publication of the Papers: institutional damage (need to protect the presidency, and keep se-crets, secret); partisan damage (the papers made the Democratic predecessors look bad); policy damage (the fear that the Nixon war effort might be hurt by the information); press damage (Nixon could use the case to make the press look like traitors); and legal damage (someone should be prosecuted for stealing the report and leaking it to the press). To indicate the importance of this case to the Nixon administration, there was serious consideration given to having the president himself argue the case before the Supreme Court. In the end, it was decided that this was too risky.

Nixon seemed most concerned with the damage publication of the report might do to his war efforts. He was concerned that publication of the Papers would undermine the whole Vietnam effort and give his critics new ammunition.[55]

Chuck Colson has called the events surrounding the Pentagon Papers issue "the beginning of the end." It was here that the administration really began to "cross the line."[56] Indeed, the events which followed release of the Pentagon Papers relate directly to the downfall of the Nixon presidency.

The administration went to court to try to halt publication of the Pentagon Papers. Simultaneously, a secret effort to discredit and defame Daniel Ellsberg was also going on. Chuck Colson, who pleaded guilty to obstructing justice in the Ellsberg trial, said on June 24, 1971: "The president on numerous occasions urged me to disseminate damaging information about Daniel Ellsberg, including information about Ellsberg's attorney and others with whom Ellsberg had been in contact."[57]

Nixon's urgings led Colson to contact his longtime friend Howard Hunt to discuss the possibility of "nailing Ellsberg." Colson taped his conversation with Hunt and gave Ehrlichman a transcript along with the recommendation that he hire Hunt. The seeds that would grow into the Plumbers were planted.

THE PLUMBERS

Frustrated by the Supreme Court decision to allow publication of the Pentagon Papers, frustrated by the FBI's inability to stop information leaks, suspicious of the loyalty of the FBI,[58] CIA, and other government agencies, unhappy with the lack of response to their overtures to the bureaucracy on security matters, paranoid about events surrounding the antiwar movement and domestic dissent, and generally displeased with the quality of government work, the Nixon administration decided to take matters into their own hands.

In 1971, a special White House secret apparatus was organized to deal with matters such as leak plugging. The Special Investigations Unit, known as the Plumbers, because their job was to plug leaks, met in Room 16 of the Old Executive Office Building. This clandestine group began to do more than originally charged.

On June 17, 1971, only four days after the *New York Times* published its first story about the Pentagon papers, Kissinger, Haldeman, Ehrlichman, and the president met in the Oval Office to discuss Daniel Ellsberg.[59] Kissinger was worried that Ellsberg might have other material and described him (according to John Ehrlichman) as a drug user, a genius, and a threat to national security. He had to be discredited, prosecuted, and stopped.

Since Nixon felt that the FBI and other agencies were inept, uncooperative, and disloyal, the only recourse was for the White House to set up its own intelligence gathering–covert operations capacity. To head this secret unit David Young, a former NSC associate of Kissinger's, and Egil ("Bud") Krogh, a lawyer on Ehrlichman's Domestic Council staff, were chosen. Neither man had experience in covert operations, but their loyalty was unquestioned.

The main job of this unit would be to plug leaks, but they quickly expanded their activities to include a variety of other covert operations. Young and Krogh hired more-experienced hands such as E. Howard Hunt (CIA) and G. Gordon Liddy (FBI).

Krogh, who emerged as leader of the Plumbers, saw his role in somewhat expansive terms. "We were going after an espionage ring, not just Daniel Ellsberg!"[60] And indeed, such steps as firebombing the Brookings Institution[61] and burglaries were seriously discussed. One of the first acts of the Plumbers, though, showed how small and petty the Nixon people could be. In 1971, E. Howard Hunt and Chuck Colson forged top-secret State Department cables in an effort to falsely link President John Kennedy to the assassination of South Vietnam's president Ngo Dinh Diem.[62] They then tried, unsuccessfully, to get *Life* magazine to run stories based on these fake cables.

By far the biggest of the known jobs of the Plumbers related to the Pentagon Papers and efforts to embarrass and discredit Daniel Ellsberg. On June 28, 1971, Ellsberg was indicted for theft of government property and violation of the Espionage Act. The Nixon administration was determined to convict Ellsberg, but it wanted more—it wanted to discredit him and, if possible, link his activities to the Democrats (the 1972 election was only a short time away). To accomplish these goals, the clandestine arm of the administration had to be expanded and enervated. It was to be the beginning of the fall from power. As Jonathan Schell has written: "The Pentagon Papers episode was the gateway through which the lawbreaking of the war entered American society at its very highest level and became lawbreaking at home. It was the war-coming-home in its most virulent form."[63]

In an effort to "get" Ellsberg, Chuck Colson wanted information he could leak to the press that discredited and embarrassed Ellsberg.[64] But the psychiatric profile prepared by the CIA was not what the Nixon people wanted. It read in part, "There is no suggestion that Subject saw anything treasonous in his act. Rather he seemed to be responding to what he deemed a higher order of patriotism."

If the FBI and CIA were uncooperative or inefficient, the Plumbers would act. Nixon thought FBI director Hoover was dragging his feet. Nixon didn't want excuses, he wanted results. Since the FBI wasn't up to the task, the White House would do it themselves.[65]

In late August, Hunt and Liddy went to Los Angeles to "case" the office of Daniel Ellsberg's psychiatrist, Dr. Lewis J. Fielding, located in Beverly Hills. On Labor Day weekend, Hunt and Liddy, and "three Cubans" (Barker, Martinez, and De Diego) broke into Fielding's office in the hope of finding information that would prove damaging to Ellsberg. Nothing of use was found. In his memoirs, Nixon argues that he was not aware of the break-in, but defends it on national security grounds, admitting that it was in part an outgrowth of Nixon's own sense of urgency about undermining Ellsberg.[66]

Who ordered the Fielding break-in? Clearly John Ehrlichman had ordered a "covert operation" (he was convicted for ordering the break-in), with the stipulation that it be "done under your assurance that it is not traceable," but did the president know? There is no clear cut evidence that he did. But in his memoirs, Bob Haldeman relates in detail a post-presidency conversation with Nixon concerning the break-in. As Haldeman recounts the conversation, Nixon spoke as if he *had* ordered the break-in, saying at one point, "I was so damn mad at Ellsberg in those days. And Henry was jumping up and down. I've been thinking—and maybe I did order that break-in."

Haldeman then recounts how Nixon took steps that set in motion a "devious attack on Ellsberg and leakers," at one point telling Chuck Colson, "I don't give a damn how it is done, do whatever has to be done" . . . and "I don't want excuses. I want results. I want it done; whatever the cost."[67]

John Ehrlichman recalls that after repeated frustration over the job the FBI had been doing in its, in Nixon's view, meager efforts to pursue Ellsberg and stop leaks, Nixon finally gave a vague order for the Plumbers to proceed. As Ehrlichman writes, "Nixon authorized Krogh to use 'his people,' Howard Hunt, G. Gordon Liddy, et al., to find out what Ellsberg was up to."[68] Even if the president had not ordered, or even known the specifics of, the break-in of Ellsberg's psychiatrist's office, it is clear that Nixon set a tone, or a mood, and put great pressure on those around him to "get Ellsberg." The president's wish was their command, and clearly many of those who worked for the president felt confident that these covert and illegal methods would meet with the president's approval. They were correct.[69]

But when the government becomes the lawbreaker, who will stand up for law? Break-ins, burglaries, and assorted other covert activities done in the name of one man's—even the president's—view of national security needs does not a legality make. So concerned—obsessed—were the Nixon people with getting Daniel Ellsberg, that at a San Clemente meeting between Nixon and Matthew Byrne, the judge in the Ellsberg case, John Ehrlichman called Byrne aside and tentatively "offered" him the directorship of the FBI, if he handled the Ellsberg case in the right way (Byrne later threw the case out of court).[70] The impropriety of the Fielding/Ellsberg break-in was emphasized by U.S. District Court judge Gerhard Gesell, who called the break-in "clearly illegal."

But the moral and legal tone set in the White House permitted such disregard of the constitution. A secret, private, intelligence unit was established by the White House, outside of the normal channels, and engaged in a variety of illegal activities.

At a conference on the Nixon presidency held at Hofstra University in 1987, Chuck Colson discussed the impact of the Pentagon Papers on the behavior of the Nixon administration. Colson said that he saw the release of the Pentagon Papers as "the pivotal point" of the Nixon years. "When that happened," the ground rules began to change. That was when the Nixon people had, in Colson's words, "crossed that line." Egil Krogh agreed, citing the events surrounding release of the Pentagon Papers as "the seminal event of the Nixon term that resulted in the downfall of that administration." It sparked both legitimate national security fears and illegitimate personal fears, which animated behavior of an illegal nature. Internally, the process of moral deterioration became accelerated. The fall picked up speed.

Krogh concluded his Hofstra University commentary by saying that "what was done in 1971 set a precedent, a pattern that I think those who went on to work for the Committee to Re-Elect later on felt was appropriate conduct. They felt that if the White House would be willing to condone that kind of activity for national security purpose in 1971, it wouldn't be much of a stretch to condone it in 1972, 1973, for political purposes, and that's exactly what took place." Looking back, Krogh now has problems with the use of "national security" to justify illegal behavior.[71]

THE WAR DRAGS ON . . . AND ON

Nixon's efforts to end the war in Vietnam met only with frustration. Hanoi wasn't seriously negotiating, the bombing of the North seemed only to strengthen their resolve, extending the war into Cambodia and Laos had only a limited impact, the antiwar movement seemed to grow larger and angrier with each passing day, and congressional doves seemed always to be undermining the president's position. Would Nixon, like his predecessor, be dragged down and defeated by the Vietnam war? Abroad, Nixon hoped to force the North to negotiate by bombing North Vietnam and Cambodia. At home, Nixon hoped to quell domestic protest by ending the draft, bringing the troops home, and suppressing dissent. Nothing worked as planned.

By 1970, Nixon's initial hope for an early end to the war had vanished. The negotiations between the missions in Paris and between Kissinger and Le Duc Tho were failing because each side insisted on peace conditions unacceptable to the other. Nixon's alternatives seemed to be either bomb the North to a degree unacceptable by civilized standards, or back away from some of his negotiating demands and hope that Vietnamization would work. But could the president get his much valued "peace with honor" in Vietnam?

In February of 1971, the war expanded further, as South Vietnamese troops, with American air and artillery support, invaded Laos. The goal of the invasion was to invade the Laotian panhandle and defeat the North Vietnamese army at the Ho Chi Minh Trail. But the U.S.-backed forces were trapped inside the Laotian jungle and suffered enormous casualties. It was a military failure in every sense of the word.

As the war dragged on with no honorable end in sight, Nixon began to see

Vietnam as a test of his and America's prestige. America would not be "a pitiful, helpless giant," Nixon said; and H. R. Haldeman's notes of meetings with the president reflect a repeated concern for not appearing weak. For example, on June 2, 1971, Haldeman writes:

P. will not go out of VN whimpering
play hole card in Nov - bomb NV totally
unless we get our breakthru
(underlined in original)

Earlier notes by Haldeman have the president saying, "our purpose is not to defeat NVN—it is to avoid defeat of America" (underlined in original). But "peace with honor" proved no easy goal.

Vietnamization was not working. Nixon could accept defeat or escalate. A summit conference with the Soviet Union was scheduled for May of 1972, and the president was determined to get the Soviets to force North Vietnam to stop the war. Linkage, however, did not work, as the Soviets did not have as much influence over the North Vietnamese as Nixon and Kissinger had, for four years, assumed.

Le Duc Tho and Henry Kissinger met in Paris. The North was negotiating from a position of strength. Le Duc Tho told Kissinger that he would not compromise. Kissinger returned to the United States with the bad news. In a weekend meeting at Camp David, Nixon decided to escalate. On Monday, May 8, after a lengthy National Security Council meeting at the White House, Nixon handed his own draft of a speech written at Camp David to speechwriter Ray Price. Nixon would go on national television at nine that evening to announce his plans.

"An American defeat in Vietnam," Nixon said, "would encourage . . . aggression all over the world. . . . I have . . . concluded that Hanoi must be denied the weapons and supplies it needs to continue the aggression." He continued, "All entrances to North Vietnamese ports will be mined to prevent access to these ports and North Vietnamese naval operations from these ports."

The North was to be blockaded. The air force would bomb rail and roadways, along with military targets in the North. The bombing of Hanoi and Haiphong began immediately. In an effort to create the appearance of public support for these actions, the Committee to Re-elect the President spent eight thousand dollars to have false letters and telegrams of support sent to the White House.

Under the grueling pressure of round-the-clock bombing (Nixon said to his associates, "The bastards have never been bombed like they're going to be bombed this time"),[72] the North finally agreed to return to the negotiating table. In the summer of 1972, as a presidential election was approaching, the two sides met in Paris.

Attention turned to Paris and the negotiations to end the war. As the negotiations progressed, the bombings decreased. In a frantic, often confusing and contradictory process of proposal and counterproposal, Henry Kissinger kept working for an honorable way out of the war. But the North Vietnamese wanted a negotiated victory. A two-track American process of negotiation and bombing continued in the hope of driving the North to an agreement more amenable to American interests.

By the early summer of 1972, North Vietnam's politburo made a breakthrough concession. They would drop their demand for a coalition government in the South. Thieu would be permitted to remain in office. In effect, the North was agreeing to let the United States leave Vietnam and to wait for either the government of the South to collapse or an opportunity to overthrow a shaky government with a questionable military capacity. From that point on, the negotiations moved ahead. By the fall of 1972, an agreement was in sight. A cease-fire was agreed to, the North was allowed to keep its troops in the South (a major concession by Nixon), all U.S. troops were to withdraw, a government that included communists was established, and an election commission was set up to decide the fate of Vietnam.

South Vietnam was not a party to this agreement, and when Henry Kissinger took the tentative agreement to South Vietnam's president Thieu in October, things began to fall apart. Thieu correctly recognized that the agreement was South Vietnam's death warrant. He refused to allow the North's troops, numbering around 145,000 to remain in the South and refused to recognize the legitimacy of the Vietcong.

Nixon and Kissinger pressed Thieu, telling him that this was the best they could do and promising continued support to Thieu. On October 26, 1972, Radio Hanoi disclosed the terms of the agreement in hopes of forcing the United States to sign the agreement. Also on October 26, Henry Kissinger announced at a press conference that "peace is at hand." This premature announcement, less than two weeks before the 1972 presidential election, blew up in Kissinger's face. Thieu refused to accept the deal struck by Kissinger and Le Duc Tho. Kissinger urged Nixon to make a separate peace agreement with Hanoi, but Nixon refused.

Kissinger and Le Duc Tho met in mid-November of 1972 to try once again to iron out an agreement, but the introduction of President Thieu's demands led to North Vietnamese objections. Things seemed to be going in reverse. In an effort to get an agreement, Nixon informed the North that if Thieu remained intransigent, he would make a separate deal with Hanoi; further he threatened Thieu with a cutoff of U.S. support if Thieu refused to go along with the agreement. Nixon also promised Thieu that if the North violated the agreement, the United States would "save" South Vietnam from a communist takeover.[73] Finally, Nixon gave Hanoi seventy-two hours to seriously resume negotiations or face renewed, and more-massive, B-52 bombing of the North.

Nixon decided to step up the pressure. On December 18, 1972, U.S. B-52s began a twelve-day, round-the-clock bombing of North Vietnam in which the

United States dropped more tons of bombs than had been dropped in the entire 1969–71 period. The "Christmas Bombing" shocked the nation and the world. It was one of the most brutal examples of force in history. It was an effort to bomb the North into submission. As the bombs showered the North, Nixon sweetened the pot for Thieu and the South, giving them an additional billion dollars in military aid while warning Thieu that if he didn't accept the American "peace" terms, Nixon would make his own peace with North Vietnam. In the end, neither side could resist Nixon's ultimatum.

The North returned to the bargaining table, Nixon ordered a halt to the bombing, Thieu acquiesced to American pressures and promises, and in Paris on January 23, 1973, the Agreement on Ending the War and Restoring Peace in Vietnam was initialed by Henry Kissinger and Le duc Tho. Nixon claimed his "peace with honor."

Twenty-seven months after the signing of the Paris accords, the Saigon government fell to the communists, in spite of Nixon's promise to President Thieu to "respond with full force" if the North violated the agreements (Nixon told Thieu in March of 1973, "You can count on us"). Nixon had been forced from office, and America had no stomach for a return to Vietnam. The North had conquered the South by force. The Khmer Rouge controlled Cambodia.

At a January 31, 1973, press conference announcing the peace agreement, Nixon took a swipe at the press. Against great odds, we had, Nixon said, achieved "peace with honor"; "I know it gags some of you to write that phrase, but it is true, and most Americans realize it is true."

In their memoirs, Nixon and Kissinger defended their conduct during the Vietnam War and blamed Congress and the media for the 1975 fall of Saigon. While the Congress, much of the press, and a majority of the public *did* oppose the war, shifting blame to others for a failed policy in Vietnam only obscures the issue. For nearly twenty years the United States acted in Vietnam on false assumptions and incomplete information. There is enough blame to spread around. American policy in Vietnam was doomed because our operating assumptions were almost always wrong. Richard Nixon inherited a war that he expanded, then ended on terms that were bound to collapse. For America, and for Southeast Asia, the Vietnam War was a tragic mistake and a tragic failure. And for Nixon, actions stemming from that war led to his own downfall. In the end, Nixon's goal of military victory in Vietnam gave way to hopes for a negotiated settlement, which gave way to a turning of the war over to South Vietnam, which gave way to hopes of peace with honor, which finally gave way to U.S. withdrawal without humiliation. But in the end, not only did South Vietnam and Cambodia fall, but Nixon also fell victim to the war. As a direct result of actions taken stemming from the war, the seeds of Watergate were planted. Nixon thus became yet another victim of the tragedy of Vietnam.

Richard Nixon inherited a no-win war in Vietnam. In his effort to end that war, he expanded it into Cambodia and Laos. In an effort to hide the expansion of the war from public and congressional scrutiny, he misled the public and relied on excessive secrecy. To protect this secrecy, he illegally wiretapped news reporters, government officials, and others in an effort to find out who was leaking information. He went further, setting up a domestic intelligence unit, and authorized clearly illegal activities such as burglaries (the Huston Plan). He later set up the Plumbers to plug leaks, but they soon became involved in forging State Department cables and breaking into a psychiatrist's office to get the goods on Daniel Ellsberg.

Having their roots in the administration's efforts to deal with the war in Vietnam, these activities began within months of Nixon's taking office. Thus, 1969 was the start of everything for Nixon—including the end. The roots of Nixon's political and personal tragedy can be traced back to the foreign policy events of 1969 and the war in Vietnam. Nixon's concept of national security was so broad and expansive that it covered all sorts of illegal acts ("When the President does it, that means it is not illegal," Nixon told interviewer David Frost in 1977). This sweeping notion of a national security state created a framework, rationale, and justification for abuses of power that ultimately contributed to the unmaking of a president.

U.S.-SOVIET RELATIONS: THE TIES THAT BIND LOOSELY

In the immediate aftermath of the Second World War, as U.S.-Soviet rivalry heated up, the United States sought to maintain its massive economic and military superiority and the political clout it hoped would go with that superiority. American policy in the first twenty years of the Cold War reflected a confidence in superior resources, and the United States was able to pursue a policy of containment based on resources that seemed almost limitless. But the war in Vietnam made America aware of very real limits to power, and as Richard Nixon ascended to the presidency, he, more than most, saw the long-term consequences of a changing world and America's changing relationship to that new world.

In the span of twenty years, America's Cold War consensus seemed to be eroding, her resources were seen to be limited, the Western alliance proved shaky, the Russians had achieved near nuclear parity, and the emerging nations were not as compliant as before. It was a new world, and it required new insights.

Nixon recognized the need for what he called "a new era of international relations," and "a new approach to foreign policy." The postwar period, Nixon said, was over. The era of American predominance had passed. A "new structure of world peace" was needed. At the center of any new structure were American-Soviet relations. Nixon and Kissinger knew that improved relations between the United States and the Soviet Union were essential if a grand design was to work.

Given Richard Nixon's anticommunist background, it is hard to imagine how a new attitude of détente could evolve, but indeed, a new attitude and relationship was developed during the Nixon years. From staunch anticommunist to father of détente, the public education of the man showed that—at least in his overall approach to foreign policy—there truly may have been a "new" Nixon.

Nixon and Kissinger liked to think of themselves as realists and pragmatists (this in spite of harboring grandiose plans to create a "new" international structure) and felt that the old global design of global containment had dangerously overextended America's resources and was not in line with U.S. security interests. It had to give way to a more realistic worldview, and a new U.S.-Soviet relationship was to be the cornerstone of a new American foreign policy. As Tad Szulc writes:

Nixon had resolved from the first days of his administration to embark on a gradual policy of improving relations with Moscow. He approached this policy in a cold, non-ideological fashion, reasoning that only a viable relationship between the United States and the Soviet Union could guarantee world peace in the long run. . . . The president thought in power terms in erecting his "structure of peace," and the stark reality was that the Russians were a superpower and had to be treated accordingly. Otherwise, Nixon believed, Moscow would move from mischief to mischief politically, endangering international peace. [74]

Nixon wanted to move from an "era of confrontation" to an "era of negotiation" while not abandoning containment as the strategic foundation of American policy. Through a complex web of interrelated agreements, Nixon hoped to pursue containment by other means—less ambitious and less costly means. Nixon was well aware of the dangers posed by the Soviet Union, but he hoped to control or contain them via agreement and inducement.

Nixon hoped to control Soviet power through subtlety of maneuver, not sheer force or the threat of force. Through negotiations, agreements, military sufficiency, and linkage, Nixon sought to lure the Soviets into a system of détente (a strategy that emerged as much as a reaction to events as a preconceived plan) which promoted international stability on the basis of a commitment to the concept of legitimacy.

For Nixon's Grand Design to work, the Soviet Union had to be brought into the orbit of nonrevolutionary states, it had to accept the legitimacy of the status quo, and not foment revolution or systemic disruption. For the Soviet Union to do this, system maintenance, as opposed to system change, had to be made to appear in their best interest. Of course, both superpowers shared an interest in avoiding nuclear war. But did they share an interest in preserving the status quo?

Nixon himself had a variety of motives for improving U.S.-Soviet relations. In broad terms he was seeking to implement his Grand Design in the international arena, and in narrower, more immediate terms, he was hoping the Soviet Union would put pressure on its ally North Vietnam to accept Nixon's peace proposal. This is where the concept of linkage became so important to the president. Nixon hoped to modify Soviet behavior by linking one issue to another, perhaps unrelated issue, a carrot-and-stick formula. Nixon wrote in his memoirs of linkage as a new way of dealing with the Soviets. Since Nixon felt it unrealistic to compartmentalize areas of concern, he wanted to link progress in one area with progress in other areas, especially Vietnam.[75]

This policy of trade-cffs assumed that the Soviets were interested and willing to link issues together. This however, was not the case, and linkage proved a disappointment to the United States. Nixon had assumed that the Soviet Union had a level of power in North Vietnam that they simply did not have. The legacy of the old Cold War vision of "monolithic communism" controlled in Moscow obscured reality and led Nixon down a dead-end street.[76]

The Road to—and from—Détente

During the Nixon presidency, the United States and the Soviet Union did a slow, awkward mating dance that ended in frustration and disappointment for both countries. Called détente, it held forth the promise of an improved relationship and the hope of eventual peace. But the euphoria over détente did not last long, and the dashing of hopes built up in the early stages of détente led to a renewal of the heated rhetoric of the Cold War and a reaction against the belief that the United States and the Soviet Union could truly improve their relationship.

From the early stages of détente in 1969, to the high point of the May 1972 summit, this short-lived era of good feeling was a brilliantly conceived but poorly implemented strategy; it was conceptually sound, but overly personalized; a hope for the future that was oversold for personal and political reasons. The American architects of realpolitik let hopes interfere with sound analysis and presented détente as something it was not. When reality set in, bitter disappointment followed as the public turned against détente. Each side had a different conception of what détente meant and required, and the process deteriorated very quickly as each side became disillusioned. By 1978, détente had become a dirty word in the United States, and by the 1980 campaign the victorious candidate campaigned against détente.

What did détente mean? In general terms it meant a relaxation of superpower tension, a movement from confrontation to negotiation, an effort to make explicit the informal rules governing international behavior, some projects of a cooperative nature, arms control, and an overall increase in contact and communication.

Did détente fail? Actually, it was never really tried. Because each side had such different conceptions of what détente entailed, neither side was able to give it an adequate test. Détente—a French word meaning relaxation of tension—was awkwardly pursued, poorly followed up, and became an easy target when performance failed to meet promise.

Both Nixon and Brezhnev wanted improved relations, but for very different reasons. In an immediate sense, Nixon wanted Soviet aid in ending the war in Vietnam. In more general terms, Nixon wanted to reduce the risk of nuclear war and engage the Soviet Union in a web of agreements recognizing new "rules of the game" so as to moderate Soviet international behavior and establish a more stable status quo.[77] Thus, Nixon would offer a variety of incentives to the Soviet Union in hopes of inducing greater international cooperation. It was an effort to shift from the use of U.S. military might to contain the Soviet Union, to a state of "self-containment" in which Moscow recognized that it was in its own best interest to modify its behavior. Nixon was convinced that the Soviet Union would always act on the basis of self-interest, but he hoped détente would make that self-interest a bit more enlightened.[78]

Henry Kissinger, in congressional testimony, said that "the challenge of our time is to reconcile the reality of competition with the imperative of coexistence,"[79] and said that the purpose of détente was to control and moderate Soviet behavior. "Détente," Kissinger said, "is a means of controlling the conflict with the Soviet Union."[80]

Brezhnev's main goal in détente was to be treated like an equal in the international arena. The Soviet Union had sacrificed greatly to approach military parity with the United States, and thus détente represented the "official" recognition of the emergence of the Soviet Union as a co-equal superpower with the United States. In the Soviet mind, military parity also granted political parity. Détente, in their view, granted the Soviets this position and power.[81] Brezhnev saw détente as a bold new era in U.S.-Soviet relations: "What is détente? What do we mean by that term? Détente above all means overcoming the 'cold war' and transition to normal, equal relations among states. Détente means a readiness to resolve difference and disputes not by force, not by threats and sabre-rattling, but by peaceful means, at a conference table. Détente means a certain trust and ability to take into account the legitimate interest of one another."[82]

Détente did not mean that the Soviet Union would retreat from the world, or even that they would abandon any ambitions they might have (nor would the United States). It merely meant that the competition would take place with different ground rules, *and* between relatively equal competitors. In effect, détente would make historical change—which they saw as inevitable—safer.

Détente did not emerge full-blown out of the minds of Nixon and Kissinger, but developed slowly, piece by piece, as a result of efforts to move from confrontation to negotiation. In fact, the Soviet Union made the first moves indicating their eagerness to move ahead on strategic arms limitations talks (SALT) and other areas. Nixon and Kissinger, in no hurry, but interested in the prospect of improving relations, set up a "back channel" connection between Kissinger and Dobrynin (the State Department was once again excluded) and later introduced the prospect of a summit meeting with Soviet prime minister Kosygin in meetings with Ambassador Dobrynin in mid 1970. The hope of an early summit foundered on the rocks of the Cambodia invasion.

After a series of back-and-forth hints and nudges by both parties, Ambassador Dobrynin in January of 1971 finally proposed a summit meeting, but only if the United States was prepared to discuss the ongoing Berlin negotiations. The Soviets were using linkage in a way that the United States found objectionable. Finally, in September of 1971, both sides agreed to a May 1972 summit in Moscow. This was *after* President Nixon announced his trip to China, an announcement that no doubt hastened the Soviet decision to arrange a summit.

Henry Kissinger made a secret trip to Moscow from April 20 to 24, 1972, to decide on an agenda and to work on a declaration of principles that would be signed at the summit. In fact, the summit became a very carefully planned and scripted event.

THE 1972 SUMMIT

The 1972 summit in Moscow was a resounding success for President Nixon. It was a great public relations event in an election year, but it was also a substantive success, as the United States and Soviet Union reached agreement on several important fronts. It was also a vindication of the personal diplomacy of Henry Kissinger and the "summit diplomacy" of Richard Nixon. It was truly one of the high points of the Nixon presidency.

At the Moscow summit, Nixon sought Soviet assistance in pressuring North Vietnam to accept a peace settlement. While the Soviets did soften their position on this, they would not give Nixon what he wanted, because in reality they could not.

In other areas the summit was a great success. This was due in part to the type of personal diplomacy so artfully conducted by Nixon and Kissinger. Nixon told Brezhnev that during World War II, differences between the United States and the Soviet Union were "usually overcome at the top level" by Roosevelt and Stalin. "That," said Nixon, "is the kind of relationship that I should like to establish with the General Secretary."[83]

A variety of agreements were signed at the 1972 summit, dealing with everything from the establishment of a joint economic commission to the avoidance of naval accidents. But the two most significant agreements were the Basic Principles of U.S.-Soviet Relations and the SALT treaty.

The Basic Principles agreement was signed on May 29, the final day of the summit. It was, in effect, the charter for détente. While the United States would subsequently downplay the importance of the principles (in his memoirs, Nixon gives them only two sentences), the Soviet Union gave them great significance. The principles consisted of a variety of guidelines for conduct. The first stated that the United States and the Soviet Union would "proceed from the common determination that in the nuclear age there is no alternative to conducting their mutual relations on the basis of peaceful coexistence," and that despite their differences, there was a pledge to pursue "normal relations based on the principles of sovereignty, equality, non-interference in internal affairs and mutual advantage."

The second principle attempted to avoid confrontations that could lead to direct U.S.-Soviet conflict. It pledged restraint and a determination to negotiate and "settle differences by peaceful means." It also recognized that the "efforts to obtain unilateral advantage at the expense of the other, directly or indirectly are inconsistent with these objectives." Further, it renounced the use of force between the United States and the Soviet Union.

The remaining ten principles set other loosely worded ground rules for superpower behavior. Kissinger said that the principles represented "an aspiration and an attitude." He later wrote that while "these principles were not a legal contract," they did establish "a standard of conduct by which to judge whether real progress was being made and in the name of which we could resist their violation."[84]

The second major agreement signed at the 1972 Moscow summit was the Strategic Arms Limitation Talk compact. The culmination of a long, difficult process that began under Lyndon Johnson at the Glassboro summit, the SALT agreement was a major arms limitation accord.

In late 1969 the SALT talks between the United States and the Soviets took on a seriousness reflecting the sincerity of a new "era of negotiation." After long and complex bargaining and compromise, the SALT I agreement was finally reached in 1972. It was the centerpiece of the Summit, and inaugurated détente between the United States and the Soviet Union. Henry Kissinger put SALT I into perspective: "When linked to such broad and unprecedented projects as SALT, détente takes on added meaning and opens prospects of a more stable peace. SALT agreements should be seen as steps in a [détente] process leading to progressively greater stability. It is in that light that SALT and related projects will be judged by history."[85]

Under SALT, two major agreements were reached. The first was an antiballistic missile (ABM) treaty, which prohibited testing and deployment of air, space, or mobile land-based ABM systems, and limited each nation to no more than two ABM sites. It was of unlimited duration. The second major part of SALT was the Interim Agreement on the Limitation of Strategic Arms, which set ceilings on intercontinental ballistic missiles (ICBMs), submarine-launched ballistic missiles (SLBMs), and missile-carrying submarines. This agreement was set to expire in 1977, but there was an agreement to pursue SALT II negotiations to set future limits on arms.

Nixon pointed to the SALT I agreement as an indication that negotiation and not confrontation could guide superpower relations. While the president was understandably proud of this major accomplishment, the overselling of SALT soon began. Euphoria set in with the president's address to a joint session of Congress immediately after his return to Washington. Nixon began with: "Three fifths of all the people alive in the world today have spent their whole lifetimes under the shadow of a nuclear war which could be touched off by the arms race among the great powers. Last Friday in Moscow we witnessed the beginning of the end of that era which began in 1945. We took the first step toward a new era of mutually agreed restraint and arms limitation between the two principal nuclear nations."[86]

Henry Kissinger, briefing congressional leaders, spoke of working "to create a set of circumstances which would offer the Soviet leaders an opportunity to move away from confrontation through carefully prepared negotiations," and giving the Soviets "a vested interest in mutual restraint."[87] While the SALT agreement and its connection to the conceptual framework of détente was important, the president and his national security adviser oversold and overpromised what would result from the agreements. For immediate personal and political reasons, the seeds of disappointment were planted at the very outset. As public and congressional expectations soared, so too would they plummet when SALT and détente proved in future years to be merely mortal.

The Moscow summit of 1972 was to be the first of many proposed meetings of U.S. and Soviet heads of state.[88] It would be the base of détente and future improvement in superpower relations. When he returned from the Moscow summit, President Nixon told the Congress that "the foundation has been laid for a new relationship between the two most powerful nations in the world."[89]

THE 1973 SUMMIT

In June of 1973, Leonid Brezhnev came to the United States for the second Soviet-American summit. After the grand achievements of the previous years's summit, the '73 meeting would be a slight disappointment. The summit was held during the Watergate summer, and Senator Sam Ervin, head of the Senate's investigating committee, agreed to suspend his hearing during Brezhnev's visit. But the shadow of Watergate hung over the summit.

Again, it was a very carefully planned meeting, with Henry Kissinger spending five days in Moscow in May to iron out details of the summit. But there was comparatively little to plan. The SALT II talks were going slowly, and so Kissinger and Brezhnev were relegated to ironing out a series of lesser agreements, lest people think détente was faltering.

The 1973 summit opened on June 18. While not as dramatic as the 1972 summit, this meeting was part of an effort to institutionalize yearly summits between the United States and the Soviet Union. Nixon and Brezhnev did sign two significant agreements, one entitled On the Prevention of Nuclear War, the other, Basic Principles of Negotiations on the Further Limitation of Strategic Offensive Arms, as well as a host of other, lesser agreements. The president and Brezhnev also held frank, lengthy discussions on a variety of other issues, including Jewish emigration from the Soviet Union.

While the '73 summit was no match for the previous year's in drama or importance, it did renew and strengthen the personal relationship between Nixon and Brezhnev. To Nixon it also had the advantage of further pulling the Soviets into the conceptual scheme of his "structure of world peace." Nixon felt that the '73 agreements continued the SALT process of building a web of relationships to increase the Soviets' stake in protecting the status quo.[90]

THE 1974 SUMMIT

While the Watergate scandal had been only a minor annoyance at the 1973 summit, by the time the 1974 summit in Moscow took place it was a full-fledged crisis for Richard Nixon. He had spent a tremendous amount of time and energy fending off charges of wrongdoing that were getting closer and closer to the Oval Office.

As had been the case before the previous summits, Henry Kissinger was sent to Moscow in late March to set up the details of the meeting. But this was certainly not summit-as-usual. Nixon was distracted by the Watergate scandal. He was unable to focus on the summit. Kissinger wondered if anything could be salvaged.[91]

The unfolding Watergate crisis had crippled Richard Nixon, and this allowed the antidétente forces (led by Democratic senator Henry Jackson) to narrow the options of Nixon vis-à-vis the Soviets. Kissinger insisted that "Jackson and others in the anti-détente lobby were determined that Nixon should have no negotiating chips in Moscow."[92]

Nixon had stated that the purpose of the 1974 summit was threefold: (1) to strengthen relations with the Soviet Union; (2) to further develop areas of cooperation; and (3) to decrease the threat of nuclear war. Between June 23 and July 7, the summit did produce the Protocol to the Treaty on the Limitation of Anti-Ballistic Missile Systems (reducing the number of ABM systems each country could have to one) and the Treaty and Protocol on the Limitation of Underground Nuclear Weapons Tests, as well as several lesser agreements. But it was not seen as a great success because of the popular expectation that each summit should match the sweeping success of 1972.

What the '74 summit did was to further the pattern of superpower interaction and regularize summit meetings, no small feat. It continued a momentum that in subsequent years would be halted. Nixon himself considered the '74 summit a "mixed bag," and wrote in his personal diary that while the formal sessions produced very little, the informal meetings were of great value.[93]

Given the mounting pressures of Watergate, it is not surprising that Nixon was not in his best form for the '74 summit. He was distracted and disturbed, and not the Nixon of old. But the three summits and détente were a legacy Nixon cited with great pride. He had moved the nation from a period of confrontation to an era of negotiation. Nixon had succeeded, for a time, in turning the U.S.-Soviet relationship around. But it would not last.

During the Nixon years, several factors contributed to the decline of détente.

The October 1973 war in the Middle East split the United States and the Soviet Union; Watergate and the resignation of President Nixon removed détente's prime mover from power; domestic opposition to détente became more organized; and there were problems in the way détente was conceived and operationalized at the executive level. A properly conceptualized policy must integrate three elements: a grand design, a strategy for achieving the design, and appropriate tactics for implementing the strategy. In a democracy, a fourth element must be added: persuading the other political actors of the appropriateness of the vision. But Nixon never fully or clearly articulated his grand design. On a strategic level, however, Nixon had a keen sense for how to readjust commitments to match resources. Where Nixon failed in détente was in his inability to use appropriate tactics and to meet the democratic requirements of foreign policy to build a solid domestic consensus in support of his actions.

On a tactical level, Nixon and Kissinger overpersonalized détente. Their distrust of the bureaucracy and their need to control all events led to the overpersonalization of détente. Thus, when Nixon declined, so too did détente. By not institutionalizing détente, Nixon and Kissinger left no one behind with a stake or vested interest in seeing that détente continued.

Linked to this criticism is the fact that the policy of détente was never democratized and thus never legitimized. Nixon was able to develop a consensus on détente, but it was a very superficial consensus. As Henry Kissinger asserted, "The acid test of a policy is its ability to obtain domestic support," but by overselling détente, the consensus built to support it quickly evaporated, and only a few years after Nixon's resignation, the antidétente forces dominated the American political landscape.

The grand hopes for détente, that somehow the Soviet Union could be turned into a status quo power, that the risks of nuclear war could be reduced, that an era of negotiation could replace an era of confrontation, that an orderly devolution of American power could take place, was only a partial success. There was not a new era of peace, but there were successes.

Détente was a welcome change from the confrontational past, but détente (containment by other means) was not fully integrated into the foreign policy process, and with Nixon gone, there was no one left to defend it against its critics.

OPENING DOORS TO CHINA

Nixon's opening of China, often cited as the greatest diplomatic success of his presidency, was a bold, risky diplomatic stroke that transformed the Asian political balance to the United States' advantage. The risks of such a move at first appeared great, domestically and internationally, but Nixon and Kissinger saw a strategic window of opportunity, and seized it. Decades of hostility between the United States and China, as well as a career built on the shoulders of staunch anticommunism, made Nixon an unlikely choice to bring about rapprochement. But in a dramatic style characteristic of the Nixon-Kissinger approach to foreign policy, a new link was developed between the United States and China. It would change the international balance of power.

Begun and executed under a cloak of secrecy, and with the close collaboration of Nixon and Kissinger, a bold step toward normalized relations took place. There are a variety of reasons why Nixon chose to improve Sino-American relations at this time. Domestically, Nixon the conservative anticommunist could afford politically to make the move because no one could accuse him of being soft on communism. Also, after decades of poor relations, the time seemed right for a rapprochement, if both sides so desired. The fact that the 1972 election was not far off also offered a tantalizing inducement for the president.

In national security terms, Nixon could use improved Sino-American relations to pressure the Soviet Union into moderating their behavior. This might be the leverage Nixon needed to gain certain concessions from the Soviets. Also, if tensions could be reduced with China, some of the military pressure on the United States might be eased in Asia. Creating a new and more favorable military and strategic balance in Asia as well as exploiting the split between Beijing and Moscow presented a variety of beneficial options and possibilities for the United States. Rapprochement was thus deeply rooted in the Nixon-Kissinger conception of global diplomacy and their efforts to change the international balance of power.

China, after decades of relative international isolation, was also ready for more normalized relations. Motivated in large part by the deteriorating Sino-Soviet relationship (there were serious border clashes in 1969), China sought to move closer to the United States in an effort to distance itself from the Soviets as well as to further weaken Soviet influence in Asia.

The style of decision making on China was typical of the major decisions of the Nixon administration. Distrusting the bureaucracy, Nixon and Kissinger jealously guarded their policy initiatives and kept them secret—even from the State Department. Drama, secrecy, and intrigue marked the early stages of policy, and personal diplomacy was the order of the day.

Clearly Richard Nixon was the prime architect of Sino-American rapprochement. In a 1967 article in *Foreign Affairs*, Nixon even hinted at such a move, writing that "we simply cannot afford to leave China forever outside the family of nations." Added to this, Kissinger admitted to not being a China expert when he came to power.[94]

After a variety of early, delicate, and tenuous moves[95] in which simply making contact with the Chinese proved difficult, the United States and China agreed to talk. All of this was done in secret, as neither side was ready for public exposure of these initial steps. In early July 1971, Henry Kissinger, pretending to be sick with a stomach problem while in Pakistan, made a secret trip to China to meet with Premier Chou En-lai to arrange a Chinese-American summit.

"Playing the China card" had a significant impact on U.S.-Soviet relations.

If détente between the Soviet Union and the United States made China edgy, rapprochement between China and the United States would have the same impact in Moscow. It was a deft game of playing one nation off against another.[96]

As with Nixon's summits in Moscow, the Beijing summit was carefully and meticulously planned. From February 21 to 28, 1972, Nixon met with the Chinese leaders. It was a dazzling political and diplomatic event. Never before had an American president visited China. Upon meeting with Mao Tse-tung, Nixon said, "What brings us together is a recognition of a new situation in the world and recognition on our part that what is important is not a nation's internal philosophy. What is important is its policy toward the rest of the world and toward us." He later told Chou En-lai, "We know you believe deeply in your principles, and we believe deeply in our principles. We do not ask you to compromise your principles, just as you would not ask us to compromise ours." In a banquet toast Nixon declared, "So let us start a long march together, not in lockstep, but on different roads leading to the same goal, the goal of building a world structure of peace and justice."[97]

At the end of the trip, the United States and China issued the 1,800-word Shanghai Communiqué and took the first awkward steps toward normalization of relations. In his memoirs Nixon said that the communiqué "broke diplomatic ground by stating frankly the significant differences between the two sides on major issues rather than smoothing them over." Indeed, the communiqué did admit to differences over matters such as the status of Taiwan, ideology, and other issues. It also sought harmony in Pacific relations and a commitment that both China and the United States would look harshly on any efforts to gain hegemony in Asia.

The trip to China was an unabashed triumph for Nixon and Kissinger. Coming on the eve of the 1972 presidential elections, it had an added dividend for the president. In the long run, rapprochement with China was to prove one of the enduring legacies of the Nixon foreign policy.

NIXON AND THE ALLIES

Nixon's structure of peace was a complex, multilayered plan. For it to succeed, he needed to bring the Western Allies on board to support the plan. But the alliance was not as firmly under American control in 1969 as it was in 1959 or 1949.

The Europeans and Japan, so devastated by World War II, were by 1969 prosperous and thriving. With economic success came a growing independence from U.S. control and influence. But these countries did still rely upon the American nuclear umbrella for much of their defense, and the United States remained the acknowledged leader of the Western alliance.

Alliance politics, as played by Nixon and Kissinger, sought to reduce the U.S. burden but preserve the basic structure of U.S. power over the alliance.

It was hoped that in an atmosphere of greater independence and growing divergencies between the United States, Europe, and Japan, the structure of U.S. leadership could be preserved and even reinforced.

What role would the Allies play in building the structure of peace? One of the first things the new president did in 1969 was to plan a trip to Europe to meet with the heads of state. On the trip the president called for a "new partnership" in which Nixon seemed to be calling for Europe to take a greater responsibility for its own future. The key result of the trip was to give Nixon the chance to meet with the Allies.[98]

At first it appeared as if Nixon did intend to focus more attention on the strengthening of the alliance. But Vietnam and Big Power politics drew attention away from the Allies. Returning to Europe in 1973, Nixon promised "The Year of Europe," an effort to come to grips with the drifting alliance. Nixon and Kissinger were hoping for a comprehensive new approach to U.S.-European relations. But little came of this ambitious goal, and as Watergate ate away at the Nixon presidency, the Year of Europe was all but forgotten.

While Nixon was pursuing détente with the Soviet Union, Chancellor Willy Brandt of West Germany launched *Ostpolitik*, efforts at closer relations with Eastern Europe and the Soviet Union. In line with *Ostpolitik*, a Conference on Security and Cooperation in Europe—the Helsinki Conference—continued throughout the early 1970s. The Helsinki accords, signed in 1975, furthered human rights, encouraged cultural and human contacts between East and West, and were a part of the spirit of détente. Also, in 1971 a four-power agreement was signed that provided for Western access to Berlin.

Perhaps the biggest blow to U.S.-European relations was the 1971 economic shock, when Nixon took the United States off the gold standard, imposed tariff restrictions, and charted his own course in international economic policy. The lack of consultation or even prior warning shocked the Allies, and U.S.-European relations under Nixon never really recovered. From that point on the United States was seen as a less-reliable leader, and trust between the Allies declined.

The United States had come to see Japan as a rising economic competitor whose contribution to its own defense was very small. There seemed little the United States could do about this, and as Nixon pursued rapprochement with China, the United States decided not to pressure Japan to boost military spending. Japan followed the U.S. lead in China with Prime Minister Kakuei Tanaka's fall 1972 trip to China, which led to improved Japanese relations with the People's Republic.

Militarily, Nixon's policy vis-à-vis Japan was ambiguous. He wanted to reduce U.S. military commitments, and in fact, he withdrew 12,000 troops, leaving 27,000 in Japan in all of East Asia, but wanted to maintain a position of leadership in the area. Could Nixon have it both ways? The Japanese feared American devolution and retrenchment. While Nixon reaffirmed the American commitment to protect Japan with its nuclear umbrella, he announced that land forces would play a less significant role in the future.

Many of the East Asian allies, including Japan, were concerned. They were still unclear as to their role in the defense of the region. Just how far would American retrenchment go? When Nixon went to China, doubts about the future U.S. role in East Asian defense intensified. More than anything, the ambiguity of the new relationship caused fear and concern among the Japanese. Nixon never clarified matters.

In the end, the alliance was of secondary importance to Nixon. He was concerned with bigger issues abroad, and smaller issues at home. Europe and Japan were caught in the middle. As long as the Allies did not cause major problems, they had low priority, low visibility, and low status. The opportunity to develop a stronger alliance in light of changes on the international scene evaporated as Nixon treated Europe and Japan not as Allies, but often as nuisances.

CHILE AND THE OVERTHROW OF ALLENDE

While Nixon was pursuing improved relations with the Soviet Union and China, the administration still harbored great fears of communism—especially in this hemisphere. The United States has a long history of intervention in the affairs of nations in this hemisphere, and in the early 1970s, the Nixon administration, faced with a leftist government in Chile, took steps to destabilize Chile's government.

In the 1960s, the U.S. government sought to influence the internal affairs of Chile in an effort to prevent Salvador Allende, a socialist, from becoming president. The government's efforts were successful until 1970, when, in spite of the administration's effort to pursue a "spoiling campaign" against Allende, he was elected president by a narrow margin.[99]

Edward Korry, the U.S. ambassador to Chile, reported to Nixon:

Chile voted calmly to have a Marxist-Leninist state, the first nation in the world to make this choice freely and knowingly. . . . *His margin is only about one percent but it is large enough in the Chilean constitutional framework to nail down his triumph as final.* There is no reason to believe that the Chilean armed forces will unleash a civil war or that any other intervening miracle will undo his victory. It is a sad fact that Chile has taken the path to communism with only a little more than a third (36 percent) of the nation approving this choice, but it is an immutable fact. *It will have the most profound effect on Latin America and beyond; we have suffered a grievous defeat; the consequences will be domestic and international;* the repercussions will have immediate impact in some lands and delayed effect in others.[100] (emphasis in original)

A Marxist had been democratically elected, and Henry Kissinger concluded, "I don't see why we need to stand by and watch a country go Communist due to the irresponsibility of its own people."[101] According to Kissinger, Nixon told CIA director Helms "that he [Nixon] wanted a major effort to see what could be done to prevent Allende's accession to power." Nixon further told Helms, "If there were one chance in ten of getting rid of Allende we should try it; if Helms needed $10 million he would approve it. . . . Aid programs should be cut; [Chile's] economy should be squeezed until it 'screamed.' "[102] Helms would later tell a Senate committee, "If ever I carried the marshal's baton out of the Oval Office, it was that day." But there seemed no way to prevent Allende, and when he finally took over, the CIA produced an intelligence memorandum analyzing the impact of an Allende presidency. The CIA concluded that "the U.S. has no vital national interests within Chile . . . the world military balance of power would not be significantly altered" but that "an Allende victory would . . . create considerable political and psychological costs."

The "40 Committee" (composed of the attorney general, deputy secretaries of state and defense, the CIA director, the Joint Chiefs chair, and the assistant to the president for national security affairs), which replaced the "303 Committee" and was responsible for supervising covert operations within the Nixon administration, was asked to formulate a policy for dealing with the perceived threat of a Marxist government in Chile. The 40 Committee had been meeting on Chile for several years, trying to find ways to prevent Allende from becoming president. Now, with his election a certainty, it had to develop a plan of action. They decided on a series of half measures that seemed futile.

Nixon wanted more. On September 15, 1970, the president met with Kissinger, CIA director Richard Helms, and John Mitchell. According to the Senate select committee, Nixon ordered the CIA to (secretly) help organize a military coup d'état.

From that time on, a two-track policy developed toward Chile. Track I consisted of a variety of covert activities supervised by the 40 Committee with the hope of keeping Allende out of office. Track II involved efforts at promoting a military coup. While the CIA had doubts about the plan to promote a coup, it followed the president's order. But by September 23, the CIA Santiago office reported that such an effort was "utterly unrealistic."

At the same time, International Telephone and Telegraph (ITT), fearing the loss of property and revenue if Allende took power and nationalized industry, was putting tremendous pressure on the Nixon administration to block Allende's rise to power. ITT and its chairman, Harold Geneen, provided assistance in the destabilization effort in Chile.

But such efforts did not prevent Allende from becoming president, so the effort to destabilize his administration proceeded. A policy of applying economic pressure on Chile in hopes of fomenting opposition to Allende was pursued. The administration sought the help of Harold Geneen and other American businessmen in this effort.

After Allende took office, the 40 Committee authorized over $7 million in covert support to the anti-Allende forces in Chile. Nixon wanted to squeeze

Chile's economy until it, in his words, "screamed." He also wanted to give encouragement to right-wing elements in Chile's military. U.S. aid was cut off, and a "cool but correct" public posture was assumed. But it was anything but correct, and before long, Chile's economy collapsed, opposition to Allende grew, and in September of 1973 a military coup, in which Allende was killed, took control of the government. To what extent was the U.S. responsible for the overthrow of Chile's democratically elected government? A U.S. Senate report concluded:

There is no hard evidence of direct U.S. assistance to the coup, despite frequent allegations of such aid. Rather the United States—by its previous actions during Track II, its existing general posture of opposition to Allende, and the nature of its contacts with the Chilean military—probably gave the impression that it would not look with disfavor on a military coup. And U.S. officials in the years before 1973 may not always have succeeded in walking the thin line between monitoring indigenous coup plotting and actually stimulating it.

THE MIDDLE EAST

The political powder keg of the Middle East exploded into violence again in June of 1967 when Israel, acting on intelligence information, launched a preemptive strike against its Arab neighbors Egypt, Syria, and Jordan. The Six-Day War was a military triumph for Israel: it defeated three of its enemies, expanded its territory, gained control of the Palestinian population in the West Bank, and established the Israeli military as overwhelmingly superior in the region.

The United Nations called for a cease-fire and Israeli withdrawal to previous borders, but Israel did not comply. Thus, Israel maintained control of the conquered territories, and Israelis began to settle in the West Bank. While this Israeli victory was a great military triumph, it also set the stage for future hostilities and problems. When Richard Nixon became president in 1969, he inherited a crisis waiting to break out in the Middle East, and possibly a superpower confrontation.

After the Six-Day War, U.S. efforts to mollify the vying sides in the Middle East intensified. Nixon was well aware of the dangers lurking in this region. Not only were the countries of the region at each other's throats, but the Soviet Union was seeking to enhance its influence among the Arab states. How was the United States to (a) protect Israel from its unfriendly neighbors; (b) fairly represent the concerns and interests of the Arab world (the oil-producing states in particular); and (c) prevent the Soviets from gaining a stronghold in the region?

The Middle East also was of special importance to Nixon and Kissinger for reasons beyond those already mentioned. To them, the Middle East could serve as a test case and example of American power being used to promote peace and thereby restoring the credibility damaged by the war in Vietnam.

Initially Henry Kissinger had very little to do with the administration's Middle East policy. As Kissinger admitted in his memoirs, "When I entered office I knew very little of the Middle East." Beyond this, the president was concerned that the Arab leaders might be suspicious of Kissinger, a Jew. Thus, Secretary of State Rogers and the professional diplomats at State assumed the leadership role on this issue.

Nixon's early goal was to develop an evenhanded policy in the region. While Nixon was sensitive to the power American Jews held within the United States, he was also concerned that the Arab nations, especially those of the oil-rich countries, see that U.S. policy was balanced and fair. Nixon's concern for fairness in Middle East policy is reflected in notes taken by H. R. Haldeman at a September 10, 1979, meeting with the president. Nixon and Al Haig discussed the need to

quietly
    take resp for looking over anything re Israeli
be *sure* it is objective—has not been in past.
    & balanced
also I will watch them—say nothing to K

Nixon also wanted to reduce the growing Soviet influence in the region. He thus needed a genuine settlement of the differences between Israel and its Arab neighbors. Nixon was determined to actively pursue a Middle East peace settlement with new initiatives. He thus opened up U.S.-Soviet consultation on the Arab-Israeli conflict and made more positive overtures to the Arab leaders. Nixon's policy took shape in what was called the Rogers Plan.

The United States began active negotiations in the four-power talks (United States, Soviet Union, Great Britain, and France) hoping to arrive at a consensus. But the most serious talks occurred between the United States and the Soviet Union between March 18 and April 22, with Assistant Secretary of State Joseph Sisco engaging in direct talks with Soviet ambassador Dobrynin. The United States also hoped to get talks going among the belligerents, but the Arabs and Israelis were not prepared to talk, only to fight.

The administration felt that to get the peace process on track, the Soviet Union had to be brought into the process as an active participant and the United States had to visibly display that it truly would be evenhanded in its dealings with the Arabs and Israelis. There were several modifications of the Rogers Plan, but in essence it called for indirect negotiations between Egypt and Israel, a timetable for Israeli withdrawal from Egyptian lands, formal end to the state of war, agreed-upon secure borders, creation of demilitarized zones, free navigation through the Strait of Tiran, access through the Suez Canal, settlement of the Gaza Strip dispute, discussions on the Palestinian refugee issue, recognition of sovereignty and secure borders, and a promise from the "four powers" to see that the agreement was adhered to.[103]

The Rogers Plan was a bust. Israel and the Soviet Union rejected the plan, and U.S. policy floundered. In his memoirs, Nixon claims that he knew the Rogers Plan "could never be implemented,"[104] but hoped that the proposal would display an evenhanded approach and thereby make later efforts to approach the Arab leaders easier. Nixon himself never aggressively pushed the Rogers Plan, but hoped it might put the Soviets on the defensive.

While Kissinger was not the front man for the administration on Middle East policy in the first year, he began to have greater influence as time went on. By January of 1970, as the Middle Eastern situation worsened, the administration groped for a policy. All sides seemed polarized, with the Israeli air force stepping up its raids on Egypt, and the United States and Soviet Union unable to reach agreement on general principles toward peace in the Middle East. Finally, on January 31, Nixon received what Kissinger called the "first Soviet threat" of his presidency. This "threat" was conveyed in a letter from Premier Kosygin which read in part, "We would like to tell you in all frankness that if Israel continues its adventurism, to bomb the territory of the UAR and other Arab states, the Soviet Union will be forced to see to it that the Arab states have the means at their disposal, with the help of which a due rebuff to the arrogant aggressor could be made."[105]

Nixon characterized his response to Kosygin's letter as "carefully low-keyed," but it caused great concern that the Soviets would step up their activity in the region. Nixon sent a memorandum to Kissinger pointing out that " 'Even Handedness' is the right policy—But above all our interest is—what gives the Soviets the most trouble—Don't let Arab-Israeli conflicts obscure that interest." Thus, the Middle East became yet another arena for East-West conflict.[106]

At this point Rogers's star was descending, and Kissinger loomed more powerful. Nixon decided to resupply Israel and try to stem the growth of Soviet power in the region. As the Soviets began to resupply Egypt, Kissinger pressed Nixon, arguing that "the political balance would be drastically changed, and the military balances could be overthrown at any moment of Soviet choosing."[107] Kissinger dismissed the argument—whose source was the State Department—that the Israelis bore some responsibility for the conflict with Egypt, and instead concentrated on the growing Soviet influence in Egypt. From this point on, halting Soviet influence in the Middle East became the overriding concern of U.S. policy.

While Rogers and Dobrynin talked, Kissinger pressed the president to act forcefully. But Nixon, unsure of what to do, vacillated. By June, the president endorsed a revised Rogers Plan, this one a toned-down version of the first, designed to stop the shooting and start the talking. Egypt responded positively to the plan, and Nixon pressed Israel to agree to a cease-fire. The State Department had one of its few foreign policy victories!

But just as it seemed as if progress might be made in the Middle East, another crisis erupted. In September 1970, King Hussein of Jordan, one of the few pro-Western leaders in the Arab world, faced a series of hijackings and threats to his leadership in Jordan. On September 6, members of the Popular Front for the Liberation of Palestine (PFLP) hijacked a TWA plane and a Swissair plane and forced them to land in Jordan. A third plane was hijacked and forced to land in Cairo, its passengers were unloaded, and the plane was blown up. The next day a BOAC jet was hijacked and forced to land in Jordan. The PFLP had 478 hostages, all in Jordan. Amid threats a blow up the planes with the passengers aboard, King Hussein faced a dilemma: if he failed to act with force, the Jordanian army might act on its own, thereby jeopardizing his authority; if he acted too decisively, he ran the risk of being labelled traitor to the Arab cause.

Nixon, hoping to exert greater influence in the Middle East, put U.S. troops on alert in the region. On September 12, the PFLP moved the hostages to their camps and blew up the three planes. An exchange of "hostages" was agreed to. Israel would release 450 Palestinian prisoners, and the hijackers would release their hostages. But 55 Jewish hostages remained captive.

The PFLP also began terrorist attacks against Hussein's army. On September 15, Hussein replaced his civilian government with military leaders, and Jordan was in a civil war. Nixon was concerned that Syria and Iraq would intervene against Hussein. If that occurred, Nixon hinted that U.S. troops might intervene to help King Hussein. Nixon was convinced that the Soviets were behind the insurrection, and wrote in his memoirs that he could not allow Hussein to be overthrown, but was conscious of the game of nuclear dominoes being played.[108]

While Nixon may have overstated Soviet involvement and overestimated the consequences, the situation for Hussein was perilous. On September 18, Kissinger got word that Syrian tanks had crossed the Jordanian border. Amid reassurances from the Soviets that they were not behind any such efforts, Kissinger the next day received firm evidence that Syria *had* invaded Jordan. Hundreds of tanks were moving toward Irbad. Kissinger was sure the Soviets had lied to him.

American troops were on selected alert, and the United States warned the Soviets that if Syria proceeded, Israel and perhaps the United States might intercede. But by September 21, Syria was still in Jordan, and Hussein requested Israeli air support. Move and countermove seemed to be leading to a direct U.S.-Soviet conflict in the Middle East. Israel wanted assurances from the United States that if Egyptian and Soviet forces attacked Israel, the United States would come to the aid of Israel. Nixon agreed. Thus, Israel was able to give Hussein the support he needed. With Israeli aid, King Hussein's troops were able to drive the Syrian forces back into Syria, and a broader international crisis was averted.

After the Jordanian crisis, things seemed to stabilize in the Middle East. The Nixon administration drew several lessons from the crisis: (1) the evenhanded approach didn't work; (2) the Soviets were a growing threat in the region; and

(3) our best bet for stability was to boost Israel and its military. But Nixon and Kissinger may have erred in placing too much weight on the Soviet influence in Syria. Regional and internal political pressure motivated Syria more than Soviet pressure. Thus, rather than looking at the regional dynamics, Nixon continued to see the Middle East in terms of the United States versus the Soviet Union.

The very tenuous stability of the Middle East was once again shattered in October of 1973 by the Yom Kippur war. Unfortunately for Nixon, this occurred at a time when the Watergate scandal was closing in on the president. In the midst of the Watergate tapes controversy, as revelations of executive branch wrongdoing flooded out to the public, at a time when Nixon's vice president, Spiro Agnew, was forced to resign when evidence indicated that he had been accepting bribes, Nixon was distracted by his own problems. But leaders cannot pick the time they will allow crises to emerge, and the October '73 war came as a surprise to the Americans.

On October 6, 1973, two weeks after Henry Kissinger became secretary of state, Egypt and Syria simultaneously attacked Israel's northern and southern borders. Two days later, Israel launched a counterattack against Syria; a week later Israel counterattacked Egypt, crossing the Suez Canal. The Soviets resupplied Egypt and Syria with arms; the United States did the same for Israel. The military advantage was going to Israel. In an effort to boost the Arab position, the Organization of Arab Oil Producing Countries (OAPEC) announced a cut in oil production until Israel withdrew from the occupied territories. This move was clearly designed to pressure the West into softening its support for Israel.

On October 19, Brezhnev sent Nixon a message urging talks to end the hostilities.[109] Kissinger flew to Moscow, and the talks resulted in a U.S.–Soviet-sponsored United Nations resolution that was ultimately accepted by all parties. But the cease-fire quickly broke down, and the Israeli army completely encircled the Egyptian Third Army on the East Bank of the Suez Canal. Egyptian president Anwar Sadat asked the United States and Soviet Union to intervene, but Nixon refused. Brezhnev sent a message to Nixon suggesting joint intervention, threatening to intervene unilaterally if the United States failed to move. Nixon put all U.S. troops on worldwide alert shortly after midnight, October 25.[110] Whether Brezhnev or Nixon was bluffing is uncertain, but the Soviets *did not* intervene, and the United Nations eventually sent a peace-keeping force to the region to supervise a cease-fire.

Because Nixon was so distracted by Watergate, it was Kissinger who took the lead in developing the U.S. response to the October '73 war. Kissinger spoke and acted "for the president." And the Yom Kippur war changed the way the United States viewed the power situation in the Middle East. The illusion of stability based on Israeli military superiority was shattered. Also, the West began to fear that oil could indeed be used as a tool to pressure the United States and its allies. While the United States did not shift from a pro-Israeli to a pro-

Arab stance, the United States did recognize that oil might be used to blackmail the West, and the sense of vulnerability, of the limits of U.S. power, became more pronounced.[111]

Kissinger, out of the ashes of the October war, developed a more complex, step-by-step process of diplomacy whereby Egypt and Israel disengaged their forces in January of 1974, Syria and Israel agreed to a demilitarized buffer zone, and Egypt and Israel agreed to the "Sinai II" disengagement, which called for Israel to give back part of the territory they acquired in the 1967 war. Events in the Middle East created opportunities. Finally, in 1974, Kissinger was able to take advantage of the opportunities and through step-by-step diplomacy salvage a tenuous peace in the region.

As the Watergate crisis closed in on the president, Nixon, just two months before resigning from office, took a trip to the Middle East. At the time the president was suffering from phlebitis, and his doctors recommended against the trip. But the president was determined. He went to Cairo, where he received a hero's welcome. Nixon visited several other Middle Eastern countries, returning home to face the crisis that would soon drive him from office.

Overall, the Nixon administration's policies toward the Middle East took several course changes—from evenhandedness, to a view that the region was a U.S.-Soviet battleground, to a pro-Israeli tilt, to a recognition of the complexity of motives and resources of the region that led to the United States' serving a role as "honest broker." Nixon and Kissinger (and Rogers) did not ameliorate the deep-rooted difference between Arabs and Jews, but they did help keep the conflict within certain bounds.

THE INDIA-PAKISTAN WAR

On March 25, 1971, Yahya Khan, the president of West Pakistan, ordered his troops to attack secessionist forces in East Pakistan. Henry Kissinger characterized this episode as "perhaps the most complex issue of Nixon's first term."

The attack by the West Pakistani army was brutal, and it shocked the world. It was an effort not simply to defeat the secessionists, but to wipe them out. Most of the world denounced the atrocities, but not the United States. For Nixon and Kissinger, a larger geopolitical issue was at stake. Yahya Khan was a conduit for the United States to China, and Nixon did not want to jeopardize his China connection. But the war eventually drew India into the fray, would topple Yahya Khan's regime, and establish an independent state, Bangladesh.

The crisis stems from the time just after World War II when India and Pakistan won their independence from Great Britain. Pakistan united a large portion of the Moslem population, but a large segment was also split, between East and West Pakistan with India separating them. This led to wars in 1947–48 and 1965. The dominant West Pakistanis had constant troubles with East Pakistan, and in a December 1970 election, East Pakistan voted 98 percent for autonomy. The government of West Pakistan answered the call for independence by imprisoning the leaders of East Pakistan, killing thousands of East Pakistanis, and imposing martial law. A resistance movement erupted, and this led to oppression by West Pakistan. Masses of refugees fled to India, heating up the already tense relations between West Pakistan and India.

Reports of Indian assistance to the rebels infuriated the West Pakistani government, and finally on December 3, 1971, the West Pakistani air force attacked Indian airfields near West Pakistan, and the West Pakistani army moved into the Kashmir region of India. The India-Pakistan war had begun. Immediately, Indian troops moved into East Pakistan.

Even before the fighting had begun, Nixon and Kissinger decided "to tilt toward Pakistan." In spite of public neutrality, the United States began to come to the aide of Pakistan, at first denying helping Pakistan and when caught in a lie, arguing that it was merely continuing to supply arms for which Pakistan had already contracted. This policy, which ran contrary to our public position, was revealed in a dramatic and damaging leak. The United States was pursuing one policy in public, and the opposite policy in private. The United States had a long history of good relations with India, but Nixon despised Indian prime minister Gandhi.[112] Also, India was warming up to the Soviet Union, while Pakistan was our primary, though not our sole (contrary to what Kissinger later claimed) link to China.

It quickly became apparent that India would win the war in East Pakistan and a new nation would emerge. But Nixon and Kissinger, seeing the war as a test of wills between the United States and the Soviet Union, began to heat up the American effort. Nixon ordered the aircraft carrier *Enterprise* into the Indian Ocean, and he had Kissinger drop hints that unless the Soviet Union backed off, he would cancel his trip to Moscow. But India did win the war, and Bangladesh was born out of East Pakistan. In his memoirs, Kissinger devotes seventy-six pages to this incident, accusing India, with the backing of the Soviet Union, of threatening American interests in the region and attempting to jeopardize U.S. rapprochement with China. Kissinger claims that he and the president handled the crisis with "far-seeing geopolitical comprehension," "statesmanship," and a "courageous political stand."[113]

But another active participant, Deputy Assistant Secretary of State Christopher Van Hollen, presents a vastly different account of this crisis.[114] Nixon and Kissinger, seeing the Pakistani problem in East-West terms, misread the situation and assumed that the Soviets were behind the initial internal dispute in Pakistan and thus acted on an incorrect assumption. Kissinger believed that the India-Pakistan war was also an effort by the Soviets to humiliate China, with the United States caught in the middle.[115]

As Seymour Hersh points out, Nixon's assumptions "would . . . lead to a decision . . . to risk world war in a South Asia showdown with the Soviet Union. Nixon and Kissinger totally misread the situation, and the showdown they expected never took place. But if it had begun, and if China had decided to intervene on the side of West Pakistan, as Nixon and Kissinger convinced themselves it would, the United States was ready to do battle allied with China against the Soviet Union."[116] U.S. policy in the India-Pakistan war led to severe worldwide criticism, but there was very little backlash at home. The major blunder did not have a long-term negative impact on Nixon, and he continued to move toward reelection.

THE THIRD WORLD

To Nixon and Kissinger, the third world mattered little. In fact, the third world was important only inasmuch as East-West conflicts could be played out in those nations. There was no independent view or plan for the third world. Those nations were generally seen merely as pawns in big power games between the United States and the Soviet Union. Nixon and Kissinger did not appreciate the growing independence of much of the third world, and thus failed to see the third world as it was. In this sense, a great opportunity was missed.

But events in the third world kept cropping up, demanding time, attention, and resources. Especially in the areas of economic policy and military confrontation, third world issues kept "interfering" with the plans for a new structure of world peace.

Apart from Vietnam and the Middle East, the United States never gave enough attention to third world regions to develop a coherent policy. The president never visited a Latin American country (except Mexico), and he never went to Africa as president. Except for Cuba and Chile, the president and Henry Kissinger seemed uninterested in Latin America. In his inaugural address, Nixon broke with postwar tradition by not even mentioning Latin America. He was also late in appointing an assistant secretary of state for inter-American affairs.[117] Nixon sought to move away from the Alliance for Progress and pursue a lower profile in Latin America. In an October 31, 1969, speech on Latin America, Nixon criticized the Alliance for Progress approach, suggesting that the Latin American nations had to pursue their own destinies and not be made into the image of the United States.

Cuba was a different story. Because of the unique relationship of the United States to Cuba since the 1950s, Nixon was very conscious of having a Soviet satellite state ninety miles off the Florida coast. Nixon had long been a critic of what he saw as the softness of his Democratic predecessors on Cuba. In September of 1971 Nixon received reports that the Russians were constructing a nuclear submarine base in Cienfuegos, Cuba. If the Soviets were building such a base, it violated the 1962 Kennedy-Khruschev agreement reached after the Cuban Missile Crisis. When press reports began to surface, the president had to respond.

But the evidence was very ambiguous.[118] If Nixon precipitated a crisis over nothing, he could endanger the nation's security. If he failed to act, he would be at grave political risk. The president decided to exert behind-the-scenes pressure on Soviet ambassador Dobrynin, impressing upon him the gravity of the situation. There followed a confusing set of accusations and denials, and even now we do not know whether a base was being built in Cuba. But the Russians assured Nixon that no such base was being built, and no further evidence of construction surfaced.

Black Africa was of little importance to Nixon. At one point the president told Kissinger, "Henry, let's leave the niggers to Bill [Rogers] and we'll take care of the rest of the world."[119] In Africa, Nixon alternated between having no policy and pursuing the "Tar Baby" option (named that by State Department critics who warned that the policy was so sticky that if something went wrong, the United States would be unable to extricate itself from the mess).

Between August 1969 and January 1970, the NSC discussed what to do about the problems of white minority governments in the nations of sub-Saharan Africa where black majorities were demanding power. Eventually the NSC, in NSSM 39, came up with five options, only three of which were considered seriously. The first called for "closer association with the regimes to protect and enhance our economic, strategic, and scientific interests,"; the second, the Tar Baby option, called for "selective relaxation of our stance toward the white regimes" while maintaining a public position of "opposition to racial repression." The third option called for a continuation of current policy as developed by Lyndon Johnson, to continue to express opposition to the racial and colonial policies of the white minority governments, but maintain diplomatic and other relations with these countries, in ways "which do not imply our condoning of racial repression." The final two options, to cut off all ties with the white governments and to follow a complete hands-off policy, were never seriously considered. Nixon and Kissinger chose option two.[120]

The Tar Baby option called for a relaxation of pressure on white minority regimes in Southern Africa, assuming that "the whites are here to stay."[121] The black majorities would get some verbal support, but the whites would be supported in all other ways. This policy of offering aid and assistance to white leaders did not come to public attention until Terence Smith of the *New York Times* published a long article on April 2, 1972. Until that time, Nixon gave the public the impression that we were promoting black majority rights and rule. Smith's article revealed that Nixon was pursuing a policy of "deliberately expanded contacts and communication with the white governments of Southern Africa." The policy Nixon pursued in southern Africa resembled that of his predecessors but was more deliberate in its tilt toward white minority governments. Nixon wanted to preserve the status quo, and when he thought about southern Africa, which was rarely, he thought of it in broad strategic terms.

In 1975 the administration's policy collapsed under the weight of the crisis in Angola. The United States, it turned out, did not have much of a policy for dealing with the emerging issues in southern Africa. History was passing us by.

In the southern Africa nations of Angola, Mozambique, Rhodesia (Zimbabwe), Southwest Africa (Namibia), South Africa, and Zambia, four million whites ruled thirty million blacks. Nixon and Kissinger simply did not have a viable policy for dealing with this problem of white minority government in black majority nations. They continued, with modifications, the Europeanist approach of their predecessors, but placed greater emphasis on promoting stability in the midst of majoritarian uprising. As much as was possible, Nixon and Kissinger ignored developments in the southern African region and, as NSSM 39 revealed, sought to prop up white minority governments and practice benign neglect and wishful thinking where black majorities were concerned.

In the third world, Nixon constantly saw most issues in East-West terms. He was unable to see them in terms of the new structure of world peace; he was unable to move beyond Cold War stereotypes. The great foreign policy innovator was mired in a Cold War conceit that distorted his own views and assumptions and imperiled his policy initiatives.

INTERNATIONAL ECONOMIC POLICY

The international economic situation that Nixon inherited was one in which the United States was moving from a position of economic supremacy to a more-competitive, less-dominant role. The United States emerged from World War II as the unchallenged leader of the West, but by the 1970s, Japan and Western Europe were becoming economic competitors, threatening U.S. markets, trade positions, and supremacy.

At first Nixon behaved as if a new international political structure could be created without paying much attention to the economic aspects of the international order. But by 1971, economic problems loomed large, and Nixon brought Peter G. Peterson, chairman of the board of Bell & Howell, into the administration to coordinate foreign economic policy.[122] In early 1971 Nixon also created the Council on International Economic Policy (CIEP) to further coordinate foreign economic policy. Peterson eventually headed CIEP and became the president's chief assistant for international economic issues. But Peterson was far down the White House pecking order—under Kissinger in foreign policy and under Connally in economic policy. Peterson did have some impact, but he was never able to become a part of the inner core of the White House, and given Nixon's closed decision-making style, his influence, and that of CIEP, was short-lived.

Nixon and Peterson faced two immediate problems: oil and the decline of the U.S. hegemonic position in international economics. At first the United States did not take seriously the threat of the Organization of Petroleum Exporters (OPEC) to use oil as a political tool.[123] But the West was vulnerable to interruptions in the supply of oil, and if the United States was to maintain its leadership of the alliance, it had to deal with this threat. Nixon was given a report by State Department energy expert James Akins on the potential crisis, recommending oil conservation. Nixon rejected that idea, and John Ehrlichman sent a terse memo to Peter Flanagan, "Conservation is not in the Republican ethic."[124]

But oil dependency, and the vulnerability it created, could not be ignored. On June 4, 1971, Nixon sent Congress a "Special Message on Energy Resources," calling for "new sources of energy" and making no mention of conservation. In short, the United States was not prepared to deal with the problem in any meaningful way.

The difficulties flowing from the decline of the American hegemonic position in the international economic arena could not be so easily ignored. The United States, the big kid on the block (in many ways, the only kid on the block) after World War II, now faced economic challenges from the rebuilt and growing economies of Japan and Western Europe. International economic relations were destabilizing, and the United States was caught in the middle. Should the president protect the postwar international economic framework established at Bretton Woods, or should he worry about the American domestic economy?

Nixon had two options—heat up the domestic economy temporarily, or pull the rug out from under the Bretton Woods framework that served as the foundation of the international economic system. For short-term domestic political reasons, Nixon chose the latter. The 1972 presidential election was approaching, and Nixon wanted to boost his chances for reelection by stimulating the economy and putting more disposable income into the hands of average Americans. Nixon chose to heat up the domestic economy.

The postwar international order was the victim of a "Nixon shock" when in August of 1971, Nixon took the United States off the gold standard, let the dollar float, put a 10 percent surcharge on foreign goods, and imposed domestic wage and price controls. When the hegemon breaks the rules of the international order, the system begins to break down. For the sake of domestic political considerations, Nixon let the international framework disintegrate. The decline of American leadership of the Western alliance continued.

CONGRESS AND FOREIGN POLICY

While presidents tend to dominate the Congress in the field of foreign policy, and while the courts normally grant wide latitude to presidential claims of power in the field of foreign affairs,[125] on occasion, the Congress will rise up and challenge a president over foreign policy. Early in his term, Richard Nixon faced a Congress frustrated by U.S. policy in Vietnam and impatient for a sign that Nixon was ending that war. After some early scrapes with the Congress over issues such as the ABM treaty and military and economic aid proposals, Nixon and the Congress came to loggerheads over Vietnam.

Whatever trust or support Nixon had in the Democrat-controlled Congress was shattered by the bombing and invasion of Cambodia in 1970. From that point on, congressional efforts to force an end to U.S. involvement in Vietnam accelerated. The Cooper-Church amendment to the 1970 foreign military sales bill was the high-water mark for Congress. This amendment prohibited funds for U.S. forces in Cambodia. In 1973 and 1974 these restrictions were extended to forbid "the use of any past or present appropriations for financing directly or indirectly United States combat activities in or over or from off the shores of North Vietnam, South Vietnam, Laos, or Cambodia."[126]

By 1973, the president's stock had fallen, and a more activist Congress, bolstered by Watergate, attempted to further codify—and limit—the president's powers in foreign affairs. In November of 1973, over Nixon's veto, the Congress passed the War Powers Resolution, which called for congressional consultation before the president committed U.S. troops to combat, limited the time and circumstances of U.S. military involvement without congressional authorization, and gave the Congress authority to disengage American troops from hostilities. While all presidents from Nixon to Reagan have questioned the constitutionality of this act, there has been no direct challenge.

Because of what the Congress felt were excesses by Nixon in foreign policy, the early 1970s saw resurgence of congressional will to be a participant in foreign policy making. Nixon's successor, Gerald Ford, faced a very vocal and, in Ford's view, obstructionist Congress in the field of foreign affairs. If the presidency under Nixon had become "imperial," the Congress saw to it that under Ford, it was imperiled, shackled, and restrained.

CONCLUSION

Two powerful images of Richard Nixon persist. On the one hand, he is remembered as the president who resigned his office in disgrace when faced with the certainty of impeachment and conviction in the Senate. The other image is of a skilled, daring, imaginative international statesman and diplomat who refashioned America's foreign policy, ended the war in Vietnam, opened doors to China, and pursued détente with the Soviet Union. Which is the real Nixon? Both, of course. In light of all his creativity and impact in the field of foreign affairs, it is ironic that the most powerful image is still that of disgraced leader. Abroad Nixon maintains a fairly positive image, especially in Europe and the Eastern bloc. Richard Nixon the paradox.

Nixon attempted to face the dilemma of a hegemonic nation losing its power base. Economic advances by our allies, military advances by our adversaries, and resource dependency all put the United States in a less-dominant international position than at any time since World War II. Nixon set out to reorder America's international responsibilities and bring objectives in line with available resources. Kissinger said in his memoirs that the president "wanted to found American foreign policy on a sober perception of permanent national interests."[127] In this light Nixon attempted to relate interests to capabilities and produce a more viable, pragmatic approach to America's role in the world. "Nixon's was," writes C. L. Sulzberger, "the most complete conception of an overall policy for a great-power America that had been produced by any U.S. president since Woodrow Wilson." Sulzberger continued, "To denigrate Nixon's foreign policy because it was flawed by the Vietnam inheritance and overshadowed by the dirty Watergate mess is to misread Nixon's historical importance."[128] Nixon pursued a form of realpolitik that was visionary and dynamic. He attempted to secularize foreign policy. While his realpolitik may not have always held a firm handle on realism, it was always pursued with a steady and often subtle hand.

When discussing the Nixon legacy in foreign affairs, one must never lose sight of the war that he inherited, both at home and in Vietnam. The war dominated the first Nixon term and affected so much of his behavior, even the unsavory and illegal acts that led to his downfall, that one must always see Nixon through the prism of Vietnam. Given that Nixon inherited a divisive war, one must still evaluate his efforts to end that war. Nixon, while pulling American troops from Southeast Asia, went on to extend, then end the war. The price for ending the war was a brutalized Vietnam and a devastated Cambodia. While it is unfair to blame Nixon for the war, it is fair to criticize him for the secret bombing of Cambodia, and for his prosecution of the war that America lost. While Nixon claimed that the war in Vietnam was resolved as "peace with honor," that simply was not the case. Shortly after the United States pulled out, brutal communist regimes took over Vietnam and Cambodia.

Overall, how are we to evaluate Nixon's handling of foreign policy? What standards should be used to assess presidential performance in foreign affairs? A six-category test[129] can be applied that looks at: (1) *policy direction and design* (how well designed are the president's goals and tactics?); (2) *organization, management, staffing* (how effective is the presidential team?); (3) *power and security* (do the president's policies promote U.S. power and security, both in the short and long term?); (4) *consensus-building* (does the president build stable domestic support for his policies?); (5) *democratic accountability* (does the president perform his duties according to constitutional, ethical, and legal standards?); and (6) *human rights* (do the president's policies promote respect for human rights at home and abroad?).

Policy Direction and Design

Nixon attempted to readjust America's goals to match more-limited resources. His design was ambitious, comprehensive, and brilliantly conceived. He must receive high marks for conceptual design.

Organization, Management, and Staffing

Nixon and Kissinger ran a two-man show in foreign policy. The bureaucracy, including even the State Department, was excluded. This approach fit

Nixon's personality needs and operating style, but in the long run did not serve Nixon's or the nation's interests. The two-man system limited the number of issues that could be dealt with at any one time, and by overpersonalizing and underinstitutionalizing foreign policy, undermined their own ability to integrate their new approach into the mainstream of the foreign policy establishment.

Power and Security

Prolonging and extending the war in Vietnam clearly damaged American interests, but developing closer relationships with China and the Soviet Union were in the nation's short- and long-term interests. The staying power of détente is evident when one recalls that even its most strident critic, Ronald Reagan, eventually was forced to embrace détente.

Consensus-building

In this regard Nixon failed miserably. Not only did he oversell détente, but he acted as if building domestic support for his policies was unnecessary. Thus, when Nixon left office in disgrace, his policies floundered for want of public and institutional support.

Democratic Accountability

Nixon's overreliance on secrecy, his dissembling, his illegal activities, bespeak a contempt for democratic procedures and accountability. Nixon attempted to withhold information from, and deceive, Congress and the public. If, as Kissinger wrote, "the acid test of a policy . . . is its ability to obtain domestic support,"[130] Nixon must be judged a failure.

Human Rights

Nixon was concerned with power. Questions of values and human rights took a secondary position. In Chile, South Africa, Southeast Asia, and elsewhere, Nixon's focus on power overshadowed questions of rights.

In more-general terms, the political left in the United States criticized Nixon for overemphasizing power and underemphasizing morality in foreign policy; the right criticized Nixon for placing too little emphasis on ideological conflict between West and East and for giving too much away to the Soviets through détente. But whatever the criticisms, the broad outlines of Nixon's approach to foreign affairs continue to have an impact in policy-making circles to this day.

Nixon brought the "imperial presidency" to its apex.[131] He pushed presidential powers beyond their legal and politically acceptable limits. His excessively broad concept of the national security state justified in his mind a series of criminal acts that led to Watergate. The slide into abuse of power, corruption, and criminality began in the foreign policy arena with Cold War justifications and culminated in Nixon's 1977 response to a question by interviewer David Frost, "Well, when the President does it, that means it's not illegal." [132]

Nixon used the power of the presidency against his political opponents (enemies) and felt justified to do so because only he could protect the national interest against a multitude of threats. "National security" became the justification. It was also the excuse.

But the president was not completely above the law, and when the tools and tactics normally reserved for use against foreign adversaries—burglaries, break-ins, dirty tricks, and so forth—began to emerge in the domestic arena, the imperial nature of the Nixon presidency was revealed. The rule of law had to be reinforced in the face of such abuses. The crimes of Watergate had their origins in the foreign policy arena. How could Nixon, so brilliant an international strategist, have let this happen?

In foreign affairs, all presidents have a fairly high level of opportunity to act. There are fewer restraints and greater powers in foreign policy than in the domestic arena. Richard Nixon, determined to be an activist foreign policy president, used his powers to the fullest. While he could not bring about the structure of peace he sought, he did begin a transformation in superpower relations that had a significant and lasting impact.

NOTES

1. Cecil V. Crabb and Kevin V. Mulcahy, *Presidents and Foreign Policy Making* (Baton Rouge: Louisiana State University Press, 1986), p. 237.

2. Kissinger, *White House Years*, p. 57. For a more elaborate discussion of presidential policies dealing with relative decline, see: Genovese, "The Presidency in an Age of Decline."

3. Robert Osgood et al., *Retreat from Empire?* (Baltimore: Johns Hopkins University Press, 1973).

4. While Nixon has denied that his policies were designed to face an era of relative decline, he certainly acted as if that were precisely what he and Kissinger were aiming at. Now Nixon has especially harsh words for the politicians and academics who speak and write about decline; see Richard Nixon, *1999: Victory without War* (New York: Simon & Schuster, 1988).

5. James E. Dougherty and Robert L. Pfaltzgraff, *American Foreign Policy: FDR to Reagan* (New York: Harper & Row, 1986), Chap. 7. See also: Walter LaFeber, *The American Age* (New York: Norton, 1989), Chap. 18.

6. Tad Szulc, *The Illusion of Peace* (New York: Viking, 1978), pp. 7–8.

7. "Inaugural Address of President Richard Milhous Nixon," January 20, 1969, *Presidential Documents* 5 (January 27, 1969), pp. 152–153.

8. Richard M. Nixon, *U.S. Foreign Policy for the 1970s: Building for Peace* (United States Government, February 15, 1971), p. 167.

9. Nixon, *RN*, p. 395.

10. Richard Nixon, *Public Papers of the Presidents* (United States Government, 1970), pp. 116–190.

11. Stephen Garrett, "Nixonian Foreign Policy: A New Balance of Power—or a Revived Concert?" *Polity* (1976), pp. 389–421.

12. Zbigniew Brzezinski, "The Balance of Power Delusion," *Foreign Policy*, (Summer 1972), pp. 54–59; Stanley Hoffman, "Will the Balance Balance at Home?" *Foreign Policy* (Summer 1972), pp. 60–86.

13. James Chace, "The Concert of Europe," *Foreign Affairs* (October 1973), pp. 96–108.

14. M. J. Brenner, "The Problem of Innovation and the Nixon-Kissinger Foreign Policy," *International Studies Quarterly* (September 1973), pp. 255–94.

15. Edward A. Kolodziej, "Foreign Policy and the Politics of Interdependence: The Nixon Presidency," *Polity* 9, no. 2 (Winter 1976), pp. 121–157.

16. Reichley, *Conservatives in an Age of Change*, p. 112.

17. Bernard Kalb and Marvin Kalb, *Kissinger* (Boston: Little, Brown, 1974); David Landau, *Kissinger: The Uses of Power* (Boston: Houghton Mifflin, 1972); and Stephen R. Graubard, *Kissinger: Portrait of a Mind* (New York: Norton, 1973).

18. For Henry Kissinger's description of the Fallaci interview, see: Kissinger, *White House Years*, pp. 1409–1410. Also see: Seymour M. Hersh, *The Price of Power: Kissinger in the Nixon White House* (New York: Summit, 1983), pp. 608–609.

19. Quoted in C. L. Sulzberger, *The World and Richard Nixon* (New York: Prentice-Hall, 1987), p. 368.

20. Quoted in Reichley, *Conservatives in an Age of Change*, p. 109.

21. Crabb and Mulcahy, *Presidents and Foreign Policy Making*, pp. 260–267.

22. Crabb and Mulcahy, *Presidents and Foreign Policy Making*, Chap. 7.

23. Kissinger, *White House Years*, p. 142.

24. H. R. Haldeman, files from Nixon Presidential Materials, National Archives, Alexandria, Virginia.

25. John D. Ehrlichman, files from Nixon Presidential Materials, National Archives, Alexandria, Virginia.

26. George C. Herring, *America's Longest War* (New York: Wiley, 1979), pp. 217–251.

27. Szulc, *The Illusion of Peace*, p. 150.

28. Haldeman, *The Ends of Power*, pp. 82–83.

29. Nixon, *RN*, p. 381.

30. Nixon, *RN*, p. 382.

31. The secret bombing of Cambodia was the basis of one of the impeachment charges against President Nixon. The article was voted down by a 26–12 margin.

32. Szulc, *The Illusion of Peace*, pp. 54–55.

33. "Reconstruction of Cambodia Decision," *New York Times*, June 30, 1970, p. 16.

34. When the president spoke these words, American B-52s had been flying bombing missions over Cambodia for over thirteen months.

35. Les Evans and Allen Myers, *Watergate and the Myth of American Democracy* (New York: Pathfinder, 1974).

36. Evans and Novak, *Nixon in the White House*, pp. 277–285.

37. Szulc, *The Illusion of Power*, pp. 284–285. For Nixon's own version, see: Nixon, *RN*, pp. 459–466.

38. In November of 1969, the My Lai massacre—in which American soldiers killed more than 350 South Vietnamese villagers—became public knowledge. While the massacre took place in 1968, Nixon had to deal with the public outrage. His response was to spy on Ronald Ridenhour, who made the massacre known to the army and later to Congress. The revelation of the My Lai massacre proved to be a turning point in public opinion as the "middle class" began to turn against the war. See: Hersh, *The Price of Power*, p. 135; and Clark R. Mollenhoff, *Game Plan for Disaster* (New York: Norton, 1976), Chap. 9.

39. Haldeman, *The Ends of Power*, p. 79.

40. Nixon himself had used leaks on a number of occasions, such as his effort to spread damaging information about Daniel Ellsberg, and in his memoirs (p. 400), Nixon wrote of planting "a story that I knew would leak."

41. Nixon, *RN*, p. 387.

42. Nixon, *RN*, pp. 387–388.

43. Hersh, *The Price of Power*, p. 44.

44. Safire, *Before the Fall*, p. 166.

45. Hersh, *The Price of Power*, pp. 86–87.

46. Safire, *Before the Fall*, pp. 166–167.

47. Nixon, *RN*, p. 388.

48. Nixon, *RN*, pp. 469–471.

49. William Shawcross, *Sideshow: Kissinger, Nixon and the Destruction of Cambodia* (New York: Simon & Schuster, 1979), pp. 157–169; Jonathan Schell, *The Time of Illusion* (New York: Knopf, 1976), pp. 111–116; and Szulc, *The Illusion of Peace*, pp. 294–296.

50. Barry Sussman, *The Great Coverup: Nixon and the Scandal of Watergate* (New York: New American Library, 1974), pp. 207–209.

51. Nixon, *RN*, pp. 469–476.

52. Seymour M. Hersh, "1971 Tape Links Nixon to Plan to Use Thugs," *New York Times*, September 24, 1981, p. 1.

53. Martin Shapiro, *The Pentagon Papers and the Courts* (San Francisco: Chandler, 1971).

54. James F. Simon, *In His Own Image* (New York: McKay, 1974), Chap. 8.

55. Nixon, *RN*, p. 508.

56. Chuck Colson, comments at Hofstra University Conference on the Nixon presidency, November 1987.

57. Sussman, *The Great Coverup*, p. 213.

58. Upset that J. Edgar Hoover was, in Nixon's view, "dragging his feet" on the Ellsberg investigation, the president said that if the FBI was not going to pursue the case, "we shall have to do it ourselves." See: Langford, *Nixon: A Study in Extremes of Fortune* (London: Weidenfeld and Nicolson, 1980), p. 80.

59. For Nixon's version of this meeting, see: Nixon, *RN*, p. 511.

60. Hersh, *The Price of Power*, p. 397.

61. The president admits in *RN* (p. 512) that at the June 17 meeting he said that he wanted government documents removed from Brookings, "even if it meant having to get it surreptitiously."

62. Szulc, *The Illusion of Peace*, p. 475; also see Haldeman, *The Ends of Power*, p. 220; and J. Anthony Lukas, *Nightmare* (New York: Viking, 1973), pp. 84–86.

63. Schell: *The Time of Illusion*, p. 162.

64. Nixon feared that Ellsberg might have "acted as part of a conspiracy." Nixon, *RN*, p. 513.

65. Nixon, *RN*, p. 513.

66. Nixon, *RN*, p. 514.

67. Haldeman, *The Ends of Power*, pp. 114–116.

68. Ehrlichman, *Witness to Power*, p. 165.

69. Nixon, *RN*, p. 515.

70. Ehrlichman, *Witness to Power*, p. 374.

71. Commentary by Charles Colson and Egil Krogh, Hofstra University Conference on the Nixon Presidency, November 1987.

72. Barbara Tuchman, *The March of Folly: From Troy to Vietnam* (New York: Ballantine, 1984), p. 369.

73. Nguyen Thien Hung and Jerrold L. Schecter, *The Palace File* (New York: Harper and Row, 1986).

74. Szulc, *The Illusion of Peace*, p. 70.

75. Nixon, *RN*, p. 346.

76. Richard J. Barnet, *The Giants: Russia and America* (New York: Simon and Schuster, 1977), p. 28.

77. Raymond L. Garthoff, *Détente and Confrontation: American-Soviet Relations from Nixon to Reagan* (Washington, D.C.: Brookings Institute, 1985), pp. 25–36.

78. Nixon, *RN*, p. 941.

79. Prepared statement, in *Détente, Hearings before the Senate Committee on Foreign Relations*, 93rd Cong., 2d sess. (Washington, D.C.: U.S. Government Printing Office, 1975), p. 247.

80. Interview in *U.S. News and World Report*, June 12, 1975, p. 42.

81. Garthoff, *Détente and Confrontation*, pp. 36–53.

82. *Pravda*, January 19, 1977.

83. Nixon, *RN*, p. 610.

84. Kissinger, *White House Years*, p. 1250.

85. Kissinger, "Détente with the Soviet Union: The Reality of Competition and the Imperative of Cooperation State Bulletin," Statement to the Senate Committee on Foreign Relations, September 19, vol. 71 (October 14, 1974), pp. 512–513.

86. Nixon, address to joint session of Congress, June 1, 1972.

87. Nixon and Kissinger, June 15, *State Bulletin* 167 (July 10, 1972), p. 40.

88. The president had a great deal of confidence in his and Kissinger's ability to negotiate with the Soviets. In notes taken by John Ehrlichman of a November 14, 1972, meeting at Camp David, Ehrlichman wrote that the president believed that "HAK (Kissinger) is a ragmerchant—start at 50% to get 25%—That's why he's so good w/the Russians."

89. Nixon address to Congress, June 1, 1972.

90. Nixon, *RN*, p. 886.

91. Henry Kissinger, *Years of Upheaval* (Boston: Little, Brown, 1982), p. 994.

92. Kissinger, *Years of Upheaval*, p. 997.

93. Nixon, *RN*, p. 1037.

94. Kalb and Kalb, *Kissinger*, p. 216.

95. Kalb and Kalb, *Kissinger*, Chap. 9.

96. Garthoff, *Détente and Confrontation*, Chap. 6.

97. Nixon, *RN*, pp. 544–580; and Kissinger, *White House Years*, Chap. 24.

98. Kissinger, *White House Years*, Chaps. 4 and 11.

99. "Covert Action in Chile, 1963–1973." Staff Report of the Select Committee to Study Governmental Operations with Respect to Intelligence Activities, United States Senate, 1975.

100. Kissinger, *White House Years*, Chap. 17; Kissinger, *Years of Upheaval*, Chap. 9; and Nixon, *RN*, pp. 489–490.

101. Quoted in Seymour M. Hersh, "Censored Matter in Book about C.I.A. Said to Have Related Chile Activities," *New York Times*, September 11, 1974, p. 14. For a review of Nixon's covert activities in Chile, see: John Prados, *President's Secret Wars* (New York: Quill, 1986), pp. 315–324.

102. U.S. Senate, Select Committee to Study Governmental Operations with Respect to Intelligence Activities, *Interim Report: Alleged Assassination Plots Involving Foreign Leaders* (Washington, D.C.: U.S. Government Printing Office, 1975). Also see U.S. Senate, *Hearings before the Senate Select Committee to Study Government Operations with Regard to Intelligence Activities*, 94th Cong., 1st sess., 1975, chaired by Senator Frank Church. The Church Committee published a staff report entitled *Covert Action in Chile, 1963–1973*.

103. William B. Quandt, *Decade of Decisions: American Policy toward the Arab-Israeli Conflict 1967–1976*, (Berkeley: University of California Press, 1977).

104. Nixon, *RN*, pp. 478–479.

105. Hersh, *The Price of Power*, p. 223; Quandt, *Decade of Decisions*, pp. 95–96.

106. Hersh, *The Price of Power*, Chap. 18.

107. Kissinger, *White House Years*, Chap. 10.

108. Nixon, *RN*, p. 483.

109. Nixon, *RN*, pp. 920–922.

110. Nixon, *RN*, pp. 939–940.

111. Quandt, *Decade of Decisions*, pp. 200–206.

112. Hersh, *The Price of Power*, p. 447.

113. Kissinger, *White House Years*, pp. 842–918.

114. Christopher Van Hollen, "The Tilt Policy Revisited: Nixon-Kissinger Geopolitics and South Asia," *Asian Survey* 20 (April 1980), pp. 339–361.

115. Kissinger, *White House Years*, pp. 875–76, 883–86.

116. Hersh, *The Price of Power*, pp. 446–447.

117. *New York Times*, June, 1969, for various reports.

118. Hersh, *The Price of Power*, Chap. 20.

119. Hersh, *The Price of Power*, p. 111.

120. National Security Council Interdepartmental Group for Africa, *Study in Response to National Security Study Memorandum 39: Southern Africa*, Document AF/NSC-IG 69, August 15, 1969, reprinted in full in Mohamed A. El-Khawas and Barry Cohen, eds., *National Security Study Memorandum 39: The Kissinger Study of Southern Africa* (Westport, Conn.: Lawrence Hill, 1976).

121. Anthony Lake, *The "Tar Baby" Option: American Policy toward Southern Africa* (New York: Columbia University Press, 1976).

122. Szulc, *The Illusion of Peace*, Chap. 16.

123. Szulc, *The Illusion of Peace*, Chaps. 7 and 16.

124. Szulc, *The Illusion of Peace*, p. 450.

125. Michael A. Genovese, *The Supreme Court, the Constitution, and Presidential Power* (Lanham, Md.: University Press of America, 1980).

126. *Congressional Quarterly Almanac,* Washington, D.C.: Congressional Quarterly, (1973), p. 792.

127. Kissinger, *White House Years,* p. 914.

128. Sulzberger, *The World and Richard Nixon,* p. 3.

129. Adapted from: Ryan J. Barilleaux, "Presidential Conduct of Foreign Policy," *Congress and the Presidency,* 15, no. 1 (Spring 1988), pp. 1–19.

130. Henry A. Kissinger, *A World Restored: Costlereagh, Metternich, and the Problems of Peace 1812–1822* (Boston: Houghton Mifflin, 1957–1964), pp. 326–330).

131. Arthur Schlesinger, Jr., *The Imperial Presidency* (Boston: Houghton Mifflin, 1973).

132. Nixon, *RN,* p. 763.

5

Watergate and the Collapse of the Nixon Presidency

> Let us begin by committing ourselves to the truth—to see it like it is, and tell it like it is—to find the truth, to speak the truth, and to live the truth.
>
> Richard Nixon, accepting the Republican
> Presidential nomination in 1968

"Watergate" is a generic term that originally referred only to the break-in of the Democratic National Committee (DNC) headquarters located at the Watergate office complex, but has come to be an umbrella term, under which a wide variety of crimes and improper acts are included. Watergate caused the downfall of a president. It led to jail sentences for a number of the highest-ranking officials of the administration. It was a traumatic experience for the nation. Why Watergate? How could it have happened? How could someone as smart and experienced as Richard Nixon behave so criminally *and* so stupidly? How could someone so adroit and practiced in the art and science of politics behave so foolishly? How could a "third-rate burglary" turn into a national disaster? How could Richard Nixon have done it to himself?

In essence, Watergate involved three separate but interconnected conspiracies, centered in four different areas.[1] The first conspiracy was the *Plumbers conspiracy*. This involved a variety of steps taken in the first term to plug leaks and "get" political enemies, illegal wiretapping, the break-in of Daniel Ellsberg's psychiatrist's office, and other acts, done in some instances for ostensible "national security" reasons, and at other times for purely political reasons. The purpose of this conspiracy was to destroy political enemies and strengthen the president's political position.

The second conspiracy was the *reelection conspiracy*. This grew out of lawful efforts to reelect the president, but degenerated into illegal efforts to extort money, launder money, sabotage the electoral process, spy, commit fraud, forgery, and burglary, play "dirty tricks," and attack Democratic front-runners. The purposes of this conspiracy were to (a) knock the stronger potential Democratic candidates (Hubert Humphrey, Ted Kennedy, Edmund Muskie, and Henry (Scoop) Jackson) out of the race; (b) accumulate enough money to bury the Democratic opponent by massively outspending him, and (c) thus guarantee the reelection of Richard Nixon. This conspiracy was conscious, deliberate, organized.

The third conspiracy was the *coverup conspiracy.* Almost immediately after the burglars were caught at the DNC headquarters in the Watergate, a criminal conspiracy began that was designed to mislead law enforcement officers and protect the reelection bid of the president, and then after the election, to keep the criminal investigations away from the White House. To this end, evidence was destroyed, perjury committed, lies told, investigations obstructed, and subpoenas defied. The purpose of the coverup was to contain the criminal charges and protect the president. This conspiracy was less conscious, almost instinctive. It was deliberate but poorly organized.

One can divide Watergate activities into four categories: the partisan arena, the policy arena, the financial arena, and the legal arena.[2] The *partisan* activities include acts taken against those of the opposition party and those deemed to be "enemies" of the administration. They include acts such as wiretapping and break-ins, the establishment of the Huston Plan, the Plumbers, and the enemies list, forged State Department cables, and political dirty tricks.

Policy activities include the stretching of presidential power beyond legal or constitutional limits. Examples include the secret bombing of Cambodia, the impoundment of congressionally appropriated funds, attempts to dismantle programs authorized by Congress, the extensive use of executive privilege, and underenforcement of laws such as the Civil Rights Act of 1964. When Nixon's defenders answer charges against the president by saying that "everybody does it," they are most often referring to this area of behavior.

In the *financial* area, both Nixon's political and personal finances deserve mention. On the political front, the "selling" of ambassadorships, extortion of money in the form of illegal campaign contributions, and laundering of money must be included. In Nixon's personal finances, such things as "irregularities" in income tax deductions and questionable "security" improvements in his private Florida and California homes, paid for with tax dollars, are included.

Finally, in the *legal* arena, illegal activities of the Nixon administration include obstruction of justice, perjury, criminal coverup, interference with criminal investigations, and destruction of evidence. It was the criminal coverup that eventually led to Nixon's forced resignation.

Categorizing and classifying Watergate behavior does a disservice to the drama and suspense of the unfurling of this political mystery. The story of Nixon's rise and fall, of his choices at several important points in the story, of his ultimate collapse, is what makes this drama so poignant and tragic.

Watergate was a series of criminal and unethical acts committed by Richard Nixon and members of his administration that were designed to increase Nixon's political power, punish potential "enemies," sabotage the electoral process, and cover up evidence of crimes. Acts such as obstruction of justice, burglary, conspiracy, lying under oath, wiretapping, misprision of perjury, and dirty tricks were involved. It took a vigilant press, a determined court system, two special prosecutors, House and Senate investigations, a federal grand jury, an aroused public, a good deal of luck, and ultimately, Nixon's own tape-recorded words to finally force the president to resign one step ahead of impeachment in the House and conviction in the Senate.

A number of crimes and "dirty tricks" had taken place before the 1972 re-election bid (see Chapter 4), but these acts did not become public until after the '72 election. In this sense, a clear and lengthy pattern, some would say policy, of deceit, manipulation, and crimes can be traced back to the early days of the administration. For example, in March of 1969 the United States began fourteen months of secret bombings of Cambodia; in May of 1969, il-legal wiretapping was under way; in June of 1970, the Huston Plan was ap-proved; in June of 1971, the Plumbers were created and they began to act against Daniel Ellsberg, eventually breaking into his psychiatrist's office; and in 1971, the enemies list was created. But these events came to light after and as part of an investigation into a bizarre event that took place at the Democratic National Committee's headquarters located at the Watergate office complex. An examination of the Watergate scandal reveals, as does no other area, the extent to which the paranoid style animated behavior in the Nixon administra-tion.

1970 MIDTERM ELECTIONS

Frustrated in his efforts to get his way with the Democratic Congress, the president knew that he had to pick up seats in the 1970 midterm elections if he was to have any hope of passing his legislative program into law. The goal was clear, but the strategy for achieving it was not. How could a Republican Congress be elected?

Nixon knew that there was no way he could win enough House races to gain a majority there, but the Senate was another matter. He might be able to win enough seats to gain control. But history was against him; midterm elections tend to be referendums on the incumbent president, and usually there is enough discontent and/or rebalancing from the previous election's presidential coattails to that the party not in control of the White House gains an average of 30 House seats, and 2–3 Senate seats. Could Nixon reverse this history? If he had any chance, he would have to concentrate on the Senate. He was determined to do so.

To gain a 50–50 split in the Senate thereby giving the vice president the tie-breaking vote and the Republicans majority power, the Republicans had to win 7 seats from the Democrats. The overall strategy for achieving this was to use Vice President Agnew to attack, attack, attack. Agnew would become Nixon's

Nixon. The president would not actively campaign, but he beefed up Agnew's staff with many of his own people and was personally involved in the details of campaign strategy. Agnew was to paint the Democrats as far leftists and "radic-libs," soft on crime, soft on campus demonstrators, soft. His attacks were hard-hitting, and he crisscrossed the country trying to put the Democrats on the defensive.

With the attack plan in high gear, the 1970 campaign steamed ahead. But Nixon was using the campaign not only to win control of the Senate, but as an important test run for his own 1972 reelection bid. Thus, the campaign took on a broader dimension than simply the anti-Democratic theme being struck by Agnew.

Two books strongly influenced the Nixon strategy. The first, Kevin Phillips's *The Emerging Republican Majority,* posited the theory that liberalism was waning and there was an opportunity to build a new conservative, Republican majority based on bringing the white South, ethnic Catholics, and some labor into the Republican fold. Nixon planned to aim for these traditionally Democratic groups. The second book, *The Real Majority* by Democrats Richard M. Scammon and Ben Wattenberg, suggested that the vast majority of voters were unyoung, unblack, and unpoor. An electoral strategy based on this recognition, and the issues associated with it, the so-called social issues, would bring victory. Agnew would hit hard, gaining the hard-core right and the disaffected. Nixon would pursue policies aimed at converting the supposedly convertible groups. The goal was a new ideological majority.

As the campaign progressed, Agnew hit harder and harder. Then the president made a fatal mistake. In effect Nixon abandoned the laid-back approach he was himself taking and at the eleventh hour decided to campaign hard for Republicans. As Nixon campaigned, his rhetoric became more and more shrill, more and more like Agnew's. It was a major miscalculation. Nixon appeared, as John Mitchell said, as if he were "running for sheriff"!

The 1970 midterm results were good by historical standards. While Republicans lost a net of 11 governorships, giving the Democrats a 29–21 advantage, they lost only 9 House seats, so the Democrats still had an enormous 254–181 advantage, and the Republicans won 2 Senate seats, leaving the Republicans only 5 seats short of a 50–50 split. But given the opportunity, the Republicans did poorly. The hopes of creating a new Republican majority were buried on the campaign trail of 1970, as the president could not stay with his early strategy and chose to go on the offensive in Agnew-like (or early Nixon-like) style. As a test run of the 1972 campaign, 1970 was distressing.

In November of 1970, things did not look good for Nixon. In the midterm congressional elections, the president campaigned aggressively for Republican candidates, but on election night the results were disappointing. The president staked his prestige on the campaign and emerged wounded. His own prospects for reelection in 1972 seemed questionable (Of course, this was before the China and Soviet Union trips, and before the ending of the war in Vietnam).

Four days after the disappointing 1970 midterm elections, Nixon, John Mitchell, Bob Haldeman, John Ehrlichman, Robert Finch, Charles Colson, Donald Rumsfeld, and Bryce Harlow, core members of the Nixon team, met in Key Biscayne to review the election results and plan for the 1972 race. There was agreement that President Nixon's campaign activities were counterproductive and a new approach was needed. After several hours of discussion a consensus emerged that called on the president to depoliticize his activities; Nixon was to be less partisan, less quarrelsome, he would be above politics—he would run for president, not sheriff. Nixon would present a positive image, not focus on the attack or the negative. By doing this, the team felt that Nixon could win the 1972 election and help forge inroads into the new Republican majority. Agnew might be asked to go on the attack, but not the president.

The Southern strategy, so effective in 1968, would be replaced by a Northern strategy, as the focus of 1972 would be Kevin Phillips's new suburban middle class, ethnic Catholics, labor members: the Silent Majority. Agnew would continue to pound away, attack the Democrats, hit hard. The president would rise above petty partisanship and be leader of all the people. It was a brilliant campaign strategy, needing only a policy victory or two to get it off the ground. But the plan included a third prong—a clandestine strategy to "screw" the Democrats would be implemented. It was the beginning of the end for Nixon.

For the strategy to succeed in reelection and realignment, several problems had to be resolved: the war in Vietnam had to be concluded, the economy had to be given a boost, a more moderate/progressive domestic agenda had to be forged, and the president had to stay on the high road and act presidential. It amounted to a significant reorientation of the Nixon presidency in midterm.

At the same time, a siege mentality continued to dominate. Opponents were increasingly seen as enemies, political competition as war. The new campaign strategy was simply war by other means. Charles Colson played a lead role in convincing the president and Haldeman that politics, especially at the presidential level, was war, and that adversaries were enemies. It was Colson who first brought the enemies list to his superiors. But from that point on, the public Nixon would be presidential, not "political"; the dirty work would be left to others.

THE 1972 ELECTION

If things looked grim for the president in 1970, as the 1972 election approached, things looked great. By acting presidential, and after a series of policy victories, the president's chances of reelection looked very bright. But the optimism over the president's election prospect was not based solely upon Nixon's style or policy successes; it rested also upon a strategy that successfully eliminated all the president's top Democratic challengers. In effect, the president tried to pick his opponent in the 1972 race.

As the primary season got under way, Maine senator Ed Muskie appeared to be Nixon's main challenger. Muskie, a popular and seasoned campaign veteran, rated close to—and sometimes ahead of—the president in early polls. Nixon feared a campaign against Muskie and set out to tilt the race.

The Nixon team developed a two-pronged strategy that was (1) productive and (2) predatory. The productive side was designed to highlight the president's accomplishments. The predatory side was designed to attack and destroy the Democratic front-runners.

The president had an inordinate fear of losing. His insecurities combined with past experiences to lead the president to overkill in campaigns. After all, in 1960 he lost the presidency by the thinnest of margins in a race he believed had been stolen from him (the president spoke of this frequently in the early campaign strategy sessions). In 1968, after a huge early lead, Nixon beat Hubert Humphrey by only one half of one percent. The president vowed not to let this happen again. He would win, and win "big."

The campaign organization, the Committee for the Re-election of the President, known as CREEP, was first run by Jeb Magruder, but the real head was John Mitchell, who, in close contact with the White House, called most of the shots from the outset. He, along with chief fundraiser Maurice Stans, established the most highly organized, well funded presidential campaign in American history.

In addition to the normal and expected work of the president's reelection effort, a subterranean operation of illegal money-collecting and dirty tricks was employed. In an effort to accumulate enough money to run the campaign, the president's money collectors went beyond the bounds of pressuring potential donors to extorting funds.

While Nixon continually claimed that he did not know about the dirty tricks campaign (he was, he maintained, working on issues such as peace and prosperity, and had no time for the details of campaigning), a May 5, 1971, tape recording indicates otherwise. One and one half years before the election, the dirty tricks campaign was already underway. Nixon and Haldeman were discussing some of Chuck Colson's tricks against Ed Muskie, laughing and joking about oranges sent in Muskie's name to some protesters, when the conversation turned to more serious tricks. Haldeman told the president that Colson "got a lot done that he hasn't been caught at," adding, "We got some stuff that he doesn't know anything about, too."

Haldeman then responded to a question from Nixon, saying that Dwight Chapin, Nixon's appointments secretary, had established a link with "a guy that nobody, none of us knows except Dwight . . . who is just completely removed. There's no contact at all. He's, he's starting to build it now. We're going to use it for the campaign next year." (They are almost certainly referring to Donald Segretti.)

"Are they really any good?" asked Nixon. Haldeman replied that "this guy's a real conspirator type . . . thug-type guy. . . . This is the kind of guy that can get out and tear things up." Clearly Mr. Nixon was aware of the dirty tricks operation at the early stages of the campaign.[3]

Since Muskie was the front-runner, the Nixon people went after him. A memo written by Pat Buchanan reads, "We ought to go down to the kennels and turn all the dogs loose on Ecology Ed." Buchanan added, "The President is the only one who should stand clear, while everybody else gets chewed up."[4]

The predatory strategy worked beyond the administration's wildest dreams. Muskie dropped out of the race shortly after the New Hampshire primary; Jackson, Humphrey, and the rest followed until Senator George McGovern, whom Nixon considered his weakest potential opponent, got the nomination. McGovern was very liberal and had only marginal support from mainstream Democrats. The president couldn't have been more pleased if he had picked his opponent—which in a way, he had.

The result of the 1972 campaign seemed a foregone conclusion even before it had begun. Nixon had several significant foreign policy victories to point to and seemed to be ending the war in Vietnam. McGovern, on the other hand, had nothing but trouble. His choice as vice president, Senator Thomas Eagleton of Missouri, it was revealed, had experienced severe depression on several occasions and had been hospitalized. He had also received electric-shock treatment for his depression. When this became public, Eagleton was forced off the ticket and R. Sargent Shriver, former Peace Corps director and ambassador to France, was put on the ticket. But the damage had been done, and the McGovern campaign never recovered.

The Nixon campaign was carefully orchestrated, controlled, and well funded. The president stayed above the fray and was generally inaccessible to the press. As McGovern self-destructed, the Nixon camp moved forward. But a curious event took place in mid-June. In the early morning hours of June 17, five men were arrested inside the office of the Democratic National Committee headquarters in the Watergate office complex. A young security guard making his rounds discovered a piece of tape horizontally covering the lock on the door. He removed the tape but did not call the police. Later, while on another set of rounds, he discovered *another* piece of tape on the same door! This time he called the police.

A short time later the D.C. police arrived and arrested five men in the sixth-floor offices of the DNC. The men wore rubber surgical gloves, carried walkie-talkies, electronic eavesdropping equipment, cameras, and other tools. One of the men, James McCord, was a former employee of the CIA and was the security chief of CREEP. Later, two others were arrested in connection with the Watergate break-in: a former CIA operative and consultant to the Nixon White House, E. Howard Hunt, and G. Gordon Liddy, general counsel to CREEP. The White House and CREEP denied any connection to the break-in, but among the belongings of those arrested at the Watergate were papers linking the suspects to the White House.

While the newspapers reported the story, and links between the burglars and the Nixon White House seemed possible, the break-in had little impact on public opinion (this was due in part to a coverup of the crime by the White House). If the public had suspicions, they did not run deep, and on November 7, 1972, Richard Nixon was reelected in an enormous landslide. In spite of the "minor annoyance" value, the Watergate story did not damage the president. He won a reelection victory, getting 97 percent of all electoral votes and over 60 percent of the popular vote. It was the biggest landslide in presidential history.

The jubilation at containing damage from the Watergate story was short-lived. Shortly after the election, a slow stream of news stories built up to an avalanche of bad news that revealed a wide range of criminal and unethical acts committed on behalf of the president.

On January 8, 1973, the trial of the Watergate burglars began. The White House was hoping for continued silence from the conspirators. On January 12, James McCord and CREEP "undercover agent" John Caulfield met in the evening on an overlook of the George Washington Parkway, and Caulfield assured the burglars of executive clemency "from the highest level of the White House." Nixon lawyer and fundraiser Herbert Kalmbach later admitted that on January 19, John Mitchell, John Dean, and Fred LaRue asked him to raise hush money for the defendants. At the trial itself, Magruder and Herbert Porter perjured themselves, testifying that Liddy was given money only for legitimate political intelligence gathering. On January 25, McCord, who was resisting the clemency offer, met for a third time with Caulfield, who told McCord he was "fouling up the game plan." But the game plan was starting to collapse under pressure from several directions.

DIRTY MONEY

> I made my mistakes, but in all of my years of public life, I have never profited, never profited from public service. I have earned every cent. And in all of my years of public life, I have never obstructed justice. And I think, too, that I could say that in my years of public life, that I welcome this kind of examination because people have got to know whether or not their President is a crook. Well, I am not a crook, I have earned everything I have got.
>   Richard M. Nixon, at Walt Disney World, November 17, 1973

"Money," as Jesse Unruh used to say, "is the mother's milk of politics," and the Nixon team collected and spent more money (over $60 million) than any campaign in presidential history. But money was also a sticking point for the president, for in both his political and personal finances, Richard Nixon went afoul of the law, and by being too greedy, helped cause his own downfall. "Remember 1960," Nixon told Haldeman, "I never want to be outspent again."

In his first term, Nixon was the target of allegations of trading influence for money. The "ITT affair" and the dairy lobby money raised serious questions about the sense of propriety of the administration. But it was in the reelection campaign that money became the root of many Nixon evils.

The effort not to be outspent was led by former commerce secretary Maurice Stans, with Nixon's longtime personal lawyer Herbert Kalmbach as chief fundraiser. The money was collected in two stages, reflecting changes in the campaign reform laws. Money collected *before* April 7, 1971, did not fall under the stricter reporting requirements of the new regulations, so there was a major effort to get the money in "pre–April 7."

In spite of frantic efforts to get as much money as possible before the reporting requirements went into effect, some money came in "late." On April 10, a former Republican state senate majority leader named Harry L. Sears gave Stans an attaché case containing $200,000 in $100 bills. The money was illegally treated as "pre–April 7" money and proved an even greater embarrassment when it was revealed that the money was a contribution from Robert Vesco, the international financier and fugitive from American justice.

Stans and his fundraising associates sought contributions from corporations dependent on the largesse of the government. Campaign contributions from corporations are illegal, but this did not deter Stans. The pitch made to these corporate executives was "finely calibrated, depending on who they were and how much fund-raisers thought they could get." [5]

This approach brought in millions. By politely hinting that corporate contributions would help and that failure to contribute would hurt badly, the president's reelection team was able to extract political tithes from some of the biggest and most respected companies in the nation. Even a partial list is impressive: American Airlines, $55,000; Braniff Airways, $40,000; Ashland Oil, $100,000; Goodyear Tire and Rubber, $40,000; Gulf Oil, $100,000; Northrop, $150,000; and Phillips Petroleum, $100,000. This who's who of corporate America illegally contributed to the Nixon reelection effort, and all were convicted—after the 1972 campaign.

In an effort to hide the money, that is, to prevent tracing it to the source, most of this money was laundered. The laundering took several forms. American Airlines sent money from a U.S. bank to a Swiss account of an agent in Lebanon, back to another U.S. bank, then to CREEP. Still other firms gave money from slush funds, and some airlines sold bogus tickets and sent the cash to CREEP. By far the most common route to launder money was through Mexico. In fact, it was to protect the money-laundering operation in Mexico that President Nixon first became actively involved in the criminal conspiracy to obstruct justice on June 23, 1972, less than a week after the Watergate break-in.

Illegal corporate contributions proved to be an excellent source of money, as did the "selling" of ambassadorships. Several big donors were promised ambassadorships in exchange for campaign money. J. Fife Symington gave over

$100,000, but the promised post of Spain or Portugal fell through (Herbert Kalmbach pled guilty to a charge of promising a federal job to Symington in exchange for money). Vincent P. de Roulet paid over $100,000 for Jamaica. Walter H. Annenberg received Great Britain after a $250,000 contribution. Mrs. Ruth Farkas, after donating $250,000 and being promised Costa Rica, complained to Kalmbach, saying, according to the grand jury testimony, "Well, you know, I am interested in Europe, I think, and isn't two hundred and fifty thousand dollars an awful lot of money for Costa Rica?" After giving a total of $300,000, Mrs. Farkas was appointed ambassador to Luxembourg.[6] The president was well aware of the "ambassadorial auction," as notes taken by H. R. Haldeman at a meeting with the president and Maurice Stans on March 21, 1972, indicate. Stans and Nixon discussed possible appointments and how much money each donor gave. The notation on Farkas was: "Mrs. Farkas 250?—where's the play on her?"

CREEP was almost literally awash in cash. There was so much money that the Nixon campaign officials were looking for ways to spend it. Besides the normal political expenses, money was used for some abnormal campaign expenses that crossed the line of ethics and legality.

DIRTY TRICKS

Part of the Nixon predatory strategy involved attempts to sabotage the campaigns of the top Democratic candidates in hopes of destroying their campaigns and thereby running against one of the weaker Democrats in the November general election. The predatory strategy involved the use of political "dirty tricks" that often went far beyond the bounds of ethics and the law.

Nixon felt that tricks were a part of the American electoral process. After all, Nixon himself was the victim of a number of tricks at the hands of the infamous Dick Tuck. As early as the 1950 Senate race, Dick Tuck took it upon himself to become a thorn in the side of Richard Nixon.[7] Tuck played a variety of tricks on Nixon including posing as a fire marshal and giving low estimates of campaign crowd sizes to the press; posing as a campaign official and telling bands to play "the candidate's favorite song, 'Mack the Knife' " (the lyrics of which describe the pearly teeth of a shark who is back in town); putting up signs in a Chinatown rally that in Chinese ask, "What about the Hughes loan?"; and a variety of other campaign pranks that caused embarrassment for Nixon.

In the 1972 campaign, Nixon was determined to use all the tools available to him to "get" his political opponents. As early as July of 1969, Nixon, in White House notes taken by Bob Haldeman, discusses the use of dirty tricks. Haldeman makes the following notation:

Buchanan Nofzngr Moll Ke Woods
    req. mtgs—dirty tricks dept.

use power of WH more ruthlessly
in deadly battle—use all weapons.

To engage in the battle of dirty tricks, Nixon's appointment secretary Dwight Chapin hired college chum Donald Segretti. Segretti was in charge of "Operation Sedan Chair," the effort to harass the Democratic candidates with what were called "black advances." Of course, almost all of this sprang out of Nixon's "us versus them" attitude, his notion of confrontational politics, his view that politics was the law of the jungle—get them before they get you.

Nixon was a man haunted by memories of past failures, of fears of enemies. He saw the world as a hostile place, and politics as a dirty, harsh business. One had to be tough to survive, and Nixon wanted to be the winner in this game. Thus, Nixon could approve the dirty tactics and hardball politics of his campaign team. As John Dean's memo of August 1971 stated: "This memorandum addresses the matter of how we can maximize the fact of our incumbency in dealing with persons known to be active in their opposition to our Administration. Stated a bit more bluntly—how can we use the available federal machinery to screw our political enemies?"

In 1971, a file entitled "Political Enemies Project" (the enemies list) was kept by the president's special counsel Charles Colson. Along with John Dean, Colson compiled a list (released on December 10, 1973) that according to congressional investigations contained 575 names. On September 9, 1971, Colson came up with 20 names for "go status." The list included United Automobile Workers leader Leonard Woodcock, Congressman John Conyers, journalist Daniel Shorr, actor Paul Newman, and others. The White House tried, with very limited success, to get the IRS to audit the taxes of those on the list.[8] Nixon himself is quite revealing on this, as a tape of a conversation between the president, Haldeman, and Dean on September 15, 1972, dealing with *Washington Post* attorney Edward Bennett Williams indicates.

President Nixon: I would not want to be in Edward Bennett Williams' position after this election. . . . We're going after him.

Haldeman: That is a guy we've got to ruin.

President Nixon: You want to remember, too, he's an attorney for the *Washington Post.*

Dean: I'm well aware of that.

President Nixon: I think we are going to fix the son of a bitch. Believe me. We are going to. We've got to, because he's a bad man.

Dean: Absolutely . . . I've tried to . . . keep notes on a lot of the people who are emerging . . . as less than our friends.

President Nixon: Great.

Dean: Because this is going to be over someday, . . . We shouldn't forget the way some of them have treated us.

President Nixon: I want the most comprehensive notes on all of those that tried to do us in. . . . They didn't have to do it. . . . I mean if . . . they had a very close election everybody on the other side would understand this game. But now they are doing this quite deliberately and they are asking for it and they are going to get it. We have not used this power in this first four years. . . . We have never used it. We haven't used the Bureau and we haven't used the Justice Department, but things are going to change now. . . . They're going to get it right.

Dean: That's an exciting prospect.

President Nixon: It's got to be done. It's the only thing to do. . . .

President Nixon: The *Post* is going to have damnable . . . problems out of this one. They have a television station.

Dean: That's right they do.

Haldeman: They have a radio station, too.

President Nixon: Does that come up too? The point is, when does it come up?

Dean: I don't know. But the practice of non-licensees filing on top of licensees has certainly gotten more active in the area.

President Nixon: And it's going to be goddamn active here . . . the game has to be played rough.

The larger enemies list included Senators Ted Kennedy, Edmund Muskie, and Walter Mondale, the presidents of Yale and the Harvard Law School, the heads of the World Bank, Ford Foundation, and Rand Corporation, four ex–cabinet members, two ex-ambassadors, a Nobel prizewinner, and actors Carol Channing, Steve McQueen, Burt Lancaster, Shirley MacLane, and Gregory Peck, along with football player Joe Namath.

On August 16, 1971, John Dean sent Bob Haldeman a memo entitled "How to Deal with Our Political Enemies and How We Can Use the Available Political Machinery to Screw Our Political Enemies." Dean wanted to address "the matter of how we can maximize the fact of our incumbency in dealing with persons known to be active in their opposition to our Administration."[9]

The word *enemy* is unusual to American politics. Normally, one thinks of adversaries, opponents, rivals, but not enemies. But to Nixon, the word *enemy* fit. He did indeed see his opponents as enemies, and attempted to move the machinery of government against them. The Nixon administration made government into an instrument for revenge and retaliation. They attempted, not to defeat their rivals, but to destroy their enemies. Along the way they broke the law and subverted the democratic process.

Members of the administration were involved in other subterranean tricks such as fake-letter–writing campaigns to inflate the level of support for the president's policies, alleged discussions of plots to murder columnist Jack Anderson,[10] plots to sneak LSD into Daniel Ellsberg's soup prior to a speaking engagement, and forgery of State Department cables that falsely made it appear that President Kennedy had ordered or approved the assassination of South

Vietnamese president Ngo Dinh Diem and his brother, followed by an attempt to get a story based on these fake cables published in *Life* magazine.

The attitude that political enemies had to be destroyed was successfully employed in the 1972 Democratic primary campaign against front-runner Edmund Muskie. The strategy was to wage a campaign *in the Democratic primary* against the stronger Democrats, in hopes of knocking them out of the race and facing a weak Democratic opponent in the general election. Thus, Muskie became the first target.

Throughout his campaign, Muskie was the victim of a variety of dirty tricks. In February of 1972, voters in New Hampshire, site of the first primary, received late-night phone calls from people claiming to represent the "Harlem for Muskie Committee" promoting the candidacy of Muskie. Shortly before the Florida primary, letters were mailed to Democrats on stationary stolen from Muskie's headquarters, with a "Vote for Muskie" message, and containing vicious lies about Muskie's Democratic opponents. The letter claimed that "in 1929 Scoop Jackson had gotten a 17-year-old girl pregnant," that "in 1955 Scoop Jackson was arrested as a homosexual," and that on "December 3, 1967, Hubert Humphrey was arrested for drunk driving in Washington D.C. with a well-known callgirl in his car."[11]

Perhaps the most-damaging trick on Muskie took place just prior to the New Hampshire primary. The conservative newspaper the *Manchester Union Leader* published a letter signed by a Paul Morrison accusing Muskie of insulting Canadian-Americans, calling them "Canucks," and accusing Muskie's wife of being an alcoholic who would walk up and down the aisles of planes drunk, encouraging people to "tell dirty jokes."

Muskie stood on the steps of the newspaper building and denied the charges, and in the process of defending his wife, shed tears. The following day the *Union Leader* asked, "Do you want this man's hand on the button?" All attempts to locate Paul Morrison, the alleged author of the letter, were unsuccessful, but Muskie was finished as a candidate. The Nixon strategy was working. On April 4, 1972, Pat Buchanan and Ken Khachigian wrote to Haldeman and Ehrlichman that the effort to get rid of Muskie was succeeding. On April 26, Muskie withdrew from the race. The other Democratic candidates followed until George McGovern was the nominee: just as the administration had planned.[12]

Perhaps the most amazing and insidious activity in the campaign of dirty tricks and sabotage was what became known as the "Liddy Plan."[13] As chief legal counsel for CREEP, G. Gordon Liddy cast his net over a wide array of activities, most notorious of which was the plan that bears his name. In an effort to further disrupt and divide the Democrats, Liddy was to develop an intelligence-gathering/undercover operation. On January 27, 1972, at four o'clock in the afternoon, Liddy went to the office of the attorney general of the United States, John Mitchell, and presented a plan that was frightening—or should have been.

At the meeting with Liddy and Mitchell were John Dean and Jeb Magruder. Liddy, with charts and an easel, presented a plan that at first the rest of the group could not understand. That was because everything was in code. But as Liddy proceeded to explain, it became clear what "Gemstone" was all about: it was a massive and expensive plan of sabotage and surveillance of unprecedented proportions.

Carrying a $1 million price tag, the Liddy Plan called for mugging squads to beat up demonstrators at the Republican Convention, teams to kidnap leaders of the demonstrations and hijack them to Mexico until the Republican Convention was over, electronic surveillance against the Democrats at their Washington headquarters and convention sites, prostitutes to be employed ("high-class" ones, according to Liddy, "the best in the business") to lure prominent Democrats onto a yacht equipped with hidden cameras and recording equipment, break-ins to obtain and photograph documents, shorting out the air conditioning at the arena in Miami where the Democrats were to have their Convention, and other sordid acts.

John Dean called the plan "mind-boggling." The attorney general, the highest-ranking law enforcement official in the land, rather than throwing Liddy out of his office—as he later admitted he should have done—rejected the plan, not on its merits, but as too expensive, and asked Liddy to draw up a new, scaled-down version. As John Dean testified before the Senate Watergate Committee, Mitchell "took a few long puffs on his pipe," and told Liddy, "the plan . . . was not quite what he had in mind and the cost was out of the question, and suggested to Liddy he go back and revise his plan, keeping in mind that he was most interested in the demonstration problem." Jeb Magruder recalls a similar response from Mitchell: "Gordon that's not quite what we had in mind, and the money you're asking for is way out of line. Why don't you tone it down a little, then we'll talk about it again?"[14]

On February 4, 1972, Liddy returned to Mitchell's office with a scaled-down plan costing only half a million dollars. But again the attorney general demurred. Liddy was to come up with another proposal. Almost two months later, on March 30, 1972, a third meeting with Mitchell was held in Key Biscayne, Florida. Dean and Liddy were not present, but Magruder and Fred LaRue were in attendance. Toward the end of a wide-ranging meeting, Mitchell, who by that time had resigned as attorney general to become director of CREEP, turned to the revised Liddy plan. While everyone at the meeting expressed reservations, Mitchell finally approved the plan, but gave Liddy "only" $250,000.[15] Among the targets was Larry O'Brien, chair of the Democratic National Committee, whose office was located in the Watergate office complex.

Within a week, Liddy was off and running. He received $83,000 in cash from CREEP's Finance Committee, purchased bugging and surveillance equipment, and began planning the first break-in of Watergate. In attempting to figure out why Mitchell approved the revised Liddy plan, and why so many others in the administration and CREEP went along with it, Jeb Magruder offers that it was "the result of a combination of pressures that played upon us at that time." First, Liddy "put his plan to us in a highly effective way"; second, Mitchell was under pressure from the ITT affair and was distracted; third, Mitchell's wife, the high-strung Martha, was putting a strain on her busy husband; and fourth, "Liddy's plan was approved because of the climate of fear and suspicion that had grown up in the White House, an atmosphere that started with the President himself and reached us through Haldeman and Colson and others, one that came to affect all our thinking, so that decisions that now seem insane seemed at the time to be rational." He continued, "It was all but impossible not to get caught up in the 'enemies' mentality."[16]

THE BREAK-IN

Out of this atmosphere of dirty tricks, dirty money, and dirty politics came the plan to break into and bug offices in the headquarters of the Democratic National Committee. While the roots of the DNC break-in can be found in the legitimate need for campaign intelligence, things got so out of hand, sank so low, that the dirty tricks and break-ins were eventually seen as a necessary part in the reelection of the president.

Early efforts at gaining political and campaign intelligence led John Dean, at the instruction of Bob Haldeman, to contact Jack Caulfield to set up such a capability. Caulfield developed what he called "Operation Sandwedge," an intelligence-gathering operation that would have "black bag" capability. Caulfield's plan never got off the ground, and Dean continued to feel the pressure from Haldeman.[17] Dean would later testify before the Senate Watergate Committee that the White House had an insatiable appetite for political intelligence.

As part of Liddy's intelligence-gathering plan, information was to be obtained by what Liddy called a *Nacht und Nebel* (Night and Fog) operation. One such operation was to get information on what the Democrats had on the Republicans, and more specifically on Nixon. The fear was that Larry O'Brien, chairman of the DNC, might possess material that could be particularly damaging to the president. Liddy and his accomplices broke into the Democratic headquarters twice. The first time, the bugging equipment did not work properly, and the information obtained was not useful.

According to Liddy, Jeb Magruder, then deputy director of CREEP, ordered the second break-in on June 12. At a 1987 conference at Hofstra University, Magruder admitted that the break-in was deemed necessary, to "find out what information Larry O'Brien knew." The "primary purpose of the break-in was to see if O'Brien had embarrassing information linking President Nixon's close friend Bebe Rebozo to loans from Howard Hughes" that went to Nixon. "It was a planned burglary," said Magruder. Thus, while most political professionals scoffed at the break-in in its aftermath, suggesting that it had to be a rene-

6

gade operation because everyone knew that there was nothing of value at the DNC, there was a reason: the fear that Larry O'Brien had the goods on a Hughes-Nixon deal.

As Magruder said at the Hofstra conference: "These people [the Watergate burglars] were hired . . . under the insistence . . . to my recollection when I was in Key Biscayne with John Mitchell and Fred LaRue, in discussions on the phone with Bob Haldeman, that it was important for us to get the information on Larry O'Brien that regarded to the Hughes affair. . . . So the purpose as I understand it for the break-in and the wiretapping was to find out what information Larry O'Brien knew and what information we would then be able to use to keep that under wraps during the election."

To get this information, Liddy and his accomplices first broke into the DNC headquarters on May 27, 1972, and installed wiretaps. When the taps didn't work properly, a second surreptitious entry was required. On the night of June 16 and morning of the 17th, Liddy and his cohorts returned.

In the early morning hours of Saturday, June 17, 1972, after a call to police by security guard Frank Wills, five men were arrested for illegal entry to the DNC headquarters in the Watergate office complex in Washington, D.C. At first this case was treated as a routine criminal act, but the arrested men were found to have links to the White House and CIA, and one of those arrested, James W. McCord, Jr., was director of security for the Committee for the Re-election of the President (CREEP). Soon two other suspects were linked to the crime, E. Howard Hunt, a former White House aide, and G. Gordon Liddy, a former White House aide currently under the employ of CREEP. The White House denied any involvement in the burglary, with Press Secretary Ron Ziegler calling it a "third-rate burglary attempt."

Did President Nixon *know* about Gemstone, the Liddy Plan, the effort to bug the DNC.? There is no evidence to suggest that he knew of the plan in advance. While Nixon may not have ordered the break-in, he certainly created an atmosphere in which planning such crimes was tolerated and even encouraged. Bob Haldeman gives us an indication of the atmosphere when he recounts an example of what he calls "classic Nixonian rhetorical overkill" when the president ordered him to get the tax files of leading Democrats: "There are ways to get it," Nixon said, "Goddamnit, sneak in in the middle of the night." [18] On January 14, 1971, Nixon did send Bob Haldeman a memo suggesting that they needed more information on DNC chairman Lawrence O'Brien. The memo read in part: "It would seem that the time is approaching when Larry O'Brien is held accountable for his retainer with Hughes," and "perhaps Colson should make a check on this." While Nixon had an interest in O'Brien, there is no direct evidence pointing to the president having advance knowledge of the break-in. But he was actively involved in the coverup from the beginning.

THE COVERUP BEGINS

The arrests at the Watergate, occurring less than five months before the 1972 election, might have been a political embarrassment, perhaps even a serious scandal, but the White House quickly went to work on an effort to coverup the crime and contain political damage from the president and his reelection.

Initially the story of the arrests at the Watergate attracted very little attention. On June 18, the day after the arrests, the story appeared on page 30 of the *New York Times*. Few seemed to notice or care. The president and Haldeman were in Key Biscayne, John Mitchell and Jeb Magruder in California, and John Dean in Manila. But within hours of the break-in, the coverup began. On the morning of the 18th, G. Gordon Liddy called Magruder in Los Angeles and told him of the arrests in the Watergate.[19]

Liddy informed Magruder that "the four men arrested with McCord were Cuban freedom fighters, whom Howard Hunt recruited. But don't worry; my men will never talk." The coverup was immediate and reflexive. Magruder said: "We never considered that there wouldn't be a coverup," and he told the Senate Watergate Committee, "The cover-up began that Saturday when we realized there was a break-in." Or, as John Mitchell said, "What'd they expect us to do—advertise it?"

The coverup, in Magruder's words, "was immediate and automatic; no one even considered that there would *not* be a cover-up. It seemed inconceivable that with our political power we could not erase this mistake we had made." Upon hearing the news of the arrests from Liddy, Magruder immediately informed John Mitchell, and the coverup was under way. In a flurry of activity, steps were taken to sever whatever links could be established between the burglars and the White House. Magruder had one of his assistants remove the Gemstone file from his office. Liddy also removed files from CREEP headquarters. Haldeman aide Gordon Strachan used the White House shredder to destroy incriminating documents. Liddy even went so far as to volunteer to John Dean that he, Liddy, would wait on a corner and be killed if it became necessary! As Dean recalled: "He told me that he was a soldier and would never talk. He said if anyone wished to shoot him on the street, he was ready."

E. Howard Hunt's name was expunged from the White House phone directory. Hunt removed ten thousand dollars from his White House safe. John Ehrlichman ordered that Hunt's safe be opened and the contents removed. Dean ordered Hunt to leave the country, but later rescinded the order. A quick payment scheme for the burglars was put into action. But the frenetic activity lacked coherence and guidance. According to Magruder, the guidance began with a June 19 meeting with Mitchell, LaRue, Mardian, Dean, and himself. At the meeting, Magruder asked what to do with the Gemstone file. Mitchell suggested that it might be a good idea if Magruder had a fire in his home that evening.

At the June 19 meeting, according to Magruder, it was agreed that the president's reelection would suffer if the truth about the break-in and bugging became known, and a plan to cover up this act evolved out of the meeting. All top-level CREEP officials would deny, deny, deny, and they agreed on false stories to tell the FBI and prosecutors. Shortly thereafter, John Dean was assigned to keep the cover on the story and contain the damage.

On Saturday afternoon, June 17, John Ehrlichman called Ron Ziegler, who was with the president and Bob Haldeman in Florida, and told him that Howard Hunt was arrested at the Watergate and that Hunt could be traced to the White House. On the 18th, Ehrlichman again called Florida and discussed McCord and Hunt's involvement in the break-in with Haldeman. Ehrlichman was worried that it could open a can of worms, which could lead prosecutors to Haldeman, Mitchell, himself, and a host of embarrassing and illegal activities that could not stand the light of day.

On June 18, the president, then in Key Biscayne, called Chuck Colson. Nixon had reason to believe that Colson knew of, or was involved in, the DNC break-in. After all, Colson was considered the administration's hit man. According to testimony given by Colson, Nixon was so upset at McCord's involvement in the break-in that he (Nixon) threw an ashtray across the room. Nixon knew that McCord, the security director for CREEP—who was arrested inside the DNC headquarters—was a link to CREEP and the White House, and ultimately to Nixon himself. Also on June 18, Nixon put John Ehrlichman in charge of Watergate, and Ehrlichman assigned Dean to the operational role in handling the problem (U.S. House of Representatives, Evidence, Article I of Impeachment, 1974).

The following day Nixon telephoned Colson and they spoke for an hour about the break-in. According to Colson's testimony to the House Judiciary Committee, he told the president that administration officials were holding meetings in Washington to determine how best to handle the problem.

When the president returned to Washington on June 20, the coverup was already in motion. That morning, the *Washington Post* ran a story that proclaimed: "White House Consultant tied to bugging figure." The Howard Hunt link was being pieced together. If Hunt could be linked to his sponsor, Colson, it was a very short step to the president.

June 20 was the first time Nixon had the opportunity to meet with the top people involved in the break-in and coverup. On that day, the president held meetings or discussions with Haldeman, Mitchell, Colson, and others. He discussed Watergate with these aides, and when the White House taping system was revealed, a search for tapes of these meetings proved fruitless. Meetings with Mitchell were, according to a White House spokesman, not recorded; there was a mysterious eighteen-and-a-half-minute gap in a Haldeman conversation on Watergate, and a thirty-eight-second gap in the Dictabelt recording Nixon made of his daily recollections. On this, the most important day for the president, the day when he first discussed Watergate with the top principals, the recorded evidence is gone.

By June 23, less than a week after the arrests, the president was directly leading a criminal coverup. In a discussion between Haldeman and Nixon, the substance of which was not revealed until August 5, 1974, the president's chief of staff informed Nixon that the break-in occurred because Liddy was under pressure (probably from Mitchell) to "get more information," to which the president responded, "All right, fine. I understand it all. We won't second guess Mitchell and the rest. Thank God it wasn't Colson." Haldeman then informed Nixon that the FBI was beginning to close in on the source of money used for the illegal activities, saying that "the FBI is not under control," and suggested that "the way to handle this now is for us to have Walters [deputy director, CIA] call Pat Gray [acting director, FBI] and just say 'stay to hell out of this' . . . . Pat wants to [end the investigation] . . . he doesn't have the basis for doing it. Given this, he will then have the basis."

The president then ordered Haldeman to tell CIA director Richard Helms that "the President believes that it is going to open the whole Bay of Pigs thing up again. And . . . that they [the CIA] should call the FBI in and [unintelligible] don't go any further into this case period!"

Later that day in another meeting with Haldeman, Nixon orders Haldeman to tell Helms that "Hunt . . . knows too damned much. . . . If it gets out that this is all involved . . . it would make the CIA look bad, it's going to make Hunt look bad, and it is likely to blow the whole Bay of Pigs thing which we think would be very unfortunate—both for the CIA and for the country . . . and for American foreign policy. Just tell him [Helms] to lay off . . . I would just say, lookit, because of the Hunt involvement, whole cover basically this."

At 1:30 p.m. on June 23, Haldeman and Ehrlichman met with Helms and Walters and persuaded them to approach Gray in an effort to limit the FBI investigation into the break-in. Later that afternoon, Haldeman again met with the president to report on his meeting with Helms and Walters. He told the president that while he didn't mention Hunt, he did tell the CIA officials that "the thing was leading into directions that were going to create potential problems because they were exploring leads that led back into areas that would be harmful to the CIA and harmful to the Government," and that Helms "kind of got the picture. He said, he said, 'we'll be very happy to be helpful [unintelligible] to handle anything you want.' . . . Walters is going to make a call to Gray."

At almost the precise moment Haldeman was having this conversation with the president, Vernon Walters called L. Patrick Gray and told him that if the FBI pursued its investigation into Mexico, it would be jeopardizing some of the CIA's covert operations. He suggested that the investigation be limited to the suspects already under arrest. Gray complied. Thus, the criminal conspiracy to obstruct justice, to interfere with an FBI investigation, began less than a week after the arrests in the Watergate. This put the president right in the middle of a criminal conspiracy to obstruct justice. The national security excuse was a ruse. The top people in the administration were covering up a crime. But this was only the beginning.

In his memoirs, Richard Nixon explained the events surrounding the June 23 meeting as the first steps toward the end of his presidency. Admitting that he did enlist the CIA's help in limiting the FBI investigation, Nixon nonetheless defends his actions as a pragmatic way of dealing with a potential problem, not as a criminal coverup.[20]

On June 30, John Mitchell abruptly resigned as head of CREEP for "personal reasons." But Mitchell was not out of the picture. He simply moved across the hall to rejoin his old law firm and from there continued to lead the coverup. Meetings frequently took place involving Mitchell, Magruder, and LaRue in which, as Magruder recalls, "We did not discuss the Watergate affair in terms of perjury or burglary or conspiracy. We would refer, rather, to 'handling the case' and 'making sure things don't get out of hand.' "

From the day after the burglars were caught in DNC headquarters, until the November presidential election, President Nixon and his top aides conducted a plan of concealment, coverup, and containment. The goals were to prevent any damaging information from getting to the prosecutors and to make sure that no potentially explosive scandals interfered with the reelection of the president.

Within weeks, in an effort to contain and cover up, efforts were made to buy the silence of the defendants in the Watergate break-in case with promises of executive clemency and money. (John Dean testified that he told Mitchell of "the need for support money in exchange for the silence of the men in jail." Liddy and his associates eventually received over $500,000.) Officials of CREEP were pressured to commit perjury, and an elaborate effort was under way to interfere with or control the FBI investigation.

In early July, suspicion grew of a possible connection between the burglars and Nixon officials. U.S. District Court judge John Sirica, who was overseeing the Watergate grand jury, raised a number of questions, but his prodding seemed to be going nowhere.

The Democrats were trying to get political mileage out of the break-in. Larry O'Brien had filed suit, and Representative Wright Patman of Texas, chairman of the House Committee on Banking and Currency, planned to hold hearings in an effort to determine whether any banking or campaign laws had been violated in connection with CREEP activities. But the White House took steps to block the investigation, and in mid-September, things seemed to be going well for the conspirators.

In public, the president tried to distance himself from the break-in, denying any complicity for himself or any White House officials in the illegal acts, and on the whole he was believed. On August 29, at a press conference, Nixon, responding to a question on Watergate, said that "what really hurts, is if you try to cover it up." When, on September 15, an eight-count indictment in the Watergate case was handed out, the charges were limited to Hunt, Liddy, and the five burglars. The charges included stealing documents, tapping telephones, and planting eavesdropping devices. The president's strategy was working—no one in the White House was implicated. At 5:27 p.m. John Dean met with the president and Haldeman. The conversation begins:

President: Well you had quite a day today, didn't you? You got, uh, Watergate, uh, on, the, way, huh?

Dean: Quite a three months.

Haldeman: How did it all end up?

Dean: Uh. I think we can say "Well" at this point. The, uh, the press is playing it just as we expect.

Later Dean sums up his thoughts:

Dean: Three months ago I would have had trouble predicting where we'd be today. I think that I can say that fifty-four days from now that, uh, not a thing will come crashing down to our surprise.

President: Well, the whole thing is a can of worms. As you know, a lot of this stuff went on. And, uh, and, uh, and the people who worked [unintelligible] awfully embarrassing. And, uh, and, the, uh, but the, but the way you, you've handled it, it seems to me, has been very skillful, because you—putting your fingers in the dikes every time that leaks have sprung here and there. [Unintelligible] having people straighten the [unintelligible].

But Dean was still concerned about what might lie ahead, and warned the president about dissension with CREEP, to which Nixon responded:

President: They should just, uh, just behave and, and, recognize this, this is, again, this is war. We're getting a few shots and it'll be over. And, we'll give them a few shots. It'll be over. Don't worry [unintelligible]. I wouldn't want to be on the other side right now. Would you?

But Dean persisted:

Dean: We just take one at a time and you deal with it based on—

President: And you really can't just sit and worry yourself—

Dean: No.

President: About it all the time, thinking, "The worst may happen," but it may not. So you just try to button it up as well as you can and hope for the best. And—

Dean: Well it Bob—

President: And remember that basically the damn thing is just one of those unfortunate things and, we're trying to cut our losses.

Dean: Well, certainly that's right and certainly it had no effect on you. That's the, the good thing.

Haldeman: It really hasn't.

President: [Unintelligible.]

Haldeman: No, it hasn't. It has been kept away from the White House almost completely, and from the President totally. The only tie to the White House has been the Colson effort they keep trying to haul in. (White House Tape, 1974)

While most of the press played down the Watergate story in the early phase, two reporters for the *Washington Post*, Carl Bernstein and Bob Woodward, began to piece the story together, finding many loose ends that pointed toward involvement by higher-ups in the Nixon administration. On October 10, they published a story linking John Mitchell to illegal campaign acts. In spite of scathing attacks from the president's men, the *Post*, on October 25, published another damaging article, this one linking Bob Haldeman to the scandal. Slowly things were closing in on the president himself.

Why a coverup? Why didn't the president come clean early and cut his losses? Why was there virtually no discussion of *not* covering up? According to Jeb Magruder, on the Monday after the break-in, he met with Mitchell and suggested that they come clean on Watergate immediately. But Mitchell, after a discussion with Haldeman and Ehrlichman, told Magruder that they could not come clean on Watergate because they had "other reasons" to keep the lid on the story.

Indeed, "other reasons" made the coverup so important and necessary. Covering up the break-in itself was not the key; what was important was to keep a lid on all the other illegal and unethical activities that might be revealed if the "can of worms" were opened. The real enemy was an enemy from within. That is what had to be kept hidden, the dirty tricks and dirty money and crimes of the past several years: warrantless wiretaps, the Fielding break-in, the extortion of campaign funds, sabotage of elections, campaign crimes, and a host of other crimes. There simply couldn't *not* be a coverup.

UNCOVERING THE COVERUP

On July 6, 1972, Pat Gray warned the president that "people on your staff are trying to mortally wound you by using the CIA and FBI." Gray didn't know that it was the president who was leading the coverup.

In spite of all the problems attendant to keeping a lid on the story and investigations, as the election approached, it appeared that containment was indeed working. Dean had "handled" Watergate, and the reelection was assured. But after the election, the walls came tumbling down.

In an effort to control the Watergate investigation, the president, through John Dean, closely monitored the Justice Department's investigations. Dean was allowed to sit in on questioning of White House and CREEP officials, and as Dean later told the president, "I was totally aware what the bureau was doing at all times. I was totally aware what the grand jury was doing. I knew what witnesses were going to be called. I knew what they were going to be asked." When Nixon asked why Henry Peterson (the assistant attorney general who was in charge of the Watergate investigation) was "so straight with us," Dean replied, "Because he is a soldier." (White House Tape, March 21, 1973.)

This of course greatly aided the administration in its efforts to keep the investigation limited. Thus, witnesses could be encouraged to commit perjury and conceal information, and Dean could keep track of how well the coverup was holding together. Additionally, Peterson kept reporting to the president on the status of the investigation. Peterson did not know that the information he gave Nixon was going to aid in the coverup because he did not know that the president was involved in the coverup. At one point Nixon told Ehrlichman and Ziegler, "I've got Peterson on a short leash." Following pressure from Nixon, Peterson and his colleague Earl Silbert kept the investigation on a very narrow course. Again, the coverup seemed to be working. But the defendants were threatening to go "off the reservation." By late December James McCord sent John Caulfield a letter warning: "If the Watergate operation is laid at the CIA's feet, where it does not belong, every tree in the forest will fall. It will be a scorched desert. The whole matter is at the precipice now. Just pass the message that if they want it to blow, they are on exactly the right course."[21] Shortly after the election, the defendants began to fear that they were vulnerable, that Nixon didn't need their silence as much as he did prior to the election, and that they might be "forgotten." Hunt began pressuring Colson. He spoke of financial needs of the defendants. But Colson, who was taping the call, tried to get Hunt to back away. Hunt refused:

Hunt: All right, now, we've set a deadline now for close of business on the twenty-fifth of November for the resolution, the liquidation of everything that's outstanding.
Colson: Um hmm.
Hunt: And this is—I'm now talking about promises from July and August.

Later Hunt said:

Hunt: And, uh, the election's out of the way, uh, initial terror of a number of people has subsided, some people have already left the administration, and that's all to the good.
Colson: Um hmm.
Hunt: So now it's pared down to the point where a few people ought to be able to really concentrate on this, get the goddamn thing out of the way once and for all. . . .

He added:

Hunt: After all, we're protecting the guys who were really responsible. But now that's
. . . a continuing requirement, but at the same time, this is a two-way street . . .
and, as I said before, we think that now is the time when some moves should be
made and, uh, surely your cheapest commodity available is money. . . .

Colson gave the tape to Dean, who played it for Haldeman and Ehrlichman.
The threat was clear. Dean was told to "tell Mitchell to take care of all these
problems." Hunt wrote a nine-hundred-word indictment of the way they were
being handled by the administration. The defendants, he wrote, had committed the burglary "against their better judgment," but the administration was
guilty of "indecisiveness at the moment of crisis." They failed to "quash the
investigation while that option was still open," and a laundry list of other charges,
including "failure to provide promised support funds on a timely and adequate
basis; continued postponements and consequent avoidance of commitments."

Then Hunt listed some of the potentially damaging information he possessed: "Mitchell may well have perjured himself"; the Watergate crime was
"only one of a number of highly illegal conspiracies engaged in by one or more
of the defendants at the behest of senior White House officials. These as yet
undisclosed crimes can be proved"; that "immunity from prosecution and/or
judicial clemency for cooperating defendants is a standing offer"; and that
"congressional elections will take place in less than two years." The deadline
given Colson was extended until November 27, but the defendants would meet
before that time to "determine our joint and automatic response to evidence of
continued indifference on the part of those in whose behalf we have suffered
the loss of our employment, our futures, and our reputations as honorable
men. The foregoing should not be interpreted as a threat. It is among other
things a reminder that loyalty has always been a two-way street."[22]

The president of the United States was being *blackmailed.*

The threat worked. Almost immediately, $50,000 was delivered by LaRue
to Hunt's lawyer. Shortly thereafter LaRue said he needed more money.
Haldeman told Dean to give LaRue "the entire damn bundle, but make sure
we get a receipt."

On December 8, Hunt's wife, Dorothy, was killed in a plane crash. She was
carrying $10,000 in $100 bills. Hunt became increasingly despondent. Hunt
wanted clemency. Charles Colson began to push for clemency to Ehrlichman,
who, according to Dean, took the matter up with the president and then gave
Colson an assurance that the president had promised clemency for Hunt. A
few days later the president and Colson discussed Hunt's clemency:

Nixon: . . . I, uh, question of clemency . . . Hunt's is a simple case. I mean, after
all, the man's wife is dead, was killed; he's got one child that has . . .

Colson: Brain damage from an automobile accident.

Nixon: That's right.

Colson: [unintelligible] one of his kids.

Nixon: We'll build, we'll build that son-of-a-bitch up like nobody's business. We'll have [William] Buckley write a column and say, you know, that he, that he should have clemency, if you've given eighteen years of service.

Later in his conversation with Colson, Nixon indicated that clemency might be offered to the other defendants.

Nixon: . . . I would have difficulty with some of the others.

Colson: Oh, yeah.

Nixon: You know what I mean.

Colson: Well, the others aren't going to get the same . . . the vulnerabilities are different.

Nixon: Are they?

Colson: Yeah.

Nixon: Why?

Colson: Well, because Hunt and Liddy did the work. The others didn't know any direct information—

Nixon: Oh, well, I think I agree.

Colson: See, I don't give a damn if they spend five years in jail—

Nixon: Oh, no . . .

Colson: They can't hurt us. Hunt and Liddy: direct meetings, discussions are very incriminating to us. . . . They're both good healthy right-wing exuberants.

On January 8, 1973, it appeared that the administration would be able to hold the coverup together. As the Watergate trial approached, Dean, in a meeting with the president, laid out the scenario for the trial. According to notes taken by Bob Haldeman, Dean told the president:

Hunt take guilty 3 counts
    after Silbert opening stmt
    w/say no higher-ups involved
    rest w/go to trial—Rothblatt wild man
        w/Cubans
Liddy go—hope for error—lots of procedures
    etc.
    All will sit mute
        and if immunized after—w/take contempt
        better cause won't take stand
McCord will testify—but he has no firsthand knowledge
Grt concern that commitments won't be honored
    prob w/funds—LaRue on this

Three days later, on January 11, 1973, the Watergate trial began. Everyone was back on the reservation—just in time. The defendants all pled guilty except for Liddy and McCord.

After deliberating only ninety minutes, the Watergate jury found, on January 30, Liddy guilty on all six counts and McCord guilty on all eight counts. Sentencing was postponed. On February 2, Judge Sirica said he was "not satisfied" that the full story on Watergate had been disclosed. In spite of Sirica's skepticism, the coverup was holding.

But as each problem was temporarily solved, a new one sprang up. On February 7, by a 70–0 vote, the Senate established a select committee, headed by North Carolina's Sam Ervin, to investigate Watergate and related campaign abuses. In response to the committee, the president, Haldeman, Ehrlichman, Dean, and Richard Moore met at the La Costa resort in California on February 10 and 11. In meetings that lasted between eight and fourteen hours, the group agreed on a strategy; CREEP, not the White House, would assume primary responsibility for Watergate defense matters, John Mitchell would coordinate this, and, as Dean later recalled, they would "take a posture of full cooperation but privately . . . attempt to restrain the investigation and make it as difficult as possible to get information and witnesses. . . . The ultimate goal would be to discredit the hearings." H. R. Haldeman's notes of February 11 reflect this as he writes:

public stance of cooperation
    but stand ready to quietly obstruct
    paint as partisan but not from W. H.

The "La Costa strategy" became part of the coverup attempt.

Starting on February 27, John Dean began a series of meetings with the president to discuss the coverup. Dean warned the president that the containment policy might not hold up forever. (The tape of this conversation was subpoenaed during the House Judiciary Committee's impeachment inquiry, but the White House could not find the tape.) In a March 13 meeting with the president and Haldeman, Dean, speaking of the bugging of the DNC, said, "A lot of people around here had knowledge that something was going on over there," to which the president replied, "They had goddamn poor pickings. Because naturally anybody, either Chuck [Colson] or Bob [Haldeman], uh, was always reporting to me about what was going on. If they ever got any information they would certainly have told me . . . but they never had a goddamn [laughs] thing to report . . . it was a dry hole."

On the morning of February 28, John Dean told the president, "We have come a long road on this already. I had thought it was an impossible task to hold together . . . but we have made it this far and I am convinced we are going to make it the whole road and put this thing in the funny pages of the history books rather than anything serious." But on that very day, Pat Gray's confirmation hearings to be director of the FBI began. Gray ended up telling much more than anyone had intended. In what proved to be a major embarrassment, Gray admitted that he repeatedly turned over FBI files on the Watergate investigation to John Dean, in spite of the fact that Dean and other White House officials were suspects in the investigation. Gray also admitted that Dean had been allowed to sit in when the FBI questioned witnesses. Gray also suggested that Dean "probably lied." Almost out of nowhere, John Dean became a central figure in the Watergate drama, and the Senate Judiciary Committee, which was conducting the Gray confirmation hearings, wanted to talk to this previously almost unknown figure.

But Nixon did not want Dean to testify. He knew too much. Thus, executive privilege was invoked. Nixon's view of executive privilege, the constitutionally questionable "right" of a president to refuse to answer or have his staff answer to the Congress, was unusually broad, almost absolute. The president stated on March 12: "Under the doctrine of separation of powers, the manner in which the President personally exercises his assigned executive powers is not subject to questioning by another branch of government. If the President is not subject to such questioning, it is equally appropriate that members of his staff not be so questioned, for their roles are in effect an extension of the Presidency."

The Judiciary Committee was unpersuaded and voted unanimously to demand Dean's appearance. The president could not afford to have Dean testify, and eventually withdrew Gray's nomination.

As Dean's role became more exposed, he began to have doubts about whether the coverup could be maintained. On March 13, he warned the president, "There are dangers. . . . There is a certain domino situation. If some things start going, a lot of other things are going to start going." The president, as usual, was more graphic: "Sloan starts pissing on Magruder and then Magruder starts pissing on who, even Haldeman." Everyone, Dean noted, was looking to "cover his own ass."

Each passing day seemed to bring a new damaging revelation. By mid-March the president spent more and more time dealing with, or more accurately, reacting to, each new problem. The criminal investigation continued, the Senate was about to start its hearings, the press dug deeper and deeper, and the public was turning slowly against the president. A new PR line was needed.

On March 17, the president pressured Dean to write a report that "basically clears the President," in which Dean could "make self-serving goddamn statements." Progressively, the president moved further and further away from the truth. Nixon called the new line a "hang-out" approach. Haldeman called it a "limited hang-out" approach, and Ehrlichman called it a "modified limited hang-out." Whatever one called it, it was still a coverup. And John Dean could not, or at least did not, write his Watergate report clearing the president. Dean feared that he was being set up. He was right.

The March 21 meeting between the president and John Dean was pivotal in the Watergate saga. In what has been called the "Cancer on the Presidency" meeting, Dean gave Nixon a comprehensive overview of the complicity of Mitchell, Haldeman, Ehrlichman, Magruder, Colson, Kalmbach, Strachan, and himself in the Fielding and Watergate break-ins and the coverup, telling the president, "A lot of these people could be indicted." Dean told the president of the danger and reviewed the genesis of Watergate:

Dean: I think, I think that, uh, there's no doubt about the seriousness of the problem we're, we've got. We have a cancer—within—close to the Presidency, that's growing. It's growing daily. It's compounding, it grows geometrically now, because it compounds itself. Uh, that'll be clear as I explain, you know, some of the details, uh, of why it is, and it basically is because (1) we're being blackmailed; (2) uh, people are going to start perjuring themself very quickly that have not had to perjure themselves to protect other people and the like. And that is just— And there is no assurance—

President: That it won't bust.

Dean: That that won't bust.

President: True.

Dean: So let me give you the sort of basic facts, talking first about the Watergate; and then about Segretti; and then about some of the peripheral items that, uh, have come up. First of all, on, on the Watergate: how did it all start, where did it start? It started with an instruction to me from Bob Haldeman to see if we couldn't set up a perfectly legitimate campaign intelligence operation over at the Reelection Committee.

President: Hm.

Dean went on to give the president details of the Watergate crimes, much of which Nixon already knew. Dean described the Liddy Plan, Mitchell's role, the Ellsberg break-in, the dirty tricks, the Watergate break-in, and perjury by administration officials. Then Dean turned to the coverup.

Dean: Uh, I don't know what he said. Uh, I have never seen a transcript of the grand jury. Now [sighs] what, what has happened post–June 17? Well, it was, I was under pretty clear instructions [laughs] not to really to investigate this, that this was something that just could have been disastrous on the election if it had—all hell had broken loose, and I worked on a theory of containment.

President: Sure.

Dean: to try to hold it right where it was.

President: Right.

Dean went on to discuss the money demands of the Watergate defendants. These payoffs were, to Dean,

Dean: the most troublesome post-thing, uh, because (1) Bob is involved in that; John is involved in that; I am involved in that; Mitchell is involved in that. And that's an obstruction of justice.

President: In other words the fact that, uh, that you're, you're, you're taking care of witnesses.

Dean: That's right. Uh . . . But, now, here, here's what's happening right now.

President: Yeah.

Dean: What sort of brings matters to the— This is the one that's going to be a continual blackmail operation by Hunt and Liddy and the—

President: Yeah.

Dean: Cubans. No doubt about it. And McCord—

President: Yeah.

Dean then briefed the president on some of the other problems they faced.

Dean: Now, where, where are the soft spots on this? Well, first of all, there's the, there's the problem of the continued blackmail—

President: Right.

Dean: which will not only go on now, it'll go on when these people are in prison, and it will compound the obstruction of justice situation. It'll cost money. It's dangerous. Nobody, nothing—people around here are not pros at this sort of thing. This is the sort of thing Mafia people can do: washing money, getting clean money, and things like that, uh—we're—we just don't know about those things, because we're not used to, you know—we are not criminals and not used to dealing in that business. It's, uh, it's, uh—

President: That's right.

Dean: It's a tough thing to know how to do.

President: Maybe we can't even do that.

Dean: That's right. It's a real problem as to whether we could even do it. Plus there's a real problem in raising money. Uh, Mitchell has been working on raising some money. Uh, feeling he's got, you know, he's got one, he's one of the ones with the most to lose. Uh, but there's no denying the fact that the White House, and, uh, Ehrlichman, Haldeman, Dean are involved in some of the early money decisions.

President: How much money do you need?

Dean: I would say these people are going to cost, uh, a million dollars over the next, uh, two years.

President: We could get that.

Dean: Uh huh.

President: You, on the money, if you need the money, I mean, uh, you could get the money. Let's say—

Dean: Well, I think that we're going—

President: What I meant is, you could, you could get a million dollars. And you could get it in cash. I, I know where it could be gotten.

Dean: Uh huh.

President: I mean it's not easy, but it could be done. But, uh, the question is who the hell would handle it?

Dean: That's right. Uh . . .

President: Yeah. Well, what do you need, then? You need, uh, you don't need a million right away, but you need a million. Is that right?

Dean: That's right.

President: You need a million in cash, don't you? If you want to put that through, would you put that through, uh, this is thinking out loud here for a moment—would you put that through the Cuban Committee?
You need it in cash, don't you? If you want to put—

Dean: All right. Let, let me, uh—

President: Go ahead.

Dean: continue a little bit here now. The, uh, I, when I say this is a, a growing cancer, uh, I say it for reasons like this. Bud Krogh, in his testimony before the grand jury, was forced to perjure himself. Uh, he is haunted by it. Uh, Bud said, "I haven't had a pleasant day on the job."

President: Huh? Said what?

Dean: He said, "I have not had a pleasant day on my job." Uh, he talked, apparently, he said to me, "I told my wife all about this," he said. "The, uh, the curtain may ring down one of these days, and, uh, I may have to face the music, which I'm perfectly willing to do." Uh—

President: What did he perjure himself on, John?

Dean: His, did, uh, did he know the Cubans? He did. Uh—

President: He said he didn't?

Dean: That's right. They didn't press him hard, or that he—

President: He might be able to—I am just trying to think. Perjury is an awful hard rap to prove. He could say that I— Well, go ahead.

Dean: [Coughs] Well, so that's, that's the first, that's one perjury. Now, Mitchell and, and, uh, Magruder are potential perjuries. There is always the possibility of any one of these individuals blowing. Hunt, Liddy. Liddy is in jail right now; he's serving his—trying to get good time right now. I think Liddy is probably, in his, in his own bizarre way, the strongest of all of them. Uh, so there's—there is that possibility.

President: Well, you, your major, your major guy to keep under control is Hunt.

Dean: That's right.

President: I think. Because he knows—

Dean: He knows so much.

President: About a lot of other things.

Dean: He knows so much. Right. Uh, he could sink Chuck Colson. Apparently, apparently he is quite distressed with Colson. He thinks Colson has abandoned him. Uh. Colson was to meet with him when he was out there, after, now he had left the White House. He met with him through his lawyer. Hunt raised the question;

he wanted money. Colson's lawyer told him that Colson wasn't doing anything with money, and Hunt took offense with that immediately, that, uh, uh, that Colson had abandoned him. Uh—

President: Don't you, just looking at the immediate problem, don't you have to have—handle Hunt's financial situation—

Dean: I, I think that's—

President: damn soon?

Dean: That is, uh, I talked to Mitchell about that last night—

President: Mitchell.

Dean: And, and, uh, I told—

President: Might as well. May have the rule you've got to keep the cap on the bottle that much.

Dean: That's right; that's right.

President: In order to have any options.

Dean: That's right.

President: Either that or let it all blow right now.

Dean: Well that, you know, that's the, that's the question. Uh—

Dean continued to go over other possible legal problems. He told the president of the need for continued perjury in the future to protect the coverup. After Haldeman joined the meeting, they continued to explore ways of containing the mess.

President: Well, another way, another way to do it then, Bob, is to—and John realizes this—is to, uh, continue to try to cut our losses. Now we have to look at that course of action. First, it is going to require approximately a million dollars to take care of the jackasses that are in jail. That could be, that could be arranged.

Haldeman or Dean: Yeah.

President: That could be arranged. But you realize that after we are gone, I mean, assuming these [unintelligible] are gone, they're going to crack, you know what I mean? And that'll be an unseemly story. Eventually, all the people aren't going to care that much.

Later in the conversation:

President: Coming back, though, to this. So you got that—the, uh, hanging over. Now. If, uh—you, you see, if you let it hang there, the point is you could let all or only part— The point is, your feeling is that we just can't continue to, to pay the blackmail of these guys?

Dean: I think that's our greatest jeopardy.

Haldeman: Yeah.

President: Now, let me tell you, it's—

Dean: 'Cause that is—

President: No problem, we could, we could get the money. There is no problem in that. We can't provide the clemency. The money can be provided. Mitchell could provide the way to deliver it. That could be done. See what I mean?

The maintenance of the coverup continued to depend on perjury from several of the participants. But how to guarantee continued perjury? The president instructed:

Dean: You can't have a lawyer before a grand jury.

Haldeman: Okay, but you, but you, you do have rules of evidence. You can refuse to, to talk.

Dean: You can take the Fifth Amendment.

President: That's right. That's right.

Haldeman: You can say you forgot, too, can't you?

Dean: Sure.

President: That's right.

Dean: But you can't—you're—very high risk in perjury situation.

President: That's right. Just be damned sure you say I don't—

Haldeman: Yeah—

Dean: remember; I can't recall, I can't give any honest, an answer to that that I can recall. But that's it.

Finally, they return to Hunt's demand for hush money, and realize that it is a problem that must be met.

Haldeman: This is Hunt's opportunity.

Dean: This is Hunt's opportunity.

President: That's why, that's why—

Haldeman: God, if he can lay this—

President: that's why your, for your immediate thing you've got no choice with Hunt but the hundred and twenty or whatever it is. Right?

Dean: That's right.

President: Would you agree that that's a buy time thing, you better damn well get that done, but fast!

Dean: I think he ought to be given some signal, anyway, to, to—

President: Yes.

Dean: Yeah—you know.

President: Well for Christ's sakes get it in a, in a way that, uh— Who's, who's going to talk to him? Colson? He's the one who's supposed to know him.

Dean's original goal prior to this meeting was to get the president to somehow end the coverup. But by the end of the meeting the coverup expands. Exasperated, Dean told the president that the administration was not in a position to maintain the coverup.

President: Well, look, uh, what is it that you need on that, uh, when, uh, uh? Now look [unintelligible], I am, uh, unfamiliar with the money situation.

Dean: Well that, you know, it, it sounds easy to do, apparently, until, uh, everyone is out there doing it and that's where our breakdown has, has come every time.

President: Well, if you had it, where would you, how would you get it to somebody?

Dean: Well, I, uh, I gather LaRue just leaves it in mailboxes and things like that, and tells Hunt to go pick it up. Someone phones Hunt and tells him to pick it up. As I say, we're a bunch of amateurs in that business.

Haldeman: That was the thing that we thought Mitchell ought to be able to know how to find somebody who could do all that sort of thing, because none of us know how to.

Dean: That's right. You got to wash money and all that sort, you know, if you get a hundred thousand out of a bank, and it all comes in serialized bills, and—

President: Oh, I understand.

Dean: And that means you have to go to Vegas with it or a bookmaker in New York City and I've learned all these things after the fact, it's— [laughs] Great shape for the next time around. [Laughter]

Haldeman: Jesus.

The meeting concluded with an agreement to expand the coverup.

President: All right. Fine. And, uh, my point is that, uh, we can, uh, you may well come—I think it is good, frankly, to consider these various options. And then, once you, once you decide on the plan—John—and you had the right plan, let me say, I have no doubts about the right plan before the election. And you handled it just right. You contained it. Now after the election we've got to have another plan, because we can't have, for four years, we can't have this thing—you're going to be eaten away. We can't do it.

Dean: Well, there's been a change in the mood—

Haldeman: John's point is exactly right, that the erosion here now is going to you, and that is the thing that we've got to turn off, at whatever the cost. We've got to figure out where to turn it off at the lowest cost we can, but at whatever cost it takes.

Dean: That's what, that's what we have to do.

President: Well, the erosion is inevitably going to come here, apart from anything, you know, people saying that, uh, well, the Watergate isn't a major concern. It isn't. But it would, but it will be. It's bound to be.

Dean: We cannot let you be tarnished by that situation.

In the March 21 meeting, the president was fully informed on Watergate, its roots, and the continuing coverup. He was told of potential criminal liability among his top people and was warned that the coverup was cracking. The cancer on the presidency is growing, warns Dean. But rather than clean up the mess, Nixon got deeper into a coverup. He instructed in how to commit perjury, approved of hush money to maintain the silence of the Watergate defendants, and orchestrated a new coverup plan. Nixon was now in charge of the management of the Watergate coverup.

The following day, March 22, the president, Dean, Haldeman, Ehrlichman, and Mitchell met in the Oval Office to devise a way of dealing with the upcoming Senate hearings. They discussed a means to limit testimony, using executive privilege as a way to get the committee to compromise on the method of questioning White House officials.

The meeting moved to the subject of the "Dean report," with Dean saying, "I really can't say if I can do it." But the president continued to pressure Dean, with Ehrlichman telling Dean to say that "Nobody [in the White House] was involved," to which Nixon adds, "That's right."

The discussion returned to the use of executive privilege, and the president, responding to a suggestion by Mitchell, said, "All that John Mitchell is arguing, then, is that now we use flexibility in order to get on with the coverup plan." All the participants knew that they could not fully testify. As Nixon said to Mitchell, "I know we can't make a complete cave-in and have the people go up there and testify. You would agree on that?" "I agree," responded Mitchell.

Toward the end of the March 22 meeting, Nixon assured everyone, "We will survive it," and complimented Dean for being a "son-of-a-bitching tough thing," and the president added: "I don't give a shit what happens. I want you all to stonewall it, let them plead the Fifth Amendment, coverup or anything else, if it'll save it—save the plan. That's the whole point."

Then the president, commenting to Mitchell, said, "Up to this point the whole theory has been containment, as you know, John," and Mitchell answered, "Yeah."[23]

The following day everything hit the fan.

On Friday, March 23, an unexpected crack in the coverup developed. In open court, Judge John Sirica dropped a bombshell when he made public a letter written to him by convicted Watergate burglar James McCord. McCord's letter charged that the Watergate defendants were under "political pressure" to plead guilty and remain silent, that perjury had been committed, and that higher-ups were involved. It was the first crack in the coverup wall. Soon, the walls would come tumbling down on Richard Nixon.

The following week McCord testified for four hours in a closed-door session before the Senate Watergate Committee. He declared that Colson, Dean, Magruder, and Mitchell had prior knowledge of the Watergate break-in.

Dean began to feel the noose closing around his neck. The McCord letter and his fear that Nixon was setting him up (taking Dean's own advice and cutting the losses), plus the continued pressure to write a "Dean report," led Dean to consider a trip to the prosecutors in hopes of getting a deal. Finally, on March 26, when Haldeman told Dean that the White House was cutting Magruder and Mitchell loose, he realized that everyone—except the president—was expendable. Dean, fearing that Magruder would crack, called criminal lawyer Charles Shaffer. On April 2, Dean's lawyers told the prosecutors that their client was ready to cooperate. On April 8, John Dean began to talk. Magruder, seeing the writing on the wall, also decided to cooperate with the prosecutors. The coverup continued to crack.

ALL FALL DOWN

April was a particularly bad month for the president. With Dean and Magruder talking to the prosecutors, he had to see that the coverup might collapse on his shoulders. In mid-April the world began to shatter for Nixon. He called April 14 "the day when everything began to fall apart." The president had devised an "hors d'oeuvre strategy," as Nixon told Haldeman and Ehrlichman, "Give 'em an hors d'eouvre and maybe they won't come back for the main course." But who would be a tasty hors d'oeuvre? John Mitchell, of course. On April 14 Nixon, Haldeman, and Ehrlichman decided to try to get John Mitchell to take the fall for Watergate. He refused. Ehrlichman's unsuccessful effort to persuade Mitchell to take the rap for the president led Mitchell to conclude that he was "too far out" and would not take the fall. Mitchell defended himself by pointing out that the genesis of Watergate came from pressure exerted from within the White House.

If Mitchell would not shoulder blame and protect Nixon, who would? It was decided that John Dean would be made presidential scapegoat, the sacrificial lamb. The new strategy devised by Nixon, Haldeman, and Ehrlichman was to have Dean write a report that "basically clears the President and the White House staff of involvement." If Dean would submit such a report, the president could go public and say, "Look, this is what I relied on. Dean deceived me." But Dean refused, suspecting he was being set up, and instead continued to talk to the Justice Department in hopes of getting a deal from the prosecutors. At the same time, Jeb Magruder continued to meet with government prosecutors and tell all. The net was closing in on the White House.

On April 14, the president, Haldeman, and Ehrlichman discussed their own complicity in the coverup. The president began by saying that "Dean only tried to do what he could to pick up the pieces, and everybody else around here knew it had to be done." "Certainly," Ehrlichman said. Later Ehrlichman, the only one of the three who was not aware of the taping system then in operation, said, "There were eight or ten people around here who knew about this, knew it was going on, Bob knew, I knew, all kinds of people knew."

"Well, I knew it, I knew it," Nixon added.

The management of Watergate, up to now scattered and only semicoordinated, began to frustrate the president. Aware that the edges of the coverup were cracking and that it was in danger of falling apart completely and engulfing him, he suggested getting "everyone" together, "They've gotta have a straight damn line."

The president's desperate efforts to save the coverup seemed doomed the following day, April 15, when Attorney General Richard Kleindienst informed Nixon that Haldeman and Ehrlichman were "being drawn into the criminal case," and that John Dean was their chief accuser. Kleindienst advised the president to dismiss his two top aides.

At nine o'clock on the evening of the 15th, Dean met with the president and told him, according to Dean's testimony to the Senate, that he "had gone to the prosecutors," told them of his own involvement and that of others, but had not discussed with them the president's role in Watergate. The president asked Dean a number of leading questions that made him "think the conversation was being taped," and Nixon said of his March assurance to Dean that he could get $1 million "to maintain the silence of the defendants," that "he had, of course, only been joking."

The president knew Dean had to go, but he was still hoping to put the blame on Dean. When they met on April 16, Nixon gave Dean two draft letters, one requesting a leave of absence, the other a letter of resignation. Dean refused to sign either, again fearing he was being set up for a fall.

The following morning the president discussed the John Dean problem with Haldeman and Ehrlichman. Dean has "decided to save his ass," the president said. And on April 17, Haldeman told Nixon, "I must admit the guy [Dean] has really turned into an unbelievable disaster for us." "I'm trapped," the president concluded, "I've trapped myself" (Haldeman notes, April 17, 1973).

In an April 30 television address, the president, bowing to the inevitable, announced the resignations of Haldeman and Ehrlichman. He also announced John Dean's dismissal. He denied any personal involvement in the break-in or coverup, but conceded that "there had been an effort to conceal the facts." Nixon claimed that he was misled by subordinates into believing that no one from his administration or campaign organization was involved. With Haldeman and Ehrlichman gone, the presidential cocoon so comfortably spun around Nixon evaporated.

In his memoirs, Nixon admits that the April 30 speech was less than truthful, giving the impression that he was unaware of the coverup until March 21. Instead of "exerting presidential leadership," Nixon admitted embarking upon an "increasingly desperate search for ways to limit the damage."[24]

The president was unprotected, his "Berlin Wall" was gone. If Nixon was isolated before, he was even more alone and isolated in May as the Senate Watergate hearings began. At this time the Nixon high command took a new shape. General Alexander Haig assumed Haldeman's role as chief of staff. And, bowing to pressure to appoint a special prosecutor in the Watergate case, new

Attorney General Elliot Richardson announced that former solicitor general and Harvard law professor Archibald Cox would serve in that capacity. Cox immediately went to work accumulating evidence.

THE (MIS-)MANAGEMENT OF WATERGATE

From a management standpoint, Watergate was a disaster. In both its "routine" and "crisis" stages,[25] Watergate is a study in mismanagement.[26] Nixon himself admitted that "history will justifiably record that my handling of the Watergate crisis was an unmitigated disaster."[27]

Organizational objectives were never clearly defined; *planning* was casual, reactive, and haphazard; *personnel* were not chosen whose skills matched their assigned tasks (Dean once said that the White House staff was poorly equipped for the jobs they were asked to do, suggesting that such tasks were better suited to "Mafia" types); *control* was never clearly spelled out, and no one was coordinating the process; *information* was poorly channeled, with different people knowing different parts but no one knowing everything; *communication* was sporadic and uncoordinated; *group-think*, with the White House staff adopting Nixon's "everyone is out to get us" approach, distorted facts and painted an unrealistic picture of the problems; *misperception* was rampant in Nixon and his top staff; the *quality of character* of the president and his men was such that no one said, "Stop! This is illegal, and it must end"; and CREEP was *overcapitalized* to such a degree that it was looking for ways to spend the money.

In the end, the "prime measure of management is effectiveness."[28] By this standard, Watergate was badly mismanaged. At almost every turn, the president and his men made the wrong move.[29] This is surprising because Nixon was not a bad manager overall; he and the men around him were bright. But Nixon and his men were tainted with resentment for, and fear of, the world of politics which they absorbed from the boss. Nixon's fears, hatreds, and paranoia distorted the administration's perceptions and judgments, and in the end this view inhibited the managerial side of Watergate.

In planning and discussing ways to contain Watergate, one notices (from listening to the tapes) that all participants, including and especially the president, show a lack of organized thinking. Discussions seem random and unfocused. Ideas, plans, proposals are scattered throughout the conversations, but there is no direction; no one took over and lent coherence to the discussions. Everything was haphazard and loose. No clear orders were given, no fully rational or organized plan emerged.

One might think that this phenomenon is restricted only to Watergate and is the result of the participants' reluctance to give order and coherence to what deep down inside they knew were criminal acts. It might have been difficult for these men to be explicit about committing crimes. But, this form of behavior was not peculiar to discussions of Watergate and the coverup. In fact, such free-flowing discussions characterized Nixon's style. He used meetings to discuss, not decide. Rarely were direct orders clearly given in the midst of discussions. There was no organized and coordinated action plan. In this sense, was Watergate a "cancer" growing on the presidency, isolated and idiosyncratic; or was it a reflection on Nixon's whole presidency and operating style writ large? In general, the management style operating during Watergate bears a striking resemblance to other decision areas in that such decisions reflected an overpersonalization and underinstitutionalization of policy. Watergate was an aberration for the presidency broadly speaking, but not for the Nixon presidency, because it was the result of the mix of process and personalities so much a part of the Nixon operating style.

SENATOR ERVIN'S COMMITTEE

When the Senate Select Committee on Presidential Campaign Activities (usually referred to as the Ervin Committee or Watergate Committee) opened its hearings on May 17, the president was already in a precarious position: Dean, Magruder, and McCord were talking, Haldeman and Ehrlichman had been jettisoned from the administration, the president's popularity was slipping, and the press was pursuing lead after lead on Watergate. The fact that the Senate hearings would be televised nationally only worsened things.

The hearings got off to a slow start, with the committee initially calling witnesses on the periphery of power. Everyone was waiting for John Dean. Finally, on June 25, John Dean took the chair and began to read his prepared opening statement in a monotone voice: "To one who was in the White House and became somewhat familiar with its interworkings, the Watergate matter was an inevitable outgrowth of a climate of excessive concern over the political impact of demonstrators, excessive concern over leaks, an insatiable appetite for political intelligence, all coupled with a do-it-yourself White House staff, regardless of the law."

Thus began a 245-page statement in which Dean blew the lid off the administration. The portrait Dean painted was devastating: wiretapping, burglary, enemies lists, secret funds, money laundering, dirty tricks, Plumbers, intelligence surveillance, character assassination, obstruction of justice, coverup. But all Dean had was his word—no documentation, no corroboration. Dean's assertion that the president was right in the middle of the mess came down to his word against the president's. How would the dilemma be resolved?

The answer fell into the lap of the committee on July 16 after several staff members had questioned Alexander Butterfield in preparation for his appearance before the committee. In that questioning Butterfield revealed the existence of a White House taping system. Butterfield was rushed to give testimony. Minority counsel Fred Thompson asked, "Mr. Butterfield, are you aware of the installation of any listening devices in the Oval office of the President?" "I was aware of listening devices, yes, sir," was Butterfield's reply. "Are you aware of any devices that were installed in the Executive Office Building office of the President?" asked Thompson. "Yes, sir."

The president had secretly tape-recorded all conversations in the Oval Office, the president's office in the Executive Office Building, the Lincoln Room, and at Camp David. Another bombshell. The tapes could confirm or shatter Dean's charges against the president. It was no longer Dean's word against the president's. There was proof.

The Senate immediately requested the tapes, as did the special prosecutor. Nixon refused. The Senate and special prosecutor subpoenaed several of the tapes, and Nixon still refused, citing executive privilege. The Senate Watergate Committee and Archibald Cox took the president to court over the tapes. On August 29, Judge John Sirica ruled that the president must turn over the subpoenaed tapes. The president appealed the ruling, and on October 12, the U.S. Court of Appeals upheld Sirica's order. The president decided to appeal to the Supreme Court.

As the battle for the tapes began, the Senate committee continued to hear from witnesses. Mitchell, Ehrlichman, and Haldeman all contradicted Dean and pointed the finger at Dean as being the real culprit in the coverup. But as the Senate's investigation wound down, the battle for the tapes heated up.

As if things weren't bad enough for President Nixon, the Justice Department was also investigating charges of corruption against Nixon's vice president, Spiro Agnew. Allegedly, Agnew had taken cash payments—bribes—in exchange for government contracts while Agnew was an official and later governor of Maryland. According to the charges, Agnew was accepting bribe money while he was vice president.

An investigation by the U.S. attorney in Baltimore found approximately fifty possible criminal violations, including bribery, extortion, conspiracy, and tax evasion. After reviewing the evidence, Agnew's attorneys negotiated a plea bargain: Agnew would resign as vice president, plead *nolo contendere* (no contest) to a single charge of income tax evasion, the Justice Department would enter the evidence into the public record, and Agnew would escape a prison sentence. Walter Hoffman, the judge in the case, told Agnew that the no-contest plea was "the full equivalent of a plea of guilty." On October 10, 1973, Spiro Agnew resigned as vice president. Two days later, President Nixon nominated Gerald Ford as vice president. Ford was confirmed and was sworn in on December 6, 1973.

The battle for the tapes continued, with the president insisting that Archibald Cox, who was technically part of the executive branch, cease from pressing the president to produce the tapes. In an effort to get a compromise, Nixon offered Cox a surprise deal: the Stennis Plan. Under this plan, Nixon would let the seventy-two-year-old conservative Democrat Senator John Stennis of Mississippi, who was still recovering from a gunshot wound, verify the accuracy of a transcript of the tapes, but not turn them over to Cox. Part of the deal included an insistence that Cox ask for no more tapes.

Cox refused, and on October 20, in what came to be known as the "Saturday Night Massacre," Attorney General Elliot Richardson resigned after refusing to fire Cox. Deputy Attorney General William Ruckelshaus also resigned; and finally Solicitor General Robert Bork was named acting attorney general, and he carried out Nixon's order to fire Cox, abolish the special prosecutor's office, and have the FBI seal Cox's offices to prevent removal of any files.

A tremendous public outcry followed, as did the introduction of twenty-two bills in Congress calling for an impeachment investigation. How much more could the president—and the nation—take? On October 30, the House Judiciary Committee began consideration of possible procedures in the event of an impeachment. Nixon finally agreed to turn over some of the tapes. On November 1, 1972, Leon Jaworski was appointed as new special prosecutor. He too sought the tapes. As pressure on the president mounted, calls for his resignation appeared. On November 17, the president, in a televised press conference, said, "People have got to know whether or not their President is a crook. Well, I'm not a crook."

The president was determined to try one last PR offensive, this one called "Operation Candor." In this operation, Nixon would publicly promise to deliver everything, but stall, stall, stall. Although the president promised on November 20 that there were no more Watergate "bombshells" waiting to explode, on the very next day Nixon's lawyers told John Sirica of a "gap" problem in the tapes. Operation Candor was dead.

The president continued to take a public beating. Within a week of his "I am not a crook" statement, Judge John Sirica revealed that there was an eighteen-and-a-half minute gap in the important June 20, 1972, tape of a conversation between Nixon and Haldeman—a meeting held three days after the Watergate break-in. Although Alexander Haig, Nixon's chief of staff, blamed the gap on "some sinister force," a panel of experts concluded that it was the result of five separate manual erasures. Judge Sirica recommended a grand jury investigation into "the possibility of unlawful destruction of evidence and related offenses," adding that "a distinct possibility of unlawful conduct on the part of one or more persons exists." The eighteen-and-a-half minute gap caused another public outcry. Calls for Nixon's resignation became more frequent—and came from more establishment-oriented, mainstream sources.

As the Ervin Committee and special prosecutor continued to battle Nixon for more tapes, the president announced that he would not hand over any more tapes because it would violate confidentiality and could have an adverse effect on the Watergate trials.

On February 6, with only four dissenting votes, the House of Representatives adopted H.R. 803, which directed the House Committee on the Judiciary to begin an investigation into whether grounds existed for the House to impeach President Nixon.

Watergate was moving closer and closer to the president. On March 1, the federal grand jury indicted seven former top presidential aides—Mitchell,

Haldeman, Ehrlichman, Colson, Mardian, Parkinson, and Strachan—for attempting to cover up the Watergate investigation by lying to the FBI and to the grand jury, and for paying hush money to the original defendants. The grand jury also turned a briefcase over to Judge Sirica, the contents of which were kept secret, but which related to the president's role in the scandal. In this briefcase was material based on which the grand jury named Richard M. Nixon, president of the United States, as "unindicted co-conspirator" in the case.

The House joined the Senate and special prosecutor in seeking White House tapes, but the president continued to resist. Finally, on April 29, in a national television address, Nixon announced that he would supply the Judiciary Committee with "edited transcripts" of the subpoenaed conversations. Nixon said that this action would "at last, once and for all, show that what I knew and what I did with regard to the Watergate break-in and coverup were just as I have described them to you from the very beginning. As far as the president's role with regard to Watergate is concerned, the entire story is there."

But the entire story *was not* there. The transcripts later proved to be incomplete and inaccurate. At the time, however, they appeared impressive indeed. The president, in his speech, had the camera pan to a table containing stack upon stack of binders that appeared to contain thousands upon thousands of pages. In reality, this was a public relations ploy. Many of the binders contained only a few pages.

Among the many White House omissions is this portion of the March 22, 1973 conversation between Nixon and Mitchell. The president says: "I don't give a shit what happens. I want you all to stonewall it, let them plead the Fifth Amendment, cover up or anything else, if it'll save it—save the plan. That's the whole point. . . . Up to this point, the whole theory has been containment, as you know, John."

This incriminating material *does not* appear in the White House transcript but is in the House Judiciary Committee's version. There were many other inaccuracies. Nixon's sanitized version was not acceptable, and the fight for the tapes themselves continued.

Leon Jaworski was methodically building a criminal case against administration officials, but a problem remained: what to do about the president? The charges against Mitchell, Haldeman, et al. hinged upon a conspiracy in which the president was actively involved. But could the president of the United States be indicted in a criminal case, or was impeachment the only avenue?

Jaworski asked his staff for legal memoranda relating to this question. The conclusion reached was that while there was a question of "propriety," there was "no explicit or implicit constitutional bar to indictment."[30] In the end, Jaworski, while admitting that there was clearly enough evidence to indict Nixon, could not bring himself to indict a sitting president.[31] Instead, the grand jury unanimously voted to name Richard Nixon an "unindicted co-conspirator."

THE MEDIA: FROM LAMBS TO LIONS

During the 1972 campaign, the press was generally supportive or neutral regarding the president.[32] But as the story of Watergate and its related horrors picked up steam, and as the trickle of negative stories built into an avalanche that eventually buried Richard Nixon, the press had an increasingly important role in shifting public opinion against the president.

The cumulative impact of day after day of revelations, day after day of TV coverage of Senate and House hearings, the unrelenting pressure of investigative reporting, and the almost daily discovery of bombshell after bombshell eventually led to Nixon's downfall.

Of course, recognizing the enormous impact of the media on the downfall of Richard Nixon should not obscure the fact that *at first* the press dealt very gingerly with Watergate—if at all. The press generally came late to the story, but when they did, they came with a vengeance.

A study by Ben Bagdikian revealed that only 15 out of the 433 Washington-based reporters were assigned to the Watergate story, and some on only a limited basis. Robert Maynard of the *Washington Post* found that of the approximately five hundred articles written by national columnists during the '72 campaign, less than two dozen dealt with Watergate. And Edwin Diamond reviewed all network TV newscasts during the campaign, and found "a straight, unquestioning serving of 'news' that—it is clear, in hindsight—advanced the cover-up."[33] CBS gave Watergate the most coverage of the TV networks, but as their White House correspondent Dan Rather noted, "CBS News was putting some stories about Watergate on the air, more than our broadcast competitors, but pitifully few." Rather blames this on "the deadly daily diet of deceit sent us from the White House. . . . They lied, schemed, threatened, and cajoled to prevent network correspondents from getting a handle on the story. And they succeeded."[34]

Nixon claimed he "had the most unfriendly press in history, it has never bothered me." Actually it did bother Nixon, as it would any president. Nixon did face a hostile press, but *not* in the campaign of 1972. And while administration officials kept complaining about "excessive press coverage" of a "third-rate burglary," there was actually very little coverage of Watergate during the campaign.

After the 1972 election, the Watergate story seemed to take on a life of its own. Day after day, story after story, seemed to engulf the president. Nixon's aides insisted the press was being unfair and that Nixon was "hounded from office" by a hostile press, and Nixon himself claimed that the press had "built this [Watergate] into a federal case." But did the press *create* Watergate, or merely *uncover* it? Edwin Diamond writes: "The record of the Watergate coverage discloses no hounding of the president. Quite the contrary. The press did not speak as a chorus with one voice. The president had his own defenders;

equally important, his [campaign] in 1972 initially came across louder than the message of Watergate."[35]

During the period of Watergate exposés, Nixon steadfastly avoided contact with the press and severely cut back on formal press conferences. Between March of 1973 and August 1974, Nixon held only six press conferences, and three question periods from groups other than the Washington press corps. At an October 26, 1973, press conference, Nixon gave this evaluation of the press's coverage of Watergate: "I have never heard or seen such outrageous, vicious, distorted reporting in twenty-seven years of public life."

"Mr. President, you have lambasted the television networks pretty well. Could I ask you, at the risk of reopening an obvious wound, you say after you have put on a lot of heat that you don't blame anyone. I find that a little puzzling. What is it about the television coverage of you in these past few weeks and months that has so aroused your anger?"

"Don't get the impression that you arouse my anger," Nixon responded.

"I'm afraid, sir," said Robert Pierpoint, "that I have that impression."

Nixon smiled and said, "You see, one can only be angry with those he respects."

From the beginning of Watergate, Nixon sought to deal with the press by avoiding direct contact, treating Watergate as essentially a public relations problem, and making end runs around the press and going directly to the people. In the end, nothing could save him. The full weight of Watergate—and the press played a significant part in revealing the story—was too much for Nixon.

THE HOUSE FACES IMPEACHMENT

In this highly charged atmosphere of eroding public confidence in the president, in which every day seemed to bring a new, more-damaging revelation, the House Judiciary Committee prepared to open the public phase of its impeachment inquiry. The case against the president had been building for over a year, but the case was made up primarily of circumstantial evidence linking the president to the scandal, with accusations from Dean, Magruder, and others. The direct evidence was still fairly thin.

As committee counsel John Doar accumulated material against Nixon, it became clear that the full weight of the accumulated evidence was devastating. But before impeachment proceedings against the president could begin, a very important question had to be answered: What is an impeachable offense?

At one end of the spectrum of thought (the president's position) was the view that impeachment could *only* be for serious crimes. Nixon's was a strictly *legalistic* view. At a March 6, 1974, press conference, Nixon, answering a question, said that "impeachment should be limited to very serious crimes committed in one's official capacity." Nixon added, "When you refer to a narrow view of what is an impeachable crime, I would say that might leave in the minds of some of our viewers and listeners a connotation which would be inaccurate. It is the constitutional view. The Constitution is very precise. Even Senator Ervin agrees that that view is the right one, and if Senator Ervin agrees, it must be the right one." (Senator Ervin did not hold this view.) At the other end of the spectrum was the view that impeachment was primarily a *political* device for removing a president, and one need not find violations of the law to vote for impeachment.

The Constitution, as it is in many areas, is rather vague regarding impeachment. The Constitution says that public officers "shall be removed from office on impeachment for, and conviction of, treason, bribery, or other high crimes and misdemeanors" (Article II, Section 4). But what are high crimes and misdemeanors?

The Founders' original proposal on impeachment first presented at the Constitutional Convention provided for impeachment for "malpractice or neglect of duty." The Committee on Detail changed the wording to read "treason, bribery, or corruption," and still later changed it to "treason or bribery." George Mason recommended that "maladministration" be added to the list, but James Madison objected on grounds that it was too vague. Finally, the wording was changed to the old British term "high crimes and misdemeanors." What then, did the Founders understand this phrase to mean?

In general, the Founders, following the British common law tradition, did not understand "high crimes and misdemeanors" in the narrow, legal sense, or in the strictly criminal sense.[36] Constitutional scholar Raoul Berger concludes that the Founders had a fairly wide view of the grounds for impeachment that included misapplication of funds, abuse of official power, neglect of duty, encroachment on or contempt of Parliament's prerogatives, corruption, and betrayal of trust.[37]

The history of impeachment in the United States offers few precedents, as only a handful of cases have reached the Senate. Several of these cases, however, *did not* involve indictable criminal offenses. In the only other attempted case of presidential impeachment, that of Andrew Johnson in 1868, the charges were almost strictly political.[38] Following this view, on February 21, John Doar submitted a report to the committee entitled "Constitutional Grounds for Presidential Impeachment," which reviewed the history of impeachment and its application to the case at hand. Doar concluded that impeachment was a remedy to be applied in cases of "serious offenses against the system of government."

A long, emotional, often heated, sometimes eloquent debate over the evidence against the president ensued. Under the glare of national television, Chairman Peter Rodino of New Jersey guided the hearings through these difficult times with evenhandedness. He knew that if the impeachment of Richard Nixon were to be legitimate and appropriate, it would require a bipartisan vote

Table 6
Vote on Impeachment Articles

Article	For		Against		
	Dems.	Reps.	Dems.	Reps.	Total
I Obstruction of Justice	21	6	0	11	27-11
II Abuse of Power	21	7	0	10	28-10
III Contempt of Congress	19	2	2	15	21-17
IV Bombing of Cambodia	12	-	9	17	12-26
V Income Tax Evasion	12	-	9	17	12-26

Source: Adapted from *Impeachment of Richard Nixon*, Report of the Committee on the Judiciary, House of Representatives, August 20, 1974.

in favor of impeachment. Would any of the Republicans vote for impeachment?

On July 19, John Doar summarized the case against Nixon for the committee. "Reasonable men," he said, "acting reasonably would find the President guilty." Doar spoke of Nixon's "enormous crimes," and accused the President of "the terrible deed of subverting the Constitution." Minority counsel Albert Jenner supported Doar's conclusion. Would the Republicans on the committee?

On July 27, the committee voted on Article I of impeachment, which accused the president of engaging in a "course of conduct" designed to obstruct justice in attempting to cover up Watergate. This article passed by a 27–11 vote, with 6 Republicans joining all 21 Democrats in the majority. The following day Article II, charging Nixon with abuse of power, passed 28–10, and on the following day, the third article of impeachment, charging the president with unconstitutionally defying a congressional subpoena, passed 21–17. Two other articles, dealing with concealing the bombing of Cambodia and with income tax evasion, both failed by 26–12 votes.

The vote against the president—especially on Articles I and II—was bipartisan (see Table 6). Rodino was able to get enough Republicans to vote against a president of their own party to ensure that the public would see that the case against Nixon crossed party loyalties. The Judiciary Committee would recommend to the full House that it vote to impeach Richard M. Nixon, thirty-seventh president of the United States. On only one other occasion, in the impeachment of Andrew Johnson over one hundred years earlier, had the House faced such a situation.

THE BATTLE FOR THE TAPES

Everyone seemed to want Nixon's White House tapes. The Senate, the special prosecutor, then the House, all wanted the recorded record to see who was telling the truth. But the president refused to part with the tapes, citing variously executive privilege, the need for confidentiality, and other reasons.

Judiciary Committee chairman Pete Rodino wanted the tapes, and by a vote of 20–18 (essentially along partisan lines) the Judiciary Committee rejected Nixon's offer of transcripts, and informed the president that he had "failed to comply with the Committee's subpoena." After battles by the Judiciary Committee and Jaworski to get the tapes from the president, the Supreme Court agreed to hear the case.

President Nixon refused to comply with the committee's subpoena, invoking a claim of "executive privilege." While there is no mention of executive privilege in the Constitution, the claim derives from a belief that it is part of the implied power of the executive function of the president. The president's claim was not entirely self-serving. Not only is there a considerable history of presidential claims of privilege and confidentiality, but it is clear that some stages of the policy-making process must remain outside the glare of public scrutiny.

Taking the case placed the Court in the center of a legal *and* political battle. It was not a foregone conclusion that the president would obey a Court ruling. He had already warned that he would only obey a "definitive" ruling, and Charles Alan Wright, Nixon's lawyer, said, "The tradition is very strong that judges should have the last word, but," he added, "in a government organized as ours is, there are times when that simply cannot be the case."

The case, *United States of America v. Richard Nixon*, revolved around the question of who decides whether a president obeys a subpoena, the Congress, the courts, or the president himself? Leon Jaworski argued that the president must comply with a subpoena in a criminal case, that our system of law is based on no man being above the law:

Who is to be the arbiter of what the Constitution says? Now, the President may be right in how he reads the Constitution. But he may also be wrong. And if he is wrong, who is there to tell him so? . . . This nation's constitutional form of government is in serious jeopardy if the President, any President, is to say that the Constitution means what he says it does, and that there is no one, not even the Supreme Court to tell him otherwise.

Nixon's lawyer, James St. Clair, thought otherwise:

The President is not above the law. Nor does he contend that he is. What he does contend is that as President the law can be applied to him in only one way, and that is by impeachment.

On July 24, in an 8–0 decision (Justice Rehnquist withdrew from the case), the Supreme Court ruled that President Nixon must give to Judge Sirica (who was presiding in the Watergate coverup trial) the tapes, which were evidence in a criminal case. While acknowledging a heretofore unrecognized constitutional basis for the claim of executive privilege, the Court ruled that in this case, the president was required to turn over the tapes. The decision read in part:

A President and those who assist him must be free to explore alternatives in the process of shaping policies and making decisions and to do so in a way many would be unwilling to express except privately. . . . The privilege is fundamental to the operation of government and inextricably rooted in the separation of powers under the Constitution. . . . Nowhere in the Constitution . . . is there any explicit relevance to a privilege of confidentiality, yet to the extent this interest relates to the effective discharge of the President's power, it is constitutionally based.

But this privilege was not without limits. As the Court noted:

Neither the doctrine of separation of powers, nor the need for confidentiality of high level communications, without more, can sustain an absolute, unqualified presidential privilege of immunity from judicial process under all circumstances. The President's need for complete candor and objectivity from advisers calls for great deference from the courts. However, when the privilege depends solely on the broad undifferentiated claim of public interest in the confidentiality of such conversations, a confrontation with other values arises.[39]

On August 5, Nixon finally released the tapes, and his fate was sealed. The June 23, 1972, tape became the "smoking gun," with undeniable evidence of criminal complicity, and when its content became known, it decimated the president's defense. When he released the tapes, the president admitted that some of the tapes "are at variance with certain of my previous statements." Nixon *had* lied, covered up, obstructed justice, not for national security reasons, but to protect himself. There was no way Nixon could survive. Even his staunchest supporters turned on the president. It was over.

When the tapes were released, nearly all Nixon's support evaporated. Nixon loyalist Senator Hugh Scott said that the tapes showed "a shabby, disgusting, immoral performance by all those involved." Representative Mann of South Carolina said that "the more that people know about him, it seems the more trouble he's in." Conservative publisher William Randolph Hearst, Jr., said Nixon was "a man totally immersed in the cheapest and sleaziest kind of conniving." Impeachment in the House and conviction in the Senate were now certainties. Public opinion, which had been turning against the president since January, was now overwhelmingly against the president. Gallup Pool data (see Table 7) reveals the quick, sharp shift in public opinion.

The June 23 tape not only revealed that Nixon was directing a criminal coverup in the first week after the break-in, but also showed Nixon to be a small, petty person. This tape, and others, contained revealing personal glimpses into Nixon the man, and much of what was revealed showed a side of Nixon

Table 7
Percent Believing in Nixon's Complicity

May 11-14	56
June 1-4	67
June 22-25	71
July 6-9	73
August 3-6	76

Source: Gallup polls (adapted from *Congressional Quarterly Weekly Report*, Washington, D.C., 1974).

never before shown to the public. Nixon appeared small, petty, political in the worst sense of that word.[40]

But it was not these indications of Nixon's smallness that proved to be his undoing. The tapes also contained irrefutable proof that Richard Nixon had committed indictable crimes, lied about his knowledge and involvement, and obstructed justice and directed the coverup from June of 1972.

THE RESIGNATION

The final days were a nightmare for Nixon. He became progressively alone and isolated. He began to drink heavily. Son-in-law Edward Cox later remarked that "the president was up walking the halls last night, talking to pictures of former presidents—giving speeches and talking to the pictures on the wall."[41] Theodore H. White said the president was "an unstable personality," and "a time bomb which, if not defused in just the right way, might blow the course of all American history apart." Chief of Staff Al Haig ordered the president's doctors to deny Mr. Nixon all pills.[42]

In the final days a virtual coup took place. With the president behaving in an unstable manner, Al Haig took over day-to-day operations of the White House, and Secretary of Defense James Schlesinger ordered all military commanders to accept *no orders* from Nixon unless Schlesinger himself countersigned the order![43]

As those around the president began to see resignation as the only viable alternative, a slow, delicate process of coaxing Nixon to accept the inevitable began. With his popularity in the low 20 percent range and falling, with impeachment and conviction a certainty, all that remained was for the final decision to be made.

In the late afternoon of August 7, Hugh Scott, minority leader in the Senate, John Rhodes, minority leader in the House, and Barry Goldwater, elder statesman of the Republican party, met with Nixon in the Oval Office. Al Haig warned them, "He is almost on the edge of resignation and if you suggest it, he may take umbrage and reverse." In the meeting, the word *resignation* never came up. Instead the three Republican leaders assessed Nixon's waning support in the Congress. Scott told Nixon the situation was "gloomy." "It sounds damn gloomy," Nixon replied. Goldwater said it was "hopeless." Without using the words, the three visitors made it clear that Nixon would be impeached and convicted. When they left, Nixon went upstairs in the White House to tell his family it was over. The president broke the news to his family and, according to his daughter Julie, asked, "Was it worth it?"

Nixon friend and longtime speechwriter Ray Price prepared two resignation speeches: Option A, which in essence was the one Nixon delivered, and Option B, in which Nixon admitted much more and took blame and responsibility for his actions.

In a fifteen-minute television address delivered on the evening of August 8, 1974, the president announced that "I shall resign the presidency effective at noon tomorrow." In the speech Nixon showed little remorse, and cited as his reason for leaving: "In the last few days it has become evident to me that I no longer have a strong enough political base in the Congress to justify continuing in office." He added, "I regret deeply any injuries that may have been done in the course of the events that led to this decision. I would say only that if some of my judgments were wrong—and some were wrong—they were made in what I believed at the time to be in the best interest of the nation." Nixon neither protested his innocence nor admitted guilt. It was a controlled, carefully crafted speech.

The next morning, the Nixon family went to the East Room for a farewell to the president's staff. In an emotional talk, Nixon rambled almost uncontrollably, then pulled himself back together, rambled, then controlled himself. He spoke about his father:

I think they would have called him sort of a little man, common man. He didn't consider himself that way. You know what he was? He was a streetcar motorman, first, and then he was a farmer, and then he had a lemon ranch. It was the poorest lemon ranch in California, I can assure you.

Then his mother:

Nobody will ever write a book, probably, about my mother. Well, I guess all of you would say this about your mother—my mother was a saint. And I think of her, two boys dying of tuberculosis, nursing four others in order that she could take care of my older brother for three years in Arizona and seeing each of them die, and when they died, it was like one of her own. Yes, she will have no books written about her. But she was a saint.

Nixon spoke of his background, of sorrow and hatred, of troubles and heartaches, and he wept.

He then walked to his helicopter for the first leg of a journey that would take him to San Clemente. When the plane was midway across the American heartland, he was no longer president of the United States.

On August 9, 1974, shortly before noon, Nixon's letter of resignation was delivered to Secretary of State Henry Kissinger. It read in its entirety: "Dear Mr. Secretary: I hereby resign the office of President of the United States. Sincerely, Richard Nixon." He was the first president ever to resign from office. Upon being sworn in as president, Gerald Ford said that "our long national nightmare is over," and said that the wounds of Watergate were "more painful and more poisonous than those of foreign wars."

The Judiciary Committee filed its report with the full House. In the end, *all* thirty-eight members recommended impeachment. On August 20, the House accepted the committee's report and recommendations by a vote of 412–3, without taking any action on it. The ten Republicans on the Judiciary Committee who earlier voted against all the impeachment articles issued the following statement:

Our gratitude for his having by his resignation spared the nation additional agony should not obscure for history our judgment that Richard Nixon, as President, committed certain acts for which he should have been impeached and removed from office.

They added:

We know that it has been said, and perhaps some will continue to say, that Richard Nixon was "hounded from office" by his political opponents and media critics. We feel constrained to point out, however, that it was Richard Nixon who impeded the FBI's investigation of the Watergate affair by wrongfully attempting to implicate the Central Intelligence Agency; it was Richard Nixon, who created and preserved the evidence of that transgression and who, knowing that it had been subpoenaed by this Committee and the Special Prosecutor, concealed its terrible import, even from his own counsel, until he could do so no longer. And it was a unanimous Supreme Court of the United States which, in an opinion authored by the Chief Justice, whom he appointed, ordered Richard Nixon to surrender that evidence to the Special Prosecutor, to further the ends of justice.

The tragedy that finally engulfed Richard Nixon has many facets. One was the very self-inflicted nature of the harm. It is striking that such an able, experienced and perceptive man, whose ability to grasp the global implications of events little noticed by others may well have been unsurpassed by any of his predecessors, should fail to comprehend the damage that accrued daily to himself, his Administration, and to the Nation, as day after day, month after month, he imprisoned the truth about his role in the Watergate cover-up so long and so tightly within the solitude of his Oval office that it could not be unleashed without destroying his Presidency.

THE PARDON

Would Nixon, as ex-president, have to face criminal charges? After all, the conspiracy to obstruct justice had Nixon as an "unindicted co-conspirator." The answer came less than a month after Nixon left office.

On Sunday, September 8, 1974, President Gerald Ford called a news conference in which he announced that he had granted former president Nixon "a full, free, and absolute pardon . . . for all offenses against the United States which he, Richard Nixon, has committed, or may have committed, or taken part in during the period" of his presidency.

Some suggested that Ford and Nixon, or Ford and Haig, made some sort of deal: resignation in exchange for a pardon.[44] But no proof exists, and all parties to the decision deny that any deal—implicit or explicit—was made. But the pardon, granted in the absence of criminal charges, leaves unanswered questions and creates disconcerting problems. To what extent was Nixon criminally guilty? Is a president above the law? How does one accept a pardon for acts he claims never to have committed?

The Republicans took a beating in the midterm elections following Richard Nixon's resignation. Fighting an uphill battle against the recent legacy of Watergate, the Republicans had little hope of doing well. In the House, the Republicans lost 48 seats, and in the Senate they lost 5 seats. While numerically this may not seem drastic, one must remember that the Democrats already had large majorities in both chambers. Given their already clear control of the Congress, these numbers are indeed impressive.

The Case Against Nixon

Since Richard Nixon was not brought before the court of justice, some defenders still maintain that while some mistakes were made, Nixon did not "really" commit an impeachable or indictable offense. This view flies in the face of overwhelming evidence to the contrary. What then were the offenses of Richard Nixon? Leaving policy disagreements aside, of what is Richard Nixon guilty? What crimes did Nixon order, tolerate, and encourage?

Richard Nixon is the most investigated president in history. Part of his defense is that other presidents did what he did—but because of the intense investigations, he got caught and they didn't. He also maintains that while he did make some mistakes, the evidence, when looked at in its entirety, shows that he committed no impeachable or indictable offenses, in spite of a grand jury naming him an "unindicted co-conspirator." Bob Haldeman refers to Nixon's own description of his involvement in Watergate as a cry of "innocence," and of Nixon's rationale of this innocence as "ignorance."[45]

Indeed, that *is not* the way it was. Richard M. Nixon, thirty-seventh president of the United States, engaged in a variety of illegal and unethical acts while president. Among them are the following:[46]

(N) *Obstruction of Justice:* On June 23, 1972, just six days after the Watergate burglars were caught, Richard Nixon—as tape recordings prove—instructed Bob Haldeman to have the CIA stop the FBI investigation into the sources of funds used by the burglars (the money came from Nixon campaign funds).

(N) *Conspiracy to Obstruct Justice:* As the March 21, 1973, tape clearly shows, Nixon conspired with others to continue the coverup of Watergate. The following day the president, talking with John Mitchell, discussed "stonewalling," and saving the "plan." The conspiracy to obstruct justice included paying money for the silence of the Watergate defendants, offers of clemency, etc.

(N) *Conspiracy:* In several areas, Nixon conspired with other members of the administration to break the law. The grand jury, convinced of this, named Nixon an "unindicted co-conspirator."

(N) *Conspiracy to Misuse Government Agencies:* The administration sought to have the IRS harass people on Nixon's "enemies list."

(N) *Coverup of Crimes:* Again the June 23, 1972, tape is important. It reveals that at least from that date, Nixon was engaged in covering up crimes. Numerous other examples of Nixon's coverup can be gleaned from the tapes; for example, on September 15, 1972, Nixon tells Dean, "So you just try to button it up as well as you can," on March 21, 1973, Nixon to Dean: "It's better to just fight it out and not let people testify," on March 22, 1973, Nixon to Mitchell: "I want you all to stonewall it, let them plead the Fifth Amendment, cover up or anything else, if it'll save it—save the plan." The coverup took several forms at different times, from a block-the-investigation, to a containment, to a modified-limited-hangout, to a circle-the-wagons, to a give-'em-an-hors-d'oeuvre approach. But the goal was the same: save the president.

(N) *Illegal Wiretaps:* Without obtaining a court order, Nixon approved seventeen wiretaps on newsmen and government officials.

Destruction of Evidence: Apart from the eighteen-and-a-half-minute gap (and other gaps) in the June 20, 1972, tape, examples of destruction of evidence include burning sensitive documents (Magruder) and "deep sixing" incriminating evidence from Hunt's safe (Gray). Relevant CREEP records were also destroyed.

Presentation of False Material to Congress: The transcripts of taped conversations that Nixon submitted contained many discrepancies, with several compromising statements expunged from the Nixon-sanitized version. For example, the White House transcript of a portion of the March 22, 1973, tape has Nixon saying he needed flexibility "in order to get off the coverup line." In the committee transcript the line reads, "in order to get on with the coverup plan."

Election Fraud: A variety of efforts to undermine the Democratic party's leading candidates was undertaken, including theft of campaign material, dissemination of false and libelous material, dirty tricks, misinformation, and political espionage, leading up to the break-in and bugging at the DNC headquarters. This effort successfully undermined the democratic and electoral process.

Forgery: The administration forged State Department cables falsely linking President Kennedy to political assassinations and attempted to get reporters to write stories based on these lies.

(N)   *Perjury and Suborning of Perjury:* On several occasions, the president advised potential witnesses to lie or give incomplete answers to the grand jury and congressional committees. He also coached witnesses to give testimony that would not contradict "the plan." On March 21, 1973, he told Dean, who was to meet with prosecutors, "Just be damned sure you say I don't . . . remember, I can't recall, I can't give any honest, an answer to that, that I can recall. But that's it." And on April 14, 1973, he directed Ehrlichman to coach Gordon Strachan in giving testimony before the prosecutors so his story would match Magruder's. Several members of the administration lied before the grand jury.

(N)   *Money Laundering:* In order to hide illegal or questionable campaign contributions, money was laundered, usually via Mexico. Nixon was aware of this, as the June 23, 1973, tape confirms.

Extortion of Campaign Funds: Pressure tactics and threats were used to get corporations and individuals to contribute money to the president's reelection campaign.

(N)   *Bribery and Hush Money:* Beginning on June 29, 1972, just twelve days after the Watergate break-in, over $450,000 was paid to the burglars to buy their silence. Nixon, as the March 21, 1973, tape indicates, was aware of and discussed the paying of money to the defendants. On that day Nixon told Haldeman of Hunt, "His price is pretty high, but at least, uh, we should, we should buy the time on that, uh, as I, as I pointed out to John." That evening, $75,000 in cash was delivered to Hunt's lawyer.

(N)   *Questionable "Security" Improvements in Nixon's Private Homes:* At public expense, a fireplace fan, a heating system, new windows, handrails, a shuffleboard court, a fiberglass flagpole, twelve brass lanterns, furniture, an ice maker, and other nonsecurity improvements were made in Nixon's San Clemente and Key Biscayne homes. The Joint Congressional Committee on Internal Revenue Taxation eventually determined that over $90,000 of nonsecurity improvements were made on Nixon's homes.

(N)   *Income Tax Violations:* Back dating of Nixon's donation of his vice presidential papers to the National Archives allowed the President to claim a $482,018 income tax deduction. This was later disallowed after an IRS investigation.

(N)   *Money for Favors:* In the ITT, Vesco, Dairy, and other cases, favorable governmental decisions followed contributions to the president's campaign coffers.

Burglary: In the Watergate break-in, there is no direct evidence that the president knew in advance of the crime.

(N)   *Huston Plan:* The president approved a domestic intelligence plan even though he was aware that some elements of the plan were clearly illegal. Shortly after approving the plan, it was scrapped.

(N)   *Clemency Offers:* Nixon, on several occasions, discussed offering clemency to the Watergate burglars. In fact, the burglars were given the impression that they would be granted clemency.

(N)   *Plumbers:* Nixon approved the creation of a private presidential investigation unit, first to plug leaks, but which later engaged in such acts as breaking and entering (Fielding break-in).

(N)   *Failure to Fulfill Oath of Office:* Richard Nixon took an oath to faithfully execute the law, but failed, for example, to act when his subordinates informed him that certain crimes had been committed (this is due in part to the fact that the president was involved in some of these crimes).

(N)   *Failure to Comply with Subpoenas:* Nixon failed to honor congressional and special prosecutor's subpoenas and withheld information requested by the courts. This resulted in charges of contempt of Congress against the president.

(N)   *Interference with Prosecutors:* Henry Peterson, who originally was assigned to handle the Watergate prosecution for the Justice Department, repeatedly fed Nixon information on the status of his investigation, and Nixon used this information to help him and his staff avoid prosecution. "I've got Peterson on a short leash," Nixon once told John Ehrlichman.

(N)   *Obstruction of a Congressional Investigation:* Nixon tried to interfere with and influence testimony given by various staff members before the Ervin Committee.
       Agnew: The vice president was forced to resign from office as part of a plea bargain for which he avoided prosecution and jail while pleading *nolo contendre* to income tax violation.

(N)   *Nixon's Lies:* Repeatedly the president lied in speeches and news conferences about his involvement in and knowledge of Watergate and the coverup. The Judiciary Committee staff compared the information in the tapes with Nixon's public statements and found numerous examples of dishonesty in the president's public claims of innocence and ignorance.

(N)   *Betrayal of the Public Trust:* The cumulative impact of Watergate was a legacy of suspicion and distrust. It left a mark on the way we viewed and practiced politics.

While this list is not exhaustive, it highlights some of the main areas in which Nixon went beyond the bounds of law and ethics.[47] By his actions in Watergate, Nixon undermined the rule of law and the oath of office he took. The House Judiciary Committee laid Watergate squarely at the feet of the president: "From the beginning, the President knowingly directed the cover-up of the Watergate burglary—this concealment required perjury, destruction of evidence, obstruction of justice—all of which are crimes. It included false and misleading public statements as part of a deliberate, contrived, continued deception of the American people." As Arthur Schlesinger has written:

If he really had not known and for nine months had not bothered to find out, he was evidently an irresponsible and incompetent executive. For, if he did not know, it could only have been because he did not want to know. He had all the facilities in the world for discovering the facts. The courts and posterity would have to decide whether the *Spectator* of London was right in its harsh judgment that in two centuries American history had come full circle "from George Washington, who could not tell a lie, to Richard Nixon, who cannot tell the truth."[48]

THE MEANING OF WATERGATE

Watergate, that generic word by which we refer to a range of crimes and improprieties, raised legal issues, political issues, *and* moral issues. It spoke to who we are and what we believe. It tested our system and ourselves.

Would the United States remain a "limited government" under the rule of law, or had we become an imperial nation with an imperial presidency?[49]

For Nixon, the question is, how could someone so smart and seasoned behave so stupidly?[50] It was a "third-rate burglary" made into a first-rate coverup and into a world-class scandal.

In the end, Nixon remains unable or unwilling to admit guilt in Watergate. While he calls his handling of Watergate stupid and a failure, he continues to "stonewall" on his own guilt. In a television interview with David Frost in May of 1977, Nixon told the interviewer, "I did not commit, in my view, an impeachable offense." But he did admit:

I let down the country. I let down our system of government and the dreams of all those young people that ought to get into government, but who now will think it's all too corrupt. . . .

Yep, I, I, I let the American people down, and I have to carry that burden with me for the rest of my life. . . . And, so, I can only say that in answer to your question, that while technically, I did not commit a crime, an impeachable offense . . . these are legalisms. As far as the handling of this matter is concerned, it was so botched-up. I made so many bad judgments. The worst ones, mistakes of the heart rather than the head.

Watergate spawned a variety of legislative responses. In the aftermath of Nixon's abuses, the Congress went through a period of legislative activism that resulted in the passage of the Budget Control and Impoundment Act (1974), the War Powers Act (1973), the Case Act (1972), the Federal Election Campaign Act (1974), the Ethics in Government Act (1978), the Presidential Records Act (1978), the National Emergencies Act (1976), the Government in Sunshine Act (1976), the Federal Corrupt Practices Act (1977), the Foreign Intelligence Surveillance Act (1978), plus laws relating to privacy in banking and to setting up a vehicle for creating special prosecutors, and the Freedom of Information Act (1974).

"EVERYBODY DOES IT"

Was Nixon different in his behavior from other presidents? A refrain one often hears from Nixon's defenders is "Everybody does it, Nixon just got caught!" Is this true? And if everybody does do it, why pick on Nixon? Victor Lasky asks, "Precisely what is Nixon accused of doing, if he actually did it, that his predecessors didn't do many times over?"[51] If "everybody does it" is true, this is the most damning indictment of the United States and its government imaginable. To suggest that every president, or even most presidents, engaged in the voluminous crimes such as those that make up Watergate is to accuse the government of being rotten and corrupt, deceitful and petty, antidemocratic and immoral. Those defenders of Nixon who use the excuse that everybody does it, show contempt for the United States and cynicism about human beings. Everybody *doesn't* do it! Gerald Ford didn't. Jimmy Carter didn't. And while some presidents engaged in some sordid behavior, none can compare to Richard Nixon.[52]

The defense of Nixon that says that it is "just politics," or everybody does it, is both false and dangerous. False because while other presidents *did* engage in immoral and illegal behavior, not one comes close to Nixon in volume, type, or degree of presidential involvement. Nixon's was a systematic abuse of power and subversion of law. It is dangerous because such an attitude breeds disrespect for the government and contempt for our political institutions. Aside from that, the "everybody does it" excuse is no justification for misconduct.

What John Mitchell called the "White House horrors" is without precedent in the United States. The United States is far from perfect, and past presidents are not without sin, but historian C. Vann Woodward sums up the difference between Nixon and his predecessors nicely:

Heretofore, no president has been proved to be the chief coordinator of the crime and misdemeanor charged against his own administration as a deliberate course of conduct or plan. Heretofore, no president has been held to be the chief personal beneficiary of misconduct in his administration or of measures taken to destroy or cover-up evidence of it. Heretofore, the malfeasance and misdemeanor have had no confessed ideological purpose, no constitutionally subversive ends. Heretofore, no president has been accused of extensively subverting and secretly using established government agencies to defame or discredit political opponents and critics, to obstruct justice, to conceal misconduct and protect criminals, or to deprive citizens of their rights and liberties. Heretofore, no president has been accused of creating secret investigative units to engage in covert and unlawful activities against private citizens and their rights.[53]

One of the primary differences between Watergate and the scandals of previous administrations is that the scandals of the past almost always involved greed for private financial gain, and the president was the unwitting victim. Past presidents were not knowingly a part of the corruption. In Watergate, the greed was for power, and the president was a direct participant in the corruption.

WATERGATE AND THE RISE OF THE NATIONAL SECURITY STATE

After World War II, when the United States became the hegemonic power of the West, it needed a dominant military presence to maintain leadership of the alliance. With these new global responsibilities came the rise of the "national security state." This of course led to a concomitant rise in the power of the presidency. If the president was the chief architect of America's foreign policy, and if the United States was to have an expanded—hegemonic—role in international affairs, it seemed inevitable that presidential power would increase. It had a distorting impact on our constitutional democracy and created a framework for the rise of presidential power and the abuse of power by the president; it created the national security state.[54]

In a system based on the concept of limited government, the rule of law, and a separation of powers, how is one to reconcile this tremendous rise in power in one office? How will the checks that are supposed to balance, work? Can one limit *and* expand presidential power over foreign affairs? Or, is the Constitution, an eighteenth-century document, ill suited to the demands of a world power in the twentieth century? Within the constitutional framework, foreign policy always was, as Edward S. Corwin noted, an "invitation to struggle" for supremacy. Should that supremacy now shift permanently to the executive?

In the Nixon presidency, "national security" served as both a reason and an excuse. So many of the roots of Watergate can be traced back to the national security presidency. Nixon was fighting a war in Vietnam and trying to plug leaks, repel demonstrators, and disarm critics, and he used both the national security apparatus *and* his own private, secret Plumbers unit to advance his goals.

But did Nixon have to go to extremes to advance his goals? And did he have to use the tools and tactics of foreign policy (dirty tricks, sabotage, subversion) in the U.S. domestic arena? It is the domestication of foreign policy tools which in large part led historian Arthur Schlesinger, Jr., to describe the American chief executive as an "imperial presidency," a presidency above and beyond the constraints of law.

The power of the phrase *national security* can distort perception. It is a potent bromide, as Egil Krogh, who was in charge of the Plumbers, noted:

I see now that the key is the effect that the term *national security* had on my judgment. The very words served to block my critical analysis. . . . To suggest that national security was being improperly invoked was to invite a confrontation with patriotism and loyalty and so appeared to be beyond the scope and in contravention of the faithful performance of the duties of my office. . . . The very definition of *national security* was for the President to pursue his planned course.[55]

When the president invoked the term *national security*, all checks were to fall, all doubts to diminish. The term was used to justify, or hide, lying, break-ins, sabotage, subversion, secret wars, and more. But these acts were always justified with the magical phrase *national security*. In the end, so much of what went on in the name of national security was not to protect the national interest but to further Richard Nixon's political interest. Nixon's sweeping notion of national security blinded his own people to what they were doing.

"THE SYSTEM WORKED!" (OR DID IT?)

After the fall of Nixon, one heard the popular refrain: "The system worked!" Existing safeguards, structures, and procedures protected liberty and reestablished the rule of law. After all, Nixon was caught and forced to leave office. But a haunting feeling remains. Did the system work, or did other forces bring about the downfall of Richard Nixon?

"The system" is the complex web of interrelated governmental and nongovernmental actors who serve as a check on power. In Watergate the system included the media, Congress, the courts, the public, the CIA, the FBI, the Justice Department, the special prosecutor's office, and the grand jury. How well did the system perform its function?

The *media* began like a lamb but ended like a lion. While they were manipulated by Nixon during the 1972 campaign, after the election a herd mentality developed and they turned on Nixon. The *Congress*, especially in the Ervin and House Judiciary committees, played a very important role in the downfall of Richard Nixon. They moved slowly, methodically, but they moved against the president. The *courts*, especially Judge Sirica, and the Supreme Court at the end, were clearly a key in the downfall of Nixon. Again, they acted slowly, but effectively. The *public*, at first giving Nixon a landslide reelection victory eventually turned on the president like the media. The *FBI* and *CIA* were used and manipulated, as was the *Justice Department*. The grand jury was essential in getting to the bottom of Watergate. Finally, the *special prosecutor's office*, treading on new ground, played an indispensable part in the process. In the end, the system had to act in concert to bring down Nixon. For so many to act in concert is highly unusual. This speaks to the great difficulty of controlling a determined president. The system is indeed vulnerable when, even with all these political actors working against the president, it was the "luck" of a taping system which finally brought Nixon down! This suggests that the system is actually a rather weak check on presidential abuses of power. "Watergate," wrote Walter Lippmann, "shows how very *vulnerable* our constitutional system is. If the national government falls into the hands of sufficiently unprincipled and unscrupulous men, they can do terrible things before anyone can stop them."

The system worked more than anything else because of luck, accident, and ineptitude. After all, the first break-in of the Watergate was a botched job, as the bugs weren't properly installed. This necessitated a second break-in, at which time the burglars were caught. And why were they caught? Because a piece of tape, used to keep the door's lock from catching, was placed across the lock so it could be seen. But even this did not alert the guard who, on his rounds, simply removed the tape. When the burglars returned to the door, they taped it again, and again placed the tape *across* the lock so it could be seen on the outside. When security guard Frank Wills made his *second* rounds of the building and saw the tape across the same door for a second time, he was alerted and called the police.

What if Nixon had not taped himself? There would have been no "smoking gun" and Nixon might have survived. What if the coverup had been better managed? It might have held together. What if Nixon had destroyed the tapes before their existence had become known? He would not have had to defy a subpoena—one of the acts on which an article of impeachment was based.

Nixon and Haldeman recognized the role luck played in the Watergate story, as evidenced by this March 20, 1973 taped exchange on how Watergate was "discovered":

Nixon: . . . a lot of bad breaks . . .

Haldeman: Yeah.

Nixon: We got a bad break with the Judge, for example.

Haldeman: Monumental bad breaks and a string of 'em—one leading to *another.*

Nixon: This judge, that . . .

Haldeman: . . . one lousy part-time night guard at the Watergate who happened to notice the tape on the, on the locks on the doors. If he hadn't seen them—the thing probably would never have busted. If you hadn't had Watergate—you wouldn't have had Segretti. You wouldn't have had any of that stuff."

In another sense, the system refers to the two-hundred-year-old constitutional framework and the assumptions upon which it is based. This Madisonian system, described in *Federalist* No. 51, believed that "ambition must be made to counteract ambition," that by separating power, viable checks might protect the liberty of the citizen.

The framers of the Constitution saw human nature neither in excessively benign nor unmercifully harsh terms. Man was capable of great good and great evil. The Founders knew man's darker side, his darker impulses, and sought to control this while also empowering government. In a way, it was precisely for the Richard Nixons of the world that the separation of powers and checks and balances were created.

The impeachment process itself was shown to have very limited utility. The system of accountability is slow, cumbersome, and difficult. It can be used only in truly extraordinary circumstances. And while we do have *periodic* accountability (elections), and *ultimate* accountability (impeachment), we do not have a system of *daily* accountability (routine and continuous).

Finally, it was the system that allowed Nixon to rise to the highest office in the land, in spite of the many clues from his career as to what "the real Nixon" was like. It was the system that Nixon used and manipulated for so long. Thus, the system both nourished and destroyed Richard Nixon.

WHY WATERGATE?

Throughout the complex web of crimes and dirty tricks, wiretaps and obstruction of justice, one keeps coming back to the gnawing question, why? Why Watergate? What caused the administration to engage in the volume and type of corruption which typified Watergate?

Theories abound. The most frequently mentioned cause of Watergate is *Nixon himself*. His personality, past experiences, operating style, and worldview in many ways infected those around him and led to the abuses of Watergate. While some go so far as to say that Nixon's personality made Watergate inevitable,[56] others suggest more cautiously that he made Watergate possible or probable. Nixon was, in Jeb Magruder's words, "a man of enormous talents and enormous weaknesses" who had "a fatal flaw": "an inability to tolerate criticism, an instinct to overreact in political combat." Nixon's hatreds and passions "fed on one another, grew more and more bitter, until once he achieved the Presidency Nixon could not resist the urge to use his awesome powers to 'get' his enemies."

Magruder continues, "A President sets the tone for his Administration. If President Nixon had said, 'I want each of you to do his job, to obey the laws, and not to worry about our critics,' there would have been no Watergate. Instead, the President's insecurities, aggravated by the constant opposition of the media, liberal politicians, and the anti-war activists, led to an atmosphere in the White House that could create the plumbers, the enemies lists, and Watergate."[57]

Nixon's distrustful style, his insecurities, his fears bordering on paranoia, his vindictiveness, all created a mood, an operating style that allowed, even encouraged, subordinates to act in illegal and unethical ways, for the moral and ethical tone of the White House reflected the president and his style.

Other views regarding the causes of Watergate range from the Vietnam imperative (which sees Watergate as a direct response to the events surrounding that war), to a "climate of the times" view[58] (which sees America as a corrupt society, and Watergate as merely a symptom of a sick society), to the "Nixon was victimized by his staff" approach (in which Nixon was unaware of the evils being done in his name), to the "everybody does it" view (which sees corruption as the inevitable outgrowth of a too-powerful presidency), to the "CIA trap" approach (which has Nixon being set up by the CIA), to the "capitalist politics as usual" view (which sees Nixon as a representative, not aberrational figure, of capitalist corruption).[59]

The question remains: why Watergate? I would suggest that Watergate can best be understood if one sees several "wars" being waged simultaneously. There was, most importantly, the war within Nixon. Nixon's distrust, insecurities, obsessions, fears, and hatreds created an infectious atmosphere that warped those who served him and set Watergate in motion.

There were other wars as well. The *war in Vietnam*, which Nixon inherited and had such a difficult time ending, added to the pressures that, when combined with the Nixon personality, led to disaster. Next, the *war at home*, with its antiwar demonstrations and social upheaval, put added strain on the Nixon White House. Finally, there was the *partisan war*. Nixon saw democratic elections as war, and adversaries as enemies.

So much of life to Nixon was war. This way of looking at the world is what caused Watergate. Ultimately, Nixon was unable to distinguish between the democratic competition for electoral office and enemies in war. To Nixon, war and politics melted together. He saw them as one and the same. Nixon's descent was the result of Nixon the man: secretive, compulsive, insecure, suspicious. Nixon was ultimately the victim of his own paranoid style and worldview.

A strong presidency does not have to produce a corrupt president. But Nixon's presidency was a projection of Nixon the man. In the end, Watergate was the dark side of Richard Nixon come to life. Nixon speechwriter William Safire has written: "Whose fault was Watergate? Nixon's of course . . . Nixon's own decisions brought Watergate about, and there is no tiptoeing away from that. The root decision to put in the wiretaps on newsmen was his, with Kissinger, Haig, Mitchell, Ehrlichman, and Haldeman right with him. The approval of the Huston burglary proposal was Nixon's; the motivation of Krogh to 'get' Ellsberg was Nixon's . . . he was not guilty of all those crimes; but they were all his fault."[60]

Nixon lacked a moral and philosophical center. Other than winning, it is difficult to discern any deeply held values in Nixon. *Winning*, that was all. Defeated enemies was the end, there was no moral or ethical guidance on the means. "There is no independent sense of morality there," said Nixon aide Hugh Sloan. Indeed, moral qualms were seen as a sign of weakness.

CONCLUSION

The abuses known as Watergate were the most pervasive and systematic subversion of the political rights of American citizens, and sabotage of the democratic electoral process, in the history of the United States. Never before had so many done so much to so many at so high a level in violation of laws and norms of this nation. Watergate went beyond the presidential corruptions of the past, for while most previous corruption involved isolated crimes or greed for money, Watergate was systematic, comprehensive, aimed at the rights of citizens and the democratic electoral process, and the president was right in the middle of the corruption. In the end, he brought himself down: his own deeds, his own words. "I gave them a sword," Nixon told David Frost, "and they stuck it in and twisted it with relish."

Among the casualties of Watergate are a president who was named as an unindicted co-conspirator by a grand jury and who was eventually forced to resign (he was also disbarred), a vice president who pleaded no contest to income tax evasion and who was forced to resign, an attorney general who went to jail, a former secretary of commerce who went to jail, a chief of staff who went to jail, a president's counsel who went to jail, a president's chief domestic adviser who went to jail, a president's appointments secretary who went to jail, a president's personal attorney who went to jail, and the list goes on. Over two dozen administration figures went to jail because of Watergate.

Beyond this, Watergate so disillusioned the American citizens that trust in government declined sharply, public cynicism toward government grew, a backlash occurred that ushered in a spate of corrective legislation and saw a candidate for president elected in 1976 in part because he promised the American public, "I will never lie to you."

Thomas Paine once said that in America, the Constitution is king. The downfall of Richard Nixon struck a blow for the concept that no man is above the law, not even the president. While Nixon could attempt to justify his actions in a 1977 interview with David Frost by saying, "When the President does it, that means it is not illegal," this view was flatly rejected by nearly all segments of the American system. The words of Justice Brandeis remained operative: "If Government becomes the lawbreaker, it breeds contempt for law." Reverence for the laws, Abraham Lincoln once said, should "become the political religion of the nation." But sadly we have moved away from Lincoln's view.[61]

What responsibility do "the people" bear for Watergate, for the rise and fall of Richard Nixon? After all, Nixon the politician had been on the political scene since 1948; his slashing campaign style, his character flaws, his ethical lapses were a part of the public record. All the elements in Nixon that led to the abuses of Watergate were operative and observable in embryonic form in his previous political behavior. Do "the people" bear some measure of blame or responsibility for Richard Nixon? There is a saying, "In a democracy, people tend to get the government they deserve." Did we "deserve" Watergate? This sobering possibility is brought home forcefully by historian Henry Steele Commager, who has chillingly written:

The basic problem posed by Watergate and all its attendant horrors is neither constitutional nor political; it is moral. It is not a problem posed by an Administration in Washington; it is one posed by the American people.

After all, we can never get away from the most elementary fact: The American people reelected Mr. Nixon by a majority of nearly eighteen million votes. Either they did not know what kind of man he was, in which case they were inexcusably negligent or inexcusably naïve, or they did know what kind of man he was and did not care or perhaps liked him as he was—as some Americans still like him the way he is. The latter explanation is probably nearer to the truth.

Did he not—indeed, does he not—represent qualities in the American character that are widespread and even taken for granted? In himself and in the curious collection of associates he gathered around him, he represents the acquisitive society, the exploitative society, the aggrandizing society. He represents what is artificial, meretricious, and manipulative. He represents the American preference for the synthetic over the real, for advertising over the product, for public relations over character, for spectator sports over active games, and for spectator politics over participatory democracy.

He represents, too, the widespread American conviction that anything can be bought: culture, education, happiness, a winning football team—or the Presidency.[62]

In a very real sense, the American public can be accused of falling asleep at the wheel of democracy. Of all the checks which are to balance our political system, none is more powerful than alert and aroused public opinion. A thoughtful, responsible, aware public is the best defense against tyranny. There is no substitute for an aroused citizenry, no hope unless there is a rebirth of what Thomas Cronin calls "citizen politics." Richard Nixon exposed one of the vulnerabilities of the American political system. "The system" will not protect us; we must be vigilant.

Reinhold Niebuhr wrote that "man's capacity for justice makes democracy possible, but man's inclination to injustice makes democracy necessary." This is the rationale of the Founders of the American republic. It expresses a sensitivity to the duality of the human condition, of the paradoxical nature of man. The Founders sought to incorporate this view into the establishment of a limited government, under the rule of law, with a division of power, a separation and sharing of power, and a system of checks and balances. They did not seek to paralyze political leadership, merely to keep it under control. Richard Nixon never understood this. Fortunately, the framers of the Constitution did.

After Watergate, the Congress passed a variety of laws designed to discourage future Watergates and abuses of power. As important as these laws may be, they are not sufficient to the task. Laws are not self-executing. A nation of laws depends upon the people to enliven the law. A dedicated citizenry is the only hope against tyranny. As Learned Hand said, "Liberty lies in the hearts of men and women; when it dies there, no constitution, no law, no court can save it; no constitution, no law, no court can even do much to help it."

NOTES

1. In his book, *The Whole Truth: The Watergate Conspiracy* (New York: Random House, 1980), Sam Ervin sees two conspiracies, what I refer to as the second and third conspiracies.

2. Paul J. Halpern, in his edited volume, *Why Watergate?* (Pacific Palisades, Calif.: Palisades, 1975), pp. 1–3, provides the first three categories; I have added the fourth.

3. Seymour M. Hersh, "1971 Tape Links Nixon to Plan to Use 'Thugs,' " *New York Times*, September 24, 1981, p. 1.

4. Schell, *Time of Illusion*, p. 146.

5. J. Lukas, *Nightmare*, p. 128.

6. Lukas, *Nightmare*, pp. 134–137.

7. David Felton, "The Bugging of Mack the Knife," *Rolling Stone*, October 11, 1973, pp. 22–24.

8. Lewis Chester, Cal McCrystal, Stephen Aris, and William Shawcross, *Watergate* (New York: Ballantine, 1973), pp. 78–89.

9. Theodore H. White, *Breach of Faith: The Fall of Richard Nixon* (New York: Atheneum, 1975), pp. 135–136.

10. G. Gordon Liddy, *Will: The Autobiography of G. Gordon Liddy* (New York: St. Martin's, 1980), pp. 207–208.

11. Larry Berman, *The New American Presidency* (Boston: Little, Brown, 1986), pp. 274–277.

12. *The Senate Watergate Report*, 2 vols. (New York: Dell, 1974).

13. Jeb Magruder, *An American Life: One Man's Road to Watergate* (New York, Atheneum, 1974), pp. 185–215. See also: White, *Breach of Faith*, pp. 181–218.

14. Magruder, *An American Life*, p. 195.

15. Mitchell denies approving the plan; LaRue believed that no firm decision was made one way or the other at the March 30 meeting; but Magruder is certain that Mitchell approved the plan.

16. Magruder, *An American Life*, pp. 214–215.

17. John Dean, *Blind Ambition* (New York: Simon and Schuster, 1976), pp. 66–71.

18. Haldeman, *The Ends of Power*, p. 170.

19. Magruder, *An American Life*, p. 231.

20. Nixon, *RN*, p. 646.

21. New York Times Staff, *The End of a Presidency* (New York: Bantam, 1974), p. 161.

22. Lukas, *Nightmare*, pp. 257–259.

23. For a more thorough review of this time period, see: Ervin, *The Whole Truth*, pp. 40–58.

24. Nixon, *RN*, p. 850.

25. For discussion of crisis management and the presidency, see: Michael A. Genovese, "Presidential Leadership and Crisis Management," *Presidential Studies Quarterly* (Spring 1986), pp. 300–309; and Genovese, "Presidents and Crisis: Developing a Crisis Management System in the Executive Branch," *International Journal on World Peace* (Spring 1987), pp. 81–101.

26. For a review of the management of Watergate, see: Max Ways, "Watergate as a Case Study in Management," *Fortune* (November 1973), pp. 109–201.

27. Richard M. Nixon, *Six Crises* (New York: Warner, 1979), p. xii.

28. Ways, "Watergate as a Case Study," p. 109.

29. For a view that suggests that Nixon and his top aides acted rationally, see: Douglas Muzzio, *Watergate Games: Strategies, Choices, Outcomes* (New York: New York University Press, 1982).

30. Richard Ben-Veniste and George Frampton, Jr., *Stonewall: The Real Story of the Watergate Prosecution* (New York: Simon and Schuster, 1977).

31. Leon Jaworski, *The Right and the Power: The Prosecution of Watergate* (New York: Readers's Digest Press, 1976), pp. 99–101.

32. Joseph C. Spear, *Presidents and the Press: The Nixon Legacy* (Cambridge: MIT Press, 1984), 209–211. Spear sees four stages; I have added the first two.

33. Edwin Diamond, *The Tin Kazoo* (Cambridge: MIT Press, 1975), p. 217. Also see Chap. 11, "Myths of Watergate."

34. Dan Rather, "Watergate on TV," *Newsday*, December 16, 1973, p. 9.

35. Diamond, *The Tin Kazoo*, p. 218.

36. Raoul Berger, *Impeachment: The Constitutional Problems* (New York: Bantam, 1973); and U.S. Congress, House Committee on Judiciary, *Impeachment: Selected Materials*, H. Doc. 93-7, 93rd Cong., 1st sess.

37. Berger, *Impeachment*, pp. 628–629.

38. Michael Les Benedict, *The Impeachment and Trial of Andrew Johnson* (New York: Norton, 1973); and Gene Smith, *High Crimes and Misdemeanors: The Impeachment and Trial of Andrew Johnson* (New York: McGraw-Hill, 1976).

39. "Symposium: United States v. Nixon," *UCLA Law Review* 22, no. 1, (October 1974).

40. Lukas, *Nightmare*, pp. 519–520.

41. Carl Bernstein and Bob Woodward, *The Final Days* (New York: Simon and Schuster, 1976), p. 395.

42. Bernstein and Woodward, *The Final Days*, pp. 100–102, 204, 230–270, 437–438, and 498.

43. White, *Breach of Faith*, p. 35; and Lukas, *Nightmare*, p. 559.

44. Seymour M. Hersh, "The Pardon: Nixon, Ford, Haig, and the Transfer of Power," *The Atlantic Monthly* (August 1983), pp. 55–78.

45. Haldeman, *The Ends of Power*, p. 216.

46. Those crimes/acts for which there is evidence of President Nixon's *direct* involvement are preceded with (N).

47. For other lists of Nixon's violations; see: Leon Jaworski, *The Right and the Power*, Chap. 11, "The Case against the President"; and Michael Myerson, *Watergate: Crime in the Suites*, Chap. 2, "A Report on Law and Order."

48. Schlesinger, *The Imperial Presidency*, p. 379.

49. Schlesinger, *The Imperial Presidency*.

50. Nixon himself called his handling of Watergate "stupidity at its highest level." See: Jack Nelson, "Nixon Calls Watergate Highest Stupidity," *Los Angeles Times*, April 6, 1984, p. 1.

51. Victor Lasky, *It Didn't Start with Watergate* (New York: Dial, 1977), p. 1.

52. C. Vann Woodward, ed., *Responses of the Presidents to Charges of Misconduct* (New York: Dell, 1974); H. R. Miller, *Scandals in the Highest Office* (New York: Random House, 1973); and Shelley Ross, *Fall from Grace* (New York: Ballantine, 1988).

53. C. Vann Woodward, "The Conscience of the White House," in Woodward, ed., *Responses of the Presidents*, p. xxvi.

54. Kenneth E. Sharpe, "The Real Cause of Irangate," *Foreign Policy* (Fall 1987), pp. 19–40.

55. Daniel Candee, "The Moral Psychology of Watergate," *Journal of Social Issues* 31, no. 2 (1975), pp. 183–92.

56. Eli Chesen, *President Nixon's Psychiatric Profile* (New York: Wyden, 1973), p. 160.

57. Magruder, *An American Life*, p. 348.

58. Magruder, *An American Life*, p. 349.

59. Myerson, *Watergate: Crime in the Suites*; Les Evans and Allen Myers, *Watergate and the Myth of American Democracy* (New York: Pathfinder, 1974), and Kirkpatrick Sale, "The World behind Watergate," *New York Review of Books*, May 3, 1973, pp. 12–14; Carl Olglesby, "In Defense of Paranoia," *Ramparts* (November 1974), pp. 23–27.

60. William Safire, *Before the Fall: An Inside View of the Pre-Watergate White House* (New York: Doubleday, 1975), p. 657.

61. See, for example, the popular approval of Ollie North, who admitted to lying, misleading Congress, destroying evidence, etc.

62. Henry Steele Commager, "Watergate and the Schools," in David C. Saffell, ed., *American Government: Reform in the Post-Watergate Era* (Cambridge, Mass.: Winthrop, 1976), p. 6.

6

Conclusion: The Nixon Legacy

> No man will ever bring out of the Presidency the reputation which carries him into it.
>
> Thomas Jefferson

In attempting to unravel the mystery of Richard Nixon, one is struck with how many mysteries remain. While Nixon has inspired more scholarly and popular writing than any other president, so much remains hidden, shrouded in secrecy, obscured by shadows. In part this is because the former president has limited access to himself and fought to keep private many of his presidential papers. It is also because Nixon is such a complex, contradictory figure. He defies simple analysis and unambiguous evaluations. He is more than, and different than, the sum total of his many parts.

THE POST-PRESIDENCY

Richard Nixon just won't go away. He is in our memory, our consciousness, and our history, and he remains a prominent, if often reviled, part of the political landscape. He continues to be one of the most fascinating characters in modern America and has managed to reemerge from oblivion to be once again a figure of note.[1]

Plays (*Secret Honor*, later made into a movie) and an opera *(Nixon in China)* have been written about him since he left office. He continues to write books and articles about politics, especially foreign policy (e.g., *Leaders*, *The Real War*, *Real Peace*, 1999). He continues to advise Republican presidents and candidates, visit foreign countries and meet with their leaders, and was recently admitted to the French Academy of Arts. T-shirts bearing his picture and inscribed with "He's Tan, Rested, and Ready, Nixon in '88" appeared during the

1988 presidential campaign. His comeback was hailed in a May 19, 1986, *Newsweek* cover story under the title "He's Back."

But he never really left. He is still working, still fighting. But now he is fighting for his place in history. The efforts at the resurrection and rehabilitation of Richard Nixon have an eye toward how history will view his performance and legacy. The struggle for history has become what Stanley Kutler calls Nixon's "final crisis." He is running for the title of ex-president, and the respectability that goes with that title.

WHO IS RICHARD NIXON?

Richard Nixon remains a man difficult to understand. Friends, associates, critics, and commentators see many different things in the man. Was he, as many of his former associates noted, a man with two very different, conflicting parts: the good and bad Nixons, the light and dark sides? In this sense, was the battle for Nixon the battle of his better self against his worse self, a battle that was ultimately lost to the forces of darkness? Or, was Nixon a paradox, a contradictory figure who could be so brilliant, yet make so many needless mistakes in Watergate; lead an anticommunist movement, then embrace China and the Soviet Union; praise the free market, then impose wage and price controls; preach about self-sufficiency, then propose the Family Assistance Plan? Nixon as paradox could do all these things, embrace all these beliefs, travel these many roads. Or, was Nixon little more than a political chameleon, changing color and political stripes to fit the whim of the day?

In the final analysis, Nixon was all these things, because the core of Nixon, the true Nixon, could be summed up in one phrase: he was a man obsessed with *self-promotion*. This self-promotion took form in his paranoid style of operation. That paranoid style poisoned his administration and led to his self-destruction.

Fundamentally, Nixon had no central philosophical beliefs, no deep ethical moorings. He was amoral, not immoral. His central pursuit was a rather narrow and short-term self-interest. This allowed him to shed what seemed to be deeply felt and long-held beliefs when it suited his career. While his chameleonlike quality suited his rise to power, it did not guide him in the uses of power.

Nixon was in many ways a rootless wanderer, the product of a family that did not nourish his needs or give him stable roots; a man who was sensitive to the snubs of the "better sort," who never did accept Nixon; who got his big break by upsetting incumbent Jerry Voorhis for a seat in Congress. From that point on, only one thing mattered: winning, showing them, getting ahead.

There may have been, as so many of his former associates noted, a good and a bad Nixon, but in the end, it was the Nixon self-promotion that won out. Thus, his downfall is not a great tragedy in which the good or innocent protagonist is done in by a fatal flaw. No, Nixon's demise is the logical outcome of self-promotion gone mad. Nixon was brilliant but amoral, experienced but insecure, capable but manipulative, obsessed with power but consumed by weakness, power-seeking but paranoid. He was neither trusting nor trusted. He was the author of some stunning successes in foreign policy and the author of a demeaning and destructive string of political misdeeds that culminated in Watergate. Nixon was a big thinker but a small person, brilliant but deeply flawed. His mental elasticity, a sign of pragmatism to some, was really a reflection of his own opportunism. He was a polarizer, a divider. Nixon saw life as a battle against a hostile world, where enemies waited around every corner.

Nixon was a man who felt hurt. He seemed to remember all the hurts, to store them up until he saw the world peopled with enemies. The White House tapes are full of references to enemies out to "do us in," to "get us." "This is war," Nixon would say, "They are after us." "Nobody is a friend of ours. Let's face it!" he told John Dean. Nixon set out to destroy this menace that he had so exaggerated. In the process he ruined himself.

He was a troubled man who governed in turbulent times. That mixture sparked a fire that destroyed Nixon's presidency and damaged the nation. The combustible mixture of Nixon's personality with the events and forces of the political environment produced a poisoned outlook and a poisoned atmosphere. In different times, the negative aspects of Nixon's psyche might not have been challenged, pricked, activated to the extent they were. A Nixon presidency in 1960 might have had a significantly different ending than a Nixon presidency of 1968 and beyond.

THE NIXON PRESIDENCY

In a substantive sense, the Nixon presidency was filled with action: some grand accomplishments, and some tragic failures. In foreign affairs he inherited a war in Vietnam that could only have been won at the highest of costs. He extended, then ended that war, the first war America lost. He fathered détente with the Soviet Union and opened the door to China. He pursued a bold, creative strategy for developing a new international order, but failed to succeed in this daring initiative.

In domestic politics his agenda was very limited. After flirting with Disraeli-like reforms, Nixon retreated to a more conservative, then obstructionist approach. On the economic front, Nixon retreated from international leadership, imposed wage and price controls at home, and artificially boosted the domestic economy shortly before the 1972 election. His economic policies were shortsighted, and while they aided his own reelection effort, they hurt the U.S. economy in the long run.

As a manager, Nixon generally employed a formal, hierarchical style. This tended to isolate Nixon, but that was what he wanted, needed. The wall he built around himself did not in the long run serve his interests, but it is what he insisted upon. The fortress mentality that was the Nixon White House collapsed around the president and buried him in its rubble.

An examination of the Nixon presidency reinforces the view that personality is of prime importance in presidential politics. Because of Nixon's tendency toward paranoia, his administration took on a siege mentality. This infected every aspect of his presidency. From the way Nixon organized and ran his administration, to the policy arenas, to Watergate, Nixon's personality stamped a distinctive leitmotif on his presidency and eventually led to his downfall.

In process terms, Nixon often mishandled the major relationships of his presidency. Be it the Congress, the public, the bureaucracy, or even his own staff, Nixon did not organize functionally, follow through on policy initiatives, or realistically articulate his goals. Even in foreign policy, the jewel of his administration, the major relationships were often poorly handled.

Nixon's must be judged a failed presidency in which Watergate was not the fatal cancer that destroyed an otherwise functional presidency, but was the logical, almost inevitable outgrowth of an overpersonalized, poorly organized, and overly politicized administration. Watergate was not an isolated cancer, unrelated to the rest of administrative action, but was deeply rooted in the core of administrative practice across the Nixon presidency.

Judged on his own terms, on how well he achieved his goals, Nixon's must also be seen as a failed presidency. Many of his foreign policy advances failed to stand the test of time (détente and China being exceptions), and his domestic and economic policies left a mixed legacy at best. But it is, and shall always be, Watergate on which the Nixon legacy hangs, literally and figuratively. Judged by the totality of the deeds and misdeeds of his presidency, Nixon's term in office was a failure.

How well suited was Nixon to his times? He attempted to govern in tough, conflictual times, a period of heightened tension. The war in Vietnam and the domestic protest it spawned, the cultural movements afoot in the nation, all worked against Nixon. But he exaggerated the threats against himself, and often sought to exploit these tensions. He overly personalized the criticisms against him and his policies. In turbulent times, the challenge of leadership is to direct and manage change, to ease the transition. In this sense, Nixon failed to lead. Nixon did not create the conflicts and tensions of the 1960s, but he did little to manage them or channel the energies of change to constructive ends. Nixon was ill suited to rule in a time of turbulence.

And then there is Watergate. In the end, there is always Watergate. Nixon's guilt is undeniable; his responsibility, clear; his action, criminal.

How do the pieces of the Nixon presidency fit together? What are we to make of this man who rose and fell so many times, who achieved the highest prize, only to be forced to give it up in disgrace? In the half-light of historical distance, how is Richard Nixon to be judged? Over fifteen years after his resignation, how are we to evaluate the presidency of this most controversial of presidents?

Nixon Compared

By almost all measures, Richard Nixon rates poorly. While all rating systems are subjective and highly speculative, by almost any sort of criteria Nixon comes out near the bottom of the list.

In two polls of scholars taken in the early 1980s, Nixon ranks thirty-fourth out of thirty-six presidents in one poll and next to last in the other.[2] If one looks only at the post–World War II presidents, Nixon is ranked lowest. A 1985 poll of the general public conducted by Louis Harris and Associates looked at the modern presidents by leadership categories. When asked which president was best in domestic affairs, Nixon was named by only 3 percent. But in foreign affairs, Nixon was named by 24 percent, the highest ranking. On the "moral standards" question, Nixon was the lowest-rated president.

It has been over fifteen years since Nixon left office, and revisionist historians will have many opportunities to reevaluate the Nixon presidency. If past is prelude, we should expect to see a leveling-off of presidential reputations, and a certain moderating of presidential reputations. The good presidents are generally seen as not quite as good; the bad, as not quite as bad. Thus, Eisenhower, who in the 1960s was regarded as an average or even slightly below average president, is now seen as above average.[3] Kennedy, who left office in the near-great category, is now seen as above average.[4] This leveling-off will happen with Richard Nixon as well.

To what extent might Nixon's reputation rise with time? As the emotion subsides and we are better able to step back and take another look at the totality of his presidency, we will more clearly see the good with the bad. While Nixon will not rise sharply, it is possible that he will move up from the failure category to the below-average category. But Watergate will always hound Richard Nixon, as it should.

NIXON AND THE FUTURE OF THE PRESIDENCY

How can we avoid future Watergates and other forms of presidential corruption? The Founders of the constitutional republic hoped to discourage corruption and the arbitrary use and abuse of power by *separating* power, *dividing* power, *sharing* power, between three semi-independent, semi-autonomous branches of government. By having ambition counteract ambition, and power counteract power, no one could, for long, overwhelm the others. The rule of law embodied in the Constitution, not the will or whim of one man, was to be the guiding light. By instituting a system of checks and balances, the system had safeguards against tyranny. But would this system work? Overall, the system has worked well at preventing tyranny. While many of today's critics bemoan the excessive checks built into the system,[5] few would argue against the proposition that it has indeed been a viable safeguard against excessive arbitrary rule.

But this system of multiple checks frustrates presidents.[6] The system was designed in many ways to frustrate leadership. Given the high level of public expectations and the limited amount of independent authority granted to the president, is it any wonder that presidents feel constrained and frustrated?

How does a president overcome the checks built into the system? By a full use of the formal powers a president has to command and a full use of the informal powers a president has to persuade. But since few presidents have the range of skills or the level of opportunity necessary to move on both these fronts, presidents will sometimes be tempted to move beyond the law, beyond the limits of their authority.[7] When presidents take this step, as Nixon did during the Watergate period, how can they be checked?

Since the presidency has become the most powerful institution in America's government, only the combined efforts of an active Congress, an alert citizenry, an independent court system, a free press, and a professional bureaucracy can save the republic. In a way, these were all the things that Richard Nixon feared and perceived as enemies.

In the post–World War II period an added threat to liberty and constitutional government has emerged: the national security state.[8] Richard Nixon used national security as both a reason and an excuse for a variety of illegal acts. It was the new national security presidency that led to the imperial presidency. What are the limits, or what is the balance, between the rights of citizens and the national security needs of the state? Can democracy withstand the pressures and demands of the emerging national security state? This tension is likely to remain with us into the next century. Its solution rests again with an active, concerned, alert, and educated citizenry.

THE FATAL FLAW

Nixon, the most political of political men, was unable to make the important distinction between *politics* and *governance*. Politics is what one does to get elected; governance is what one does in attempting to lead or govern the nation. Nixon saw everything as politics—as the law of the jungle, as a tough, competitive world where you have to get them before they got you.

Governance is what is done for the good of the country. It is selfless, whereas politics tends to be selfish. Governance is high principle and vision put to the use of the state. Nixon—with the notable exception of certain parts of his foreign policy—seemed never able to move beyond politics to governance. As political columnist Hugh Sidney said, "He may have understood the world but he didn't understand the oath of office he took."[9]

To Nixon, politics was not about *persuasion*, but about *manipulation*. Thus, his political character—his view of politics as war, of adversaries as enemies—did not embrace leadership as a persuasive force, but as a means to manipulate the people and machinery of government. He saw politics as *conflict manage-

ment, not *community building.* In this sense, he limited himself to the narrowest interpretation of Harold Lasswell's definition of politics as "who gets what, when, and how." In all of this, one can see Nixon's missed opportunities. His own view of politics—so limited, so narrow, so cynical—prevents him from breaking out of his self-imposed limits and moving from politics to governance.

What ultimately brought Nixon down? It was the deadly combination of perilous times mixed with the poisoned aspects of his personality and outlook that led to Nixon's self-destruction. Nixon brought himself down.

Great presidents face tough, demanding times and elevate themselves and the nation. Nixon, when faced with tough times, demeaned himself, his office, and the nation. Nixon had the opportunity to be great, but he failed the most important test of leadership: character. In life as in political leadership, there is no substitute for character. All the experience, intelligence, political savvy, skill, and perseverance add up to little if there is a fatal flaw of character. There are certain things honorable people do not do. Nixon's lack of moral understanding, his lack of character, proved to be his undoing.

NOTES

1. Robert Sam Anson, *Exile: The Unquiet Oblivion of Richard M. Nixon* (New York: Simon and Schuster, 1984); and James C. Clark, *Faded Glory: Presidents Out of Power* (New York: Praeger, 1985), Chap. 28.

2. For a list of several different rankings of U.S. presidents, see: Larry Berman, *The New American Presidency* (Boston: Little, Brown, 1987), pp. 124–125. For more information on the two polls cited above, see Arthur B. Murray, "Evaluating the Presidents of the United States," in David C. Kozak and Kenneth N. Ciboski, eds., *The American Presidency: A Policy Perspective from Readings and Documents* (Chicago: Nelson-Hall, 1985).

3. Fred I. Greenstein, *The Hidden-Hand Presidency: Eisenhower as Leader* (New York: Basic, 1982).

4. Herbert S. Parmet, *JFK: The Presidency of John F. Kennedy* (New York: Penguin, 1983).

5. James L. Sundquist, *Constitutional Reform and Effective Government* (Washington: Brookings Institute, 1986); Donald L. Robinson, *"To the Best of My Ability": The Presidency and the Constitution* (New York: Norton, 1987); and James M. Burns, *The Power to Lead: The Crisis of the American Presidency* (New York: Simon and Schuster, 1984).

6. Michael A. Genovese, "The Textbook Presidency, Revisited," *Presidency Research* (Spring 1989), pp. 8–16.

7. In the Reagan presidency, Reagan, unable to persuade the public or move the Congress in support of his goal to fund the Nicaraguan Contras, engaged in behavior, or allowed members of his administration to engage in behavior, that was beyond the law and in direct violation of the law in an effort to achieve his goals. See: *The Tower Commission Report* (New York: Bantam, 1987); and see: Jonathan Marshall, Peter Dale Scott, and Jane Hunter, *The Iran Contra Connection* (Boston: South End, 1987).

8. Kenneth E. Sharpe, "The Real Cause of Irangate," *Foreign Policy* (Fall 1987), pp. 19–40, William S. Cohen and George J. Mitchell, *Men of Zeal* (New York: Penguin, 1988); and Jane Mayer and Doyle McManus, *Landslide: The Unmaking of the President, 1984–1988* (Boston: Houghton Mifflin, 1988).

9. Quoted in Thompson, *The Nixon Presidency*, p. 307.

Bibliography

Aberbach, Joel D., and Bert A. Rockman. "Clashing Beliefs within the Executive Branch: The Nixon Administration Bureaucracy." *American Political Science Review*, June 1976: 456–468.

Abrahamsen, David. *Nixon vs. Nixon: An Emotional Tragedy*. New York: Farrar, Straus, and Giroux, 1977.

Agnew, Spiro T. *Go Quietly . . . or Else*. New York: Morrow, 1980.

Ambrose, Stephen E. *Nixon: The Education of a Politician, 1913–1962*. New York: Touchstone, 1987.

Anderson, James E. "Managing the Economy: The Johnson Administration Experience." Paper delivered at the 1980 annual meeting of the American Political Science Association, Washington, D.C., August 27–30, 1980.

Anson, Robert Sam. *Exile: The Unquiet Oblivion of Richard M. Nixon*. New York: Simon and Schuster, 1984.

Arnold, Peri E. *Making the Managerial Presidency*. Princeton, N.J.: Princeton University Press, 1986.

Ball, Howard. *No Pledge of Privacy: The Watergate Tapes Litigation*. Port Washington, New York: Kennikat, 1977.

Barber, James D. "The Nixon Brush with Tyranny." *Political Science Quarterly*, Winter 1977–1978: 581–597.

———. "President Nixon and Richard Nixon: Character Trap." *Psychology Today*, October 1974: 112–118.

———. *The Presidential Character: Predicting Performance in the White House*. Englewood Cliffs, N.J.: Prentice-Hall, 1985.

Barnet, Richard. *Giants: Russia and America*. New York: Simon and Schuster, 1977.

Ben-Veniste, Richard, and George Frampton, Jr. *Stonewall: The Real Story of the Watergate Prosecution*. New York: Simon and Schuster, 1974.

Berger, Raoul. *Executive Privilege: A Constitutional Myth*. Cambridge, Mass.: Harvard University Press, 1974.

———. *Impeachment: The Constitutional Problems*. New York: Bantam, 1974.

Berman, Larry. *The New American Presidency*. Boston: Little, Brown, 1987.

Bernstein, Carl, and Bob Woodward. *All the President's Men.* New York: Simon and Schuster, 1974.

———. *The Final Days.* New York: Simon and Schuster, 1976.

Bickel, Alexander M. "Watergate and the Legal Order." *Commentary*, January 1974: 19–25.

———. *Watergate, Politics, and the Legal Process.* Washington, D.C.: American Enterprise Institute, 1974.

Black, Charles L., Jr. *Impeachment: A Handbook.* New Haven: Yale University Press, 1974.

Block, Herbert. *Herblock Special Report: Words and Pictures on Nixon's Career from Freshman Congressman to "Full, Free and Absolute Pardon."* New York: Norton, 1974.

Bork, Robert H. *Constitutionality of the President's Busing Proposals.* Special Analysis No. 24. Washington, D.C.: American Enterprise Institute for Public Policy Research, 1972.

Brenner, Michael J. "The Problem of Innovation and the Nixon-Kissinger Foreign Policy." *International Studies Quarterly*, September 1973: 255–294.

Breslin, Jimmy. *How the Good Guys Finally Won: Notes from an Impeachment Summer.* New York: Ballantine, 1976.

Brodie, Fawn McKay. *Richard Nixon, The Shaping of His Character.* New York: Norton, 1981.

Brower, Sid. *The Watergate Papers.* Beverly Hills, Calif.: Waterbug Productions, 1973.

Brown, Seyom. *The Crisis of Power: An Interpretation of United States Foreign Policy during the Kissinger Years.* New York: Columbia University Press, 1979.

Brzezenski, Zbigniew, "The Balance of Power Delusion." *Foreign Policy*, Summer 1972: 54–59.

Bullock, Paul. *Jerry Voorhis: The Idealist as Politician.* New York: Vantage, 1978.

Burke, Vincent J., and Vee Burke. *Nixon's Good Deed: Welfare Reform.* New York: Columbia University Press, 1974.

Burlington, Bo. "Paranoia in Power," *Harper's*, October 1974: 26–37.

Burns, James MacGregor. *The Power to Lead: The Crisis of the American Presidency.* New York: Simon and Schuster, 1984.

Buschel, Bruce, A. Robbins and W. Vitka. *The Watergate File.* Edited by Rod Nordland. New York: Flash, 1973.

Campbell, Colin, S. J. *Managing the Presidency.* Pittsburgh: University of Pittsburgh Press, 1986.

Candee, Daniel. "The Moral Psychology of Watergate." *Journal of Social Issues*, 1975: 183–192.

Caputo, David A. "General Revenue Sharing and Federalism." *Annals of the American Academy of Political and Social Science*, no. 372, 1975: 5–9.

———. "Richard M. Nixon, General Revenue Sharing and American Federalism." Paper presented at Hofstra University Sixth Annual Presidential Conference, November 19–21, 1987.

Cavan, Sherri. *20th Century Gothic: America's Nixon.* San Francisco: Wigan Pier, 1979.

Chace, James. "The Concert of Europe." *Foreign Affairs*, October 1973: 96–108.

Chambers, Whittaker. *Witness.* New York: Random House, 1952.

Chesen, Eli S. *President Nixon's Psychiatric Profile.* New York: Wyden, 1973.

Chester, Lewis, Godfrey Hodgsen, and Bruce Page. *An American Melodrama: The Presidential Campaign of 1968.* New York: Viking, 1969.

Chester, Lewis, Cal McCrystal, Stephen Aris, and William Shawcross. *Watergate: The Full Story.* New York: Ballantine, 1973.

Clark, James C. *Faded Glory: Presidents Out of Power.* New York: Praeger, 1985.

Cohen, Richard M., and Jules Witcover. *A Heartbeat Away: The Investigation and Resignation of Vice President Spiro T. Agnew.* New York: Viking, 1974.

Cole, Richard L., and David A. Caputo. "Presidential Control of the Senior Civil Service: Assessing the Strategies of the Nixon Years." *American Political Science Review,* June 1979: 389–400.

Commager, Henry Steele. *The Defeat of America.* New York: Simon and Schuster, 1974.

Committee for the Re-election of the President, John M. Mitchell, Campaign Director. "The Nixon Years . . . Life of Leadership," campaign brochure, 1972.

Conlan, Timothy. *New Federalism: Intergovernmental Reform from Nixon to Reagan.* Washington, D.C.: Brookings Institute, 1988.

Cox, Archibald. *The Role of the Supreme Court in American Government.* New York: Oxford University Press, 1976.

Cox, Trisha Nixon. "My Father and Watergate." *Ladies Home Journal,* April 1974: 42–47.

Coyne, John R., Jr. *The Impudent Snobs: Agnew vs. the Intellectual Establishment.* New Rochelle, N.Y.: Arlington House, 1972.

Crabb, C., and Kevin V. Mulcahy. *Presidents and Foreign Policy Making.* Baton Rouge: Louisiana State University Press, 1986.

Cronin, Thomas E., et al. *U.S. vs Crime in the Streets.* Bloomington: Indiana University Press, 1981.

Dash, Samuel. *Chief Council: Inside the Ervin Committee—The Untold Story of Watergate.* New York: Random House, 1976.

David, Lester. *The Lonely Lady of San Clemente: The Story of Pat Nixon.* New York: Crowell, 1978.

Dean, John Wesley. *Blind Ambition: The White House Years.* New York: Simon and Schuster, 1976.

———. *Lost Honor.* Los Angeles: Stafford, 1982.

Dent, Harry S. *The Prodigal South Returns to Power.* New York: Wiley, 1978.

Diamond, Edwin. *The Tin Kazoo.* Cambridge: MIT Press, 1975.

Dickinson, William B., and Janice Goldstein, eds. *Watergate: A Chronology of a Crisis.* 2 volumes. Washington, D.C.: Congressional Quarterly, 1974.

DiClerico, Robert E. *The American President.* Englewood Cliffs, N.J.: Prentice-Hall, 1979.

Dommel, Paul R. *The Politics of Revenue Sharing.* Bloomington: Indiana University Press, 1974.

Donovan, Robert J. *Eisenhower: The Inside Story.* New York: Harper and Row, 1956.

Dougherty, James E. and Robert L. Pfaltzgraff. *American Foreign Policy: FDR to Reagan.* New York: Harper and Row, 1986.

Doyle, James. *Not above the Law: The Battles of Prosecutors Cox and Jaworski.* New York: Morrow, 1977.

Drew, Elizabeth. *The End of a Presidency.* New York: Bantam, 1975.

————. *Washington Journal: The Events of 1973–1974.* New York: Random House, 1975.

Efron, Edith. *The News Twisters.* Los Angeles: Nash, 1971.

Ehrlichman, John. *The Whole Truth.* New York: Simon and Schuster, 1979.

————. *Witness to Power: The Nixon Years.* New York: Simon and Schuster, 1982.

Eisenhower, David. "The Last Days in the Nixon White House." *Good Housekeeping,* September 1975: 89–91.

Eisenhower, Dwight D. *Mandate for Change: The White House Years 1953–1956.* New York: Doubleday, 1963.

————. *Waging Peace: The White House Years, a Personal Account, 1955–1961.* New York: Doubleday, 1965.

————. *The White House Years.* Garden City, N.Y.: Doubleday, 1965.

Eisenhower, Julie Nixon. *Pat Nixon: The Untold Story.* New York: Simon and Schuster, 1986.

Ellsberg, Daniel. *Papers on the War.* New York: Simon and Schuster, 1972.

Ervin, Samuel J. *The Whole Truth: The Watergate Conspiracy.* New York: Random House, 1980.

Evans, Les, and Allen Myers. *Watergate and the Myth of American Democracy.* New York: Pathfinder, 1974.

Evans, Rowland, Jr. and Robert D. Novak. *Nixon in the White House: The Frustration of Power.* New York: Random House, 1971.

Fairlie, Henry. "Lessons of Watergate: An Essay on the Possibility of Morality in Politics." *Encounter,* October 1974: 59.

Fishel, Jeff. *Presidents and Promises.* Washington, D.C.: CQ Press, 1985.

Ford, Gerald R. *A Time to Heal: The Autobiography of Gerald R. Ford.* New York: Harper and Row, 1979.

Friedman, Leon. *United States vs. Nixon: The President before the Supreme Court.* New York: Chelsea House, 1974.

Frost, David. *I Gave Them a Sword: Behind the Scenes of the Nixon Interviews.* New York: Morrow, 1978.

Gardner, Lloyd C. *The Great Nixon Turnaround: America's New Foreign Policy in the Post-Liberal Era.* New York: New Viewpoint, 1973.

Garrett, Stephen A. "Nixonian Foreign Policy: A New Balance of Power or a Revived Concert?" *Polity* 8, 1976: 389–421.

Garthoff, Raymond. *Détente and Confrontation: American-Soviet Relations from Nixon to Reagan.* Washington, D.C.: Brookings Institute, 1985.

Gartner, Alan, Colin Greer, and Frank Riessman, eds. *What Nixon Is Doing to Us.* New York: Harper and Row, 1973.

Genovese, Michael A. "The Supreme Court as a Check on Presidential Power." *Presidential Studies Quarterly* 6, no. 1-2, Winter/Spring 1976: 40–44.

————. "Presidential Leadership and Crisis Management." *Presidential Studies Quarterly,* Spring 1986: 300–309.

————. "The Presidency and Styles of Economic Management." *Congress and the Presidency,* Autumn 1987: 151–167.

————. "Presidents and Crisis: Developing a Crisis Management System in the Executive Branch," *International Journal of World Peace,* Spring 1987: 81–101.

————. *The Supreme Court, the Constitution, and Presidential Power.* Lanham, Md.: University Press of America, 1980.

——. "The Textbook Presidency, Revisited," *Presidency Research*, Spring 1989: 8–16.

George, Alexander L. "Assessing Presidential Character." *World Politics*, January 1974: 234–282.

Gold, Gerald. *The White House Transcripts: Submission of Recorded Presidential Conversations to the Committee on the Judiciary of the House of Representatives by President Richard Nixon.* New York: Viking, 1974.

Goldwater, Barry. *With No Apologies.* New York: Morrow, 1979.

Goodman, Walter. *The Committee.* New York: Farrar, Straus, and Giroux, 1968.

Graubard, Stephen. *Kissinger: Portrait of a Mind.* New York: Norton, 1973.

Grayson, Cary T., Jr., and Susan Lukoski. *The Impeachment Congress.* Washington, D.C.: Potomac, 1974.

Greenstein, Fred I. *The Hidden-Hand Presidency: Eisenhower as Leader,* New York: Basic, 1982.

Grossman, Michael, and Martha Kumar. *Portraying the President: The White House and the News Media.* Baltimore: Johns Hopkins University Press, 1981.

Halberstam, David. *The Powers That Be.* New York: Knopf, 1979.

Haldeman, H. R. *The Ends of Power.* New York: Times Books, 1978.

Halpern, Paul J., ed. *Why Watergate?* Pacific Palisades, Calif.: Palisades, 1975.

Hamilton, Alexander, James Madison, and John Jay. *The Federalist Papers.* New York: New American Library, 1961.

Hart, Robert P. *The Sound of Leadership: Presidential Communication in the Modern Age.* Chicago: University of Chicago Press, 1987.

Herbers, John. *No Thank You, Mr. Presdient.* New York: Norton, 1976.

Herring, George. *America's Longest War.* New York: Wiley, 1979.

Hersh, Seymour M. "1971 Tape Links Nixon to Plan to Use 'Thugs,' " *New York Times*, September 24, 1981, p. 1.

——. "The Pardon." *The Atlantic Monthly*, August 1983: 55–78.

——. *The Price of Power: Kissinger in the Nixon White House.* New York: Summit, 1983.

Hess, Stephen. *Organizing the Presidency.* Washington, D.C.: Brookings Institute, 1988.

Higgins, George. *The Friends of Richard Nixon.* Boston: Little, Brown, 1975.

Hoffman, Paul. *The New Nixon.* New York: Tower, 1970.

Hoffman, Stanley. "Weighing the Balance of Power." *Foreign Affairs*, July 1972: 60–86.

Hoopes, Townsand. *The Devil and John Foster Dulles: The Diplomacy of the Eisenhower Era.* Boston: Little, Brown, 1973.

Hughes, Arthur J. *Richard M. Nixon.* New York: Dodd Mead, 1972.

Hughes, Emmet John. *The Ordeal of Power: A Political Memoir of the Eisenhower Years.* New York: Atheneum, 1963.

Humphrey, Hubert H. *The Education of a Public Man, My Life and Politics.* Garden City, N.Y.: Doubleday, 1976.

Hung, Nguyen Tien, and Jerrold L. Schecter. *The Palace File.* New York: Harper and Row, 1987.

Hyland, William G. *Mortal Rivals: Superpower Relations from Nixon to Reagan.* New York: Random House, 1987.

Jamieson, Kathleen Hall. *Packaging the Presidency: A History and Criticism of Presidential Campaign Advertising.* Oxford: Oxford University Press, 1984.

Jaworski, Leon. *Confessions and Avoidance: A Memoir.* Garden City, N.Y.: Doubleday, 1979.

———. *The Right and the Power: The Prosecution of Watergate.* New York: Reader's Digest Press, 1976.

Jenness, Linda, and Andrew Pulley. *Watergate: The View from the Left.* New York: Pathfinder, 1973.

Jensen, Ralph. *Let Me Say This about That.* New York: Holt, Rinehart, and Winston, 1972.

Kalb, Marvin, and Bernard Kalb. *Kissinger.* Boston: Little, Brown, 1974.

Kellerman, Barbara. "Richard Nixon and the Family Assistance Plan." In *The Political Presidency.* New York: Oxford University Press, 1984.

Keogh, James. *President Nixon and the Press.* New York: Funk and Wagnalls, 1972.

Kernell, Samuel. *Going Public: New Strategies for Presidential Leadership.* Washington, D.C.: Congressional Quarterly, 1986.

Kernell, Samuel, and Samuel L. Popkin, eds. *Chief of Staff: Twenty-five Years of Managing the Presidency.* Berkeley: University of California Press, 1986.

Kessel, John H. *The Domestic Presidency: Decision-Making in the White House.* North Scituate, Mass.: Duxbury, 1975.

King, Gary, and Lyn Ragsdale. *The Elusive Executive: Discovering Statistical Patterns in the Presidency.* Washington, D.C.: Congressional Quarterly, 1988.

Kissinger, Henry. *White House Years.* Boston: Little, Brown, 1979.

———. *Years of Upheaval.* Boston: Little, Brown, 1982.

Klein, Herbert. *Making It Perfectly Clear.* Garden City, N.Y.: Doubleday, 1980.

Kotz, Nick. *Let Them Eat Promises: The Politics of Hunger in America.* Garden City, N.Y.: Anchor, 1971.

Laird, Melvin R. *The Nixon Doctrine.* Town Hall Meeting. Washington, D.C.: American Enterprise Institute for Public Policy Research, 1972.

Landau, David. *Kissinger: The Uses of Power.* Boston: Houghton Mifflin, 1972.

Lasky, Victor. *It Didn't Start with Watergate.* New York: Deal, 1977.

Liddy, G. Gordon. *Will: The Autobiography of G. Gordon Liddy.* New York: St. Martin's, 1980.

Light, Paul C. *The President's Agenda: Domestic Policy Choice from Kennedy to Carter.* Baltimore: Johns Hopkins University Press, 1982.

Littwak, Robert S. *Détente and the Nixon Doctrine: American Foreign Policy and the Pursuit of Stability, 1969–1976.* Cambridge: Cambridge University Press, 1984.

Lukas, J. Anthony. *Nightmare: The Underside of the Nixon Years.* New York: Viking, 1976.

Lurie, Leonard. *The Impeachment of Richard Nixon.* New York: Berkeley, 1973.

———. *The Running of Richard Nixon.* New York: Coward, McCann, and Geoghegan, 1972.

McCarthy, Mary. *The Mask of State: Watergate Portraits.* New York: Harcourt Brace Jovanovich, 1974.

McCord, James W., Jr. *A Piece of Tape: The Watergate Story: Fact and Fiction.* Rockville, Md.: Washington Media Services, 1974.

McGinniss, Joe. *The Selling of the President, 1968.* New York: Trident, 1969.

Magruder, Jeb Stuart. *An American Life: One Man's Road to Watergate.* New York: Atheneum, 1974.

Mailer, Norman. *St. George and the Godfather.* New York: Arbor House, 1972.

Malek, Fred. "Federal Political Personnel Manual: the 'Malek Manual.' " *The Bureaucrat* 4 (January 1976): 13–21.

Mankiewicz, Frank. *The Final Crisis of Richard M. Nixon.* New York: Quadrangle Books, 1974.

————. *Perfectly Clear: Nixon from Whittier to Watergate.* New York: Popular Library, 1973.

Mazlish, Bruce. *In Search of Nixon: A Psychohistorical Inquiry.* Baltimore: Penguin, 1972.

Mazo, Earl. *Richard Nixon: A Political and Personal Portrait.* New York: Harper, 1959.

Mazo, Earl, and Stephen Hess. *Nixon: A Political Portrait.* New York: Harper and Row, 1968.

Miller, H. R. *Scandals in the Highest Office:* New York: Random House, 1973.

Miller, Merle. *Plain Speaking: An Oral Biography of Harry S Truman.* New York: Putnam, 1974.

Miller, Roger L., and Raburn M. Williams. *The New Economics of Richard Nixon.* New York: Harper's Magazine, 1972.

Mollenhoff, Clark R. *Game Plan for Disaster: An Ombudsman's Report on the Nixon Years.* New York: Norton, 1976.

Morris, Roger. *Haig: The General's Progress.* New York: Playboy Press, 1982.

————. *Uncertain Greatness: Henry Kissinger and American Foreign Policy.* New York: Harper and Row, 1977.

Mosher, Frederick. *Watergate: Implications for Responsible Government.* New York: Basic, 1974.

Moynihan, Daniel P. *The Politics of a Guaranteed Income: The Nixon Administration and the Family Assistance Plan.* New York: Random House, 1973.

Murphy, Reg, and Hal Gulliver. *The Southern Strategy.* New York: Charles Scribner's Sons, 1971.

Muzzio, Douglas. *Watergate Games: Strategies, Choices, Outcomes.* New York: New York University Press, 1982.

Myerson, Michael. *Watergate: Crime in the Suites.* New York: International, 1973.

Nathan, Richard P. *The Plot That Failed: Nixon and the Administrative Presidency.* New York: Wiley, 1975.

Neustadt, Richard. *Presidential Power: The Politics of Leadership with Reflections on Johnson and Nixon.* New York: Wiley, 1976.

New York Times Staff, eds. *The End of a Presidency.* New York: Bantam, 1974.

————. *The Watergate Hearings: Break-in and Coverup.* New York: Bantam, 1973.

Nixon, Richard M. "Asia After Vietnam." *Foreign Affairs,* October 1967: 111–125.

————. *Bridges to Human Dignity.* Parts 1 and 2. New York: Nixon for President Committee, 1968.

————. *The Challenges We Face.* New York: McGraw-Hill, 1960.

————. *Leaders.* New York: Warner, 1982.

————. *A New Road for America: Major Policy Statements, March 1970 to October 1971.* Garden City, N.Y.: Doubleday, 1972.

————. "Nixon: The First Year of His Presidency." *Congressional Quarterly,* 1970, p. 128.

————. *1999: Victory Without War.* New York: Simon and Schuster, 1988.

————. *The Nixon Presidential Press Conferences.* New York: Earl M. Coleman Enterprises, 1978.

————. "Nixon: The Second Year of His Presidency," *Congressional Quarterly*, 1971, p. 180.

————. *Real Peace*. Boston: Little, Brown, 1984.

————. *The Real War*. New York: Warner, 1980.

————. *RN: The Memoirs of Richard Nixon*. Grosset and Dunlop, 1978.

————. *Six Crises*. New York: Warner, 1979.

————. *Submission of Recorded Presidential Conversations to the Committee on the Judiciary of the House of Representatives by President Richard Nixon, April 30, 1974*. Washington, D.C.: U.S. Government Printing Office, 1974.

————. *The White House Transcripts: Submission of Recorded Presidential Conversations to the Committee on the Judiciary of the House of Representatives by President Nixon*. New York: Batnam, 1974.

Nixon, Richard M., in conjunction with the staff of the *Washington Post. The Presidential Transcripts*. New York: Delacorte Press, 1974.

O'Brien, Lawrence F. *No Final Victories: A Life in Politics—From John F. Kennedy to Watergate*. Garden City, N.Y.: Doubleday, 1974.

Olglesby, Carl. "In Defense of Paranoia." *Ramparts*, November 1974: 23–27.

————. *The Yankee and the Cowboy War: Conspiracies from Dallas to Watergate*. Kansas City, Mo.: Sheed Andrews and McMoel, 1976.

Orman, John. "Covering the American Presidency." *Presidential Studies Quarterly*, Summer 1984: 381–390.

Osborne, J. *The Fifth Year of the Nixon Watch*. New York: Liveright, 1974.

————. *The Fourth Year of the Nixon Watch*. New York: Liveright, Norton, 1973.

————. *The Last Year of the Nixon Watch*. Washington, D.C.: New Republic, 1975.

————. *The Nixon Watch*. New York: Liveright, 1970.

————. *The Second Year of the Nixon Watch*. New York: Liveright, Norton, 1971.

————. *The Third Year of the Nixon Watch*. New York: Liveright, Norton, 1972.

Osgood, Robert E., et al. *Retreat from Empire? The First Nixon Administration*. Baltimore: Johns Hopkins University Press, 1973.

Panetta, Leon E., and Peter Gall. *Bring Us Together: The Nixon Team and the Civil Rights Retreat*. Philadelphia: Lippincott, 1971.

Pfiffner, James. *The Strategic Presidency: Hitting the Ground Running*. Chicago: Dorsey, 1988.

Porter, William E. *Assault on the Media: The Nixon Years*. Ann Arbor: University of Michigan Press, 1976.

Powers, Thomas. *The Man Who Kept the Secrets: Richard Helms and the CIA*. New York: Knopf, 1979.

Price, Raymond. *With Nixon*. New York: Viking, 1977.

Randell, Leo. *The Mind of Watergate: An Exploration of the Compromise of Integrity*. New York: Norton, 1980.

Rather, Dan. "Watergate on TV." *Newsday*, December 16, 1973: 9.

Rather, Dan, and Gary Paul Gates. *The Palace Guard*. New York: Harper and Row, 1974.

Rathlesberger, James, ed. *Nixon and the Environment: The Politics of Devastation*. New York: Taurus Communications, 1972.

Reichley, A. James. *Conservatives in an Age of Change: The Nixon and Ford Administration*. Washington, D.C.: Brookings Institute, 1981.

Robinson, Donald L. *"To the Best of My Ability": The Presidency and the Constitution.* New York: Norton, 1987.

Saffell, David C. *Watergate: Its Effect on the American Political System.* Cambridge, Mass.: Winthrop, 1974.

Safire, William L. *Before the Fall: An Inside View of the Pre–Watergate White House.* Garden City, N.Y.: Doubleday, 1975.

Sale, Kirkpatrick. "The World Behind Watergate." *New York Review of Books,* May 3, 1973: 12–14.

Schell, Johnathan. *Time of Illusion.* New York: Random House, 1975.

Schlesinger, Arthur, Jr. *The Imperial Presidency.* Boston: Houghton Mifflin, 1973.

The Senate Watergate Report: The Final Report of the Senate Select Committee on Presidential Campaign Activities. New York: Dell, 1974.

Shannon, William V. *They Could Not Trust the King: Nixon, Watergate, and the American People.* New York: Collier, 1974.

Shapiro, Martin. *The Pentagon Papers and the Courts.* San Francisco: Chandler, 1972.

Sharpe, Kenneth E. "The Real Cause of Irangate," *Foreign Policy,* Fall 1987: 19–40.

Shawcross, William. *Sideshow: Kissinger, Nixon, and the Destruction of Cambodia.* New York: Simon and Schuster, 1979.

Shuman, Howard E. *Politics and the Budget: The Struggle Between the President and the Congress.* Englewood Cliffs, N.J.: Prentice-Hall, 1984.

Silk, Leonard. *Nixonomics.* New York: Praeger, 1973.

Simon, James F. *In His Own Image: The Supreme Court in Richard Nixon's America.* New York: McKay, 1973.

Sirica, John. *To Set the Record Straight: The Break-In, the Tapes, the Conspirators, the Pardon.* New York: Norton, 1979.

Smith, Gene. *High Crimes and Misdemeanors: The Impeachment and Trial of Andrew Johnson.* New York: McGraw-Hill, 1976.

Sobel, Lester A., ed. *Kissinger and Détente.* New York: Facts on File, 1975.

Sorenson, Theodore C. *Watchmen in the Night: Accountability after Watergate.* Cambridge: MIT Press, 1975.

Sorley, Lewis. *Arms Transfers under Nixon: A Policy Analysis.* Lexington: University Press of Kentucky, 1983.

Spear, Joseph C. *Presidents and the Press: The Nixon Legacy.* Cambridge: MIT Press, 1975.

Spero, Joan. *The Politics of International Economic Relations.* New York: St. Martin's, 1985.

Stans, Maurice H. *The Terrors of Justice: The Untold Side of Watergate.* New York: Everest House, 1978.

Stien, Herbert. *Presidential Economics: The Making of Economic Policy from Roosevelt to Reagan and Beyond.* New York: Touchstone, 1984.

Stone, David M. *Nixon and the Politics of Public Television.* New York: Garland, 1985.

Sulzberger, Cyrus Leo. *The World and Richard Nixon.* Englewood Cliffs, N.J.: Prentice-Hall, 1987.

Sussman, Barry. *The Great Coverup: Nixon and the Scandal of Watergate.* New York: Signet, 1974.

"Symposium: United States vs. Nixon." *UCLA Law Review,* October, 1974.

Szulc, Tad. *The Illusion of Peace: Foreign Policy in the Nixon Years*. New York: Viking, 1978.

Thompson, Fred. At *That Point in Time: The Inside Story of the Watergate Committee*. New York: Quadrangle, 1975.

Thompson, Kenneth W., ed. *The Nixon Presidency: Twenty-two Intimate Perspectives of Richard M. Nixon*. Lanham, Md.: University Press of America, 1987.

Tuchman, Barbara. *The March of Folly: From Troy to Vietnam*. New York: Ballantine, 1984.

Tufte, Edward R. *Political Control of the Economy*. Princeton, N.J.: Princeton University Press, 1978.

Ungar, Sanford J. *The Papers and The Papers: An Account of the Legal and Political Battle Over the Pentagon Papers*. New York: Dutton, 1972.

United Press International and The World Almanac. *The Impeachment Report: A Guide to Congressional Proceedings in the Case of Richard M. Nixon, President of the United States.* New York: New American Library, 1974.

U.S. Congress. House. *Impeachment of Richard M. Nixon, President of the United States*. Washington, D.C.: U.S. Government Printing Office, 1974.

———. *Statement of Information*, Book 3, Part 1. Washington, D.C.: U.S. Government Printing Office, 1974.

U.S. Congress. House Committee on the Judiciary, Peter W. Rodino, Jr., Chairman. *Debate On Articles of Impeachment*. Washington, D.C.: U.S. Government Printing Office, 1974.

U.S. Congress. Joint Committee on the Internal Revenue Taxation, Wilbur D. Mills, House Chair., Russell Long, Senate Vice Chairman. *Investigation into Certain Charges of the Use of the IRS for Political Purposes*. Washington, D.C.: U.S. Government Printing Office, 1973.

U.S. Congress. Joint Committee on Printing. *Congressional Pictoral Directory*, January 1971. Washington, D.C.: United States Government Printing, 1971.

U.S. Congress. Senate Committee on Commerce. *Freedom of Communications, Part II: The Speeches, Remarks, Press Conferences, and Study Papers of Vice President Richard M. Nixon, August 1 through November 7, 1960*. Washington, D.C.: U.S. Government Printing Office, 1961.

———. *Freedom of Communications, Part III*. Washington, D.C.: U.S. Government Printing Office, 1961.

U.S. Congress. Senate Select Committee on Presidential Campaign Activities, Sam J. Ervin, Jr., Chairman. *The Final Report*. Washington, D.C.: U.S. Government Printing Office, 1974.

von Hoffman, Nicholas. *Make-Believe Presidents: Illusions of Power from McKinley to Carter*. New York: Pantheon, 1978.

Voorhis, Jerry. *The Strange Case of Richard Milhous Nixon*. Middlebury, N.Y.: Popular Library, 1982.

Washington Post Staff. *The Presidential Transcripts*. New York: Dell, 1974.

———. *The Fall of a President*. New York: Dell, 1974.

Watergate Chronology of a Crisis. Vols 1 and 2. Washington, D.C.: Congressional Quarterly, 1974.

The Watergate Hearings: Break-in and Cover-up. New York: Viking, 1973.

Ways, Max. "Watergate as a Case Study in Management." *Fortune*, November 1973: 109–210.

Weisband, Edward, and Thomas Franck. *Resignation to Protest: Political and Ethical Choices between Loyalty to Team and Loyalty to Conscience in American Public Life*. New York: Grossman, 1975.

Whitaker, John C. *Striking a Balance; Environment and National Resources Policy in the Nixon-Ford Years*. Washington, D.C.: American Enterprise Institute, 1976.

White, Theodore H. *America in Search of Itself: The Making of the President, 1956–1980*. New York: Harper and Row, 1982.

———. *Breach of Faith: The Fall of Richard Nixon*. New York: Atheneum, 1975.

———. *The Making of the President, 1960*. New York: Atheneum, 1961.

———. *The Making of the President, 1968*. New York: Atheneum, 1969.

———. *The Making of the President, 1972*. New York: Atheneum, 1973.

Whiteside, Thomas. "Annals of Television Shaking the Tree." *The New Yorker*, March 17, 1975.

Wills, Garry. *Nixon Agonistes: The Crisis of the Self-Made Man*. Boston: Houghton Mifflin, 1971.

Winter, Ralph. *Watergate and the Law: Political Campaigns and Presidential Power*. Washington, D.C.: American Enterprise Institute for Public Policy Research, 1974.

Witcover, Jules. *Marathon: The Pursuit of the Presidency, 1972–1976*. New York: Viking, 1977.

———. *The Resurrection of Richard Nixon*. New York: Putnam, 1970.

Woodward, C. Vann. *Responses of the Presidents to Charges of Misconduct*. New York: Dell, 1974.

Index

About the Author

MICHAEL A. GENOVESE is Associate Professor of Political Science at Loyola Marymount University, Los Angeles. He is the author of *The Supreme Court, the Constitution, and Presidential Power* and *Politics and the Cinema*, as well as many journal articles.